Cambridge

Children and the Movies: Media Influence and the Payne Fund Contro-versy analyzes the first and most comprehensive investigation of the in-fluence of movies on American youth, the Payne Fund Studies. First published in 1933, these studies are important for their insights and con-clusions regarding the effects of movies on behavior. They are, more-over, a landmark of modern social science research, demonstrating the rapid evolution of this discipline in American academic institutions over the first three decades of the century. Based on newly discovered pri-mary sources, whose contents are published here for the first time, this volume also reproduces a long-missing Payne Fund study.

Cambridge Studies in the History of Mass Communications

General Editors

Garth Jowett, University of Houston
Kenneth Short, University of Houston

Other Books in the Series

Cinema and Soviet Society, 1917–1953, by Peter Kenez
Hollywood's Overseas Campaign: The North Atlantic Movie Trade, 1920–1950, by Ian Jarvie
Ronald Reagan in Hollywood: Movies and Politics, by Stephen Vaughn
Hollywood Censored: The Catholic Legion of Decency and the Hays Code, by Gregory Black

Children and the Movies

One of the Payne Fund studies, with unique art moderne cover design.

Children and the Movies

MEDIA INFLUENCE AND THE PAYNE FUND CONTROVERSY

Garth S. Jowett
University of Houston

Ian C. Jarvie
York University, Toronto

Kathryn H. Fuller
Virginia Commonwealth University

CAMBRIDGE
UNIVERSITY PRESS

Published by the Press Syndicate of the University of Cambridge
The Pitt Building, Trumpington Street, Cambridge CB2 1RP
40 West 20th Street, New York, NY 10011-4211, USA
10 Stamford Road, Oakleigh, Melbourne 3166, Australia

First published 1996

Printed in the United States of America

Library of Congress Cataloging-in-Publication Data
Children and the movies : media influence and the Payne Fund
controversy / Garth S. Jowett, Ian C. Jarvie, Kathryn H.
Fuller.
p.   cm. – (Cambridge studies in the history of mass communications)
Includes bibliographical references.
ISBN 0-521-48292-5 (hc)
1. Children and motion pictures.   2. Payne Fund, Inc.   3. Motion
pictures – Moral and ethical aspects.   I. Jowett, Garth.
II. Jarvie, I. C. (Ian Charles).   III. Fuller, Kathryn H.
IV. Series.
PN1995.9.C45C373   1996
305.23 – dc20   95-15279
                                                                     CIP

A catalog record for this book is available from the British Library.

ISBN 0-521-48292-5 Hardback

Contents

About the Authors

Garth S. Jowett is a Professor in the School of Communication, University of Houston. He is the author of *Film: The Democratic Art, Movies as Mass Communication* (with James M. Linton), *Propaganda and Persuasion* (with Victoria O'Donnell), and numerous other publications in the areas of film, popular culture and propaganda studies. His primary interest is the way in which societies adjust to the introduction of new media systems. He is advisory editor for the Sage Publications' Foundations of Popular Culture series and (together with Kenneth Short) for the Cambridge Studies in the History of Mass Communications series. He is currently working on a history of the American film industry in the 1950s.

Ian C. Jarvie, who teaches philosophy at York University in Toronto, has published extensively on the sociology and social history of film. His area of special interest is how society inscribes itself in film and how film affects society. He is associate editor of the *Historical Journal of Film, Radio and Television*. His most recent book, *Hollywood's Overseas Campaign: The North Atlantic Movie Trade, 1920–1950,* was awarded the Kraszna-Krausz Prize in 1993 for the most outstanding book on the study of the film industry. He is presently writing a sociological study of the pornographic feature film.

Kathryn H. Fuller is an Assistant Professor in the Department of History at Virginia Commonwealth University, where she teaches twentieth-century U.S. social history. She is interested in the history of popular culture, and has a book forthcoming from Smithsonian Institution Press on small-town film exhibition and audiences in the silent film era. She is currently working on a biography of a pair of rural itinerant film exhibitors.

Foreword

Homo sapiens is the storytelling animal. Most of what we know, or think we know, we never personally experience. We live in a world erected by and experienced through the stories we hear and see and tell.

Storytelling is my shorthand for the way we live in a world much wider than the threats and gratifications of the immediate environment, which is the world of other species. Through stories we guide relationships; assume roles of gender, age, status, class, vocation and lifestyle; and find models of conformity or targets for rebellion.

Unlocking incredible riches through music, gesture and movement, conjuring up the unseen to animate the imagination through imagery, creating towering works of fiction, fact and the command through poetry, songs, tales, reports and laws – that is the real magic of human life. The motion picture has all of that magic and was the first medium to put it all together in audiovisual-moving, and soon realistic, imagery. The trouble and turmoil that were created mark a shift in the great historic and ongoing cultural debate from religion to science and from art to social control. Behind the story of this book is the story of that long-forgotten (and perhaps still not fully completed) historical shift.

Scottish patriot Andrew Fletcher once said that if he were permitted to write all the ballads, he would not care who made the laws of the nation. Every change in the writing of all the ballads threatens the existing structure of informal but binding controls. The shift from oral to written communication agitated ancient philosophers. The industrial revolution in storytelling brought about by the printing press ushered in the Reformation. In the controversy that followed their introduction, popular novels were charged with making the new, vulnerable (mostly young, mostly female) readers immoral, indolent and lazy. And then came the most sweeping change of all, the one that requires no literacy and that retribalizes media society: the electronic transformation, beginning with motion pictures.

The most pervasive controls are exercised along age, class, and gender lines. Threats to these controls mobilize both those who wish to keep them, typically one's "elders and betters," and those who would recapture or share them, including public officials, the clergy, parents, teachers and social scientists.

This fascinating book, *Children and the Movies: Media Influence and the Payne Fund Studies,* has all the elements of this classic cultural drama, played out with every new communication technology. The volume's meticulous and balanced scholarship, indeed like that of some of the Payne Fund studies themselves, anticipates many of the conflicts, controversies, confusions and cross-purposes that characterize much current research and discussion about the social impact of electronic media.

The historical shifts of culture power, like continental drifts, change the map of social concerns and the arena of social contest. Where military, religious and political forces dominated the field, now the distribution of media attention, imagery and helpful or harmful publicity enters into affairs of state and of persons. The typical strategic approach to keeping or gaining control of that process is to focus on those thought to be more dependent, more vulnerable and arguably more in need of protection: children and youth.

The corruption of children and youth has thus been the target of choice of all great cultural debates, from Socrates to media violence. However, concern with children is, in many ways, more a decoy than the real object of concern. (Otherwise, it would be difficult to explain why, during the "family values" and youth violence controversies of the late 1980s, more than a million children were added to the poverty rolls, until the proportion of impoverished children reached one in five.) The contest is over the distribution of culture-power.

The scholarly, theoretical and political perspectives and conflicts of the Payne Fund researchers and writers can well be seen against such a complex configuration of symbolic and social forces. The story of these studies may be read as a prism through which the full spectrum of cultural policy disputes is illuminated.

Time and distance were necessary to achieve that historical perspective. When I was a graduate student, the Payne Fund Studies were required reading, but soon after, they were dismissed as obsolete and crowded out, at least temporarily, by "value-free" scientific apologists. It is time to reclaim them, with all their varied but passionate commitments to human values in research and action. Most of all, they can serve to remind us of the question that is behind all the "media wars": How do we test and make cultural policy in the electronic age?

GEORGE GERBNER

Acknowledgments

The authors are indebted to the Payne Fund and the Western Reserve Historical Society for the travel grant that enabled them to visit the Payne Fund Papers Collection in Cleveland, and to meet elsewhere for consultation and coordination as the project developed, and to Kermit Pike, the director of the WRHS Archive for his encouragement and facilitation of this grant. At the WRHS we were ably assisted by Anne Sindelaar and the other members of the staff when we "took over" for a few days. At the Archives of the Hoover Institution on War, Revolution and Peace, Jowett and Jarvie were helped immeasurably by assistant archivist Carol Leadenham and archivist Anne Van Camp. Mary Racine at Cambridge University Press expertly supervised the editing and production of the book.

Garth Jowett wishes to thank the University of Houston for two Limited Grant-in-Aid grants that facilitated travel and research. He also thanks Dr. George Gerbner, in whose offices, as a graduate student in 1969, he first encountered the black art-moderne-style volumes of the Payne Fund Studies sitting neatly on a bookshelf. In many ways, this chance encounter precipitated the long string of events that led to the development of this book.

Ian Jarvie wishes to thank York University for his Generic Research Grant.

Kathryn Fuller wishes to thank Garth Jowett and Ian Jarvie for their advice and encouragement throughout her explorations of the Payne Fund Studies, as well as Ronald Walters and Douglas Gomery for their guidance, and her friends who have read the work in many stages, especially Martha Kearsley, Mary Lou Helgesen and Douglas Fuller.

A very special thanks goes to Patricia Marsh Cavanaugh, who despite her taxing job as the associate registrar at the University of Houston, used her valuable free time to undertake the arduous task of retyping into the computer the single-spaced, carbon copy of "The Community – A Social Setting for the Motion Picture" (which was to have become the Payne Fund study *Boys, Movies and City Streets*) so that it could be edited for this volume.

For permission to reproduce materials from their holdings, we thank the Western Reserve Historical Society, the Hoover Institution on War, Revolution and Peace, the Ohio State University Library and the Rocke- feller Archive Center.

Portions of Chapter One first appeared in *Communication,* 13, no. 3 (Fall 1992). Portions of Chapter Four first appeared in the *Historical Journal of Film, Radio and Television,* 13, no. 4 (Fall 1993).

Dramatis Personae

BIOGRAPHICAL SKETCHES OF PARTICIPANTS
IN THE PAYNE FUND STUDIES

MORTIMER JEROME ADLER (1902–) was educated at Columbia University, where he taught psychology from 1923 to 1930, and completed his Ph.D. in 1928. A fierce opponent of Dewey's "progressive education," he caught the eye of Robert Hutchins, who made special arrangements to bypass the philosophy department and bring him to the University of Chicago in 1930. He remained there until 1952, when he left to create his own Institute of Philosophy. With Hutchins, he was a force behind the Great Books publishing program and the Aspen Institute, and he was involved in the redesign of the *Encyclopaedia Britannica*. Among many philosophical books, his *Art and Prudence* (1937) rewards any student of the Payne Fund materials, and his *Philosopher at Large* (1977) chronicles how an intellectual became willingly involved with the movie industry.

HERBERT BLUMER (1900–1987) earned B.A. and M.A. degrees from the University of Missouri and received his Ph.D. in sociology from the University of Chicago (1928), where he studied with George Herbert Mead and Robert Park. He taught sociology at the University of Chicago from 1928 to 1939. He then moved to the University of California at Berkeley, where he was a leading scholar of symbolic interactionism and social psychology and longtime department chair (1952–1967). Blumer was elected president of the American Sociological Association in 1955 and wrote influential articles on methodology, collective behavior and

Sources: Who Was Who in America, obituaries in the *New York Times, American Sociological Review, American Journal of Sociology*, biographical dictionaries of educators and social scientists, and Edward James, *Notable American Women, 1607–1950* (Cambridge: Belknap Press, 1971), "Ella P. Crandall," pp. 398–399.

racial prejudice, gathered in *Symbolic Interactionism: Perspective and Method* (1969). A man of many talents, he was a professional typist as a teenager and played college football at the University of Missouri and professional football with the Chicago Cardinals for six seasons (1925–1930 and 1933).

FRANCES PAYNE BINGHAM BOLTON (1885–1977) was born to a wealthy family in Cleveland, Ohio. She married Chester Bolton (1882–1939), a member of the Ohio State Senate from 1923 to 1928 and U.S. Congressman representing the 22nd Ohio district from 1929 to 1939. In the late 1910s she inherited a large fortune from an uncle, Oliver Hazard Payne, oil refiner and industrialist. Interested in nursing, she endowed the Frances Payne Bolton School of Nursing of Western Reserve University. She met Ella Phillips Crandall through public health organizations and founded the National Committee for the Study of Juvenile Reading in 1925 with Crandall and Harvie Clymer as administrators. The organization was renamed the Payne Study and Experiment Fund in 1927, which was abbreviated to the Payne Fund in 1929. Chester Bolton died suddenly in 1939 and Frances took over his congressional seat, winning a special election in 1940 at the age of fifty-five. She served in Congress from 1940 to 1969, earning honors for her work in race relations, foreign affairs, health and aid to African and international students.

WERRET WALLACE (W. W.) CHARTERS (1875–1952) earned a B.A. at McMaster University, and an M.A. and a Ph.D. in education from the University of Chicago (1904), where he studied with John Dewey. He taught education at the universities of Missouri, Illinois and Pittsburgh. He served as professor of education at the University of Chicago from 1925 to 1928 and as professor of education and director of the Bureau of Educational Research at Ohio State University from 1928 to 1947. Prominent in the study of audiovisual and technical aspects of education, he was the author of *Curriculum Construction* (1923), *The Teaching of Ideals* (1927) and many articles and coauthored books. He continued to lead the Bureau of Educational Research into the study of educational radio (funded by Frances Bolton and the Payne Fund) into the 1940s and served as director of the Bureau of Manpower Training for the War Manpower Commission from 1942 to 1943.

HARVIE M. CLYMER (18??–19??) had ten years of experience in juvenile magazine publishing with *American Boys* and *Boys Life* and had served as a national director of the Boy Scouts of America when he joined Frances Bolton's National Committee for the Study of Juvenile Reading as director in 1925. In 1926 he traveled in Europe and Russia researching children's reading habits. In 1927 he became president of the Payne Study and Experiment Fund. Clymer served as a conservative administrator who remained very mindful of public reaction to all Payne Fund activities. He left the Payne Fund under a cloud in February 1931 over personal and professional conflicts with Frances Bolton. The details of the remainder of his professional life are unknown.

ELLA PHILLIPS CRANDALL (1871–1938) was trained in nursing at the Philadelphia General Hospital and directed the school of nursing at a Dayton, Ohio, hospital from 1899 to 1909. In 1909 she became a supervisor in Lillian Wald's Henry Street Visiting Nurse Service in New York City. She taught public health nursing at Columbia University Teachers College from 1910 to 1912 and served as executive secretary for the National Organization for Public Health Nursing (1912–1920), where she established professional standards in nursing training and service across the nation. She was described as "a dedicated, almost fiery woman" and "forceful and persuasive, yet leavened by a keen sense of humor" and "interested in a wide variety of topics from ancient civilization to telepathy and mysticism." From 1920 to 1925 she acted as administrative official of several groups interested in improving the health of the poor, women and children. Frances Bolton, who was on the board of directors of the National Organization for Public Health Nursing, shared Crandall's interests in nursing, children and mysticism. Bolton's biography claims Crandall first suggested studying juvenile reading habits and opening the New York office of the National Committee for the Study of Juvenile Reading in 1925. She served as executive secretary of the Payne Study and Experiment Fund from 1927 to 1938. She retired due to ill health and died that year of pneumonia.

PAUL GOALBY CRESSEY (1900–1955) earned a B.A. degree at Oberlin College and an M.A. at the University of Chicago in 1929. He did further graduate work at New York University and taught there as an adjunct while serving as associate director of the Motion Picture Project of the Boys' Club study from 1931 to 1934. He was the author of the highly regarded *Taxi-Dance Hall: A Sociological Study in Commercialized Recreation and City Life* and articles on methodology, informal education and juvenile delinquency. From 1934 to 1937 he taught at the

University of Newark, and from 1937 to 1942 continued course work as a graduate student and lecturer in community organization at New York University, where he completed his Ph.D. in 1942. He worked as a public opinion analyst for the Office of War Information during 1942–1943, and served as executive director of the Social Welfare Council of the Oranges and Maplewood, New Jersey, from 1943 to 1950, where he supported community centers for children of slum areas. In 1950 he became professor of sociology at Ohio Wesleyan University. He died suddenly on 7 July 1955 in Montclair, New Jersey.

EDGAR DALE (1900–) earned B.A. and M.A. degrees from the University of North Dakota, and received his Ph.D. in education from the University of Chicago (1928), where he studied with W. W. Charters. He was a member of the editorial staff of Eastman Teaching Films at Eastman Kodak during 1928–1929. He conducted research at the Bureau of Educational Research at Ohio State University and served as professor of education from 1929 to 1970, becoming very well known in the field of educational communications and training a generation of media scholars. He was a consultant for the Office of War Information and its Bureau of Motion Pictures during World War II. He wrote many books and articles on audiovisual education, including *Teaching with Motion Pictures* (1937), *How to Read a Newspaper* (1941) and *Building a Learning Environment* (1971).

HENRY JAMES FORMAN (1879–1966) was born in Russia, earned a B.A. degree from Harvard University and did graduate work at the École des Hautes Études Sociales in Paris. After spending two years on the staff of the *New York Sun,* he rose through the editorial ranks of the *Literary Digest, North American Review* and other magazines, serving as managing editor of *Collier's Weekly* (1914–1918). After the war he became a frequent contributor to popular magazines and was the author of a dozen novels, travel guides, historical works and plays. Following the appearance of *Our Movie-Made Children* (1933), Forman published books with spiritual themes, including *The Story of Prophecy* (1936) and *Have You a Religion?* (1941).

FRANK N. FREEMAN (1880–1961) was professor of education at the University of Chicago and the author of numerous books, including *How Children Learn* (1917), *Visual Education* (1924), *Motion Pictures in the Classroom* (1929) and *An Experimental Study of the Educational*

Influences of the Typewriter in the Elementary School Classroom (1932).

PHILIP M. HAUSER (1909–) wrote an M.A. thesis in the sociology department of the University of Chicago stemming from his Payne Fund research on the use of movies in correctional institutions. He also completed his Ph.D. at the university and remained on its faculty for his entire career. He specialized in juvenile delinquency studies and served as chairman of the sociology department for many years.

WILL HARRISON HAYS (1879–1954) was born in Indiana and remained closely tied to the Republican machinery in that state all his life. He earned a B.A. degree at Wabash College and was called to the bar in 1900. He practiced law in the firm of Hays and Hays. The consummate back-room political operative, he rose through the state ranks to become chairman of the Republican National Committee from 1918 to 1921 and in that post he organized President Harding's election campaign. His reward after victory was the job of postmaster general (he was nicknamed "General Hays" throughout his life), which he resigned in order to assume the presidency of the newly created Motion Picture Producers and Distributors Association in 1922. After retirement in 1945 he remained a consultant. The ghost-written *Memoirs of Will Hays* was published in 1955, and affectionate and amusing portraits of him appear in Edmund G. Lowry's *Washington Close Ups* (1921) and Raymond Moley's 27 *Masters of Politics* (1949).

MARK A. MAY (1891–19??) earned B.A. degrees from Maryville College (Tennessee) and the University of Chicago (1912), attended Union Theological Seminary and received an M.A. and a Ph.D. from Columbia (1917). He taught at Syracuse University from 1919 to 1927, then served as professor of educational psychology and director of the Institute for Human Relations at Yale from 1927 to 1960. He was the author of *How to Study in College* (1924), *Studies in Deceit* and *Testing the Knowledge of Right and Wrong* (with Hugh Hartshorne; 1927–1928), *The Education of American Ministers* (with Frank Shuttleworth; 1934), *Competition and Cooperation* (with Leonard Doob; 1937) and *Learning from Films* (with A. A. Lumsdaine; 1958).

RAYMOND MOLEY (1886–1975) earned a B.A. degree at Baldwin-Wallace College, an M.A. at Oberlin and a Ph.D. at Columbia University (1918). He worked as a schoolteacher and superintendent in Ohio from

1907 to 1914, and taught politics at Case Western Reserve University
from 1916 to 1919. After four years as director of the Cleveland Foundation, he became associate professor of government at Columbia University in 1923, then served as professor of public law from 1928 to
1954. He was briefly assistant secretary of state in 1933. From 1933 to
1937 he edited *Today* magazine, then joined *Newsweek* as a contributing editor and served in that capacity until 1968. He was director of
research for the New York State Crime Commission during 1926–1927
and for the New York State Commission on the Administration of
Justice from 1931 to 1933. He also wrote free-lance for other public
figures, including the Republican Will Hays. His *Are We Movie Made?*
(1938) was a popular summary of Mortimer Adler's critique of the
Payne Fund Studies. In 1945 he wrote the only official history of the
Motion Picture Producers and Distributors Association, *The Hays Office* (1945).

ROBERT E. PARK (1864–1944) worked as journalist between 1887 and
1898 before earning an M.A. degree from Harvard and a Ph.D. from the
University of Heidelberg (1904). He taught and conducted research at
the Tuskeegee Institute and other African-American educational institutions from 1905 to 1914. He joined the University of Chicago as a
lecturer in sociology in 1914 and served in that capacity until 1923,
when he became a professor of sociology, a position he held until 1933.
He was the coauthor of *Introduction to the Science of Sociology* (with
Ernest Burgess; 1921) and author of *The Immigrant Press and Its Control* (1922) and *The City* (1925). He was involved in the planning of the
Payne Fund Studies between 1927 and 1929. He traveled and lectured
on sociology in Japan during 1929–1930, taught at the University of
Hawaii and at Yenching University in China in 1931–1932 and studied
race relations in India, Africa and Brazil in 1933. He served as a visiting
professor at Fisk University from 1936 until his retirement. In a 1938
article, "Reflections on Communication and Culture," Park argued that
movies had "devastating" and "subversive" effects on local culture.

CHARLES C. PETERS (1881–1973) received a Ph.D. from the University
of Pennsylvania (1916). He taught at Ohio Wesleyan University from
1917 to 1927, then served as professor of education and director of
educational research at Pennsylvania State College between 1927 and
1945. He wrote many books, including *Human Conduct* (1918), *Objectives of Education* (coauthored with David Snedden, 1929), *Foundations*

of Educational Sociology (1932) and *The Curriculum of Democratic Education* (1942).

CHRISTIAN RUCKMICK (1886–1961) received a Ph.D. from Cornell University. He taught at the University of Illinois from 1913 to 1921, then served as professor of psychology at the University of Iowa from 1924 to 1938. He was the author of numerous books and articles, including the *German–English Dictionary of Psychological Terms* (1928), *The Mental Life: A Survey of Modern Experimental Psychology* (1928) and the *Psychology of Feeling and Emotion* (1936). He invented the affectometer and other psychological measurement instruments. He served as chief civilian psychologist for the U.S. Army induction center at Peoria during World War II, and after the war held a variety of employee training positions, including employment with the Ethiopian government and TWA's Ethiopian operations between 1946 and 1952.

WILLIAM MARSTON SEABURY (1878–1949) was the great-great-grandson of Reverend Samuel Seabury, the first Episcopal bishop in the United States. He passed the bar exam in 1899 and worked as a lawyer in New York City. He served as legal representative of the motion picture industry, but by the mid-1920s he was increasingly disillusioned and concerned about film's impact on public morals. Working with William Short in 1927, he proposed forming a national committee to fight unfair practices in the film industry. He disagreed with Short about the need for research studies and was maneuvered out of the National Committee for the Study of Social Values in Motion Pictures in December 1928. He was the author of *The Public and the Motion Picture Industry* (1926) and *Motion Picture Problems: The Cinema and the League of Nations* (1929), and he was subsequently awarded the decoration of University Palms and nominated Officier d'Academie (France) in recognition of his writing on the international and economic aspects of motion pictures and their relation to public welfare.

WILLIAM HARRISON SHORT (1868–1935) was born on a farm near College Springs, Iowa. He earned B.A. and M.A. degrees from Beloit College and graduated from Yale Theological Seminary in 1897, in which year he was also ordained as a Congregational minister. He served as a pastor in Wisconsin and Minnesota from 1897 to 1908. He then moved east to become secretary of the New York Peace Society, a position he held between 1908 and 1917. He was also secretary and member of the executive committee of the League to Enforce Peace from

1915 to 1923. During 1922–1923 he served as secretary of the 20th Century Fund, then became executive director of the League of Nations Non-Partisan Association during 1923–1925. Then in 1926–1927 he was treasurer of Rollins College, in Winter Park, Florida. He became associated with Frances Bolton's National Committee for the Study of Juvenile Reading in 1927 and was founder and director of the National Committee for the Study of Social Values in Motion Pictures (renamed the Motion Picture Research Council) from 1927 to 1935. He was the author of *A Generation of Motion Pictures* (1928) and many newspaper and magazine articles. He died of a heart attack on 10 January 1935 in Philadelphia while traveling to promote the Payne Fund Studies and the work of the Motion Picture Research Council.

FRANK K. SHUTTLEWORTH (1899–1958) earned B.A. and M.A. degrees at the University of Iowa and a Ph.D. from Yale University. He conducted research at the Institute of Human Relations at Yale in the early 1930s. He was the coauthor of *A Guide to Literature for Character Training* (with Edwin Starbuck; 1928). He taught for several years at Yale and Iowa and served as professor in the Department of Student Life at the City College of New York from 1939 into the 1950s. He remained interested in the emotional problems of adolescents, and he taught a popular noncredit course on courtship and marriage.

GEORGE D. STODDARD (1897–1981) was director of the Child Welfare Research Station of the University of Iowa from 1928 to 1942. He subsequently served as president of the University of the State of New York from 1942 to 1946 and commissioner of education in New York, then as president of the University of Illinois between 1946 and 1953. At Illinois he was involved in a political ruckus over research on a cancer cure, and was dismissed for his liberal leanings but honored by the American Civil Liberties Union. From 1956 to 1967 he was professor and dean of the School of Education at New York University. He was the author of numerous books, including *Child Psychology* (1934), *The Meaning of Intelligence* (1943) and *On the Education of Women* (1950) and an autobiography, *The Pursuit of Education* (1981). He advised General MacArthur on rebuilding the educational system of Japan during the postwar occupation, was involved in UNESCO as a delegate and as chairman of commissions, served on the board of Lincoln Center in New York and was active in promoting educational television.

FREDERIC M. THRASHER (1892–1962) received his B.A. degree from DePauw University, and his M.A. and Ph.D. from the University of Chicago, where he studied sociology with Robert Park. He was the author of *The Gang: A Study of 1313 Gangs in Chicago* (1927) and several articles on juvenile delinquency. He served as professor of educational sociology in the School of Education at New York University from 1927 until the 1950s. He was director of the Bureau of Social Hygiene–funded Boys' Club study between 1928 and 1936. He also edited and wrote the preface for a popular volume on Hollywood films, *OK for Sound* (1945).

LOUIS LEON (L. L.) THURSTONE (1887–1955) earned an M.E. degree in electrical engineering from Cornell, where he designed a motion picture camera and projector, and a Ph.D. from the University of Chicago (1917). He was interested in the application of psychology to engineering. He was a professor of psychology at the University of Chicago from 1923 to 1953 and the author of *The Nature of Intelligence* (1924), *Fundamentals of Statistics* (1924) and *The Measurement of Attitudes* (1929), as well as several books on factor analysis. He served as president of the American Psychological Association in 1932 and founded the journal *Psychometrika*. He was professor of education at the University of North Carolina from 1953 to 1955, where he founded the Psychometric Laboratory.

SUPPORTING PLAYERS: Jessie A. Charters was professor of education at Ohio State University. Wendell Dysinger was a graduate student in the psychology department of the University of Iowa who subsequently became dean of MacMurray College (Illinois). Perry W. Holaday was a graduate student connected with the Child Welfare Research Station at the University of Iowa who later held a position in the Indianapolis Public Schools. Ruth C. Peterson was a graduate student in psychology at the University of Chicago. Samuel Renshaw was professor of experimental psychology at Ohio State University. Vernon Miller and Dorothy Marquis were also associated with the psychology department at Ohio State University.

MOTION PICTURES AND YOUTH

THE PAYNE FUND STUDIES

W. W. CHARTERS, CHAIRMAN

MOTION PICTURES AND YOUTH: A SUMMARY, by W. W. Charters, Director, Bureau of Educational Research, Ohio State University.

Combined with

GETTING IDEAS FROM THE MOVIES, by P. W. Holaday, Indianapolis Public Schools, and George D. Stoddard, Director, Iowa Child Welfare Research Station.

MOTION PICTURES AND THE SOCIAL ATTITUDES OF CHILDREN, by Ruth C. Peterson and L. L. Thurstone, Department of Psychology, University of Chicago.

Combined with

THE SOCIAL CONDUCT AND ATTITUDES OF MOVIE FANS, by Frank K. Shuttleworth and Mark A. May, Institute of Human Relations, Yale University.

THE EMOTIONAL RESPONSES OF CHILDREN TO THE MOTION PICTURE SITUATION by W. S. Dysinger and Christian A. Ruckmick, Department of Psychology, State University of Iowa.

Combined with

MOTION PICTURES AND STANDARDS OF MORALITY, by Charles C. Peters, Professor of Education, Pennsylvania State College.

CHILDREN'S SLEEP, by Samuel Renshaw, Vernon L. Miller, and Dorothy Marquis, Department of Psychology, Ohio State University.

MOVIES AND CONDUCT, by Herbert Blumer, Department of Sociology, University of Chicago.

THE CONTENT OF MOTION PICTURES, by Edgar Dale, Research Associate, Bureau of Educational Research, Ohio State University.

Combined with

CHILDREN'S ATTENDANCE AT MOTION PICTURES, by Edgar Dale.

MOVIES, DELINQUENCY, AND CRIME, by Herbert Blumer and Philip M. Hauser, Department of Sociology, University of Chicago.

BOYS, MOVIES, AND CITY STREETS, by Paul G. Cressey and Frederick M. Thrasher, New York University.

HOW TO APPRECIATE MOTION PICTURES, by Edgar Dale, Research Associate, Bureau of Educational Research, Ohio State University.

List of the Payne Fund Studies taken from the frontispiece of the published volumes. Note the addition of "Boys, Movies, and City Streets," which was never actually published.

Introduction

THE PAYNE FUND STUDIES AND THEIR
CONTINUING SIGNIFICANCE FOR
COMMUNICATIONS RESEARCH

Among early efforts to research the effects of mass communications, the most extensive are the reports contained in eight black-bound volumes published by Macmillan, between 1933 and 1935, under the series title "Motion Pictures and Youth." Also known as the "Payne Fund Studies" (PFS), these pioneering works were undertaken when the mass media consisted only of the press, recorded music, the movies and the radio. Of these, the movies were of greatest concern to reformers and educators because of their enormous attraction to (unsupervised) children. (Radio was not neglected, however, as Robert McChesney's Appendix A in this book reminds us.) Hence the PFS focused all their energy on one research problem: how were movies affecting the youth of America? For its time, the research was thorough, innovative and plausible. Yet the PFS are only beginning to be accorded the recognition that are their due or studied as exhaustively as they deserve to be. By reconstructing the curious history and fate of the studies, and by publishing for the first time some of the lost materials, the present volume hopes both to explain this neglect and to restore the PFS to a place of honor in the history of communications research comparable to that accorded to Lazarsfeld and Stanton's *Radio Research*, Hovland, Lumsdaine and Sheffield's *Experiments in Mass Communications* and the work of Columbia's Bureau of Applied Social Research.

The Chicago School and the Origins of Communications Research

The PFS are important both as ground-breaking works in a new field and as examples of sophisticated social science. If they mark the beginning of large-scale mass communications research, then the cradle of that research was the University of Chicago. Strong in all the social sciences, Chicago had, according to Edward Shils, become dominant in one. He writes that between the First World War and the end of the Second, by which time it had suffered something of an eclipse, the Department of Sociology at Chicago was the "center par excellence of sociological studies in the United States."[1] The two presiding professors during the department's early years, Charles R. Henderson and Albion W. Small, were Baptist ministers who shared a conception of sociology as an area of social concern, an arena for civic improvement. "But a proper sociology, Small agreed with [his colleague] W. I. Thomas, aimed to substitute actions based on knowledge for actions based on feeling."[2] So conceived as a scientific search for reliable knowledge on which to base social action, sociology was to become a professionalized social science simultaneously pursuing descriptive and observational research and theory, with an agenda set by theoretical and philosophical considerations rather than by public opinion. For twenty years the professorial figure dominating much of this research was the former journalist Robert H. Park.

The effort to turn sociology into a science – whether pursued through general theory or more rigorous empirical research – involved the detached and objective study of society and allowed no room for an ameliorative approach, which involved explicit normative commitments. The new research methods that Thomas and Park developed diverged markedly from the approach of the social survey movement, even though they were well aware of it.[3]

In circumstances to be explained in Chapter One, the Rev. William H. Short was persuaded that the children of America could be saved from the movies only if reformers' actions were based not merely on feeling but on knowledge. It was not surprising, then, that his 1928 quest for research talent eventually drew him to the University of Chicago. Chicago's was the largest and most prestigious sociology department in the

United States, and features of urban life were its raw material. A modest, one-woman study of children and the movies had already been published.[4] As historian Dorothy Ross explains, the charity and reform work in the city inspired the concrete empirical work that flourished at the university. "The inspiration . . . came largely from Hull House and the urban charity movement. Hull House widened the sympathies of its academic visitors and the writings of Jane Addams [who ran Hull House] were regularly consulted. . . . More specifically, *Hull House Maps and Papers* (1895) began the urban studies and use of maps for which Chicago sociology later became famous."[5]

The presiding sociology professors at Chicago in the 1920s, Small, Park and Ernest W. Burgess, had focused much of the department's research on the city. They had looked at its underside, its diversity, its changing face. As early as 1915 Park had argued that the vocations of ordinary people should be studied.[6] Since movies were a characteristic urban phenomenon, it should not be hard to see why Park was himself among those who submitted a research proposal to Short.[7] Urban centers seemed to be cauldrons where a new and possibly un-American social experiment was being conducted and where social pathologies were emerging that might threaten the United States that leading thinkers thought they knew. And with the growth of cinema chains and radio networks in the cities, these troubles might be exported to rural America. Instead of urban studies viewing city life as a degeneration of that in small towns and rural areas, they saw conditions in the cities as possible harbingers of what was to be visited on their country cousins.

Short found abundant talent at Chicago in sociology and cognate fields. His eventual choice for research director, W. W. Charters, taught education there, although he was soon to move to Ohio State. There were impressive younger faculty members, like Herbert Blumer and L. L. Thurstone, and outstanding students, like Philip Hauser and Paul G. Cressey. There was Frederic Thrasher, who had received his Ph.D. in 1926 with a dissertation titled "The Gang: A Study of 1,313 Gangs in Chicago," published as a book the following year. He too moved: to New York University, where he undertook a large-scale research endeavor known as the Boys' Club study. A movie component was eventually grafted onto it, as detailed in Chapter Two. A mass of material was accumulated on the Boys' Club but none of it was ever published.[8] Thrasher later recruited Paul G. Cressey to look after the movie project.

Cressey's 1929 master's thesis, "The Closed Dance Hall in Chicago," published as *The Taxi-Dance Hall* in 1932, is one of the gems of Chicago sociology. So although the Payne Fund research was conducted at Penn State, Ohio State, Yale and New York University, much of its lineage and inspiration traces back to the University of Chicago.

Morris Janowitz, writing in the *Encyclopedia of the Social Sciences,* suggests that the use of propaganda during the First World War (and its subsequent investigation by the Creel Committee) raised some questions: Were the hopes of the politicians and the fears of the public justified? Were people susceptible to persuasion by modern communications? Could these media be used to control people? Could they mold people for the worse? These questions, he claims, lay behind such early studies as the PFS.[9] As it turned out, Janowitz opines, what the Payne Fund researchers found was not anything to exacerbate fears.[10] Janowitz notes that, at this stage, mass communications research was responsive to public opinion and concern. In this respect, it only partially conformed to the trend of work at the University of Chicago and deviated from much of social science research. Mass communications research was then, and is to this day, more closely tied to the public agenda than to social science research in general.[11]

Behind the growth of the social sciences and their research, if we follow Dorothy Ross, is the following argument. The Declaration of Independence created a unique culture. The United States envisaged itself as a society of robust and independent yeomen, largely rural, largely classless, neither Jacobin nor reactionary: an exception in the history of nations. In the post–Civil War period, the emergence of the city, the development of capitalism and the influx of lower-class immigrants shook people's faith in this exceptionalist myth. In these respects, the United States was turning out to be much like Old World countries. The underlying project of the social sciences, Ross argues, was to show that, despite uncomfortable parallels with the Old World, American exceptionalism remained intact. Adding to Ross, we may note that mass communications were, in the 1920s, the major new challenge to the exceptionalist myth, for they erupted into a republic that had not anticipated anything like them and they seemed set to disrupt it. Profit-driven and pandering, they were made in and by the very segment of society, urban immigrants, that was thought to threaten the republic's identity. Could the political system as envisaged by the founders survive the assault on the population by the mass media?

Equally significant for the assessment of the PFS was the intellectual sophistication of the studies. Since there had been no large-scale mass communications research before, since the questions to be addressed were not new but had not previously been broken down into re-searchable form, the authors of these studies were pioneers both in research methods and in research design. They had to devise ways to answer intuitive questions with empirical research: Did movies affect children's sleep? Did movies teach? Did movies affect attitudes? Did movies affect conduct? Could one identify and quantify the content of movies? Was there a cause-and-effect relationship between movies and crime? Their research methods ranged from physiological studies (using such devices as the psychogalvanometer and the wired bed; see photo section), through questionnaires, to open-ended interviews, autobiographies, content analysis and statistically standardized tests. All of these research techniques, in refined forms, continue to be used today. The Payne Fund pioneers and research designers were far from flawless in their use of these new means, but it is from their errors and oversights that more cautious and reliable methods were developed.

The Eclipse of the Payne Fund Studies

Why, then, have these volumes of research stemming from a major school of social science, both informative and methodologically innovative, only begun to be accorded the recognition they deserve as excellent early mass communications research? The answer is complex and will emerge in more detail in the three chapters of Part One.

For the purposes of this introduction, we can divide the question into global aspects having to do with changes in the social sciences themselves, and localized factors having to do with the reception of the PFS by the public and by the academy.

One factor was the decline of the Chicago school by the early 1930s, as well as criticism of the school by rival institutions, who in turn promoted themselves. The social process model of society that underlay so much Chicago work came under attack and was replaced by sampling and other techniques from survey research and statistics,[12] as well as the personality and social structure approach associated with the names of Parsons and Merton at Harvard. In this approach, theory came first: to identify something as a social problem you had first to articulate your view of society and its processes and specify norms and expectations. It was then possible to distinguish between social problems that were integral to the social system (e.g., suicide and crime) and those alleged to have exogenous causes that could be corrected if those causes were eliminated. (Prohibitionists thought of alcohol as an exogenous cause of social ills, and nowadays the language of enforcement personnel and some politicians suggests that they view drugs similarly. Functionalists would be inclined to view both as endogenous problems of failed integration.) [13]

Functionalism was a much-strengthened version of the tendency at Chicago for research problems, despite the stress on theory, to coincide with the public agenda. In classic Chicago studies, social problems were treated as deviations from the proper course of society. The later functionalist view knew no proper course; society was an integrated and functioning system and many of its so-called problems were unintended consequences of nonproblematic parts of the system. A good example is the argument about prostitution by the Harvard-trained sociologist Kingsley Davis. Davis endeavored to show that prostitution was correlated with the strength of the family system and a regime of social status.[14] A standard social problem was treated as a functional correlate of a central social institution and hence not as a problem to be ameliorated in isolation or without cost.[15]

By the time the first of the PFS appeared in 1933, the work had come to seem curiously untheoretical, even by contemporary standards. Perhaps this was because the functionalist notion of theory was stronger than that espoused by Park and those under his influence. A slew of empirical research had been carried out by the Payne Fund scientists operating with no agreed-upon model of society. At least, none was articulated. But theoretical questions, visions of society, were coming to the fore in the rivalries among university sociology departments just mentioned. In these disputes, the issues surrounding the socialization of children had a modest place. Much more important was the understanding of the acting adult in the institutional and psychological setting. Thus the work of Lasswell on Communist propaganda and of Cantril and Merton and Lazarsfeld on radio listening seems much more contemporary than the PFS.[16] These later pioneers of communications research were already in touch with the kinds of thinking about society that began to emerge in the 1930s and that have existed to the present day.

These changes in the social sciences partially explain why the PFS were orphaned; to complete the picture we have to add the influence of more local historical developments. First and foremost was the self-destruct device built into the studies. As the results of the research came in and were discussed, the researchers became increasingly divided between those whose prior doubts about the movies had been reinforced by the data (a majority) and those who concluded that the data gave no cause for alarm and that perhaps the entire approach they had been using was sociologically and psychologically naive.

We see emerging in discussions within the PFS what we might now take to be the standard dilemma of all social scientists researching public policy issues. It was not standard at the time. Scientific work is currently seen as the servant and not the determinant of policy. Indeed, research is supposed to strive for neutrality on policy issues. This was still a new position at the time the PFS were being made. As noted, several of the senior professors at Chicago had backgrounds of policy activism. All of the Payne Fund researchers were trained professionals. Short was not a professional but an activist. He had recruited researchers sympathetic to his views, researchers cool to his views and researchers who shared his disappointment at Hollywood's failure to make movies that were uplifting or educational. Edgar Dale, who confined his study to enhancing the positive socializing role of movies, seems to have stood a little outside the scientific discussions of the rest of the researchers. Yet it was projects developed out of his work that the Payne Fund continued to support for nearly twenty years.

These complicated divisions among the researchers were sharpened when the manuscript of Henry J. Forman's popular summary of the results was circulated for comments. Forman was a free-lance writer commissioned to produce a trade book summing up the research. What he produced was an antimovie polemic more strident than the Rev. Short's earlier Payne Fund project, *A Generation of Motion Pictures* (1927). Short and Charters, no friends of the movies, worked hard to get the Forman manuscript toned down. Scientific results were more persuasive, they felt, when presented in a somewhat lower key. Previewed as articles in *McCall's,* then published as *Our Movie Made Children* (1933), this best-seller became *the* representation of the PFS in the public mind and gave the false impression that the researchers had lent themselves to a moralizing crusade.[17] It diverted attention from the scientific achievement of the studies and forced the authors to distance themselves from Forman's opinions. As Chapter Three details, this danger had been seen too late to be averted.[18]

Worse was to come with regard to the standing of the work in scientific opinion. Mortimer J. Adler, who taught both philosophy and law at the University of Chicago, and who maintained a long-standing philosophical skepticism about the value of social science research for public policy, incorporated a lengthy and scathing critique of the scientific reasoning of some of the studies in his *Art and Prudence* (1937). A delighted movie industry had Raymond Moley summarize Adler's high-powered ideas in a "brochure" of 1938.[19] Clearly energized by his contempt for Forman's pretensions as a moral tutor, Adler scored heavy hits on the Payne Fund reports authored by Blumer; Blumer and Hauser; Peters; Dale; Renshaw, Miller and Marquis; and Dysinger and Ruckmick. His rhetorical case was strengthened when he singled out three of the more quantitative reports – by Shuttleworth and May, Holaday and Stoddard, and Thurstone and Peterson – as exemplary social science.

But it was Adler's overall argument that was the killer: even were the facts established as thus and so, he reasoned, it did not follow that any particular course of action was thereby recommended.[20] As contemporary philosophers would say, no value conclusions could be drawn from facts. Although the charge that the researchers had overlooked this point was unfair, it stuck. In truth, the Payne Fund researchers were well aware that social science and social policy were different things, and they had all along hoped to distance themselves from any recommendations and conclusions.[21] But the institutional overlap between the Research Committee, headed by Charters, and the Motion Picture Research Council, headed by Short (and only secretly funded by the politically shy Payne Fund), was too obvious. Furthermore, in the absence of an overall vision of society and a comparative perspective on the contributions of other social institutions to problems associated with the movies, the social scientists were hard-pressed to keep a safe distance from Short and Forman's campaign. After all, it was Short who had initiated the research, molded much of the approach and selected the researchers. It was not hard for Adler to identify unacknowledged value assumptions built into the research itself. Thus rival scientists could impugn the scientific credentials of the PFS work simply from its association with Short and Forman.

What had happened is very simple. The researchers were men and women of science but they had no clearly articulated framework in which to present their results simply as advances in science. Short and Forman were crusaders and publicity hounds. They presented the research in a moral context and as a call to action. Thus the scientific work was discussed by Adler, for example, largely in a moral context. But, unlike Short and Forman, he found it morally worthless. Thus the choice for the public seemed either to consider the work valuable and join the crusade or to repudiate the crusade and the work. Much of the social science community seems to have chosen the latter course. Shoved aside and only now being seriously contemplated are the scientific merits of the work independent of the moral context in which it was hijacked.

A contingent local historical fact but one, again, that hastened the demise of the PFS is that, during the period in which they were being prepared, the organized motion picture industry was engaged in self-reform. If the studies could be interpreted as pointing to any adverse effects, these were already moot under the reforms prompted by the League of Decency and the efforts of the Production Code Administration of the Motion Picture Producers and Distributors of America, created by Will H. Hays.[22] Insofar as the Payne Fund research identified any dangers, these drastic self-censorship efforts to make movies inoffensive, or else unintelligible, to school-age children would have allayed fears. Few reformers were wholly convinced by these "cleanup" efforts, but more sophisticated thinking about how movies affected society was required if the campaign against them was to continue. The failure of the reformers to sponsor further research may help explain why the moral panic they had tried to generate subsided after 1935.

It would be controversial to argue that the failure to publish one of the key projected studies, that on the role of the movies in inner-city areas served by boys' clubs (announced as *Boys, Movies and City Streets*), contributed to the studies' neglect. After all, the gist of the findings had been described by both Charters and Forman. Yet that projected volume was central. Would it show that, in New York, some connection could be made between undesirable social behavior and movie attendance? The self-reporting by delinquent youths seemed to suggest a connection. When the principal researcher, Paul G. Cressey, tried to write up the material, however, he found himself unpersuaded that the research question as defined could be so answered. As the reader of this volume will see, he thought through the results and found that society simply did not work the way the original research design implicitly assumed. What we publish here are his first attempt (Chapter Four) and his redesign of the problem (Chapter Five). Read with his 1938 article,[23] these texts show Cressey to be an intellectual bridge between the kind of thinking about society Chicago had sponsored in the 1920s, when the PFS project was set up, and the more modern-seeming thinking about society emerging in the later 1930s.

A final local reason for the eclipse of the PFS is that the researchers who had struggled so hard to finish the studies almost immediately turned their backs on this line of research and made their careers elsewhere. Some of the younger researchers disappeared from the social sciences.[24] Those who stayed in academe went on to gain fame for different kinds of work.[25] Perhaps the internal dissent of the group (see Chapter Two) and the studies' disastrous reception were strong signals to put the PFS behind them.

The Continuing Relevance of the Payne Fund Studies

Whether or not these are the historical reasons for the relative neglect of the PFS, the question remains, of what interest are they today? Are they of purely historical concern, or can they be profitably studied in their own right? The answer is that they are of considerable intrinsic interest. The effects of mass communication are a continuing intellectual and public policy problem, and any study of them remains far from tractable. From the past efforts of the PFS we can learn both what went right and, even more so, what went wrong. Furthermore, the Studies help us to historicize the subject of mass communications research, to demystify it by studying its painstaking and halting construction.

With concerns expressed successively about children and crooners, children and radio serials, children and horror comics, children and television, children and rock music, children and rap lyrics and children and video games, it might hardly seem necessary to make a case for the ongoing relevance of the PFS.[26] The nature of the socialization process remains poorly understood; the degree of its dependence on what might be termed the major or central institutions of family, school and church, as opposed to such informal pressures as peer group and mass media, is controversial. The PFS were done at a time when the difficulties were not fully grasped. These studies, including some of the material published here for the first time, showed how complex was the problem of raising children to be good citizens in the socially dense milieu of urbanized America.

It is also important to realize that the best researchers of the late 1920s were not all naive adherents of what has been caricatured as the "hypodermic" or "magic bullet" theory of mass communications, in which media messages were assumed to have a direct and immediate effect on the viewer's consciousness as if they were injected like a drug into the bloodstream. There are traces of that idea in the PFS,[27] but to some degree it was tested and gone beyond. Dissatisfaction with Blumer's research approach led Cressey to redesign the New York University study in the middle of the project (see Chapter Three), a decision that probably contributed to its failure to be published as a monograph. In 1938 Cressey was able to publish an overview that is still viable today.[28]

So, besides learning from the gropings and errors of the past, we need to acknowledge the degree to which past scholars got it right and, more particularly, to acknowledge the clear continuities of ideas and research techniques between the Payne Fund and present-day work. Studies of media content, learning, attitude change and values all owe debts to the PFS.[29] We may wonder why these continuities were ever elided or denied. The answer is to be found in the sociology of the academic world. Successive generations of scholars feel a need to define their work for themselves and their students by contrasting it with some other, unenlightened or former approach. The most common way is to malign not the work of their teachers, on whom they depend, but that of their teachers' teachers – a strategy sometimes called "academic grandfather-killing," as Jarvie has noted.[30]

The PFS also have relevance as historical documents: they tell us something about the society of the time and its preoccupations, and something of the state of the art in the social sciences. These researchers worked on the cutting edge, devising new ways to investigate as they went along. And they themselves were as critical of their efforts as we could be. A society that forgets its own history is one doomed to repeat its own mistakes. Insofar as leaders of public opinion and academics continue to be interested in the isolation, study and "cure" of social problems, it would be advisable for them to be aware of what has gone before.

More generally, the PFS clearly grew out of the difficulty that certain dominant and elite groups in the United States had with the rapid social changes of the twentieth century and, particularly in the cities, the communications revolution. Mass communications were new sources of social control that did not run along the grooves of established power and class relations. They served the masses without special regard for the elites. The pennies to the newspaper boy and the nickels to the box office called the tunes for mass communicators.[31] It is particularly striking that the burgeoning movie industry was seen as being in the hands of newcomers to the United States and that power and influence were going to those who had not fully assimilated the values cherished (or, at least, officially endorsed) by traditional elites. Yet if the United States was to perpetuate its image, some kind of control over the movies and their socializing effects seemed imperative. We may consider it a major lacuna in the Payne Fund series that no study of the ownership and control of the industry was undertaken. Short was aware of this need but, as explained in Chapter One, the political sensitivities of the Payne Fund made it skittish about any such project. In the end, the man Short negotiated with, Howard T. Lewis of Harvard Business School, wrote a monograph on his own.[32]

Excluding the press, where debate has been hampered by First Amendment protection, we have seen this same public policy battle fought and refought over radio, television, rock and roll, music videos and video games. In the PFS we have the first and most extensive attempt to take these issues at face value. Their researchers looked to see if intuitive concerns could be given concrete, measurable expression in research. While they had partial success, as have all subsequent efforts, they also ran into intractable problems. There was the fundamental doubt as to whether what they were measuring was an artifact of their techniques. And there was the general doubt as to whether the problem itself did not imply a rather simple model of how society and the socialization process worked. Since that day, no way has yet been found to resolve the dilemma of cause and effect: do crime movies create more crime, or do the criminally inclined enjoy and perhaps imitate crime movies? As the PFS showed, quite possibly both horns of the dilemma are true. The problem was that quantifying and weighing the two factors was next to impossible, certainly in a scientific way. No one denied that movies disseminate both implicit and explicit propaganda, including values and ideas elites may find disagreeable. Yet their very appeal to the masses makes it difficult to articulate a democratic and egalitarian case against them.

The Organization and Origins of This Book

This volume began as a quest for a missing book. It gradually became a quest to understand the origins and history of the PFS and their connection to the Payne Fund and its media projects, which the authors were convinced were very important and badly neglected. The book thus consists of both explanatory chapters and original documents from the unpublished materials discovered in the files of the Fund and Motion Picture Research Council. The major document is "The Community – A Social Setting for the Motion Picture" (Chapter Four), an *ur*-version of what was to have become Cressey and Thrasher's *Boys, Movies and City Streets*. Following that is a chapter outline (Chapter Five) of somewhat later date showing how the project had matured in Cressey's mind. This is in many ways the most intellectually impressive of the documents reproduced herein. It helps us considerably to understand why Cressey had trouble finishing the project and also why it was unlikely to please its sponsors. His 1938 article summarizing the theoretical position he had reached is reproduced in Appendix B. Chapter Six reproduces material from Herbert Blumer's studies of movies: some of the autobiographies his subjects wrote to describe the role of movies in their lives, and his unpublished essay, "Movies and Sex." Introductions place each of the documents in context, and the biographical sketches of the main dramatis personae, at the beginning of the book, will help the reader keep clear who is who. It remains to say something about how this volume came about.

When researching the *bibliographie raisonée* for his book *Movies and Society* (1970), Jarvie, then a professor of philosophy at York University, made a careful study of the Payne Fund volumes; but he also made a careless mistake. Unable to lay his hands on one volume listed in the series – *Boys, Movies and City Streets* by Paul G. Cressey and Frederic M. Thrasher – he took its title and a synopsis of it from other sources.[33] When Jarvie's book was published, Jowett, then a graduate student at the University of Pennsylvania writing his dissertation (which would later become *Film: The Democratic Art*, 1976), challenged him, claiming that the book in question, though listed and summarized (by Forman in *Our Move Made Children*), had never in fact been published, since no library held it. This seemed odd, and so an informal casting around and eventually a formal search were begun. The publisher was contacted, as were the universities involved. Nothing turned up. It was even unclear whether the Payne Fund still existed and, if so, what it was. Gradually, however, other researchers entered the scene and exchanged information about Payne Fund materials that had surfaced in several places. Finally, Jarvie stumbled across the central files of the Motion Picture Research Council project in the unlikely venue of the Hoover Institution on War, Revolution and Peace. This discovery was quite serendipitous: he was examining a list of the Institution's holdings in connection with an entirely different project.

The two veteran hands, Jarvie and Jowett, were joined by Kathryn Fuller, a social historian who was interested in film audiences. Jarvie and Jowett both made extended research trips to Palo Alto; Fuller made several trips to Columbus, Ohio, where the papers of the Payne Fund research director, W. W. Charters, were housed; and Fuller, Jarvie and Jowett rendezvoused in Cleveland to study the central files of the Payne Fund at the Western Reserve Historical Society. Planning for this book began there and was completed in a working session at Houston. There has been mutual consultation and critiquing among the authors, and the final book is the product of this lengthy interchange. Each author had responsibility for one of the major chapters: Jowett supervised Chapter One and coordinated the overall project; Jarvie supervised the Introduction and Chapter Three, as well as several of the biographies; and Fuller supervised Chapter Two, compiled the bulk of the biographies, annotated the primary document references and coordinated editing of the final manuscript. Even though it was our intention that the entire project appear seamless, each of us maintains independent views on some of the historical issues. We hope our work will jump-start the process of recuperating the important and lasting contribution of the Payne Fund to the development of research into the mass media.

PART ONE

History of the Payne Fund Studies

CHAPTER ONE

Social Science as a Weapon

THE ORIGINS OF THE PAYNE FUND
STUDIES, 1926–1929

This is the movement to fix and establish the status of the motion
picture as a new public utility and to keep the channels of trade
between the producer and the public open and free for all,
to the end that the motion picture may become and remain a
wholesome entertainment, at prices which will keep it within
the reach of the great masses. . . .
    Specifically, the remedy in America must include an Act of
Congress which will declare the motion picture to be a new
public utility and the business of producing, distributing and
exhibiting pictures to be charged with the obligation and duty to
eliminate the debasing influences, and to cultivate friendly
relations with the people of other nations and to promote the
moral, educational and cultural development of the people.[1]

When William Marston Seabury, who had for several years been general
counsel of the Motion Picture Board of Trade and the National Association of the Motion Picture Industry, wrote those words in his 1926
publication, *The Public and the Motion Picture Industry,* he set in
motion a chain of events that would culminate in the publication in
1933 of the twelve-volume series Motion Pictures and Youth, more
commonly referred to as the Payne Fund Studies (PFS).[2] This pioneering
research effort still constitutes the most extensive evaluation ever undertaken of the role of the motion picture in American society and its
effect on children, and the individual studies themselves constitute an
important but neglected chapter in the development of U.S. social science and particularly in the history of mass communications research.
The PFS are often cited, but seldom read, and the full history of the

social and political influences that precipitated their origins have never been fully explained.

Background: The Mystery of the Payne Fund Studies

After the initial furor that surrounded their publication in 1933, the PFS were all but ignored by media scholars. (The reasons for this are discussed in detail in Chapter Three.) They were "rediscovered" in the 1970s by the new group of film historians attempting to understand the interrelationship between the movie industry and American society and culture. Both Robert Sklar and Garth Jowett in their respective cultural and social histories of American film helped to place the PFS in historical perspective.[3] Despite these two efforts to highlight the significance of the studies, film scholars generally ignored their rich potential as a source of important historical information on the moviegoing process in the 1920s and 1930s.[4] Instead, most of the attention given to the PFS in the past decade has come from mass communications scholars as they begin to unravel the political history of communications research in the United States. Thus, in his history of the politics of television violence, Willard Rowland discussed the PFS as precursors to the later governmental studies on the effects of television on children.[5] Ellen Wartella and Byron Reeves cited the PFS as examples of the fact that not all communications research before 1940 was based on the "hypodermic needle" model, and in his survey of the history of communications research, Delia noted, "Although there would be steady refinements in methodological and measurement procedures, it would be a very long time before communication research developed beyond these studies."[6] The most detailed recent examination of the PFS is found in a textbook by Shearon Lowery and Melvin De Fleur, *Milestones in Mass Communications Research* (1988), in which they devote an entire chapter to an analysis and evaluation of the findings of the studies. The authors conclude: "Above all, the studies shifted the long-standing pattern of concern on the part of communication scholars with propaganda criticism that represented an earlier rhetorical form of analysis. In these senses, the Payne Fund Studies will remain one of the most significant milestones in the development of mass communication as a scientific field of study."[7]

    Despite all of this renewed interest, these historical assessments, descriptions and reevaluations of the importance of the PFS and their significant contribution to the history of social science in general, and communication research in particular, merely hint at their true significance. (Their important role in film studies still awaits wider recognition by most film scholars.) So, despite the fact that the rediscovery of the PFS has helped to fill in lacunae in the histories of both film and communications research, it is important to note that nowhere in the past or current literature is there an accurate history of the social, cultural and political forces that caused them to be undertaken in the first place. All of the aforementioned evaluations are based on the information contained in the published studies themselves or taken from contemporary accounts published in the aftermath of their appearance. In particular, the preface to the summary volume by W. W. Charters, *Motion Pictures and Youth* (1933), has been the source of most of the accepted history of the studies. Professor Charters, who was the head of the Department of Educational Research at Ohio State University, had been appointed the research director of this motion picture project. His account of the "initiation of the studies" not only is truncated, but fails to reflect the specific circumstances, both ideological and historical, that precipitated and structured the objectives and ultimate goals of the research. Nor does it describe the selection of the individual researchers and how they were contracted for, the way in which the subjects of the separate studies were decided upon, the methodological and interpretative differences between the researchers and the administrators or the disagreements about the manner in which the findings of the studies were eventually presented to the public. Without this background no accurate assessment of the PFS is possible. This book discusses each of these topics in some detail.

This first chapter examines the histories of the various organizations that played a role in the creation and funding of the PFS. It explains the circumstances surrounding the genesis of the studies and reviews the ideological influences that shaped the particular structure of the research program that was finally undertaken. The chapter concludes with a description of the final years of the Motion Picture Research Council (MPRC), the organizing body behind the PFS, and its eventual demise – a story that has never been revealed in print.

It is now possible to begin to unravel the history of the PFS thanks to two major archival deposits. The first of these is the files of the MPRC in the Archives of the Hoover Institution on War, Revolution and Peace at Stanford University. The MPRC, under the extraordinary direction of

William H. Short, was the guiding organization behind the creation, and eventual dissemination, of the PFS. In the seventy-eight boxes of files and supporting material in the Hoover Archives lies the remarkable record of not only the PFS, but also of the enormous concern surrounding the issue of "movie influence" during the period 1920–1940. The second major archival deposit consists of the files and papers of Frances Payne Bolton in the library of the Western Reserve Historical Society in Cleveland, Ohio. Mrs. Bolton, daughter of the wealthy industrialist Charles William Bingham and a prominent member of Cleveland society, was a congresswoman for the Twenty-second District from 1939 to 1968. It was through her personal efforts that the Payne Study and Experiment Fund was established in 1927. (The Fund was named for her maternal grandfather, Henry B. Payne, a lawyer and railroad entrepreneur, who had been a U. S. senator for Ohio from 1885 to 1891.) The eighty-one boxes of Payne Fund, Inc., material in this collection provide the indispensable key to understanding the continuous tensions between the sponsors and the researchers on the PFS project, as well as the sponsors' pragmatic concerns about the political consequences of their actions. A third archival collection – the papers of Dr. W. W. Charters in the library of Ohio State University, Columbus – also contains original material pertinent to the history of the PFS.

This chapter, like all of the material in this book, is based on an extensive examination of these archival deposits. By combining their holdings it has been possible to obtain a very clear picture of how the idea for the studies originated, what ideological impulses fueled their creation and their final structure and how the studies were conducted and disseminated after publication. Also, cross-referencing the material has provided a valuable (and a somewhat voyeuristic) insight into the different perceptions that the significant individuals in this endeavor held of each other. This latter discovery is particularly important, because these personal feelings very often resulted in major decisions regarding the objectives, methodologies and public presentation of the studies, or the structure of the institutions that were created to administer them. (These relationships are discussed in greater detail in Chapter Two.) The availability of these invaluable collections now means that we can, at long last, examine and evaluate the PFS using primary documentation. This will provide scholars with an accurate assessment of their significance both as scientific documents and as symbols of the response to the deep cultural shock wave being experienced in the United States in the 1920s.

The Problem of the Movies and the Decline of Protestant Hegemony

In 1916, Hugo Munsterberg, a well-known Harvard psychology professor, wrote his path-breaking treatise, *The Photoplay: A Psychological Study*. His concern for the movies was based on his assessment that

the intensity with which the plays take hold of the audience cannot remain without social effects. . . . The associations become as vivid as realities, because the mind is so completely given up to the moving pictures. . . . But it is evident that such a penetrating influence must be fraught with dangers. The more vividly the impressions force themselves on the mind, the more easily must they become starting points for imitation and other motor responses.[8]

When Munsterberg articulated his concern, the projected motion picture was already twenty years old, having had its first commercial showing in the United States at Koster and Bial's Music Hall in New York on the night of 23 April 1896. During the intervening two decades, the motion picture had undergone a dramatic metamorphosis from its first public exhibition as just another vaudeville curiosity and emerged from the chrysalis of the storefront nickelodeons in the working-class districts to occupy the first of the magnificent picture palaces on the main streets of U.S. cities.[9] What many observers had predicted (and some hoped) would be just another entertainment fad for the urban working class had, by 1916, become a major industry with a broad appeal and, more surprisingly, a significant social and cultural force that gained the attention of social scientists, educators, politicians, clergymen and social workers.[10]

The motion picture was the first of the major mass media of the twentieth century, setting the scene for what was to come later with radio and television. While many magazines had developed considerable national circulation in the late nineteenth century, their readership was not as widespread throughout all demographic and socioeconomic segments of the population as was movie attendance. Nor did the print media have the enormous inherent appeal of "glamour," which almost immediately became associated with the movies. It was through motion pictures, with their capacity to stir the audience's imagination and emotions, that the first real media personalities were created. By 1914, the movie studios were making these previously unknown men and women into nationally recognized "stars" with vast public followings.[11] Also, it was not long before the movies demonstrated that they were potent sources of ideas for changes in the material culture, affecting the nature of fashion, furniture design and even domestic architecture. All in all, nothing signified more dramatically the arrival of "mass culture" in the United States than the enormous public response to the motion picture.[12]

Of course, the enthusiastic public embrace of this new entertainment form did not go unnoticed by those individuals whom the historian Henry May has called the "custodians of culture," and almost immediately after their first appearance (even in their "peep-show" form) the movies were being threatened with censorship and subjected to investigations and evaluations.[13] The first critical reactions to the motion picture were very mixed, and there was little agreement as to what mechanism should be established to ensure the most advantageous use of the medium's obvious capacity to communicate to (and therefore educate) a large number of people with seeming ease. Everyone from clergymen to private detectives offered advice on how to "improve the movies," while the more zealous reformers appealed to their political representatives for action to prevent what they considered to be a gross and dangerous misuse of the medium's innate potential.[14]

Why all this fuss and concern over what on the surface seemed to be an innocuous diversion from the humdrum life of the urban working class? Clearly the movies represented a threat to the established hegemony of the Protestant groups that had imposed their morality and values on American life and culture. Since the end of the nineteenth century, this hegemony had been threatened by successive waves of non-Protestant immigration, increasing urbanization (and therefore new structures of political power) and new forms of entertainment and communication. By the end of the First World War, a growing number of Catholics and Jews were moving into positions of social, cultural and political prominence. In such a volatile society, there were bound to be clashes of value systems. As late as 1927 Andre Siegfried noted: "The civilization of the United States is essentially Protestant. Those who prefer other systems, such as Catholicism, for example, are considered

bad Americans and are sure to be frowned upon by the purists. Protestantism is the only national religion, and to ignore that fact is to view
the country from a false angle."[15] It was a tenet of faith that the United
States had achieved its high level of industrial and material civilization
because of the inherent superiority of Protestantism and its underlying
moral code, which stressed hard work and an adherence to a simple
God-fearing evangelic faith.

It is against the background of this unerring faith in the positive role
of Protestantism in American society that we must view reactions to the
motion picture. By the turn of the century, the Protestant hegemony felt
itself under attack as the power of the traditional socializing agencies of
the home, the school and the church were being challenged by potent
new sources of information in society – newspapers, cheap literature,
magazines, movies and eventually radio and television. These media
constituted a threat because they were not under the control of the
"guardians of the culture" and were the source of information and ideas
that often ran counter to the prevailing (Protestant) mores. The attempt
to establish prohibition through the Volstead Act and the Eighteenth
Amendment to the Constitution in 1919 can be seen as one of the last-
gasp attempts to maintain this Protestant hegemony in the face of the
growing importance of new immigrant cultures (especially those of Roman Catholic Irish and Italians) for whom alcohol was a natural part of
daily life.[16] Similarly, the U.S. Supreme Court's decision *Mutual v. Ohio*
(1915),[17] which condoned the legal censorship of motion pictures, must
also be viewed as an example of what can be accomplished by a group
in the last throes of a "loss of status."[18] Together, these two restrictive
measures represented a hollow triumph for the forces of Protestant
conservatism threatened by the immense changes in their "Christian"
(i.e., Protestant) environment.[19]

By the early 1920s, despite the availability and widespread application of legalized movie censorship, those who wished to place the entire
movie industry under much more rigorous forms of social control were
far from satisfied. In 1921 the industry had responded to these continuous threats with the creation of a major trade organization – the Motion
Picture Producers and Distributors of America (MPPDA) – with the
former postmaster general, and Warren G. Harding's campaign manager, Will H. Hays, as the president. An important reason for Hays's
appointment was his prominence as an elder in the Presbyterian church,
which, it was hoped, would counter the prevailing public perception that

Jews controlled the motion picture industry. This was a sagacious move on the part of the studio owners, for the politically experienced Hays immediately went to work to prevent any further inroads by state or federal censorship.[20] He devised and employed a variety of tactics to combat the increasing clamor for more stringent control of the movies, including the smashing defeat of a statewide referendum on movie censorship in Massachusetts in 1922.[21] Hays was soon called the "Movie Czar" by the press (one press wit dubbed him "the Czar of all the rushes"), and he worked hard to promote the concept of industry "self-regulation" as the cornerstone of his strategy to make the motion picture industry more responsive to public concerns. This philosophy, he claimed, was more in keeping with the "American way." However, the forces arrayed against the "evils of the movies" were convinced that the Hays Office (as the MPPDA became known) was merely using the illusion of self-regulation and other public relations strategies (such as inviting a wide variety of social and cultural groups to become a permanent part of the regulatory process) as a ploy to allow the movie industry to continue to produce films that eroded public morality. Throughout the 1920s, and especially after the introduction of sound films in 1926, there was a constant clamoring for the movie industry to be more socially responsible for its actions. While the number of protesters was relatively small compared with the millions who attended the movies every week without apparent complaint, they claimed to represent the opinion of all "right-thinking" Americans. Largely middle-class, professional and politically astute, they commanded far more attention and achieved more reaction from the industry than their number would normally have warranted. However, the studio heads were always nervous about organized protest, and they went to extraordinary lengths to either accommodate or combat it as the situation dictated.[22]

Social Science and the "Problem of the Movies"

It did not take long for the emerging group of professional social workers and social scientists to take an interest in the motion picture and to apply the techniques of the new social sciences to investigating and understanding it. The popularity of this ubiquitous entertainment form, especially with children and the working class, made it a ready target for those who either wished to improve social conditions (by providing

"suitable" forms of leisure) or to understand these new forces in society.
Social workers were the first to research and write about the role of
movies in their neighborhoods. They counted the number of movie
houses, they estimated attendance frequencies and audience composition
and they speculated on the influence of movies. The more perceptive
among them soon concluded that this entertainment was not as innocuous as it may have initially seemed. The results of these informal investigations by social workers are some of the first important observations
made about the movies and their influence on American society.[23]

Jane Addams, the famous director of the Hull House settlement in
Chicago, was among the first to comment on the possible influences of
the motion picture on the child's development, and she devoted an entire
chapter in her book *The Spirit of Youth and City Streets* (1909) to an
analysis of what she poetically called the "House of Dreams." Her
comments about the movies were ambivalent. She recognized the recreational role of movies for the city child, but she also voiced considerable
alarm at the possible harmful effects of this "unreal" world. She noted
that " 'going to the show' for thousands of young people in every
industrial city is the only place where they can satisfy that craving for a
conception of higher life than that which the actual world offers
them."[24] However, she then argued, the child's pleasure in the "House
of Dreams" was but a cruel illusion, and she cited several examples of
films that she felt filled "their impressionable minds with these absurdities which certainly will become the foundation for their working moral
codes and the data from which they will judge the proprieties of life."[25]
She claimed to know of many cases in which children had stolen in order
to obtain money for tickets, but for her the greatest harm lay in the
differences between the content of the five-cent theater shows and the
moral code of life as "prescribed by the church." Further, she lamented,
somewhat enviously comparing local children's attendance at Hull
House functions and at nickelodeon shows, "the five-cent theater is
also fast becoming the general social center and club house in many
neighborhoods."[26]

Jane Addams's attitude toward the "House of Dreams" is a mixture
of naive amazement at the popularity of the movies and a fear of the
powerful influence the entertainment seemed to have on its audience
("forming the ground pattern of their social life"). She saw in the movies
a source of neurosis, delinquency, sexual license, antisocial behavior,
bad health and even "attempted murder." Ultimately she was concerned

that the ubiquity and popularity of the movies would cause children to forgo other recreational activities of a more wholesome character. She concluded her chapter by noting:

To fail to provide for the recreation of youth is not only to deprive all of them of their natural form of expression, but is certain to subject some of them to overwhelming temptation of illicit and soul-destroying pleasures. To insist that young people shall forecast their rose-colored future only in a house of dreams, is to deprive the real world of that warmth and reassurance which it so sorely needs and to which it is so justly entitled.[27]

Jane Addams was only one of many prominent social workers and social scientists who voiced concern over the influence of the increasingly popular motion picture. It was only natural that social scientists, particularly psychologists, should turn their attention to the effect of movies on crime, especially juvenile crime. The possible connection between delinquency and film had always been a favorite complaint of reformers, educators, criminologists and even some early psychologists. Certainly it was to be expected that a medium that the highest court in the country had noted had "a capacity for evil" would be labeled as a major contributing factor in the increase in juvenile and other crime. In his seminal study, *The Individual Delinquent,* published in 1915, William Healy, pioneer in the study of juvenile delinquency, included several case studies concerning children who he alleged had been influenced by the movies to commit criminal acts. Healy offered an explanation of the connection between movies and crime that was remarkably similar to the description of motion picture psychology that Hugo Munsterberg had written in the same year: "The strength of the powers of visualization is to be deeply reckoned with when considering the springs of criminality. . . . It is the mental representation of some sort of pictures of himself or others in the criminal act that leads the delinquent onward in his path."[28] Healy's description of the psychology of the "movie experience" led him to a more subjective analysis of the "evils of the cinema." He claimed that his work had provided him with "much evidence" that "movies may be stimulating to the sex instinct" and that the real danger lay in the darkness of the hall where the pictures were shown. (It should be recalled that, until the late 1950s, American children, especially girls, were routinely placed in juvenile detention homes for the crime of "sexual delinquency.") Healy ominously noted: "Under cover of dimness evil communications readily pass and bad habits are taught. Moving picture

theaters are favorite places for the teaching of homosexual practices."
However, to his credit, Healy also recognized that some children might
be more susceptible than others to "pictorial suggestions." He thought
that the main hope for preventing these undesirable effects was to be
found "in rigorous censorship of perverting pictures, and in radical
prosecution of those who produce and deal in obscene and other demoralizing pictorial presentations."[29] Healy's suggestion that criminal proceedings be instigated against those who trafficked in "obscene and
immoral" movies was not an isolated one: similar proposals were
echoed by other reformers.

The reformers faced several obstacles in their attempts to make the
motion picture industry more responsive to their demands for greater
social responsibility. First, the general public tended to vote at the box
office, and while surveys indicated fairly widespread public concern
about the "quality of movies," this concern was of a relatively low level
and certainly did not deter the approximately 50 to 60 million Americans who went to the movies every week in the mid-1920s. Second, the
MPPDA (the Hays Office) had instituted its own self-regulatory measures, and combined with an intensive and fairly successful public relations effort involving a wide variety of major social organizations, this
provided an acceptable veneer of public responsibility.[30] Finally, despite
the efforts of social scientists like Hugo Munsterberg, Jane Addams and
William Healy, there was very little scientific evidence to substantiate
the often hysterical claims of the reform group. Most of the evidence
that had been collected about the influence of movies was observational,
based on content analysis and surveys and almost always interpreted in
a very subjective manner. By the mid-1920s, the sophisticated and rigorous methodological proofs increasingly being demanded by the social
sciences were not being offered in the debate.

It was the establishment of incontrovertible "scientific" proof of the
deleterious influence of certain types of motion pictures that appeared to
be the most promising weapon in the arsenal of the reformers. For nearly
thirty years (1896–1926) reformers had tried to convince a variety of
legal and legislative bodies that, if left unregulated, movies would be a
serious threat to the moral fiber of society. The failure to provide clear
proof of this assertion had always been a handicap in making their
case and frustrated their efforts to rally the public to understand the
significance of, and to support, their cause. The evidence for this frustration can be clearly seen in the testimony offered in the succession of

congressional hearings on the motion picture industry conducted in 1914, 1916 and again in 1926.[31] The goal of these hearings was the establishment of a federal motion picture commission to oversee the prior censorship of all motion pictures at the national level. Representative W. D. Upshaw of Georgia, one of the sponsors of the 1926 bill, in his introductory remarks to the hearing, noted:

It is a bill not for meticulous and meddlesome censorship of pictures already produced at heavy expense; it is intended, rather, to purify this great fountain of influence at its source, so as to prevent its poisonous and devastating overflow upon the plastic youth of America. . . .

In proposing a commission to license only such pictures as do not violate decency nor outrage "that righteousness that exalteth a nation," we are simply proposing to stand at the door of our homes, our churches, and our schools and fight back the wolves of immorality, that are crouching to destroy the hope and strength of the Nation.[32]

Not only did Upshaw's evocation of moralistic and religious metaphors reflect the sentiments of many of those who saw the movies as a serious threat to the socialization of their children, it was also representative of the type of nonspecific rhetoric that reformers generally relied upon to make their case against the movies.[33] It was this wide-ranging, essentially Bible-centered rhetorical strategy that was articulated again and again in numerous articles, books, sermons and government bills, all aimed at arousing sufficient public concern over the "morals of the movies."

Ultimately, the 1926 bill, like all of the previous ones, failed to gain sufficient votes to establish a federal motion picture censorship bureau. This failure was a clear signal that, by the mid-1920s, such rhetorical attacks on the movies no longer had much effect on the public, and especially on the politicians who made the laws. This left the reformers (who were still largely from Protestant groups, although the Catholic church was now beginning to show some concern about movies) frustrated and angry. It was not only that the general public had seemed to lose interest in this issue, but that an arch-Protestant – Will Hays – was actually helping to bamboozle the public into believing that the movie industry was being responsible and responsive to the public's needs. The "open door" public relations policy that Hays had formulated invited groups to cooperate with, rather than fight, the movie industry. On the whole, this worked quite well to defuse the opposition, but there were prominent defections, among them the National Congress of Parents and Teachers in October 1924 and the General Federation of Women's Clubs in February 1925. These and other defections were a sign that there was still deep concern about the morals of the movies. The question was, what would be necessary to attract the attention of those who could really bring the movie industry to heel? What kinds of evidence of harmful movie influence would be required to make parents, teachers and especially politicians sit up and take notice?

It was out of this frustration and genuine concern for the moral welfare of the nation that the MPRC was formed, under the guidance of the Rev. William H. Short. The MPRC became one of the most prominent and interesting of the several reformist groups dedicated to the development of more stringent forms of legalized social control over the movie industry. The one large difference between the MPRC and the other, mostly religiously based groups[34] was the fact that the very creation of the MPRC was based on a decision to move beyond the outmoded rhetorical attacks of the past. When Short first embarked upon his quest for a method of bringing social control to the motion picture industry, he was still largely in the rhetorical camp. However, his initial investigations and discussions immediately after taking office very quickly soured him on the value of such a course of action. His establishment of the MPRC was henceforth guided by his desire to undertake a series of studies to determine, with empirical social science techniques, exactly what the influence of movies was on America's youth. Only "scientific" proof of the potentially harmful influence of the movies would persuade the federal government to establish a national motion picture censorship office. This was Short's goal, and for nine years (1926–1935) he would devote himself to organizing, administering and publicizing research that would assist in making this case.

The Germ of an Idea: Short, Seabury and the Payne Fund, 1926–1927

The genesis and history of the MPRC revolve around three men: William Marston Seabury, who precipitated the creation of the organization; Short, who ran the MPRC office essentially as a one-man enterprise; and

W. W. Charters, the research director of the PFS. Of these three, by far the most important was Short, without whose tireless energy and single-minded zeal the PFS would never have been undertaken.

William Harrison Short was born on a small farm near College Springs, Iowa, on 4 December 1868. He studied at Beloit College in Wisconsin and went on to complete a divinity degree at Yale Theological School in 1897. He served as an ordained minister in Congregational churches in Wisconsin and Minnesota between 1897 and 1908, at which time he was appointed secretary of the New York Peace Society. Short became deeply involved in the peace movement and served on many peace committees before the First World War. He was one of the original members of the committee that drafted the first covenants for the establishment of the League of Nations between 1914 and 1918. Between 1922 and 1925 he served as the secretary of the Twentieth Century Fund and as the executive director of the League of Nations Non-Partisan Association. He became the treasurer and business manager of Rollins College in Florida in 1926. Short was not trained as a social scientist, but his voluminous correspondence with the PFS researchers indicates that he had acquired a firm grasp of scientific research principles.

The establishment of the MPRC can be traced to two series of events. The first involved the work of the National Committee for the Study of Juvenile Reading (NCSJR), which had been established in 1925 by Mrs. Frances Bolton in order to examine methods of increasing interest in reading among young people. It was out of this organization that the Payne Study and Experiment Fund itself would emerge in 1927. On 3 June 1925, Short sent a letter to the National Committee indicating that "my knowledge of children leads me to believe that many of them are losing hold of the simple, sincere things of life – or perhaps are never getting hold of them at all. It is a confusing and complex life into which our children are plunged."[35] While there is a lack of available correspondence between that date and the next year, clearly Short went about establishing himself with Mrs. Bolton's group. On 7 June 1926, H. M. Clymer, director of the NCSJR, wrote to Short requesting his opinion on the magazine for boys that the committee was contemplating. He also asked Short if he could contact Henry Ford through Ford's attorney, Alfred Lucking, as a potential underwriter for the magazine project.[36] Short replied two days later to say that he would make the contact only if he was certain he could "sell himself on the proposition."[37] Short was obviously convinced of the project's validity, because

on 15 July he wrote to Lucking asking to meet with him on behalf
NCSJR.[38] On 6 August, Short reported on this meeting to Ella Phi
Crandall, associate director of the NCSJR, using stationery from t
Hotel Statler, Detroit. The meeting had not brought about the desirec
involvement of Henry Ford, but Lucking had suggested approaching
Raphael Hermann, a millionaire. Short noted that "the mission you gave
me has been more favorably begun than I dared hope."[39] There is no
evidence that anything ever developed with Hermann, but on 27 August
Crandall wrote to Short regarding his request for membership on the
NCSJR Board for Lucking and himself, extending an invitation for him
to join.[40] It was in this way that Short first established a relationship
with Mrs. Frances Bolton and her assistants in her philanthropic ven-
tures.

The NCSJR had begun as an organization intended to develop a
program of reading materials promoting citizenship. By 1927 the committee's interests had expanded to include the effects of movies and
radio on youth. (The substantial involvement of the Payne Fund in
funding educational radio is covered in Appendix A of the book.) In one
of its reports – "A Proposal for: Out of School Education Through
Recreational Reading" – the committee mentioned motion pictures as a
major secondary agency in such education.[41] It was out of this realization of the increasing significance of these "secondary" agencies in the
recreation and socialization of children that Mrs. Bolton and her entou-
rage became receptive to funding both motion picture and radio projects. Also, Short had established himself with the Bolton group, although
there is every indication that he was always considered rather pushy and
somewhat self-serving.[42] Short was at this time the business manager
and treasurer of Rollins College in Florida and looking for a new position. On 13 July 1927, he wrote to Chief Justice William Howard Taft
that his work at Rollins College was over after eighteen months, and
that Florida was no longer a good place to continue financial campaigns.
He was at that time in New York "readjusting my business relationships," and asked permission to use Taft's name as a reference.[43] One
of the business relationships that Short was seriously considering had
originated in 1927 when he was contacted by a New York lawyer,
William Marston Seabury.

Thus the second series of events in this important chapter in social
science and motion picture history began with a number of letters between Seabury and Short in early 1927. Seabury, after several years as a

industry, had become concerned with the issue of
⸏ he traced largely to the unfair industry trade
⸏ing and blind selling. In his book *The Public*
Industry, Seabury had proposed that a public
⸏ to "consider and grapple with the problems
⸏ picture as controlled by the monopolized indus-
⸏ title for this organization would be the "Public Service
⸏ture League."[44] On 16 February, he asked Short to consider
⸏ning to New York to run this new organization. Short had some
reservations but expressed keen interest in the idea of an organization
that would bring about social reform in the motion picture industry.
(There is some indication that by this time Short had run into trouble at
Rollins College and was desperately seeking a new position.)[45] In a
letter dated 14 March, Seabury sought to allay Short's concerns:

> ... in referring to the adoption of a program let me hasten to assure you
> that I do not refer to my program. I mean any program which competent
> educators, economists and publicists are prepared to recommend after they
> know the industrial and commercial facts which are essential to a compre-
> hension of the subject and the problems it represents. ...
>
> I am sure that I need not review the immense potentialities of an associa-
> tion of the kind I have pictured, especially under your able direction and
> guidance.
>
> ... it seems to me that work of the kind that you are capable of doing in
> an organization of the kind proposed should command a salary of not less
> than $15,000 a year and that those funds would be well expended if they
> were sufficient to induce you to devote your undivided efforts to such
> an enterprise.[46]

Short was still a member of the NCSJR, which had examined activities
that competed for the child's leisure time, and he had come to believe
that "the motion picture was one of the most important of the agencies
impinging on the life of the youth of our day."[47]

By May 1927, Short and Seabury had conducted an extensive exchange of views, and Short had also broached the subject of the creation
of a national motion picture office with his fellow members on the
NCSJR. The members of this organization enthusiastically agreed to
help found the office on the condition that "an adequate program of
fact-finding be undertaken prior to determining a program of propaganda and action."[48] This proviso is very significant, not only because it

laid the groundwork for the PFS, but also because it was the eventual cause of the split between Short and Seabury. Once Short had received the approval and encouragement of the NCSJR to set up a separate organization to examine the role of movies in the lives of children, he and Seabury proceeded to seek funding for the establishment of an office in New York. It was due solely to Short's connections with the NCSJR that he was able to approach the newly established Payne Study and Experimental Fund to ask for the funds to set up this new organization. Unfortunately, the only account of how the funding was obtained comes from Short's own brief history written in 1928:

Through the agency of the directors of the National Committee for the Study of Juvenile Reading an appropriation was secured from the Payne Study and Experimental Fund which was financing the Reading Committee and other projects. This appropriation totaled $65,800, to be expended throughout a period of two years beginning on September 20th, 1927. . . .the first purpose of the project was designated in the application to the Fund to be the "conduct of further study of the industry, with special purpose of bringing together a greater array of facts than is now available." After these facts had been obtained, and only then, was the formulation of a program of action contemplated.[49]

Thus the initial purpose of the funding was to pull together all of the pertinent "facts" about the motion picture and role of the motion picture industry, and only then was "a program of action" to be developed and submitted for further funding. Short seemed determined not only to go about this endeavor systematically and thoroughly, but also to stretch out the possibility of this sinecure as long as he could.

The initial funding came not from Mrs. Bolton, but from her sister, Elizabeth Blossom. A letter dated 22 September 1927 from Ella Phillips Crandall, secretary of the Payne Fund, to Mrs. Blossom spells out the details of this grant. Mrs. Blossom was to donate a total sum of $65,800 to be paid in regular monthly installments over a two-year period in order to "underwrite a preliminary study preparatory to determining the advisability of attempting to overcome the present shameless monopoly within the Motion Picture Industry and perhaps to inaugurate a program of activity that will assume both national and international scope." The identity of the donor was to be protected, and the letter noted "that you emphatically prohibit the use of your name in this connection and make your contribution to the project through the _____ Fund (name still to be determined) which you and Mrs. Bolton have now established." The project was set to begin on 27 September 1927.[50]

Short moved to New York and prepared to set up an organization to be called the National Committee for the Study of Social Values in Motion Pictures, with himself as director. His salary was to be $12,000 a year. He secured an office for this organization in a suite with the newly created Payne Fund. A small committee was assembled consisting of Frances Bolton, who had become chairman of the Board of Trustees of the Payne Study and Experiment Fund; Harvie M. Clymer and Ella Phillips Crandall, directors of the Juvenile Reading Committee and president and secretary of the Payne Fund respectively; Mrs. Walter McNab Miller, an executive in the American Child Health Association and an officer in the Federation of Women's Clubs; Dr. George Millard Davidson; and Short. This committee, which met frequently and informally, decided that the preliminary study the Payne Fund had authorized should be as complete as possible and that "it should be unprejudiced and non-partisan in character," and made available in printed form.[51]

From the very first, it was obvious that Short was seeking to provide clear evidence with which to launch an attack on the motion picture industry. In a memorandum written to Clymer and Crandall on 27 September 1927, Short offered several questions for consideration regarding motion pictures. The first question suggested that "the art of the movies has been seized upon by people interested primarily, if not solely, in amusement." To make his point with a hypothetical example, he asked how the monopolization of print in its early period would have affected the world. He concluded: "In a word is it possible to get evidence in this field against the motion pictures that will shock people who are accustomed to the license in pictures and in writing that is so widely indulged in today?"[52] Despite Short's private attitude of hostility to the motion picture industry, he quickly realized that his public demeanor had to be much more neutral and controlled if he was to maintain his relationship with the Payne Fund and to achieve his goal of obtaining evidence with which to bring the motion picture industry to heel. In the official history of the MPRC, as written by Short, this pretense of scientific objectivity was maintained:

The whole discussion regarding the motion picture was found to be in the realm of opinion and that for years almost every phase of it had been in controversy. It was felt that if this committee were to make any important contribution to the discussion, its first essential task must be to carry it over into the realm of fact. This could be done only by scientific studies made under the most exacting scientific conditions and under the best educational auspices.[53]

This veneer of scientific objectivity contrasted sharply with the open hostility that Seabury had developed toward the motion picture industry on the basis of his personal experiences. In a memorandum (presumably to the newly established board), Seabury set forth his view of the functions of this new organization, which he called the "Public Motion Picture Federation." Its primary purpose, he suggested in the typical legal style, should be as follows:

1. Opposition to all trade abuses and unfair practices which contribute to and promote the monopolization of the industry and the production and exhibition of undesirable pictures.
2. The substitution, in their place, of sound policies, formulated and expressed in legislative measures which will make applicable to the motion picture industry the same economic principles which now control other American industries; which principles will require the commercial reconstruction of the industry in a manner which will produce better pictures at small costs and bring a larger audience to see desirable pictures when exhibited at reasonable admission prices; and which will minimize or eliminate waste and protect the public in its investment and other interests in the industry.

Seabury then suggested that this Public Motion Picture Federation could achieve its goals through the following methods:

a. Truthful publicity disclosing among other things, the waste, extravagance and incompetence of the existing regime, its economic absurdities and its dangers to existing investors. It involves opposition to the Hays Association [sic], its standard of uniform contract, its Arbitration system, its Film Board of Trade, the control of theaters by producers, block booking, circuit booking, the conspiracy of the producers and the Hays Association against the stars and their excessive salaries while the more extensive extravagance of the producers, the extravagances of the distribution and exhibition branch continue unabated, and opposition to all production distribution and exhibition waste.
b. Enforcement of existing laws (1) By Department of Justice (2) By Federal Trade Commission (3) By Petition to Congress to force the appointment of a competent, politically impartial, special prosecuting attorney. (a) To enforce and to render effective the Federal trade Commission's decision

of July 9th, 1927 (b) To dissolve the Hays Association as a combination in unlawful restraint of trade (c) To enforce the anti-trust laws in their application to the motion picture industry. (4) Extensive publicity to each and all of the foregoing activities.

c. Federal Legislation.
The abolition of the exclusive exhibition contract system by the enactment of the proposed motion picture supplement to section 8 of the Clayton Act [antitrust legislation].

d. State Legislation.
The passage of acts, in the several states, prohibiting the exhibition of pictures which are injurious to the public, in any respect.

In the second section of his memorandum, entitled "International Program," Seabury offered similar suggestions for using the auspices of the League of Nations to create an international cinema committee "to examine and to formulate a solution of all cinema problems" within its jurisdiction. The ultimate objective was "the practical curtailment and control of the existing international monopoly, the prevention of its continued expansion and the production and exhibition throughout the world of new and better pictures."[54] This memorandum, suggesting a series of deliberate and provocative political courses of action, could hardly have been more diametrically opposed to the careful research-based plan that Short had in mind. There is no known direct response to Seabury's plan, but the subsequent treatment of Seabury clearly suggests that the Payne Fund group was very concerned about his desire to mount a frontal attack on the motion picture industry. It would be up to Short to find a way to ensure that Seabury's volatile suggestions did not become an official part of the group's efforts.[55]

The Creation of an Organization: The Short–Seabury Conflict, 1927–1928

Immediately upon assuming office, Short busied himself with two major projects in an attempt to create a veneer of scientific respectability and acceptance. First, in November 1927, on a trip to Washington, D.C., he met with a significant number of influential social scientists, including Dr. Leo S. Rowe, president of the American Academy of Political and Social Science; Dr. Vernon Kellogg of the National Research Council; and Dr. H. G. Moulton, director of the Brookings Institute of Economics and chairman of the Committee on Problems and Policies of the Social Science Research Council. In summing up the success of the trip in a letter to Clymer, Short noted:

Our convictions that important researches should be made in the motion picture field were more than confirmed by the visit. The motion picture industry is quite too important to be dealt with in any cavalier fashion. Its problems have been approached from many angles, but to a very great extent without a proper basis of knowledge.

The problems to be studied are of course those that affect the welfare and interest of the public, especially the youth who attend the picture shows. Without first making these studies any program of action we might draw up would be branded as the work of mere zealous propagandists, and would almost certainly fall more or less wide of the mark. But when these studies have been authoritatively made our feet will be upon firm ground.[56]

The second of Short's activities was the compilation of "existing opinion" on the role and impact of movies. This volume, entitled *A Generation of Motion Pictures: A Review of Social Values in Recreational Films*, was published on 21 June 1927 for the use of the committee and other interested parties. Over the years, Short was to circulate many copies of this document as a means of arousing interest in the PFS project. In the four hundred pages of what Robert Sklar has described as a *vade mecum* of the movies' horrible influence on society, Short collected excerpts from sermons, books, articles, trade publications and every sort of negative comment he could find. As Sklar notes: "It was a dazzling display of erudition, versatility and precept, of indignation and high moral tone. But it was hardly worth the paper it was written on."[57] Short himself recognized that these "literary" opinions were insufficient to arouse public interest, and this made the need for "scientific" data even more urgent. He pointed out that "the absence of an adequate and well-authenticated basis of fact has probably had much to do, hitherto, with preventing agreement of the civic-minded forces of the country on policies and programs of action for dealing with the problems of the screen."[58]

In the early decades of the twentieth century, social science had become an increasingly popular tool for dealing with a variety of social and economic problems, especially within the federal government. The use of statistically quantifiable data was now standard in many U.S. institutions and was increasingly relied upon as a basis for policy making.[59] By the late 1920s it would have been unthinkable for Short to undertake his program of movie reform without the backing of reputable social scientific research. The very act of compiling the material for *A Generation of Motion Pictures* had underscored the inadequacy and impotency of literary-based complaints. If Short and his committee were to attract the attention of policy makers, he would need far more substantial evidence that the movies were, in fact, harmful to the public. For this reason he worked with patience and diligence to create a suitable body of research. He noted in his report to the Payne Fund: "The fact that we have a definite plan of fact finding rather than an immediate plan of propaganda was distinctly pleasing. . . . Especially since the deceptive propaganda of the war does the public demand that facts be developed by surveys and scientific study programs. Without these they distrust statements of alleged fact, from whatever sources they may come."[60]

It was on the very point of the need for a lengthy preliminary period of study that Short and Seabury would part. It did not take long for this split to occur. In a series of remarkably frank letters the two men staked out their positions. Seabury, who had originated the idea of a national committee to deal with the motion picture problem, suddenly found himself on the outside, looking in at Short's rapid takeover of the agenda for the organization, which Short had named the National Committee for the Study of Social Values in Motion Pictures. In a letter dated 10 October 1927, Seabury wrote to Short that "at our conference on October 5th I received the impression that you have determined to undertake and continue by yourself the project which I formulated and in which I asked you to join me. . . . I did not invite you to take the plan or project to yourself and to exclude me from it." Seabury indicated his concern that the financial underwriting of his new book, which he had hoped would come from the new organization, had not been itemized in the budget. He was also deeply hurt that he had been excluded from the initial organizing committee because "you conceived the idea that perhaps it would be wiser if I were not a member of such committee lest mythical embarrassments might arise to other members of it if I became a part of it." Finally, Seabury had assumed that he would either be co-director of the office, receiving adequate compensation, or at least be appointed a legal counsel with a retainer of $100 per week. Now it appeared as though neither stipend would be forthcoming, and he was to be simply "one of the attorneys" for the committee. Seabury claimed that the funding had been obtained with the understanding that he would play a vital role, and if this was to change, then "I as well as the

donor would have a right to complain and so far as I am concerned I am
entirely confident of my ability to prevent you from proceeding with this
project without me, if I should desire to do so." (In this threat he entirely
underestimated his own political undesirability and the influence that
Short had with Mrs. Bolton and the Payne Fund.) He asked Short to
form a new membership organization, legally chartered in New York,
and that this organization contract with both him and Short for their
services for the two years that funds were available. He plaintively
noted: "It is most unfortunate that so soon as funds appear on the
horizon we almost instantly misunderstand each other. I had thought
that we were unusually sympathetic mentally and I still wish to do
everything in my power to bring about a better understanding between
us." Seabury requested that Short assure him that he was still to be part
of the project, as "I prefer to know this now rather than one, two or
three months from now."[61]

The MPRC files contain a candid undated, handwritten note by Short
preparatory to his lengthy reply to Seabury. It is clear from Short's
private thoughts that Seabury was considered a liability to the project.
He noted that "Clymer and Crandall will not enter into any contract
with W. M. S." The problem was that Short and the other members of
the inner circle did not want to draw attention to themselves at this point
and thereby attract the interest and inspection of the movie industry and,
more specifically, the Hays Office. Short's note to himself makes this
clear: "That this is a preliminary period of organization, not one of
crusade. . . . Pending the adoption of a program by our conferees, and
completion of a permanent organization, we must not commit our
movement to an attitude of hostility to the M. P. Industry. To do so
would forfeit the cooperation of the great majority of those whom we
shall invite to sit in with us." Seabury's outside activities and his books
had already labeled him as an opponent of the movie industry, and Short
noted, "We shall not be embarrassed by Mr. Seabury's activities, or by
his known hostility to the M. P. Industry." The note outlined a plan of
action for dealing with and satisfying Seabury, and concluded with the
suggestion to "get him away from the idea of a small, closed corporation
the main object of which would be to hold onto the project and keep
out everybody of whom we might be doubtful and to replace the idea in
his mind by the idea of a large movement composed of all earnest people
who want to secure better pictures and are convinced *that it must be
done outside of the industry.*"[62]

Short formally replied to Seabury on 18 October and apologized for allowing himself to "be so wholly employed day and night as to leave little time for conference." Short recounted their correspondence dating back to February and suggested that Seabury had indicated full confidence at that time in Short's ability to run the organization. Short also reminded Seabury that he had been part of the NCSJR before their discussions began, that this organization "had a study of the motion picture, especially in its relation to youth throughout the world, as part of its program," and that it was only this fortunate combination of circumstances that "alone made it possible to secure a pledge of funds with which to make the study that we are beginning." Short also pointed out that there had been general agreement between the two that because of Seabury's "well-known critical attitude towards the people in control of the Motion Picture Industry," it was better that Seabury was not a member of the committee or board of this organization; his contribution as counsel was more acceptable. He also made it clear that "while early publication is most desirable," the initial budget did not allow for the full amount of the subvention to Macmillan for the publication of Seabury's new book. The most that could be offered was $500 or "a little more" of the total estimated cost of $2,000. He closed by assuring Seabury of his "most kindly feelings and my desire that our relations shall be of the closest during the entire period in which we are working with the exceedingly important problems you have done more than any other to state and clarify."[63]

Between October 1927 and December 1928 Seabury remained on a retainer of approximately $100 per month for his services as legal counsel. Short asked his advice on several matters, and he prepared several lengthy memoranda on the film industry, but it was very clear that Seabury was no longer part of the long-term plan. It must have been a very frustrating year for Seabury, especially as Short moved steadily toward developing a plan for the proposed scientific studies. Finally after a meeting in early December 1928, Seabury had had enough. His anger and disappointment were obvious in a sharply worded letter he wrote to Short on 13 December:

As I understand you at our conference yesterday afternoon, you and your committee now feel that during your proposed period of study, which you estimate will consume from three to five years, the committee will not have funds which will enable it to continue to pay my compensation as its counsel, although you assure me that the committee would be happy to have me continue to act as its counsel if I serve without compensation.

As I explained to you it is not possible for me to do this. It is not a matter of compensation, so far as I am concerned, it is one of action.

I would not care to circumscribe my activities by continuing to identify myself as counsel to a committee which contemplates no activity other than studies for so prolonged a period of time, since if I continue to act in this capacity for your committee it might embarrass my acting in a similar capacity to one or more other committees which will engage in more serious and I believe more important work.[64]

Sour grapes notwithstanding, Seabury's approach to the problem was still rooted in the older, nonscientific, rhetorical style of criticism, although he personally relied a great deal on economic data in preparing his memoranda and books on the practices of the movie industry. He was also impatient to start his international program through the League of Nations. He outlined his primary objections to Short:

Neither I nor the public require specialists, however learned, or distinguished in any field, to express their opinion as to the exact kind of pictures which are harmful or the exact degree of their influence or the precise measure of the injury which their exhibition inflicts upon the public everywhere. . . .

As I have many times said, it is more important to study the causes of existing conditions which involve the economic and commercial phases of the subject, than it is to examine further into the effects of motion pictures. It is only from a study of the causes that a sound conclusion concerning the remedies can be reached. . . .

Since it is evident to me that not only do you not wish to pursue the course that I have outlined but that you would be unwilling to supply funds to permit this work to go forward under my direction, I prefer to resign my association with your committee and devote myself to the effort to interest another group of public spirited persons who would be prepared to follow the course I have outlined rather than to pursue studies, many of which have already been made and which, while interesting academically, are in my opinion practically worthless, especially unless they are preceded by the film inspection and the statistical inquiry which I suggested.[65]

Short was only too happy to accept Seabury's resignation in a letter the next day, and he suggested that Seabury's plan was not in competition with his own, but complementary. However, Short was still adamant that only through acceptable scientific studies could the industry be made to listen to pleas for greater moral responsibility:

In the absence of such proof the motion picture industry seems able to make a substantial section of the public believe that the indictment of the motion picture while supported by a great deal of weighty opinion, is "not proven." We have come to feel that until such proof is secured, it is hardly possible to obtain that united action of the great national organizations and classes – such, for example, as the parents of the Nation – that seems essential to the carrying out of any substantial program.[66]

On 27 December, Short wrote to Seabury telling him that his letter of resignation had been accepted by the committee. He could not help but add a final twist: "The Committee thought it well to discuss the question raised in your letter as to the value of the entire study program. It found itself unanimously of the opinion that the studies are important and should be made."[67] After this, William Seabury played no further role in the structuring of what was to become the body of work known as the Payne Fund Studies. He went on to publish a rather interesting and substantial study, *Motion Picture Problems: The Cinema and the League of Nations,* in 1929, which in its 421 pages contains no mention of his work with William Short or the National Committee for the Study of Social Values in Motion Pictures.

The final break between Seabury and Short in December 1928 concluded the first phase of the origins of the PFS. With Seabury gone, Short was free to pursue his own plan for developing a major series of scientific studies that would serve as the platform for launching a well-organized attack on the motion picture industry. During the last year of his initial funding from the Payne Fund, Short organized two conferences with a variety of social scientists interested in doing research on the influence of movies. (The development of the research agenda, the securing of the researchers and the political infighting that ensued are dealt with in Chapter Two.) W. W. Charters, director of Educational Research at Ohio State University, served as adviser and chairman of both sessions, and he was then officially invited to serve as the research director for the major part of the research program. In his presentation before Short's National Committee on 15 December 1928, Charters underscored the importance of the scientific nature of the endeavor: "My understanding is that it is not the purpose of these studies to throw bricks at the moving picture industry, but rather to make a study of what the possibilities of moving pictures are in our social life, and to present measures by which the influence of moving pictures may be gauged or scaled. . . . It is my understanding . . . that this is not to be a negative study, but rather a positive study."[68]

A Tentative Relationship: Short and the Payne Fund

After the two years of preliminary work had been completed and an agenda for a comprehensive research program had been established, Short applied for, and received, all of the funding for the major studies from the Payne Fund. However, during these years, from 1927 to 1929, Short's relationship with the Payne Fund became more and more tentative, as his agenda for the eventual creation of a legislative form of "moral" control of the motion picture industry became increasingly obvious. The correspondence in the archival files reveals how Short initially sought to ingratiate himself with Mrs. Bolton and the Payne Fund officers by offering his assistance on a variety of issues; but in the long run his obstinate single-mindedness and open hostility toward what was seen to be a powerful and politically dangerous industry lobby (the Hays Office) made him a dangerous ally, to be kept at a safe distance. At first, however, Short's energy, enthusiasm and the impressive array of important political connections he claimed kept him very much in favor with the Payne Fund group, and he was invited to participate in their ultimately futile efforts to secure funding for a proposed boys' magazine.[69]

Mrs. Bolton's personal relationship, and therefore that of the Payne Fund, with Short's committee seemed to vacillate between cautious endorsement and political distancing. A memo dated 15 November 1927 outlined her thoughts:

Mrs. Bolton was emphatic in her belief that all of us must consider making it a vital and fundamental rule that the new Payne Fund shall be guarded scrupulously against attack or criticism from the motion picture interests or that portion of the public which approves the present motion picture leadership. For this reason the Payne Fund should not be mentioned as the donor of funds for the motion picture study. The statement that funds come from an anonymous donor is to be preferred.[70]

The nature of the relationship between the National Committee and the Payne Fund continued to be an issue of contention in early 1928 as the program of action began to take shape. In a letter to Mrs. Bolton in January, Clymer suggested that he and Miss Crandall had been

thinking considerably more about the use of the name of the Payne Study and Experiment Fund by Mr. Short. . . . At first, with Mr. Seabury very much in the picture, with his reputation as a determined critic of the motion picture industry . . . and with the probability that Mr. Short's work would subject him and his committee to much enmity from the motion picture industry and sympathizers, it was then very necessary to protect the new Fund.

Since that time Mr. Seabury has come around to many of our views [this, as we now know, was not an accurate perception], and Mr. Short's study and planning has spread out and has so obviously taken the form of a non-partisan judicial effort that the Payne Fund may gain more than it would lose by a definite identification with the motion picture study.

. . . an occasional letter by Mr. Short on the Payne Fund letterhead to prominent people whom he is approaching may be to our advantage.[71]

Clymer was able to convince Mrs. Bolton of the potentially positive aspects of this association, and on 23 January 1928, he sent a memo to Short indicating that Mrs. Bolton had written that: "I think it is all right for Mr. Short to say frankly to those who need information that he is being financed by the Fund."[72] Therefore, in this early stage of the development of the research program, Short was free to seek the support of individuals and organizations under the relatively prestigious auspices of the Payne Fund, and with the implication of Mrs. Bolton's patronage. This was an important achievement for this ambitious and socially conscious would-be reformer of the movies.

Throughout the entire project, but especially in this early phase of organization, Short constantly feared the potential power of the motion picture industry to thwart his efforts. Bitter memories of the unleashed political clout exhibited by the Hays Office in the 1922 Massachusetts censorship referendum lingered among the movie reformers, and the massive public relations campaign that had been developed by the MPPDA, incorporating a wide variety of national groups, represented a formidable obstacle.[73] Mr. and Mrs. Bolton, important members of the Republican political organization in Ohio, were not eager to run head-on into Will Hays and the motion picture industry.[74] For that reason the work of the National Committee was kept relatively quiet and there was little public fanfare of its early achievements.[75]

Short, however, kept a very close watch on the public relations efforts of the motion picture industry. One of his prime targets for infiltration was the General Federation of Women's Clubs, a large and influential organization whose relationship with the Hays Office tended to wax and wane. As an example, in July 1928 Short went to Evanston, Illinois, to meet (in three "conferences") with Mrs. A. C. Tyler, who was the chair of the Motion Picture Committee of the General Federation of Women's Clubs. In a subsequent report, Short noted that she was "definite in her conviction that nothing can be accomplished without the results of the series of studies, as proposed." He also noted that Mrs. Tyler "urges that we hold entirely aloof from the Hays Organization and the motion picture industry. . . . Suggests that it should be understood that any member of our committee who wished to cooperate in any way with that group should first resign from ours." Short also noted that Mrs. Tyler voiced a concern shared by many other national organizations working with the motion picture industry:

Told of ways in which the Hays group immediately cultivates the members of any committee appointed by the General Federation. Puts them on the Hays committees and otherwise destroys their value for the Federation. Very discouraged regarding the possibility of accomplishing anything along lines previously followed.[76]

This interview must have confirmed for Short that any form of association with the industry, especially through the Hays Office, was to be avoided. As is discussed in the next chapter, Short's discovery that a few of the researchers had been in contact or cooperated with the motion picture industry almost led to their dismissal from the research program and certainly tainted their subsequent work in Short's eyes. His somewhat justified paranoia about the politics of the motion picture industry, especially the potential dangers to his efforts from the public relations arm of the Hays Office, would remain until his death.

The National Committee for the Study of Social Values in Motion Pictures (NCSSVMP) was formally incorporated in late August 1928. Short was elected pro tem chairman, but his appointment as director of the motion picture project was made retroactive to 20 September 1927 and was to continue for an indefinite period thereafter. It was at this meeting that Seabury was also appointed as counsel to the committee, and the budget was approved for the second year of operations.[77]

The formal establishment of the NCSSVMP and Short's appointment as director of the motion picture project immediately raised questions about Short's personal relationship with the Payne Fund. Again these concerns seemed to stem from the fear of antagonizing the motion picture industry. In late September, Clymer wrote to Short suggesting:

1. That the present small committee with a limited number of necessary accessions shall become a study committee of the Payne Fund and that this committee shall be renamed. This will save the title "The National Committee for the Study of Social Values in Motion Pictures" for your propaganda organization and period of work.
2. That this study group remain active as a Payne Fund Committee until such time as its findings have accrued and have been tested and your propaganda program is ready for inauguration. Then this committee to remain as a comparatively inactive body while your proposed great national propaganda group organizes and functions in that phase of your work, wholly independent of the Payne Fund.[78]

Short immediately replied that this arrangement was "entirely practicable and natural at this time" and that it was "desirable that the Payne Study and Experimental Fund take charge at this stage and direct the work through the study period which is about to open." The strategy was obvious: the Payne Fund would gain some legitimate prestige as an important philanthropic foundation (like the Rockefeller or Carnegie Foundation) from its association with the largely academic research efforts, but it did not want to be connected with any of the subsequent "propaganda" and other legislative efforts that would result from the publication of the research findings. As Short noted, the plan was, "when the study period is ended and it has become desirable to carry on a campaign of public education and propaganda, to organize again a citizens' committee independent of The Payne Fund that would take the findings of the study period and make use of them in the interest of public welfare."[79] Thus the strategy was to separate the organizations underwriting and actually doing the studies from the apparently spontaneous citizens' group that would spring up to utilize the findings to effect social and legislative action.

The evolution of the relationship of the Payne Fund to the research program, and its projected aftermath, continued to occupy a considerable part of Short's time for the next six years, particularly in this early period, when neither of the two parties was in total agreement as to what the correct course of action should be. On 19 October 1928, Clymer and Crandall jointly sent a memorandum to Short outlining, yet again, the nature of this relationship as they now saw it. They suggested to Short that at the upcoming meeting in Columbus, Ohio (in November), the recommendations of "facts" to be studied come from "people of practical experience" in dealing with the moral issues of the movies,

and they specifically named such well-known industry critics and reformers as George A. Skinner, former president of Educational Films
Corporation of America; Dora H. Stecker, a Cincinnati social worker
and film exhibitor, who had been a longtime spokesperson in the anti-
block-booking crusade; and Mrs. Robbins Gilman, a prominent member
of the General Federation of Women's Clubs. Each of these individuals
had long been a nemesis of the motion picture industry, and it is surprising that Clymer and Crandall nominated them, considering the Payne
Fund's desire to avoid any confrontation with the Hays Office at this
early stage.

In the same memo Clymer and Crandall finally came to the realization
that they needed to correct some of Short's terminology and curb any
discussion of how the final results of the studies would be applied:

We urge the complete and permanent elimination of the word "propaganda," and the substitution of "popular education." We would also eliminate from any statement of purpose at this time all reference to a possible
legislative program, with the understanding that this will naturally develop
in the course of time if and after all constructive efforts shall have failed. . . .

We would also urge that before any organized educational program is
undertaken, the industry be given knowledge of your studies and their
purposes, and urged to avail themselves of their opportunity to do the
corrective work. This is not to be interpreted as indicating that we are too
optimistic about the industry's response, but rather a desire that the Council
[presumably the citizen's council that would spontaneously emerge after the
studies had been published] shall have the advantage of having offered the
industry its chance.[80]

The memo concluded by reiterating that the committee doing the research — "if identified with the Payne Fund — will continue only as a
research body and share no responsibility for the 'popular education'
program." This suggestion to Short indicates that neither Clymer nor
Crandall had any real conception of what Short and now Charters had
in mind. Their nomination of Skinner, Stecker and Gilman as sources of
the "facts" to be examined by the research program was completely
antithetical to what Short intended, namely, a program of reliable social
science research, and not industry-performance-based legislative research. A clash between these two perspectives was therefore inevitable,
and it occurred at the first Columbus meeting of the interested parties in
early October 1928.

Social Science or Legislative Action: The Two Philosophies, 1928–1929

The first organizational meeting of the parties interested in the proposed program of research assembled in Columbus, Ohio, on 5–6 October 1928. This was followed up by another meeting in Columbus on 24–25 November. During these two meetings, proponents of the groups' competing philosophies – those who wanted to undertake industry studies, with a view to immediate legislative action (the Seabury position), and those who wished to undertake a lengthy series of scientific studies (the Short position) – had their say. While no transcripts of the meetings exist, we have learned what transpired by piecing together the various reports, official and unofficial, contained in the archives.

One source of insight about the individuals involved is a lengthy letter from Charters to Ella Crandall written much later, on 4 December 1934, in which he recounted his version of the history of the PFS. His description of this first meeting is interesting because he characterizes each of the major players:

> At this meeting we assembled two groups. One was composed of "friends of the movies" who knew the practical issues and problems involved but did not know the answers – the militant Mrs. Gilman, the practical Miss Stecker, the judicial Mr. Seabury, the enigmatic Mr. Skinner, the dynamic Mr. Short, and a dozen other practical people. The other group consisted of brilliant Thurstone, clever May, theoretical Park, longheaded [sic] Stoddard, thoughtful Freeman, realistic Blumer, green, young Dale, and a half dozen others – as vigorous a group of investigators in their fields as would be assembled in America. The Payne Fund officials intelligently listened and watched on the sidelines to see whether the assembly had the breadth of intellectual grasp and the practical reach to justify confidence in their undertakings.

It is interesting that Charters placed Short on the "practical" and not the scientific side. Charters's perception of Short's talents at this early stage no doubt quickly changed as Short's championing of the scientific research became the major feature of these meetings.[81]

After the first meeting, Short wrote a letter to Mrs. Bolton in which he did not even hint at conflict between the two groups. He claimed that the general research program had been reshaped along the following lines:

We propose to develop factual data regarding the social influences of motion pictures on the basis of which a national policy in motion pictures may be formulated; and to make whatever studies, either technical or non-technical, may be required to secure the desired facts.

However, despite his mention of technical (industry) studies, no doubt as a sop to the "friends of the movies," none were ever undertaken. Short went on to emphasize:

It is of course most important that these studies be made as thorough and as authoritative as is possible in the present state of scientific inquiry in the field of the social sciences. They should be inclusive of all the major bodies of facts in the field of motion pictures. We are trying to use the time between now and November 24th to insure these two things.[82]

Short and, by now, Charters were using their time to ensure that the scientific research would predominate in any program. It was with the appointment of Charters as the director of the research program that the nature of the intended research became more tangible and, most important, credible to the Payne Fund officials.

There were still some doubts about the nature of the program, as can be seen in a letter written by Clymer to Mrs. Bolton in late November, just before the second conference. Apparently both Clymer and Crandall had given "concentrated mental effort" to the course of the studies and had been in conference with both Skinner and Short. Clymer noted:

At least three of us — that is, Miss Crandall, Mr. Skinner and I, came back from Cleveland feeling that the so-called "friends of the movies" group had not accomplished anything of value. Lack of leadership and lack of preparation were at least partly responsible. Another factor was that everyone had been warned that this was a research conference.

. . . the "friends" group should have some very definite ideas about what tools [studies] they will find effectively usable when their phase of activity arrives. So, they should not be dominated by the research idea only; the ultimately [sic] "firing line" group should have a lot to say about studies made.[83]

Clymer backed Mrs. Bolton's suggestion that the two groups meet separately before coming together in joint conference and that "the friends group might find a strong chairman who would talk on equal terms with the research leader." Clymer also reported confidentially that Mrs. Gilman had told Skinner that "she was so disappointed with the Columbus conference that she had doubts about attending the next one. She is quoted as having said that she saw no use for the studies recommended by the research group." Apparently Mrs. Gilman was sending Short "pages of suggestions" for a propaganda campaign, but had "no hope for success" in that direction; instead, her full enthusiasm was behind Skinner's proposal of "education by substitution" (making educational films). Mrs. Gilman nevertheless had decided to go to the second meeting in Columbus, because she "believes that we have the substitution plan in the background." From this letter it is obvious that Skinner, with his grandiose ideas of producing higher-quality films, was having a considerable influence on the Payne Fund officials. Clymer noted, somewhat apprehensively, "We have not dared to tell Mr. Short, for fear of upsetting everything." It was also apparent that Charters was now seen as the real intellectual force behind the research program, since Clymer ended his letter with this suggestion:

Our thought is that Dr. Charters should have full knowledge, as Skinner has, of the changes going on in the industry due to the coming in of the big electrical company groups, television, etc.; also that Charters' thinking might be different along study lines in view of what Mr. Skinner has already accomplished and what he hopes to do.[84]

The second meeting of the group in Columbus on 24–25 November did very little to resolve the differences in research philosophies.

It was after the second meeting in Columbus in late November 1928 and a subsequent private meeting between Seabury and Short on 12 December that Seabury tendered his resignation. Seabury clearly had no reservations about upsetting Short by revealing to him in his letter of resignation (discussed in detail earlier in this chapter) that his research proposals were not universally appreciated within the group.[85] As previously noted, Short was only too eager to accept Seabury's resignation, and he took the time to reply to Seabury's assertion that the scientific studies would provide no new evidence. Short explained at some length why the studies were necessary and attacked the proposition that further industry studies were required, noting that "the past thirty years have seen many betterment programs come to naught, and the knowledge of these has made us loathe to plunge unprepared into the fray." The crux of the issue was the need to provide some sort of tangible, scientifically acceptable proof of the harmful effects of motion pictures. Short wrote:

In the absence of such proof the motion picture industry seems able to make a substantial section of the public believe that the indictment of the motion picture while supported by a great deal of weighty opinion, is "not proven.". . .

. . . It is because we have come, through much inquiry, to believe that effective action must await the evidence that can come only [this word was added in pencil to the carbon] from far-reaching studies and surveys that we have adopted our study programs. . . . What we need now is to lay corner-stones in the structure for a movement in the experimental approach to the analysis of this problem.[86]

Despite Short's optimistic determination to forge ahead with the scientific studies, he had still not convinced all members of the group assembled at the two Columbus meetings. The day after the November meeting, Clymer sent a handwritten note to Mrs. Bolton in which he indicated that "Dr. Charters opened by saying that there had been a revolution in his mind since the last conference, that he thought the tendency had been more destructive than was wise and should be pointed more to constructive ends." According to Clymer, Charters felt that Short's anti-industry bias was too strong and that he now recognized that "the 'Friends of the Movies' [rechristened Public Relations Committee] is *the* important group because upon them devolves the final responsibility for *use* of studies." Clymer also noted that there was much interest in Skinner's idea of producing movies, and Charters apparently said that "everyone here has in mind a picture he would like made!" There was still confusion about exactly what kind of program was going to be undertaken, because Clymer quotes Skinner as saying that "Mrs. Gilman is well in line now – evidently because she assumed that we are not merely to make studies." This letter provides clear evidence that the "friends of the movies" faction was still convinced after the second meeting that industry practice studies, and potentially the actual production of high-quality or educational movies, were part of the agenda for this group.[87] It was now up to Short, with help from Charters, to correct this misapprehension before the third, and final, organizing conference slated for June 1929.

It was the appointment of Charters to head up the university research program that provided the credibility for the scientific work, and with his help Short was now able to turn the committee's interest away from industry studies or film production. This change of heart is clear in a letter from Clymer to Bolton written three days after a meeting of the NCSSVMP on 15 December 1928, and just a few days before an important meeting at the Bolton residence in Cleveland later that month.

Clymer told Mrs. Bolton that he had consulted Charters at some length
on a variety of other Payne Fund projects, including the work on juvenile
reading and radio. Tucked away in this letter is the key to why the Payne
Fund finally agreed to go ahead with social scientific studies as the
central part of its program. Clymer's advice to Mrs. Bolton was based
on his conversation with Charters:

I told him that it was my feeling that the Payne fund would be unwise to put
itself in a position of inviting attack or revenge from the Hayes [sic] people,
and added that it was a serious matter to Mr. Bolton if through your
association with motion picture work, political animosity was aroused. Dr.
Charters instantly saw the point, raised no argument about it, said that he
could answer for his group of research men *but thought it was the other
people we would have to watch*.[88]

Charters also advised Mrs. Bolton to withdraw from membership in the
NCSSVMP and offered his opinion that it was not the Payne Fund's
function to engage in the "crusade sort of thing, but rather to handle the
study and research side." Charters even suggested that Short not be a
member of the Payne Fund Motion Picture Research Committee. Clymer
noted: "This is rather further than I ever dreamed, but Charters's reasons are that he wants the research committee to be a 'university group
beyond the possibility of suspicion of bias.' " Clymer was clearly impressed with Charters's apparent objectivity, and he pointed out that
Charters had given a "very excellent description of some 14 or 15
studies scheduled for beginning. These studies are almost entirely what
he characterizes as 'psychological studies' as differentiated from such
topics as the economic, the legal, etc."[89]

It was Charters's ability to differentiate and explain the political
significance of the two types of studies that finally determined what sort
of program the Payne Fund would be prepared to fund. The Payne
Fund lawyer, Berton L. Maxfield of New York City, was present at the
December meeting, since he had indicated some previous concerns about
the involvement of the Fund and the Bolton family in motion picture
activities. Maxfield and Clymer were both relieved to hear Charters
suggest that the NCSSVMP form another, entirely separate group, with
lawyers, economists and the like, to handle the rest of the studies.
Clymer noted that "I still had some fears as to our engaging in the
study of the legal and trade practices." The key point for Clymer was
the following:

Dr. Charters's masterly exposition of the value of the studies was so impressive to the more judicially minded Maxfield, and had done much to reconcile me to making the first "psychological studies" at least, even though we had no guarantee of public relations action behind them that I had so long insisted upon. Charters said "these first studies would have provided a very significant service for the whole question of moral education."

Clymer informed Bolton that Maxfield's assessment of the proposed undertaking was that, "excluding the proposed study on the scandals in the lives of motion picture people, which he says is full of dynamite, the others may be made with proper safeguards." Maxfield also suggested that the Payne Fund retain a veto over any study proposed and that he read the final printed reports to guard against libel. Finally, Maxfield wanted to work out carefully "the clearest possible appearance of separation between the National Committee and the Payne Fund."[90] Thus Charters's ability to articulate the social scientific studies and their long-range value, together with Maxfield's legal concerns, was sufficient to convince the Payne Fund officials to stay away from further legal and economic studies of the motion picture industry. The interests of Stecker, Gilman and Skinner and the other "friends of the movies" were simply overridden, and by the next conference, in June 1929, the foundation for a comprehensive program of social scientific research was firmly set.[91]

In March 1931, when most of the studies were half-completed, Short officially changed the name of his National Committee to the Motion Picture Research Council. It is only through an examination of the voluminous correspondence and other papers of the MPRC that Short's pivotal role is revealed, and it soon becomes obvious to anyone perusing them that William Short was the Machiavellian mastermind who kept the organization going (he often worked for months on end without his salary). Operating the MPRC essentially as a one-man office with a secretary, he became the focal point around which revolved all of the relevant correspondence between the sponsors of the research (the Payne Fund), the researchers themselves and Charters (who was based in Columbus). In this way he was privy to everything that was going on (he received copies of almost all letters), and he often played one person against the other by using private communications.

It is at this point that the detailed history of the PFS, particularly the development of the research program, is continued in the next chapter.

The Vindication of Seabury: The Final Years of the Motion Picture Research Council, 1935–1940

William Harrison Short died suddenly from a heart attack on 10 January 1935 in Philadelphia, on his way to New York from Washington; he was sixty-six years old. He was conducting business for the MPRC at the time, no doubt working tirelessly to raise funds for the continuation of its activities. He had lived long enough to oversee the publication of the twelve PFS, but he died without realizing his dream of establishing a federal motion picture commission. After the publication of the studies, Short had hoped that their findings would create such an outcry that an outraged public would demand the establishment of such a federal agency. This outcome would have justified his nearly six long years of work and would also have vindicated his persistent belief that the key to forcing control on the motion picture industry was to provide substantive scientific proof of the deleterious effects of the movies. As is pointed out in Chapter Three, this was not to be, and Short was forced to continue the fight against the motion picture industry using whatever issues he could find to make his point.

While it is difficult to ascertain what was on Short's mind at the time of his death, he was almost certainly a disappointed man, forced to exhaust himself in order to obtain the funding necessary to continue his work. Almost immediately after the publication of the studies in late 1933, the Payne Fund notified Short that it was no longer willing to provide almost all of the funding for the MPRC. Short then retained the firm of Tamblyn and Brown to raise $200,000 for the MPRC funding for 1933–1934, but this venture was obviously a failure, because on 28 December 1933 the Payne Fund provided an interest-free loan of $5,000 to Short, with repayment due by 1 July 1934.[92] Another blow came in early March 1934 when Crandall wrote to Short asking him to omit in his fund-raising material any further references to the fact that the Payne Fund had spent more than $200,000 on the scientific studies.[93] Later that same month a further rejection came when Crandall, "pursuant to the policy we thought necessary to maintain regarding the program of the MPRC," refused an invitation to an MPRC luncheon, as well as an invitation to serve as a member of the National Committee.[94] The final ignominy came in November when the Payne Fund officials, apparently feeling charitable, notified James G. Blaine, the treasurer of the MPRC, that they would waive their claim to repayment of the loan in the amount of $3,000.[95] Short died less than two months later.

With Short's death, the MPRC was thrown into complete disarray. He had essentially run the office as a one-executive, one-secretary operation, processing an enormous amount of correspondence, filing newspaper and magazine clippings, making speeches, writing articles, working to increase the number of MPRC chapters and members throughout the country and generally maintaining a strong interest in every aspect of the motion picture industry on which his work impinged. He was tireless and apparently tenacious, but he could do only so much. When his heart gave out, no one remained who could continue his work in exactly the same way, and the MPRC was forced to seek new directions for its activities. First, however, the organization had to find a new home and director.

In February 1935, John H. Finley of the MPRC Executive Committee wrote to Ella Crandall asking if the Payne Fund was interested in the disposition of the MPRC files and other materials.[96] Crandall wrote back that it would have more interest in preserving the files than any other agency after the dissolution of the council, and offered to act as a depository for the records and other relevant matter.[97] The Payne Fund then stored the files, destroying some of a "non-essential" nature, until they could be disposed of in a more appropriate manner. The records remained with the Payne Fund for only a short while, before being shipped across the country to California in April 1935. This came about when Dr. Ray Lyman Wilbur, president of Stanford University and honorary president of the California Chapter of the MPRC, arranged for this chapter to take over the operation of the organization as of 1 June 1935. The MPRC was officially dissolved in New York State on 24 June 1935.

Dr. Wilbur was apparently eager to "perpetuate the movement" and was especially interested in the future of H.R. 6472 (the Pettingill bill), a congressional attempt to outlaw block booking in the motion picture industry.[98] The files of the MPRC from mid-1935 to its eventual dissolution in the 1940s[99] indicate that the organization devoted itself almost entirely to combating the motion picture industry through the support of legislation aimed at curbing and controlling industry practices. The concentration on this type of legislative activity in the final years of its existence was the supreme irony, because that is exactly what Seabury had hoped for when he first envisaged what was to become the MPRC.

Short's dogged insistence that only the irrefutable proof of the harmful effects of movies provided by scientific studies would induce the public to rise up and act had been proved wrong. Short had eclipsed Seabury, and his position had won out. It took five years of hard work before scientific studies were published, and even after their findings had been deliberately distorted to suit Short's purposes, there was no spontaneous public outcry for federal action against the motion picture industry. Short had discovered what many other reformers had known since the turn of the century – the general public did not really perceive the movies as a serious threat to society. The public voted its basic approval of movie content at the box office, and while there was a decline in movie attendance for economic reasons during the Depression, the movies were still as popular as ever.[100]

In the end, the motion picture industry was placed under a form of social control by a combination of internal and external forces. The MPPDA was able to strengthen its self-regulatory code with the assistance of the outside threat of the Roman Catholic Legion of Decency in the period after 1933.[101] In the long run, it was legislative action such as the Paramount Divorce Decree that forced the industry to alter its distribution and exhibition practices, but by then it was too late, as the inexorable march of television across the land fundamentally redefined the nature of the moviegoing experience in the United States.

It would be wrong to say that the PFS had played a major role in the reformation of the motion picture industry. Despite what Charters and others may have suggested, there is really nothing to substantiate such exaggerated claims.[102] The studies themselves, after a brief flurry of interest, were all but ignored for forty years. Nevertheless, the twelve published studies, and the draft of the unpublished study presented here for the first time in sixty years (see Chapter Four), represent an important benchmark in the evolution of social science and are a major source for increasing our understanding of the role of moviegoing in American society.

CHAPTER TWO

Movie-Made Social Science

THE ENTERPRISE OF THE PAYNE FUND
STUDIES RESEARCHERS, 1928–1933

Until recently, discussion of the Motion Picture and Youth research series, popularly known as the Payne Fund Studies (PFS), has been constrained by the necessity of relying on the evidence and conclusions put forth in the eight volumes published by Macmillan in 1933. The recent discovery of documentary sources pertaining to the PFS in the papers of the Motion Picture Research Council (MPRC), the Payne Fund, and PFS research director W. W. Charters has provided new insight into film reform movements, the genesis of the PFS and their lasting impact on the film industry and on the development of social science. This new evidence also allows us to reconsider the PFS themselves, to deconstruct the unified, fully formed character of the published volumes and to reassess the process by which the research agendas of the participating social scientists were conceptualized and carried out.

The Payne Fund program's shape and content, like that of most experimental endeavors, evolved over several years. In the fall of 1928, the research group undertook an initial series of fourteen projects on the relationship between movie attendance and children's emotions, attitudes and conduct. They annually regrouped to modify or close projects gone awry, or to propose new studies of film's impact on moral values, sexual attitudes and delinquent behavior. Several of these additional studies involved sociologist Paul G. Cressey, who joined the research group in 1931. Except for Cressey and Thrasher's ill-fated "Boys, Movies and City Streets" project, the PFS research was largely complete by mid-1932. The ten reports that were ultimately published in the fall of 1933 represented the product of nearly five years of effort and more than twenty separate research proposals and projects.

Even though his name did not appear on the published volumes, it is important to keep in mind the extent to which the PFS owed their existence to the personal efforts of Rev. William Short. Like Frankenstein's monster, the studies were his creation and the scapegoat of his reformist desires. Short was a widely read, intelligent layman probably more capable than some of the academics involved in the studies. He doggedly inserted himself in every phase of the university-based Payne Fund research programs, from critiquing project proposals to analyzing research data to summarizing the findings. While this chapter reconstructs an account of how individual academics undertook investigations and composed the PFS, for better or worse all the reports indelibly bear Short's imprint. Short labored incessantly to shape the researchers' questions and results to forward his imperatives. As the next chapter will demonstrate, he would do even more while publicizing the results of the studies.[1]

The PFS were undertaken during a period of methodological and ideological conflicts in the social sciences. Debates over whether academic reaction to social problems should favor value-oriented social policy or value-neutral objective study led Charters and most of the sociologists and psychologists involved in the Payne Fund program to stress objectivity over advocacy. They wished to reserve judgments about the effects of movies on children until the outcomes of their experiments were known and conclusive evidence could be gathered. Whatever concerns the academics had about interpretation and ultimate uses to which the studies would be put, however, Short did not make any such distinctions between science and reform.

Because Short did not recognize the possibility of indeterminate or positive results in the search for evidence of the movies' impact on children, to the casual observer the PFS might seem to be illustrations of long-discredited "hypodermic needle" or "direct influence" theories of media effects. Indeed, they largely follow behaviorist models of media reception and content analysis, which communications scholars have since reconsidered. But when we look more closely at the actual undertaking of the studies, we see that they reached cautious conclusions that emphasized limited, indirect models of media influence and the extent to which individual social and environmental differences moderated film's impact on the young.

While the PFS researchers could not conclusively identify precise levels and mechanisms of movies' influence on children's attitudes, behavior, health and perception, their efforts did not represent a failure of social science. The conflicting methods and goals of the academic researchers and Short combined to make the PFS series seem confused and disorganized because Short and the researchers differed in their goals. While the researchers commenced the project with some sympathy for Short's negative presuppositions about motion pictures' influence, their research experiences opened many areas of contradiction and complexity. As part of their experimentation in a new research area, the PFS group invented and extended new analytical tools and techniques, and they raised important questions about media effects. It was also fairly inevitable that they would make errors of procedure, logic and interpretation. They saddled themselves with topics that were too broad, experiments that failed and assumptions that were initially naive, misguided or biased. It took time for them to hone appropriate methods, but time for experimentation and failure was a luxury that Short felt he could little afford. Even if the Payne Fund researchers' projects failed, they did so only in that they did not provide support for Short's beliefs that the movies directly, and detrimentally, influenced children.

Taken as a whole and without the conflicts generated by the researchers' relationship with Short, the PFS are valid social science projects demonstrating the complexity and intangible qualities of media influence. The Payne Fund researchers' concerns that society should strive harder to produce a healthier, less violent culture for children to grow up in were sincere. Sixty subsequent years of debate about the role of movies (or television, radio, comic books, rock music or video games) in promoting violence and sexual license among the young demonstrates how difficult it is to study these matters, how much communication and social science scholars still don't know and how important the issues remain for us today. In their experimentation with research methods and design, and through their results and interpretations, the PFS make as important an intellectual contribution to the history of the social sciences as to the history of film.

Securing the Academic Participants

In November 1927, while awaiting the (private) publication of his polemic, *A Generation of Motion Pictures,* Short began a search for qualified social scientists to undertake the program of research he sought on the influence of movies on children's morals and conduct. He traveled to interview representatives of such august bodies as the American Academy of Political and Social Science, the National Research Council, the Character Education Institute, the Brookings Institute of Economics and the Social Science Research Council. Short sought recommendations for securing the services of the most prominent academics in sociology, psychology and education whose research centered on child development and who studied how values were imparted and absorbed, the measurement of attitudes and behavior and the causes of juvenile delinquency. The advice he obtained, and Short's own considerable knowledge of current social science literature, led him to the universities of Chicago, Yale, Iowa, Wisconsin, Michigan and Minnesota. It can be argued that Short preselected his research group, choosing social scientists who already shared his beliefs that movies had a suspect influence on children.[2]

At Columbia University in March 1928, Short met with Mark A. May, visiting from Yale. May was completing a massive research program called the Character Education Study. In Minneapolis in early July, Short interviewed Max and Grete Seham, of the University of Minnesota, authors of *The Tired Child* (1926), a study of children's health and the sources of fatigue. In Iowa City (combining interviews with visits to his relatives), Short met with George Stoddard and Christian Ruckmick of the University of Iowa's Department of Psychology and its Child Welfare Research Station.[3]

Short spent a hectic week in Chicago in July 1928, conferring with venerable social reformer-colleagues Jane Addams at Hull House and Jessie Binford at the Juvenile Protection Agency. He interviewed Alice Miller Mitchell of the Wiebolt Foundation, who would soon publish an investigation of Chicago-area students' moviegoing habits called *Children and Movies* (1929). He spoke to these women about fund-raising and how to get introductions to University of Chicago faculty, for Chicago's reputation in research and scholarship was supreme and involvement with its faculty would aid Short's plan tremendously.[4]

Short's first destination at the University of Chicago was the School of Education. There he found Frank Freeman, who had recently published *Motion Pictures in the Classroom* (with Ben Wood, 1929) and had authored numerous studies exploring the processes by which children learn. On this trip Short would also stop in Detroit to meet W. W. Charters, professor in the University of Chicago School of Education (and former student of John Dewey), who had just completed direction of a research program of national scope, the Commonwealth Teacher Training Study. Charters had also published extensively, including *The Teaching of Ideals* (1927), written with the research input of his wife and colleague, Jessie Charters. Charters was in the process of moving to Ohio State University to head the university's Bureau of Educational Research.[5]

In the sociology department at the University of Chicago, Short sought out Robert Park, noted teacher and scholar of urban social issues. Park was highly enthusiastic about the possibilities of Short's project, as he and his Chicago colleagues had encouraged graduate students to immerse themselves in the city's problems to gain sufficient knowledge to diagnose its ills. Park had more than a passing interest in the effects of mass communications, having worked as a journalist and having studied the role of news and the press in community life. Park enlisted a young faculty member (and former Chicago graduate student), social psychologist Herbert Blumer, to be the junior scholar on the project. Short probably also interviewed University of Chicago attitude psychologist L. L. Thurstone on this trip. During the summer, Short also traveled to the universities of Wisconsin and Michigan (there to speak with sociologist Kimball Young, who would later be a critic of the published PFS); Short also corresponded with at least a dozen other prominent academics around the country about possible research positions.[6]

Once he had secured the financial support from the Payne Fund that enabled him to start planning this massive project, Short left his interviews in the summer of 1928 enthused by his prospects for creating a strong program of innovative research that could be completed with dispatch, so he could put the "facts" thus obtained into action against the film industry as soon as possible.[7]

Many of the researchers Short contacted were intrigued by the opportunity to investigate the influence of movies. May proposed extending his work on the Character Education Study, which gauged the attitudes of thousands of children toward ethical questions, by measuring children's attitudes toward situations found in the movies. The Sehams proposed a multifaceted study of the ways children's health was affected by attendance at motion picture shows. Stoddard thought he could use films to measure the processes by which children absorb facts and information. Freeman suggested a case study to explore the extent to which students would use information gained from films to change their behaviors. Thurstone, author of ground-breaking articles on attitude measurement, suggested that he could quantify the impact of movie themes on changes in viewer attitudes. Park proposed that he and Blumer could analyze case study data on juvenile delinquents already gathered by the Chicago courts and social welfare agencies to chart the impact of the movies on young people's identity and values formation.[8]

When he was first approached by Short, Charters claimed that motion picture studies were an untested area of social science research:

Although this was my first acquaintance with the movie situation I saw that from the scientific point of view this problem was a natural. The influence on children of any medium as widely attended as motion pictures was a grave and serious question; no investigations had been conducted in the field; but the techniques of investigation had been developed and were ready to use.[9]

While Charters, like many academics of the 1920s, had not considered film worthy of serious study, during the decade a few social scientists had begun exploring film as a source of propaganda or knowledge. Harvard psychologist Hugo Munsterberg had published *The Photoplay: A Psychological Study* in 1916. Columbia University psychologists had utilized movies in intelligence testing of New England villagers as a sugar-coated information source on which subjects could be quizzed. Frank Freeman and other education scholars had investigated film's possibilities as a teaching tool, and the Yale Historical Films group was producing movies for the classroom. Other social scientists had considered movies a "social problem" to be "solved," an outside influence upsetting the natural balance of traditional society. Park's Chicago colleague, Ernest Burgess, concerned about rising juvenile delinquency rates and the challenges movies posed to family values, had sat on the Chicago Board of Film Censorship since 1920. And Robert and Helen Lynd would note with dismay how firmly movie stars were entrenched as admired role models by the youth of Muncie, Indiana, in their seminal study, *Middletown,* which would be published in 1929. Motion pictures had contributed to a base of sociological and educational research studies in the 1920s, but never before on a scale as large as that contemplated by Short.[10]

Despite intellectual and aesthetic prejudices against popular commercial culture and the movies, many of the prominent scholars Short interviewed were amenable to joining a large research program on motion pictures. The 1920s saw the first wave of major social science research projects undertaken with outside institutional funding. What began with the U.S. Army's research programs on intelligence tests during the First World War had resulted in large foundations, like the Rockefeller, the Commonwealth Fund, the Social Science Research Council, the Carnegie and the Russell Sage, and the federal government (President Hoover's commission) making available substantial sums of money for social research that were eagerly sought after by social scientists. Many academics and their universities wanted to get their share of money from these research programs. The Payne Fund was largely unknown in this milieu, and had no real track record, but it held out the promise of a source of future largess. The potential of generous funding was a lure for the reticent researchers that overcame any squeamishness about the true intent of Short's proposed movie study. To be fair, however, the scope of the research to be undertaken, and its high visibility, was an obvious lure to young scholars wishing to make a name for themselves. The movies, after all, had become a central part of American culture by the late 1920s.

Organizing the Research Program: The First Year

The first year of the Payne Fund research program, from late 1928 through 1929, was for the social scientists a crucial period in the development of appropriate research methods, a year of frustrations, numerous setbacks and an occasional triumph. The researchers' experiences during this time shaped the scope of the studies by setting limits on what was deemed possible, and also by opening up alternative topics and modes of inquiry. The process of defining the content of the final published studies would continue for several years.

One of Short's first moves was to appoint Charters as director of research to coordinate the research program. Charters had a reputation as an organized, hardworking facilitator who was able to coax enormous amounts of work from students and colleagues. He had an informal demeanor and liked to be called "W. W.," "the Chief" or "the Boss." As Edgar Dale later recalled:

The role that Mr. Charters played was that of manager or director. He did not tell these men what ought to be studied or suggest techniques which would be especially fruitful. Rather, he attempted to bring the whole investigation under one tent. The phrase I remember Mr. Charters using again and again was "try to nail down some particular points." He tried to get the investigators to be more modest in their research plans, to attempt less, and try to "get something nailed down."[11]

At their initial three-day October 1928 conference, the academics in attendance (Park, Freeman, Charters, Jessie Charters, May and Stoddard) mulled over the many research questions Short had presented in a document called "What We Need to Know as a Basis for a National Policy in Motion Pictures." The heart of Short's proposal was the measurement of the movies' influence on children. He was most desirous of pursuing six categories of research: (1) the number of children reached by the movies; (2) a quantitative measure of their influence; (3) the positive, negative or neutral qualities of their influence; (4) differentiations of their influence ascribed to gender, age, intelligence level and "temperament"; (5) their influence on children's information processing, attitudes, emotions, conduct and aesthetic and moral standards; (6) their influence on such "important matters" as respect for authority, marriage, forms of crime, health, hero worship and international understanding. Short and the assembled academics prioritized these research projects into a list of twenty-one proposals, and decided to concentrate on isolating and quantifying film's impact on young viewers, postponing surveys of the film industry itself and projects drawing aesthetic judgments about film. Charters reported to Short and the "friends of the movies" that the group had concluded that

before you could do very much with this problem of seeing whether the influence of motion pictures was good or bad, it was necessary to be able to measure the influence. It so happens that the kind of influence to be measured – on attitudes, information, conduct, and the like – has not yet been subjected to these measures. We do not know how much influence a motion picture or a series of motion pictures has. Therefore scales have to be made. I might add . . . that it is a technical job. It is a very difficult job to measure these things with reasonable degree of sensitiveness and accuracy.[12]

While the social scientists involved in the PFS would critique one another's research designs during the ensuing experimental phase of the project, rarely did they directly debate whether quantitative or qualitative methods would be most useful.[13] Some of the researchers, especially psychologists Thurstone and Stoddard, favored statistical data collection and analysis as more scientific techniques, while the University of Chi-

Table 1. November 1928

Researcher(s)	Study: Working Title
W. W. Charters	Film Content
W. W. Charters	Child Attendance at Movies
W. W. Charters	What Is a Good Picture?
Jessie Charters	One to One Correspondence of Child and Film
Jessie Charters	Parents, Teachers and Observers
Stoddard	Getting Information through the Movies
Freeman	Educational Influence of Classroom Films
Ruckmick	Children's Emotions
Seham and Seham	Children's Health
May	Attitude Tests
Thurstone	Attitude Scales
Park and Blumer	1,000 Cases of Delinquency
Park and Blumer	Youth Conduct and the Movies
Short and Snedden	Literature Survey on the Role of the Motion Picture

cago—trained sociologists (Park, Blumer, Thrasher and Cressey, but also Yale psychologist May) championed the use of less measurable but more expressive case studies, interviews and "life histories." Although largely unspoken during the experimental phase, conflicts over methodology probably contributed to dissension and animosity among the research group during the studies' publication and promotion (see Chapter Three).

After their preliminary work in October, the Payne Fund research group met again in Columbus on 24–25 November 1928 to finalize the assignment of experiment topics. They further reduced the field from twenty-one to fourteen broadly conceived initial project proposals, a list that differs significantly by topic and author from the eight ultimately published reports familiar to scholars (Table 1).[14]

Charters and Short organized the proposed studies into complementary pairs approaching questions about the influence of movies with various research methodologies. Thus both Stoddard and Freeman would tackle how much children learned from movies and how they applied their new knowledge. Ruckmick and the Sehams would investigate the extent to which children's health and emotions were affected by movie attendance. Thurstone and May would experiment with two measurement techniques to gauge how children's attitudes were influenced by film. Park and Blumer would use two methods of analysis to study connections between movies, values formation and juvenile delinquency.[15]

Half of these initial projects fell through, however, soon after the researchers returned home. Four of the fourteen initial research proposals proved unworkable. The Sehams' elaborate study on the effect of movies on children's health looked, on closer inspection, to be much too expensive to undertake. Short's own study, an extension of A Generation of Motion Pictures, to be coauthored with educational sociologist David Snedden, was canceled because the Payne Fund board felt it involved no scientific gathering of facts. The two projects assigned to Mrs. Jessie Charters, professor of parental education at Ohio State, also were never begun. She had proposed doing intensive case studies of individual child viewers, interviews with parents and surveys of elementary school teachers' attitudes toward the impact of moviegoing on young students. Jessie Charters was actively involved in the first six months of the PFS project and attended the meetings, but she claimed to have become overwhelmed with other academic work and begged off the research committee. Then W. W. Charters delayed beginning his three projects until he could get the remaining studies off the ground, leaving the research group with seven projects to pursue in its first year.[16]

INFORMATION STUDIES

Two Payne Fund studies undertaken in 1928–1929 explored the influence of motion pictures on children's intake and retention of information. Stoddard, director of the Iowa Child Welfare Research Station at the University of Iowa, with graduate student P. W. Holaday, constructed a battery of experiments in which children of various ages were shown a movie such as Tom Sawyer or an animal film like Rango and then tested on their recall of factual information about setting, characters and plot. This project was one of the few Payne Fund studies whose experiments were conducted without complications. While children grasped and remembered a significant amount (60 percent) of what they viewed, several modifying factors kept movies from directly imprinting "sophisticated ideas" on their brains. Stoddard and Holaday found that young children reacted more strongly to exciting scenes of action and movement and to familiar themes or contexts than to scenes involving situations outside their own limited experiences.[17]

Frank Freeman's study was to have enriched the conclusions of the Stoddard and Holaday study by measuring the extent to which children translate knowledge gained while watching films into changed behavior. Over a number of weeks, Freeman screened for young students a series of instructional films about dental care and the dangers of tooth decay (*Tommy Tucker's Tooth* and *Clara Cleans Her Teeth*). Then he compared the frequency of their toothbrushing with that of a control group who did not watch the films. Freeman found that the "movie children" did not take better care of their teeth; in fact, they brushed less often than the control group. These results dismayed Freeman, the Payne Fund group and Short, who had hoped to find more clear-cut evidence of movie impact. That children resisted the messages conveyed by film was not for them an acceptable conclusion, and Freeman blamed the "lack" of results on the very poor quality of the dental films. Although Freeman completed his report, which would be eventually published as a research note in the *Journal of Educational Sociology,* his unhappy experience was indicative of the Payne Fund researchers' early frustrations.[18]

ATTITUDE STUDIES

Psychologists in the late 1920s developed tests and scales in order to compare one person's attitudes with another's so they could be collectively quantified, measured and analyzed. L. L. Thurstone's pioneering work, published as *The Measurement of Attitude* (with E. J. Chave, 1929), is acknowledged as "the first highly sophisticated technique developed for recording attitude." Payne Fund scholars Thurstone and May were both prominent researchers in this new field, although their methodologies differed significantly. Their studies, although among the more trouble-plagued of the PFS, were considered crucial to the research program.[19]

Mark May and Yale graduate student Frank Shuttleworth for their Payne Fund research developed inventories of attitudes children held toward various categories of people and ethical situations, including some characters and scenes encountered in the movies. Were chorus girls or cowboys depicted in the movies as being as honest as college professors? How did students rate each other on popularity, kindness and respect paid to them by the teacher? May and Shuttleworth planned to compare the responses of children who were frequent moviegoers with those of youngsters who never attended. The trouble was, they could not locate any children between New Haven and New York City who never went to the movies. May and Shuttleworth kept stumbling over the fact that even children who almost never saw films were nevertheless exposed to a popular culture inundated with movie references. Film's indirect influence on children was practically inescapable and could not be isolated and measured separately, which of course was one of the central findings of *Middletown* and which Cressey's study would also emphasize. Short was somewhat aware of this problem when he discussed May's study with Charters, but he rationalized that the May–Shuttleworth study measured the "excess" movie influence found by comparing children of the two extremes.[20]

May and Shuttleworth determinedly pushed on with the analysis of their data, but they were able to isolate only the most minuscule differences between the groups. The movie children had slightly lower deportment grades in school, but were slightly better liked than their nonmovie fellows. Movie children also were found to read more books and magazines than their counterparts (findings that horrified Short), but close inspection determined that movie children's reading diet was higher on "light" topics and lower on *Scientific American* and *National Geographic*. Despite these efforts to make the study useful for his arguments that movies were ruining our youth, Short was highly concerned about the lack of conclusive results from the May–Shuttleworth study, and urged them to keep testing.[21]

Where May and Shuttleworth had attempted to measure broad attitude differences, Thurstone attempted to examine very specific attitudes held by young people and then see if exposure to films could sway them to alter their views. Thurstone and University of Chicago graduate student Ruth Peterson concentrated on race, ethnicity and nationalism as issues on which people held strong or extreme attitudes. They devised questionnaires about subjects' attitudes toward Germans and Jews and designed scales to chart subjects' reactions to such statements as "Germans are better than Norwegians" and "All Jews are trustworthy." Then they showed subjects two mainstream films that portrayed Germans and Jews in a favorable light (*All Quiet on the Western Front* and *My Four Sons*). Thurstone and Peterson's plan was to test a group's attitudes about ethnicity, show the films, remeasure the attitudes to see if there had been any movement and then chart the persistence of attitude changes.

In their 1929 experiments, Thurstone and Peterson tested high school students in Hyde Park, an urban neighborhood of middle-class and working-class German-Jewish families in which the University of Chicago was located. Thurstone and Peterson found, however, that students' opinions about Jews and Germans were too emotionally charged and contradictory, given their own ethnic heritage, to gauge accurately. Disappointed, the researchers speculated that Chicago's densely populated ethnic neighborhoods offered opportunities for factors other than movies to shape residents' opinions of the honesty, patriotism and moral values of Germans and Jews. They also fretted that few results came from a single film screening and that they could not locate additional Hollywood films with Jewish or German themes. The initial results of both the May and Thurstone attitude studies were much less clear and conclusive than the researchers may have anticipated, and Short and the Payne Fund group thus considered them to be in serious trouble.[22]

HEALTH AND EMOTION STUDIES

Many social scientists in this era held that analyzing external display and control of the emotions was critical to measuring children's internal health and intellectual development. Thus several members of the Payne Fund research group suggested studying the mechanics and implications of the movies' impact on children's emotions. Christian A. Ruckmick and graduate student Wendell Dysinger of the psychology department at the University of Iowa proposed attaching film-watching children to heart monitors and psychogalvanometers to gauge suddenly accelerated heartbeats, blood pressure and galvanic resistance in children's skin associated with sweaty emotional reactions like excitement, arousal, fear and nervousness (see photo section). The researchers measured children's responses to adventure films such as *Charlie Chan's Chance* and *The Feast of Ishtar*; they were disappointed in not being able to find a current film that would produce fearful reactions as extreme as had *The Phantom of the Opera*. Nevertheless, Ruckmick and Dysinger concluded that reactions to scenes of danger peaked with nine-year-olds, but steadily lost effect among sixteen-year-olds and adults, as older subjects had to learn to firmly distinguish between fiction and reality. Responses to erotic scenes grew steadily among ten- and eleven-year-olds, peaked in the sixteen-year-old group and again dropped off after adolescence with what the researchers termed the "adult discount." This Payne Fund project was completed with relatively few problems and would produce results that have held up well in subsequent investigations.[23]

To replace the Seham sleep-and-health study, abandoned because of its too-broad focus and great expense, Charters in June 1929 tapped Samuel Renshaw, Vernon Miller and Dorothy Marquis of the psychology department at Ohio State University, who conducted experiments on how children's sleep habits and nighttime restlessness might be affected by moviegoing. They studied two groups of children at the Ohio Bureau of Juvenile Research, which operated a state children's home. One set of youngsters were taken out to the movies every night, while the other children saw no films. Researchers then wired the children's bedsprings to monitor how often the children tossed and turned at night. The data from these experiments showed few patterns. Nevertheless, Renshaw, Miller and Marquis proceeded to draw out some of the most naive, biased or antimovie conclusions in the Payne Fund program. They categorized nonmovie children who slept soundly through the night as well rested, but the researchers intimated that movie stimulation could induce a druglike stupor in film-viewing children. They construed tossing in bed at night as healthy for nonmovie children and for moviegoers as the physical manifestation of disturbing, movie-inspired dreams.[24]

BEHAVIOR STUDIES

The final project undertaken from the original 1928 list also examined external signs of movie-influenced behavior. Robert Park had proposed two studies comparing the conduct of middle-class high school and college students with those of juvenile delinquents and imprisoned criminals. To what extent could movies have influenced these young people to be honest, or to steal? How did adolescents negotiate the many suggestions made in the movies that beautiful young people could have fame and wealth, cars and clothes and boundless sexual gratification, with so little effort?

Park, much like Jane Addams, felt that children "begin very early to formulate life projects" through role playing, fantasy and imaginative games. But children could be exposed to moral values in dime novels and movies that were contradictory to what they were taught at home or in school and church. Park believed the child's preoccupation with role playing and creating conceptions of the self was essential to the development of character and that concentration on one role "subdued" and "suppressed" the others. "I am particularly interested to learn how, when, and to what extent the moving pictures serve to inflame the imagination and start reveries, which may after a long period, sometimes years, eventuate in actions which are anti-social or the reverse," Park wrote, venturing to wonder if Leopold and Loeb (University of Chicago students then much in the news for their shocking murder of a young boy) had absorbed their ideas from the movies.[25]

Park was an important and influential member of the PFS research group, attending the September and November 1928 meetings, but a fellowship opportunity arose for him in early 1929 to travel to China and Japan. He turned the Payne Fund project entirely over to Blumer, although he did ask Short whether he could conduct comparative studies of movie influence while overseas. The Payne Fund board regretfully said it must limit the project.[26]

Herbert Blumer took over the business of soliciting autobiographies from University of Chicago undergraduates and comparing them with a thousand existing life histories of juvenile delinquents. Blumer soon obtained about a hundred written statements from University of Chicago students and about as many from local high school students and young working women. The students were asked to link specific movies, film genres and habits of movie theater attendance to the formative stages of their lives. Enthusiastic about the quality of the essays, Blumer sent several to Short. (Some of these recently discovered autobiographies are included in this volume; see Chapter Six.) Blumer put the delinquency portion of his project on the back burner.[27]

Short, still impatient for very clear evidence of causality, desperately wished to explore links between delinquency, crime and the movies. With Park's departure for the Orient, Short welcomed the interest of Frederick Thrasher, who joined the PFS research group in early 1929. Thrasher was a Chicago alumnus whose book, *The Gang*, a highly regarded study of delinquent youth in Chicago, included a chapter on the influence of movies and dime novels on gang attitudes and behavior. Thrasher taught educational sociology at New York University and had just launched a huge $36,000 study, funded by the Bureau of Social Hygiene, to study the Jefferson Park Boys' Club in East Harlem's Italian slums and the possibilities of its positive influence on boys' character and behavior. Thrasher proposed a study comparing moviegoing with other factors influencing delinquency among the boys of this tenement district, which Short and Charters enthusiastically approved. From the first, this Payne Fund study would attempt to place the effects of movies in a context of other social and environmental influences on young viewers. Thrasher placed responsibility for data gathering in the hands of a graduate assistant, Orville Crays, who began flailing away at research based on the other PFS in an attempt at a grand synthesis.[28]

Regrouping: The 1929 Meeting and Second Research Year

By the June 1929 conference, the Payne Fund researchers and their projects had survived a strenuous seven-month shakedown period. Stoddard and Holaday's information study and Ruckmick and Dysinger's emotional reactions study had gone smoothly, but the others had stumbled through experimental and conceptual missteps and down blind research alleys. It is important to note that the Payne Fund academics had undertaken the challenging task of developing research methods for the new and little understood area of media effects. Unanticipated or contradictory conclusions are a natural, expected and valuable aspect of scientific research, but most of the Payne Fund researchers, driven perhaps by their initial assumptions and Short's desires, construed the outcomes of their studies so far as a lack of results. The mood of this 1929 meeting was downbeat as the academics assessed what they perceived as the damage. The group decided that Freeman's study, for one, might as well be shelved for lack of results. "After completing all he could do," Charters wrote, "Mr. Freeman decided that he would not publish it [as a Payne Fund Study volume], because he could not get the right set up to prove anything about the problem which was assigned to him."[29]

Also in serious doubt of completion were both attitude measurement projects. The May–Shuttleworth study's inconsequential results made Short furious enough to consider pulling the plug on it. In Thurstone's absence from the conference, the methodological and data problems of his study were hotly debated among the other Payne Fund researchers. Thurstone, too, contemplated abandoning his study. "Certainly the showing of a single film is not going to throw the student attitudes all over the scale," a frustrated Thurstone wrote to Charters after the

Table 2. June 1929

Researcher(s)	Study: Working Title
Charters	Film Content (not begun)
Charters	Child Attendance at Movies (not begun)
Charters	What Is a Good Picture? (not begun)
Stoddard and Holaday	Getting Information through the Movies
May and Shuttleworth	Attitude Tests
Thurstone and Peterson	Attitude Scales
Ruckmick and Dysinger	Children's Emotions
Renshaw et al.	Children's Sleep
Blumer	College Students' Conduct
Blumer	1,000 Cases of Delinquency (not begun)
Thrasher	Boys' Club
Freeman	Dental Health Education (closed)

meeting. Thurstone responded to Blumer's skeptical critique of his research:

Society would be in a bad state if a single motion picture film should throw attitudes a long distance on the scale. It is of course not likely that in the experiments we should happen to find one of those rare films that affect attitude by a conspicuous amount. Our problem is to ascertain whether films actually seen by the students have some effect that is measurable. I believe that our measuring methods are sufficiently refined to detect it.[30]

Blumer admitted during the conference that the scope of his study was increasing exponentially, but so far he had been able to draw few conclusions and still hadn't done any research on delinquency. Thrasher reported that Crays was getting nowhere with statistical data gathering, and Thrasher had no clear statement of what this integrative study might accomplish. Things looked bleak when the Payne Fund researchers made their plans for the next year of the program. Five original projects continued into the second research year, supplemented by the Thrasher and Renshaw studies, the three yet to be started Charters studies and the Blumer delinquency project not yet begun (Table 2).[31]

Charters and Short deemed it necessary to express "a final note of confidence" at the end of the conference. "The difficulties that have to be faced and overcome in researches as complex as the one engaged in were commented upon" by all the Payne Fund researchers. As they went back to their work in the fall of 1929, Short kept in close touch with the researchers, brainstorming methods of experimentation and analysis that might get the Thurstone, May and Thrasher projects back on track and ideas that would help Blumer and Thrasher to find links between movies and juvenile delinquency. There is some evidence that Charters felt pressured both by the Payne Fund administrators and by Short to show results for all the money that had been expended so far. In November 1929, Charters could assure an anxious Crandall merely that "the one definite thing that I can report is that all of the projects are being worked upon vigorously by all the investigators." Meanwhile, Short fretted to Charters that

I should much dislike to see our research eventuate in any such fashion . . . that motion pictures are comparatively . . . or perhaps quite harmless. . . . We may be disappointed in our efforts to measure the effects of various kinds of films on the several aspects of life and character that are being examined. But to reach the conclusion that there is no influence would be quite a different matter.[32]

Charters had nagging doubts about all the studies; he responded to Short, "As the studies take shape I am not sure that we are going to have data that will be comprehensive enough for the purposes of your committee. I should like to talk it all over with you in order to review again just what we need to do to make sure that we are squeezing everything out of these experiments that can be squeezed." These concerns persisted through the 1929–1930 research year. As late as June 1930, Short grumbled to Charters that the Research Committee's most pressing job was to make clear the "distinction between our failure to find results and their non-existence."[33]

ATTENDANCE AND FILM CONTENT STUDIES

Charters finally began work on his studies of children's movie attendance and analysis of Hollywood film themes in the second year of Payne Fund research. Critics of the movies had skirmished for years with the film industry over the extent of children's attendance at the movies. Social critics, counting heads at Saturday matinees, estimated that 70 to 90 percent of the movie audience consisted of children (up to twenty-one years old). The Hays Office surveyed evening attendance at New York City's most elegant movie palaces and counterclaimed that only 8 percent of the audience consisted of children.[34]

In the fall of 1929, Charters put the attendance study in the hands of graduate student Eleanor Morris. For a week in October, she and her assistants "clocked" children's attendance at fifteen Columbus, Ohio, movie theaters. Assistants were expensive to hire, however, they might not accurately estimate moviegoers' ages and they had covered only a small proportion of the city's sixty-nine theaters – for efficiency, Morris had concentrated on the huge downtown picture palaces, but children most often attended the smaller and older neighborhood theaters. Charters was dissatisfied with these incomplete results. As with the other studies, however, Charters and Short agreed to keep searching for better experimental strategies.[35]

For the film content study, Charters sought the consultation of his former graduate student at the University of Chicago, Edgar Dale, who had taken a job with Eastman Kodak. Charters soon brought Dale to Ohio State University to assume full direction of both the content and attendance studies, freeing Charters to oversee the far-flung researchers. "Dale finds that doing student questionnaires through the schools gives better information than clocking," Charters wrote approvingly to Short. Dale concluded that 37 percent of the Columbus movie audience (and, by extrapolation, the nation's audience) consisted of young people twenty-one years of age or younger (a figure close to their percentage of the population).

In this early effort to devise a content analysis study, Dale attempted to formulate what he termed a "foolproof" yardstick or "measuring rod" by which anyone could measure the content (and aesthetic and moral worth) of a film. Dale and his assistants drew up a rather elementary list of major narrative themes; then he categorized several years' worth of Hollywood features from published summaries in film trade journals. Dale concluded that some 78 percent of movie themes revolved around love, romance, sex and crime, a rather simplistic categorization that would probably describe the major themes of Western literature; this figure nevertheless would be used in subsequent MPRC publicity as evidence guaranteed to shock and titillate parents of young moviegoers. Dale's early effort demonstrated some of the problems of trying to connect empirical content analysis with issues of representation and aesthetic values that have continued to concern media critics and communication scholars to the present day.[36]

In the spring of 1930, Thurstone and Peterson succeeded in refining their attitude scales. They relocated the site of their experiments from Chicago to isolated small towns with more homogeneous populations, such as Genoa, Mendota and Princeton, Illinois. There they screened *The Birth of a Nation* and measured young people's attitudes toward African-Americans and Chinese, ethnic groups unfamiliar to locals. They also measured attitudes toward war and crime, issues that engendered more distinct reactions of approval and disapproval. These changes brought the researchers more consistent results. Although the children initially held a broad array of attitudes toward each ethnic group studied, a single film viewing seemed to affect their approval rankings significantly. Thurstone and Peterson concluded that, while a powerful film could temporarily modify opinions, young people's social attitudes generally conformed to group values and resisted easy redirection by mass media.[37]

THE STANDARDS STUDY

Short had felt from the beginning that the PFS needed a clearly identified set of "American value standards" (that he and the other members of the MPRC assumed would match their conservative, native-born, white Protestant assumptions) against which to compare the values portrayed in Hollywood films. Such a standard values list would be a useful complement to Dale's content analysis of Hollywood film themes. Short thought that, if the researchers could identify American moral attitudes toward sexual or criminal behavior and if Dale found Hollywood films deficient in comparison, then the movie industry could be forced to mend its ways.

In the fall of 1929, Short appealed to a higher authority in his quest to find a written set of standard American moral values by contacting prominent philosopher (and Charters's graduate adviser) John Dewey. In an interview with Short, Dewey suggested that the Payne researchers examine and categorize film values before critiquing cultural standards. "He doubts whether any compilation of standards, made in advance, and without direct relation to an analysis of the films, would fit the need very closely," Short reported back to Charters. Dewey advised Short to poll other academic sociologists as "objective" arbiters of American values, so Short queried the Payne Fund researchers and a dozen social science luminaries. Their replies reinforced Dewey's assertion that, currently, society's values were in too great a state of flux for one standard to be defined for all viewers and that moral values should be considered in the context of particular communities or groups.[38]

Short continued to have great enthusiasm for what Charters called the "John Dewey Study." The "What Is a Good Picture?" project, originally assigned to Charters, was reconceptualized as a standards study in the spring of 1930. Charters recommended an old friend, educational psychologist Charles C. Peters of Pennsylvania State College, to undertake a study of the relationship between film practice and moral codes at the community level.[39]

Peters and graduate student Robert Wray devised scales to measure typical community standards regarding four subjects: women's aggressive role in lovemaking, public displays of kissing and caressing, parents' use of violence toward their children and democratic attitudes and practices. "In determining what the mores are in a given community it is necessary to determine the behavior which will shock people," Peters reported. After interviewing faculty members and students at State College to determine their constructions of standard, socially accepted moral viewpoints, Peters and his observers rated 142 randomly chosen current films to compare the moral values portrayed therein.[40]

Peters found female Hollywood film characters to be more forthrightly affectionate than the average community considered appropriate, but in matters of public kissing, film behavior and community standards appeared to agree. Most surprising to himself, Peters found that films presented less child abuse and more racial tolerance than the accepted standard in American society; in addition, community practices in these areas appeared to fall below the perceived national standard. These optimistic conclusions about the movies' morals did not please Short at all.[41]

The 1930 Conference and the Third Research Year

The PFS research project roster, as it stood at the time of the June 1930 meeting, was beginning to resemble more closely its final form, with Dale assuming a leadership role in the film attendance and content studies, the Peters study added to the program and Blumer soon to begin his delinquency study (Table 3). The participants presented summaries of their research to the June 1930 conference, and the group discussed the directions the various studies were taking. To Short's muffled chagrin, the researchers reaffirmed their intention of attracting no publicity about the research until the studies were completed and the results

Table 3. June 1930

Researcher(s)	Study: Working Title
Dale	The Content of Motion Pictures
Dale	Children's Attendance at Motion Pictures
Stoddard and Holaday	Getting Ideas from the Movies
May and Shuttleworth	The Social Conduct and Attitudes of Movie Fans
Thurstone and Peterson	Motion Pictures and the Social Attitudes of Children
Ruckmick and Dysinger	The Emotional Responses of Children
Renshaw et al.	Children's Sleep
Blumer	Movies and Conduct
Blumer and Hauser	Movies and Delinquency
Thrasher	Boys' Club
Peters	Moral Standards

published, although several members agreed that a popular summary volume might be necessary to interpret their results to a wider public. While an impatient Short was anxious to secure ammunition for his battles with the Hays Office, he also understood the danger to his goals of releasing partial or premature results to a sensation-seeking press.[42]

While some of the studies now continued steadily along their paths, others remained fraught with problems. The May–Shuttleworth study continued to frustrate Short. "Verdict – a universal negative, or not proven? Necessity for caution about claiming a result of inexistence because our techniques have failed to find it," he noted in the conference report. The Boys' Club movie study was also still in disarray, so Thrasher relieved Orville Crays of his responsibilities. Crays had designed a series of experiments to integrate and test methods used by Blumer, Stoddard, Dale and other Payne Fund researchers, yet his clumsily designed surveys had yielded little significant data. The Boys' Club statisticians found little to tabulate from the autobiographies Crays gathered, and East Harlem's movie theaters were found to serve mostly adult patrons. Some 2,300 boys were surveyed about their movie attitudes, but the seven questions asked – where and when they attended movies, and who their favorite stars were – did not bear much analysis. Someone (probably Short) wrote testily on the cover of Crays's report, "Are questions 1–7 of value to N.C.S.S. [MPRC]?" Boys' Club researchers Robert L. Whitley and Janet Nelson agreed to assume temporary responsibility for the stumbling study.[43]

BLUMER'S DELINQUENCY AND SEX STUDIES

In the spring of 1930, Herbert Blumer completed most of his analysis of student autobiographies for the *Movies and Conduct* report, concluding (like Park) that childhood imitation is crucial to young people's process of forming standards and that movies offer a tremendously attractive cast of characters to imitate. Blumer felt that since Hollywood films were produced outside the circle of the child's moral guardians (home, school, church), however, they held far more potential for bad influence than good. Blumer can be characterized as one of the most antimovie of the PFS researchers, and he appears to have maintained a congenial professional relationship with Short.

Blumer now turned to the promised study of "Movies, Delinquency and Crime," recruiting Chicago graduate student Philip Hauser as coauthor. Hauser surveyed prison wardens about the use of movies in the rehabilitation of inmates, and he interviewed male and female prisoners about the influence of movies on their attitudes and behavior. Much of the resulting report, however, was a mishmash of evidence assembled by Blumer from interviews and newspaper clippings previously gathered by Short – reports of crimes duplicating movie plots, the opinions of juvenile court officials and interviews with convicted felons who claimed they learned how to commit petty crimes by imitating what they had seen on the movie screen.

Blumer and Hauser were able to argue only that 10 percent of crimes committed by delinquents could be construed as movie-related, but they played these meager findings for all they were worth. "Probably the movies may be associated with the crimes in an indirect, subtle way not clear in the consciousness of the individual," Blumer reported hopefully to Short.

Short had particularly warned Blumer and Hauser against allowing the inclusion of any evidence of movies' positive influence that could be "twisted" by the film industry, and urged them to delete statements made by delinquents and criminals "that (some) pictures make them want to be real good." Hauser's own master's thesis, drawn from the same research material, deduced that movies generated mostly harmless and occasionally positive influences on prisoners' behavior. The data and conclusions of his thesis raise serious questions about the veracity of the conclusions reached in the final report, *Movies, Delinquency and Crime*. Despite (or because of) the evident biases and thinness of their evidence, Short was delighted with the Blumer and Hauser manuscript. "Of the analysis of material and the general set up, I have nothing but praise – it seems to me excellent," he wrote to Blumer.[44]

The one media effect Blumer found in common between middle-class college students and juvenile delinquents was the movies' ability to arouse sexual desire. In his other report, *Movies and Conduct,* Blumer asserted that the movies' chief fascination for young people stemmed from "the emotional agitation which they induce. . . . Ordinary self-control is lost. Impulses and feelings are aroused, and the individual develops a readiness to certain forms of action which are foreign in some degree to his ordinary conduct."[45]

Blumer was sufficiently alarmed at the outbursts of adolescent passion encountered in his interviews with University of Chicago fraternity members to compile their statements into a twenty-nine-page report he titled "Private Monograph on Movies and Sex" (published for the first time in this volume; see Chapter Six). While only mildly titillating by today's standards, this material, detailing the desires Greta Garbo, John Gilbert and Clara Bow provoked in the erotic fantasies of middle-class young men and women, was considered so inflammatory by Blumer that he presented it without analysis. Although 25 percent of the incarcerated young women interviewed by Hauser admitted that movies led them to commit "delinquent" sexual acts, and although Hauser's master's thesis documented the discipline problems erotic Hollywood films caused in men's and women's prisons, Blumer would not seriously consider pursuing this research area further. He sent "Movies and Sex" to Short only for his "confidential use."[46]

The Final Research Conference, May 1931

At the time of the final annual meeting, held in Columbus on 29–31 May 1931, it appeared that a majority of the current studies would be completed within nine months and the publishing program could be in full swing by late 1932. In addition, there was the possibility of doing a study of adolescent sex attitudes and the movies (Table 4). Each re-

Table 4. May 1931

Researcher(s)	Study: Working Title / *Completed Project*
Dale	*The Content of Motion Pictures*
Dale	*Children's Attendance at Motion Pictures*
Stoddard and Holaday	*Getting Ideas from the Movies*
May and Shuttleworth	The Social Conduct and Attitudes of Movie Fans (in trouble)
Thurstone and Peterson	*Motion Pictures and the Social Attitudes of Children*
Ruckmick and Dysinger	*The Emotional Responses of Children to the Motion Picture Situation*
Renshaw et al.	*Children's Sleep*
Blumer	*Movies and Conduct*
Blumer and Hauser	Movies, Delinquency and Crime
Thrasher	Boys' Club (in trouble)
Peters	Motion Pictures and Standards of Morality
Cressey	Sex Attitudes (not begun)

searcher at the conference presented a detailed summary of his or her evidence and conclusions. There continued to be doubts about the methods and assumptions used in the May–Shuttleworth study, but the two researchers maintained that, like prosperity, definitive results were just around the corner. Whitley and Nelson represented an absent Thrasher to report on the still-meager progress of the Boys' Club study. A very active new participant was Paul G. Cressey, who, as will be described later, had just been brought in by Short and Thrasher both to undertake the proposed sex attitudes study and to become the new research director of the motion picture project of the Boys' Club study.

On the final afternoon of the conference, the researchers held a wrap-up session in which they summarized what they thought the PFS had accomplished. All agreed that their research had located an influence of movies on attitudes, emotions and behavior, but disagreement arose over the extent and strength of those effects. Some believed that they had found conclusive evidence that movies were harmful and that the movie industry must be confronted and changed. Dale noted that "even though we can't pin specific harmful effects on motion pictures, we will be able to show that they do not have great positive moral and social values." Stoddard felt that movies had definite effects and were a "powerful force" in children's lives and so approved a social activist role for the researchers: "We are justified in making a critical analysis of everything in movies and of every possible outcome in conduct or attitude. The practical implication is that we should do everything we can to mold public opinion and set up educational forces in such a way as to improve the content of movies, aesthetically and artistically, in the directions indicated by our studies."[47]

Blumer admitted that, at heart, he simply did not know what to make of his findings, but still did not "trust" the movies:

What I am puzzled about is this. I have some difficulty in evaluating these in terms of their presumed contribution to social welfare and their presumed detriment to social welfare. As I look back on my own results, I don't know whether types of experiences that children have are something to be commended or to be regarded as harmful. I refer notably to the greater excitement resulting, the disturbance of children's sleep, strong emotions aroused, and the influence upon their play. As to the significance of this, in turn, with its social value, I feel somewhat incapable of deciding. My general feeling is not one of skepticism of findings here, but one of inability to come to any secure position in my own mind as to how much the findings which may be discovered should be interpreted as showing that the movies could be improved in this direction or should be improved in this direction.[48]

Others like Thurstone voiced doubts that they had been able to locate any concrete, measurable evidence whatsoever and cautioned against placing any blame at the movies' doorstep. "Maybe they aren't so terrible as they seem to be. I'm afraid of exaggeration in that direction," said Thurstone.[49]

Peters pleaded for a fair assessment of the movies: "We should rather be friendly defenders of movies than rigid critics on an emotionalistic basis." He noted:

When films are condemned in general, the criticism is likely to be ignored. If you can present particular things that can be remedied, then you can get somewhere. Now we have some of that sort of thing. We find in our study that, to a considerable extent, attractive characters are doing things that we wouldn't want imitated. It would be well to suggest to producers that they play up these unattractive things with unattractive characters.[50]

Peters's assistant, Robert Wray, summed up some of the general feelings: "Movies aren't as bad as I expected to find them. On the other hand, I do not know whether we know how to interpret our results. Movies have an influence on sleep and attitudes, but how great is that effect on the life of children or adults? Are effects of scenes below the line of approval [by community values] greater than those of the scenes which lie above this line? No one has shown this, although Thurstone has come nearest. We have shown how they stand, but not the influence."[51]

Janet Nelson urged that summaries of the Payne Fund research program not try to reduce disparate findings to too-sweeping generalizations about movies' effects. "There should be an emphasis on individual differences. I wish to sound a note of caution against too widespread a use of conclusions drawn on averages." Dysinger agreed that individual differences had also come out strongly in his emotional responses study. Ruckmick felt that the major changes that occurred during their investigations had been "first, toward factual emphasis on things that we suspected before; and second, toward a more constructive attitude than that which thought motion pictures were wholly bad, or bad for all classes." On the other hand, Charters warned that "it is easy to be so cautious that we destroy the positive effect by qualifications which we understand, and scholars would understand, but which would damn the whole thing for the layman."[52]

Cressey commented that, even though he was just being introduced to what the Payne Fund researchers had been doing, he was struck by the contrast in the results of controlled lab experiments and those of field studies. "Why does a laboratory situation reveal something so subjective, and on the other hand statistical and case methods do not reveal anything so constructive?" He suggested the remedy might be a large study integrating numerous research methods (a comment made perhaps to reinforce the critical need to continue the floundering Boys' Club study, but it was a sound research plan).[53]

Holaday commented: "I believe that there is now much more of a coordinated research than there was one or two years ago. The different groups are working toward a more common central objective – outlying fringes are coming more and more in contact," and long-term beneficial and detrimental effects of movies seemed to be emerging from the studies. As they prepared to depart and to begin the final year of research, Charters agreed that coming together to think about the program as a whole had been valuable: "These general statements will be useful to everybody and are the kind of thing you don't get from [the separate] findings. . . . The opinion of the total set-up is often different from the opinion of parts of the study."[54]

Paul Cressey, the Sex Attitudes and Boys' Club Studies

Short sought a new academic researcher in the spring of 1930 to pursue a sex attitudes study that interested him immensely but that other members of the group had been hesitant to undertake. Thrasher suggested his friend Paul G. Cressey, another former University of Chicago graduate student, whose master's thesis, published as *The Taxi-Dance Hall* (1932), was a brilliant study of the seamy subject of women hired as dance partners and prostitutes in the dingy tenement-district dance halls of Chicago.

In 1929, Short reported reading sociologist Edward Alsworth Ross's recent book, *World Drift* (1928), and locating passages mentioning the declining age of puberty for urban girls. Short had written excitedly to Charters that, although Ross did not come right out and affix a cause to this "problem," there might be a connection with too much viewing of passionate movie sex scenes by young girls:

It would be a most striking thing if your studies should show that this is literally true – that there has actually been a moving forward of the age of puberty during the period that the children have been viewing the motion pictures. I suppose that a physical change of this kind, if shown, would be one of the most striking things that our studies could bring out.[55]

Short began promoting to the Payne Fund researchers the idea of a study relating movie viewing to young people's sexual behavior. He encountered great interest among them, but even greater fear for their academic positions in the face of the damaging publicity such studies might provoke. "Dr. May is rather chary about dealing with this question of sexual influence," Short wrote to Charters after a trip to New Haven:

He points out the disastrous results to an inquiry, and incidentally to the professor connected with it, at the University of Missouri, because some rather innocent sex questions were included. . . . However the matter is so important that it seems to me, as I think it over, that we must somehow get at it in a fundamental way.[56]

Charters responded to Short noncommittally, "I am backing up your suggestion about attitudes toward sex conduct. I agree with you that it is important and I agree with Mr. May that it is difficult to secure information on the subject. I hope that the two points of view can be brought together."[57]

Paul Cressey's research experience in studying dance-hall prostitutes appeared to make him the perfect candidate for Short's proposed addition to the Payne Fund researchers in 1930. There was a scandal surrounding Cressey, however, that gave Short and Charters caution about bringing him on board. Accusations had been made that the unmarried Cressey had acted with impropriety in order to collect autobiographical data from the taxi dancers: he had instructed his student assistants to pay to dance with the girls, walk them home, buy them sandwiches and coffee to loosen their defenses and extract more of their stories. Jessie Binford of the Juvenile Protection Association charged sexual misconduct, and Cressey had left Chicago under a cloud. (This did not preclude his book from being published by the University of Chicago Press, however.) Short was quite supportive of Cressey and downplayed the rumors, but Charters and Ella Crandall were not convinced. Short wrote Charters several times attempting to ease his doubts with character recommendations from Blumer, Thrasher and Ernest Burgess. Charters still fumed, "I personally am considerably in doubt about the advisability of using Cressy [sic]. We ought to be able to find a reputable scientist capable of doing good work who does not have something wrong with him sexually, in connection with a sex study." But he finally relented and approved Cressey's appointment. Nevertheless, relations between Cressey, Ella Crandall and Charters, always cool, would become icier as the Boys' Club study saga continued.[58]

Paul Cressey became the white knight of the PFS in the spring, summer and fall of 1931. Short was very impressed with Cressey's abilities, plans and ideas for fine-tuning or rescuing many of the other studies. (How other researchers felt about Cressey's advice is not known.) While Short considered Cressey for both the possible sex attitudes study (which did not materialize) and the standards study, Cressey relocated to New York, ostensibly to provide much-needed research direction for Thrasher's Boys' Club project.[59]

Soon after Cressey arrived at New York University in the fall of 1931, he found he was dissatisfied with all the material collected by Crays. Cressey felt that the entire Boys' Club study would have to be reconceptualized to capture fully what he believed were the definite links between moviegoing and delinquency:

The delinquent boys recognize that the crooks in the movies get punished in the end but most of them insisted that this was not true in real life. They say they know of criminals of their own acquaintance in their neighborhoods who had not been punished. Again the movie was discredited in favor of what they have learned from real life, namely, that many crooks are not caught and punished. Hence, the supposed preachment of motion pictures that crooks pay in the end – a point so much emphasized by apologists for the movies – does not have weight in areas of a city where even the boys know that crooks often get away without being punished. Instead the movies often seem to serve as a stimulus toward planning "more perfect" crime.[60]

Short was much impressed by Cressey's statement; he wrote Charters that it was "perhaps the most illuminating of anything I have yet had regarding the material they have in hand and the work they are doing to supplement and strengthen the study."[61]

Cressey industriously launched into a new research agenda in the winter and spring of 1932, interviewing boys, compiling case studies and obtaining life histories in a new synthesis of the methodology of the other Payne Fund studies. Thrasher warned Charters, "I think perhaps Mr. Cressey has come to conceive of the motion picture end of our project in somewhat more ambitious terms." With misgivings, Charters heard out Cressey and Thrasher's requests and allotted them more money in June 1932, but stipulated: "Mr. Cressey should guarantee, without any qualifications other than sudden death, that he will have the material finished by July 1st, 1933. Mr. Cressey should not undertake the project if he feels he cannot make the promise. Since most of the material is collected, this is not an unreasonable request to make."[62]

Cressey had an intellectual epiphany in the fall of 1932. This breakthrough opened new vistas of analysis for him and was beneficial for the development of media sociology, but it was disastrous for his relationship with Charters. A year into his research and almost at the completion stage, Cressey realized that his study would "very nearly be as negative as the Shuttleworth–May study." He formulated a new thesis – that movies should not be linked to boys' delinquency, but must instead be viewed as a powerful source of "informal education" that served boys in a far more direct and practical way than did schools or the Boys' Clubs. This 180-degree turnabout would mean further delays in the project's completion as, Cressey noted with chagrin, "much of the old material from which it was originally expected that we would write the book is not going to be used." Cressey explained to Charters, "I have been forced by the weight of evidence to see the motion picture not primarily in this relationship [to delinquency and misconduct], but in its varied functions in the lives of different groups and individuals within this community." Charters responded unsympathetically, "I note your change of base [work address] and also your alibi." Charters nonetheless noted that if the newly reconfigured manuscript was as good as *The Gang* and *Taxi-Dance Hall*, "I shall be entirely satisfied."[63]

"Instead of being considered a unilateral force whose influence can be described as 'contribution' or 'effect,' " Cressey now argued, "the motion picture is seen as one whose influence is everywhere modified by differentials in community and personality." Building on the earlier work of Robert Whitley, Cressey claimed that the inviting darkness of the movie theater was a more important influence on youth than the films on the screen. In this ghetto, where traditional authorities had long been superseded, movie theaters were social centers, places for tough gangs to gather, for prostitutes to make assignations and for young teens to test sexual and cultural boundaries.[64]

In the middle of this ambitious new work, an avalanche of disasters fell upon Cressey that seem almost Wagnerian in their force – the Depression's economic crisis in the fall of 1932, Cressey's scramble for adjunct teaching posts and gasping from heavy workloads, Cressey's wife's grave medical situation resulting from a botched tonsillectomy, Thrasher's nervous collapse in the fall of 1932, Robert Whitley's suicide in January 1933 (supposedly brought on by overwork) and Cressey's own appendicitis and lengthy illness in the summer and fall of 1933. An incredible confluence of ill health and bad luck caused Cressey and Thrasher's project to fall apart just as the rest of the Payne Fund studies were being readied for publication. Short and Charters received a stream of pathetic letters from Thrasher and Cressey full of reasons why they needed extensions of time and money to complete the research and the manuscript.

Despite his problems, in December 1932 Cressey sent Henry Forman, author of the popular summary volume of the PFS, a 168-page "Preliminary Report"; this is probably the document published in the present volume (see Chapter Four). It was hurriedly put together from dictation and notes, with hand-changed text and page number corrections. It demonstrates that Cressey had totally reconstructed the project from the material he inherited, it contains impressive amounts of detail and sections of compelling narrative and it is extremely ambitious in scope and intent. Completing it would have required the collection and analysis of a substantial amount of additional data. Nevertheless, it is a fascinating document.

The litany of Cressey's disasters, woes and excuses continued through 1933, into 1934 and beyond. In August 1934, Cressey sent an eighteen-page outline for the long-delayed book manuscript to Charters (see Chapter Five). Despite its brevity and incompleteness, it is an interesting attempt to sketch a sophisticated and innovative thesis that would have made an important contribution to media effects research. In 1934 Cressey contemplated hiring a ghost writer to help him complete the long-overdue manuscript, and resentful Boys' Club project staff members attempted to make a scandal of it by contacting Charters and blackmailing Cressey for continued employment and money. Charters heard little more from Cressey until 1936, when Cressey enlisted his aid in applying for a Guggenheim fellowship to complete the manuscript. An annoyed Charters wrote to Crandall, "I had hoped that the Thrasher–Cressey book was a thing of the past, but since Cressey is working hard on it, I feel that he has some equity in the publication even though he is exasperatingly slow." Neither the funding nor the completed, published study ever materialized for Cressey. Records indicate that Cressey received a Ph.D. from New York University for the dissertation "The Social Role of the Motion Picture in an Interstitial Area," but to this date no copy of that manuscript has been located.[65]

Thrasher's Boys' Club study lumbered along, recovering from the disarray caused by the loss of chief investigator Robert Whitley in early 1933. In 1935, Thrasher submitted a 1,200-page final report of the study to the Bureau of Social Hygiene. Like Cressey's study, this report would also fail to reach publication. This may have been due in part to the Depression and the closure of the Bureau of Social Hygiene, but it might also have been due to the Rockefeller Foundation's reaction to Thrasher's conclusion that the Boys' Club had almost no discernible impact on the safeguarding or reform of troubled urban youth.

Conclusion: The Payne Fund Studies in 1932–1933

The roster of studies in the spring of 1932, when the researchers were due to have their manuscripts completed for publication, looked much like the list familiar to scholars today (Table 5).

In 1932, as Short prodded all the researchers toward the completion of their projects with an increasing impatience born of his desire to begin the public aspects of his reform campaign against the film industry, the academics squabbled among themselves over the quality, length and

Table 5. April 1932

Researcher(s)	Published Title
Dale	*The Content of Motion Pictures*
Dale	*Children's Attendance at Motion Pictures*
Stoddard and Holaday	*Getting Ideas from the Movies*
May and Shuttleworth	The Social Conduct and Attitudes of Movie Fans (publication in doubt)
Thurstone and Peterson	*Motion Pictures and the Social Attitudes of Children*
Ruckmick and Dysinger	*The Emotional Responses of Children to the Motion Picture Situation*
Renshaw et al.	*Children's Sleep*
Blumer	*Movies and Conduct*
Blumer and Hauser	*Movies, Delinquency and Crime*
Peters	*Motion Pictures and Standards of Morality*
Cressey and Thrasher	Boys, Movies and City Streets (incomplete)

In Progress	
Charters	Motion Pictures and Youth: A Summary
Forman	Our Movie-Made Children
Dale	How to Appreciate Motion Pictures

final published form of the PFS. The fragile sense of unity that had held the social scientists together as a group during the planning and fashioning of their research agendas began to unravel. Their growing antipathies blended personal animosity, departmental and disciplinary rivalries and ideological disagreements over how the Payne Fund research should be interpreted and how the conclusions should be implemented.

Psychologists Stoddard and Thurstone were the most vociferous critics who complained to Charters, claiming to be appalled by the poor writing and muddy logic of the studies closest to their own knowledge. An exacting adviser, Stoddard wrote of his own student's write-up of the experiments on how much children understand at the movies: Holaday's report was "the rottenest mss that ever disguised a study of this scope." Thurstone urged Charters not to allow the inconclusive Shuttleworth write-up of the attitudes study to be published, and Charters was inclined to agree. May hurriedly defended his project to Charters, promising to salvage something creditable from Shuttleworth's manuscript. Stoddard and Thurstone were also harshly critical of Blumer's negative, anecdotal approach and lack of valid evidence to back up his indictment of movies' influence. The two psychologists' antipathy toward Blumer seemed partially personal and partially due to disagreements over quantitative versus personal statement-oriented approaches. These internecine battles would continue to plague the social sciences, particularly at the University of Chicago.

Thurstone, May and Peters exchanged sharp memos with Short over his manipulation and misconstrual of their evidence to strengthen his case against the movies in publications and press releases prepared by the MPRC. Even Short's closest ally among the researchers, the ambitious Blumer, griped in July 1933 about the continuing delay in the publication of the series. Blumer and Thurstone separately threatened to pull their volumes from the tardy series and publish them independently. By this point, Short was too anxious to be very sympathetic, replying to Blumer: "These long delays have been vastly more disconcerting to me than they can possibly be to you or any of the other professors. My whole program has been postponed for something like a year and a half beyond the time expected."[66]

While Short was rapidly losing the vocal support of most of the academics involved in the PFS (Frances Bolton and Payne Fund executives Clymer and Crandall had broken with him in 1929), ultimately no PFS participant, no matter how disgruntled, defected before the volumes appeared. Given the perennial concerns of academics to publish or perish and the harsh constraints on research funding imposed by the Depression, the Payne Fund researchers had little desire to be left out of the publication program. Short had already shelved Freeman's study for its failure to show direct links between children's intake of film messages and changed behavior, rather than admit its findings about children's resistance to suggestion, so the researchers assumed that his threat to not publish inconclusive results was real. Several may have toned down their disagreements with Short or shaded the interpretation of their conclusions in order to gain the results they desired. After the MPRC's publicity campaign against the movie industry began, however, several researchers, like Stoddard, Thurstone and May, were vocal in their disapproval of Short and his methods. Some, like Charters and Dale, remained polite but cool and distant. (The administrative skills of Charters and Dale and their interest in issues of radio and children's education would earn them a long and fruitful association with the Payne Fund in the 1930s, 1940s and 1950s. See the Payne Fund's role in the radio regulation wars in Appendix A.) Surprisingly, even after his change of research orientation and failure to publish his study, Cressey remained on good terms with Short and would express sadness at his death in 1935.

But what had almost five years of research produced for Short and the Payne Fund researchers? The research proposals had been ambitious, and the group had originally hoped it would be able to state conclusively and authoritatively what children learned from the movies, and how and to what extent the movies influenced their health, attitudes and behavior.

The social science the PFS developed was valid when considered not in terms of Short's goals but in relation to the cautious conclusions the majority of studies reached. The PFS demonstrated that movies had a definite impact on children's emotions, attitudes and knowledge base. But everywhere that influence was modified by the viewer's age, gender, social background and a host of other factors. Hollywood films presented moral situations that often differed from community standards, but just as often as the movies "shocked" filmgoers they offered glimpses of a more egalitarian society.

The evidence was much less clear as to what extent movies by themselves affected children's sleeping patterns, popularity among classmates, academic performance at school or general conduct. The Payne Fund researchers couldn't prove that films could make a child learn new behaviors like brushing teeth or turn a child into a criminal; they couldn't prove that all Hollywood movies had blatant sexual themes (but neither did they go looking for subtle innuendo). These studies would have appeared more valid had they been presented as demonstrating young viewers' resistance to film messages. Instead, one project was abandoned and the conclusions of several others were manipulated to highlight their negative implications. While the May–Shuttleworth study particularly demonstrated the futility of trying to separate movies' effects from other influences (Blumer's, Thurstone's and most of the other studies had also operated under the assumption that this was possible), the Cressey–Thrasher Boys' Club study, after Cressey's "epiphany," took that as its main point – inevitably the influence of movies could not be considered outside the context of other popular culture and mass media stimuli or other factors in youngsters' social environments. That in and of itself was a big step forward in communication, but it would come too late to do the rest of the Payne Fund studies any good. The story of their reception and subsequent fate is told in the next chapter.

CHAPTER THREE

Aftermath

THE SUMMARIES AND RECEPTION OF THE
PAYNE FUND STUDIES

The reception accorded the Payne Fund Studies (PFS) on Motion Pictures and Youth will be discussed in this chapter with respect both to general public opinion and to the academic world. The primary goal of the PFS was, by influencing public opinion, to clinch the long-running effort to subordinate the movies to the traditional mechanisms of social control; an unintended consequence was the studies' impact on the development of the social sciences, especially media studies.

Introduction and Chronology

In Chapters One and Two we reconstructed the nearly five years of unpublicized work that went into the PFS. In 1932 the project was nearing completion, and arrangements for publicity, publication and promotion moved to the top of the agenda. Seven volumes were published in 1933, an eighth in 1935. The announced ninth volume, *Boys, Movies and City Streets,* failed to appear. The 1933 volumes came out at a time when the movie industry was still in the process of making itself over from its origins as an upstart and disreputable offshoot of show business into an established industry with branches that were integral to every American community. Emblematic of the culmination of this process was the acceptance of the local theater operator as a member of such business and community groups as the Chamber of Commerce, Rotary, Elks and Shriners.

Though not complete in 1933, this transformation of the movie industry's social status was well advanced. The movie business had been around for more than twenty-five years and had recently invested considerable capital in the conversion to sound. Movies were a staple of large sections of the population. But there remained one matter on which their integration was incomplete. Established elements of society were convinced that too many movies had an unwholesome influence, undermining the social control exercised by home, school and church. As Schumach, Randall and countless others have related, the industry tried to placate its opponents by organizing a form of self-censorship through its trade organization, the Motion Picture Producers and Distributors of America (MPPDA).[1] In 1930 a more stringent Production Code was drawn up which from 1934 on was enforced by a dedicated Production Code Administration assigned the task of evaluating ideas, stories and scripts, as well as finished films, in an effort to ensure that they offended no powerful pressure groups. By these means industry self-censorship was tightened to the point where some complained that Hollywood movies dealing with adult themes had been infantilized.[2] (Others took the view that filmmakers developed very subtle ways of coding adult content, sufficient to deceive both reformers and children.) Nothing showing at the local theater should have embarrassed its operator when he dined with fellow businesspeople.

The negative action of self-censorship was complemented on the positive side by a major studio effort to make more prestige and family-oriented films.[3] The performances of notably risqué actors such as Mae West and the Marx Brothers, and *louche* stories involving showgirls and gangsters, were "cleaned up," and more movies were made from literary and dramatic classics. The pressure on the motion picture companies was evident when the Roman Catholic church's Legion of Decency gathered more than 3 million pledges in 1934 and eventually put out regular publications rating movies on a scale from "harmless" to "condemned" (watching a "condemned" film was sinful).[4] The general hope seems to have been that, if the spirit of Anthony Comstock rather than that of Mae West presided over moviemaking, the business would be socially respectable and hence commercially more secure.

Looking back, one of the internal histories of the Payne Fund was inclined to give some credit for both the "cleanup" and the production of more wholesome pictures to the PFS volumes:

The publication of the Payne Fund Studies of the influence of motion pictures on children and youth has had effects which were perhaps no less amazing to the Fund than to the motion picture industry. While it was expected that the findings would result in action by many organizations

interested in the social effects of motion pictures, no such movement as that
which swept the country had been foreseen. As stated by the *New York
Times*,[5] criticism of motion pictures, once carried on by isolated groups,
became a national barrage from church, civic, and educational organizations. The Motion Picture Research Council initiated the organized campaign, but within a few months was overshadowed by the Legion of Decency, which enlisted millions of persons in a nation-wide movement
threatening a general boycott of films.[6]

To what extent this appropriation of credit is warranted, given that the
result is admitted to have exceeded expectations, will be assessed later in
this chapter, in the section titled "Eclipse of the MPRC."

Viewed historically, the eight PFS volumes are an impressive social
science achievement. Several of the authors went on to long and honor-
able careers in academe. Yet their work for the Payne Fund was not
immediately followed up by other academics, it was little cited by their
peers and none of the authors continued in the same line of research.
Whether this is best explained by shortcomings of the research itself, by
the use to which their results were put, by the scathing attack on their
scientific pretensions by Mortimer Adler[7] or by other factors will also be
examined in this chapter. More generally, we will ask whether the PFS
in any way prefigured or influenced the study of the mass media that
began in the late 1930s and that has continued to the present day.

With these two topics in mind – movies as an agency of social control
and the PFS as pioneering works of social science – it may be helpful to
set out a chronology of the events to be covered from 1932 to 1938.

Press releases and articles from the autumn of 1932 proclaimed that
the PFS had found important evidence for deleterious effects of the
movies on children. Notable were Henry James Forman's three articles
in *McCall's*.[8] Before the publication of the first seven volumes between
July and November 1933, the same publishing house, Macmillan, had,
in May, published in a different format a "popularization" of the studies
by Forman, entitled *Our Movie Made Children*. This trade book was
widely promoted and reviewed, with its author doing what we would
nowadays call a book tour. It was reviewed by newspapers and magazines all across the country, and both its author and the Rev. William H.
Short contributed articles and gave speeches about it for much of the
year.[9] Besides orchestrating the articles and book by Forman, Short had
fed material to Arthur Kellogg and James Rorty and tried to convince

the indefatigable antimovie campaigner Fred Eastman to editorialize about the PFS in the *Christian Century*.[10]

Our Movie Made Children was clearly an attempt to coordinate the results of the scientific work with a view to influencing public opinion. "Public opinion" refers here not to the views of the man on the street, but to the views of the leaders and groups of civil society: politicians, professional people, journalists, people of influence, the clergy and members of religious organizations, civic and fraternal organizations, voluntary agencies and pressure groups. It was from these people that progressivism and reform drew much of their strength. To maintain the conceptualization of the movies as a social problem, it was vital for Short, Forman and the Motion Picture Research Council (MPRC) to mobilize these forces.

The PFS volumes were led off by *Motion Pictures and Youth*, a monograph by the research director, W. W. Charters, which constituted a more objective summary of the scientific work than *Our Movie Made Children*. Charters's summary was originally bound in hardback with *Getting Ideas from the Movies* by Holaday and Stoddard, but in 1935 it was issued separately as a paperback. Macmillan published all the PFS volumes in uniform format, noticeably different in shape and color from *Our Movie Made Children*. The PFS set was reviewed in the periodical press[11] and in social science journals through 1935. Sales were slow but steady.[12]

There was by 1934 what the *Hollywood Reporter* described as a "campaign in favor of censorship which is growing rapidly in all parts of the country."[13] The coincident imposition of movie industry self-censorship, the rise of the Legion of Decency and the industry's promotion of wholesome movies has already been mentioned. This muted the agitation somewhat, but the attacks continued and the industry felt bound to take every opportunity to counterattack. In 1937 the Chicago philosopher Mortimer J. Adler published a closely reasoned attack on the entire set of presuppositions entertained by the sponsors of the PFS and, inter alia, the research itself, maintaining that it was too unreliable to support any conclusions and, if intended as moral instruction, was misconceived. Adler was not deterred by the cautious way in which almost all of the social scientists had phrased their conclusions.[14]

Forman's book was still selling, so the MPPDA found a way to amplify Adler's stodgy tome into a counterblast. Raymond Moley, pro-

Advertisement for *Our Movie Made Children*.

Advertisement for *Motion Pictures and Youth*.

fessor of public law at Columbia University, former member of the
Roosevelt administration, commended for his views by Adler,[15] was
commissioned to write a popular summary of the relevant parts of
Adler's book. Moley took direct aim at Forman's *Our Movie Made
Children,* calling his book *Are We Movie Made?* (1938).

Hopes and Expectations for the Payne Fund Studies

Unlike the first fruit of the National Council on the Study of Social
Values in Motion Pictures, *A Generation of Motion Pictures,*[16] which
was a collection of polemical and anecdotal condemnations of the movies culled from printed sources, the PFS were to be scientific. Their
creators included many fine young social scientists working at established universities – Chicago, New York University, Ohio State, Pennsylvania State and Yale. Short had wanted the scientists to assemble facts
about motion pictures and youth: frequency of attendance, taste preference, absorption and effects. These scientific results would be reliable,
unbiased and politically unimpeachable. The National Council, transformed into the MPRC, was, however, overtly a pressure group with an
outlook far from the detachment of science. It consisted of people who
felt the state of the movies could be likened, as Short put it, to a situation
in which the printing press was controlled by a handful of companies
who used it solely for commercial purposes.[17] The Payne Fund, while
sympathetic to this outlook, wished to be seen only as sponsoring work
that contributed to research or education and was nervous about being
drawn into politically colored or controversial action that would embarrass Mrs. Bolton's congressman husband. Thus, to keep the MPRC at
arm's length, the Payne Research and Experiment Fund had been created
and directed by Charters. While Payne money was subsidizing both the
research and the MPRC, they were legally separate.

With the research nearing completion, the MPRC had to begin to
decide what it would do with the results. First, obviously, they had to be
published. Once they were published, what was the MPRC to do about
the situation they disclosed? The original idea was to develop a "national film policy" (see the next section). In what would such a policy
consist and how would it be implemented? At different times slightly
different goals were suggested. In an address to the Society of Motion

Picture Engineers on 24 April 1933, Short outlined the following as "unoccupied fields" that might be entered:

1. The making of dramatic educational films
2. The encouragement and perhaps sponsorship of the development of children's motion pictures, specifically created and targeted like children's books
3. The promotion of better pictures for adult entertainment
4. Adult educational, documentary and scientific films[18]

The MPRC pamphlet "A New Day for the Movies and for Children," which was sent out in March 1934, stressed education through the movies and about movies, opposition to block booking and rejection of censorship as a means of accomplishing its goals.[19]

The president of the MPRC, Mrs. August Belmont, addressed a national luncheon conference in late March 1934 to launch the new phase of activity.[20] She stated that the Council's objectives were to eliminate objectionable movies, to further the development of films for children and to encourage the production of educational films for use in public and private schools and institutions.[21] Finally, Short, in the October 1934 issue of *Education*, listed five goals:

1. Movies as a free art, with no censorship or monopoly
2. Organized communities to monitor and sponsor the work
3. The fostering of motion picture appreciation
4. The separation of child and adult audiences
5. The creation of a National film institute[22]

In the summer of 1934 Belmont abruptly resigned as president, leaving the organization without a nominal leader. *Variety* speculated that the resignation was precipitated by disagreements with Short.[23] The major source of disagreement among MPRC members over the organization's goals was the possibility that eliminating objectionable movies might require censorship, something the pamphlet and Short seem to have been firmly against. The resignation may also have been sparked by conflict over what to do about the rise of the Legion of Decency.[24] As the search for a new president went ahead during the autumn, the Legion was collecting an impressive number of pledges. Then, during a stopover in Philadelphia en route from Washington to New York in

January 1935, Short died, at the age of sixty-six. It took almost six months for the Council to find a president in Ray Lyman Wilbur, president of Stanford University, and to transfer its offices and activities to the San Francisco Bay Area. This was in effect the end of its activities on the national scene (see Chapter One).

What, then, was the upshot of these eight years of research and agitation? One could summarize the various aims stated by Short and Belmont as follows. Although the MPRC never promoted censorship, it was tarred with that brush by its opponents, and meanwhile both the movie industry and the Catholic church were pursuing censorship – the former through the MPPDA Production Code, the latter through its new League of Decency, with its classification of movies by degree of objectionableness (backed up by pledges from people to eschew "indecent" pictures). Neither the MPRC nor any of the groups it worked with made movies for children, but the idea of creating a separate series of films as well as special shows for children, originally floated to the Payne Fund by George H. Skinner, was taken up by the industry itself and became a permanent fixture. An American film institute did not come into being until 1967. Block booking and the oligopolistic structure of the industry were inhibited by the antitrust suit of 1938–1948[25] and faded finally with the restructuring caused by the rise of television. Whether better pictures in the reformers' sense resulted from these efforts is hard to say. The antimovie forces were concerned exclusively with moral criteria for "betterness." They were relatively blind to aesthetics. Many of the movies found so objectionable by the MPRC – such as the early sound gangster films, the "naughty" musicals by Busby Berkeley and others, the films of the Marx Brothers and Mae West with their raunchy humor – are thought well of today by film teachers, whereas the prestige pictures, the biographies of worthy men and women, the films of classic books and plays, are looked upon as what Manny Farber called "white elephant art."[26]

If we put on our historical spectacles and adopt the mind-set of the MPRC leaders, we may concede that Hollywood did indeed succeed in its efforts to upgrade its output – at least some of the time. Community pressure was organized mostly by the Roman Catholic church through the creation of diocesan branches of the Legion of Decency, but this was one area of endeavor where Protestant and unaffiliated bodies cooperated with their traditional rivals.[27] Of the list of aims, one briefly mentioned by Short was, especially after his death, to become the main area

of endeavor of the Payne Fund regarding the movies. That was the
teaching of movie appreciation.

This grew out of an anomaly among the seven 1933 volumes – *How
to Appreciate Motion Pictures* by Edgar Dale. It was the best-seller in
the PFS series and provided the blueprint for many years of subsequent
work. Despite Short's death and the MPRC's move to San Francisco,
Dale and Charters persuaded the Payne Fund to help finance an outreach
program from Ohio State University that would assist state and local
educational authorities to develop courses in motion picture education
and appreciation.[28] Ohio State provided materials, including Dale's
books, and instructors who would go to localities and give workshops.
The Payne Fund, through the continuing involvement of Dale and Charters, was thus responsible for the U.S. branch of a worldwide movement
in the 1930s that sought to provide schoolchildren with enough understanding to discount the glamour and "false" attractiveness of the movies with sufficient appreciation of high-quality movies to create a demand for such products that would ripple outward. The history of that
film-appreciation movement has yet to be written.[29]

Dissension in the Academy

Besides the tension between the origin of the PFS in advocacy and the
Payne Fund's desire to be seen as a promoter of supposedly value-neutral
science, there was suspicion among some of the social scientists about
what would happen to their research once it was complete. Mark A.
May, L. L. Thurstone, Frederic Thrasher and possibly other researchers
(such as Samuel Renshaw and George Stoddard)[30] became apprehensive
that Short and the MPRC intended to launch an antimovie campaign
citing the scientific studies in support of their cause. May was not hostile
to the movie industry. He had collaborated on some earlier research
financed by the MPPDA[31] and began soliciting its interest again when
his Payne Fund money ran out. This provoked an exchange of letters
with Short.[32] May also gave a talk, and his collaborator, Frank Shuttleworth, published an article that did not cleave to any antimovie party
line.[33] At one point there was a plan afoot not to publish the May–
Shuttleworth study as part of the PFS series.[34] In the end Short made
what might seem a political decision not to provoke May by such
exclusion.

The tension in the group was exacerbated by a decision, made very early on in the planning of the research, to publish not just the scientific results but also a popular summary that would make them accessible to the public. Social science research of the caliber being undertaken was unlikely to reach public opinion leaders, because it would be couched in the increasingly technical and professional language of the social scientist. Thus Short, as the liaison between the MPRC and the Payne Research and Experiment Fund, became convinced that a professional writer should be brought in to present the professionals' results in a more concise and readable form. The antirhetorical language of the social sciences needed translation into terms found in the reformers' rhetorical repertoire. All along Short had intended that the research would eventually serve the MPRC goals, which had been vaguely formulated as follows: "To develop factual data regarding motion pictures on the basis of which a national film policy, socially constructive in character, may be formulated; and to make whatever studies and surveys may be required to that end."[35] Although Short was convinced, on the basis of W. M. Seabury's work and *A Generation of Motion Pictures* (see Chapter One), that there was a social problem which needed addressing, he was willing to concede that the reformers were not in possession of all the relevant facts: "It is premature to try to decide now what our program of action will be, as it must necessarily be formed on the basis of the facts we assemble or of the conditions that exist when we come to the program-forming stage."[36] Publicity for the scientific results would have to be a forerunner to everything.[37]

As the preliminary results came in and annual meetings of the researchers succeeded one another, this aim of publicizing the results crystallized around a definite idea: to commission a well-known journalist to digest the scientific research and present it in a form palatable to the public. Several articles, and then a book, were envisaged. At first Short wrote of a "vitally written" volume for the general public and of a brief popular presentation, which he proposed to do himself in collaboration with Herbert Blumer.[38] Then he consulted Otis L. Weise, editor of *McCall's,* and drew a list of names headed by Dorothy Canfield Fisher, a respected journalist of the time. After Fisher declined to undertake the task,[39] they eventually selected Henry James Forman, twentieth on the list, author of travel books and novels of uplift.[40] Like Short himself, he was paid well. He was provided with typescripts or galley proofs of all the scientific monographs (including the material that was intended to be published as *Boys, Movies and City Streets*). In about nine months Forman produced the manuscript of what became *Our Movie Made Children* as well as three articles for *McCall's*.[41] Short and Charters read the whole book in typescript, and each scientist was sent a copy of the chapter dealing with his or her results.[42] The researchers were critical to various degrees, some not just of factual or reporting slips, but of the entire tone of the manuscript, which they read as an antimovie diatribe. This view was forcefully expressed by Charters, who found himself unable to endorse the book warmly:

> I have come to the conclusion that the manuscript has a very serious weakness that is due to the anti-movie tone which has led to the pushing of arguments against the movies without restraint, and to the minimizing of points in their favor. You give the impression to readers . . . that you have a prejudice against moving pictures, and are using every possible argument both of fact and ridicule against them.
>
> Being so extremely anti-movie, I do not feel that the manuscript interprets the position of the investigators. I feel in fact that even from the anti-movie point of view the case could be strengthened if a better balance had been observed between the good and the bad in the movies — the reader would feel that you were glad to allow for the good rather than to minimize it. Greater restraint would produce a stronger document.[43]

Pressure was brought to bear on Forman to tone down his advocacy, but whereas most researchers reported that the corrections they had demanded were made satisfactorily, Charters was never satisfied with Forman's efforts. As a result, the preface he eventually contributed was studied in its detachment and, he wrote, "as far as I can go."[44]

Short, too, felt that the tone should be lightened, although, obviously, he was sympathetic to much of Forman's outlook.[45] Forman was summoned to Columbus in February to go over the typescript sentence by sentence with Charters. Despite this exercise, the book remained resolutely "anti-movie," although Forman claimed it was merely "anti-bad-movie."[46] Charters's frustration was palpable. Whereas on 14 February he could "look back upon our four day intercourse . . . [as] an interesting and pleasant memory,"[47] just over a month later in a handwritten note he remarked: "I have received all the Forman MS. I am not satisfied with it. Why does he still continue to weaken his case with thoughtful people by pounding, pounding — with superlatives piled on superla-

tives?"[48] Even slightly watered-down, the book remained an embarrassment to Charters. To tie the studies together, Charters wrote a
summary of his own, "Motion Pictures and Youth: A Summary" and
placed it at the beginning of the first PFS volume published.

There can be little doubt that there was divided opinion among the
researchers about the movies, differences that sharpened over the course
of the research. Stoddard, for example, was critical of Blumer's methods
and inferences, and both May and Thurstone became openly suspicious
of Short.[49] In this atmosphere, amid all the concern about the way the
research would be presented, Mark May, in what seems to have been a
preemptive strike, wrote a letter to the editor of the *Christian Science
Monitor* (3 January 1933), criticizing an op. ed. piece that had been
based on a report in the *New York Times* about the PFS.[50] He clearly
articulated the caution of the social scientists and his own lack of antimovie bias:

I regret very much that the *Times* quotes only the aspect of our study which
appears unfavorable to the movies. The entire study . . . reveals conditions
which were about one-third unfavorable to the movies, about one-third
favorable, and about one-third neutral. Our conclusion was that it is impossible to say from our data whether or not the movies are a causal factor in
moral conditions, or whether or not they are a concomitant factor. It is
certainly true that bad boys attend the movies, but whether they are bad
because they attend the movies or whether they attend the movies because
they are bad, or whether movie attendance and badness are in any way
related is a question we have not pretended to answer. It is equally obvious
that good boys attend the movies, and one has exactly the same argument
whether goodness is the result or the cause of movie attendance, or whether
it is entirely dissociated from it.

It is also true that certain investigators have traced to the movies certain
bad effects and others have pointed out instances where movies have had
good effects. The problem is to assess the net effect of movie attendance
upon the life of any given individual or upon the public morals of the
community. This has not been done to my knowledge.

While I have no brief either for the movies or against them, I do feel
strongly that during the last ten years there has been great improvement in
the types of pictures that are being shown. . . . As they say in the advertisements, when better films are demanded the producers will make them.
Substantial reform must come from within the industry itself.[51]

Short was not pleased and wrote with indignation to Charters:

May's attitude evidently is making trouble, and quite clearly, is intended to do so. . . . I am at present inclined to feel . . . that he has made it essential for you and both the Forman and scientific volumes to express the judgment that study [May's] did not obtain the facts in the field which it was exploring. . . . If May has gone to work to discredit the entire series of the Payne Fund studies, he must not be allowed to succeed. . . . I have been told that May is a vain and opinionated person but have refused to believe it. . . . I am considerably incensed at the ex cathedra utterances of his closing paragraphs. . . . We all know that May's study has given him no chance to reach any scientific conclusions on either of these questions. He ceases to be a scientist and ruthlessly and recklessly invades the field of Dr. Dale's study . . . he appears to be attempting to combat the Motion Picture Research Council. . . . I call you to witness at this point that I have never for an instant opposed or called in question any effort of one of the research men along scientific lines or any findings one of them brought forward.[52]

Scientists, in Short's view, did not allow themselves any opinions. That scientists are also entitled to wear the hat of a public person seems to have escaped him. This cannot have helped his relations with the researchers.

May was not quite out in left field, however. Charters wrote back to Short to claim the last word on facts and interpretations, and as to the Forman book, "The convincingness of the book and its quality of style will be greatly increased by a more balanced statement of the findings of the investigators."[53] Short responded:

My ideal for this book is that without any ranting or extreme statements it shall be written in the consciousness that American civilization is at stake. Our civilization is not to be undermined by the movies alone – there are many evil influences at work – but the movies constitute one cause and an important one. It is the cause with which we are now dealing.[54]

Two weeks later he was defensive about the Forman manuscript; it was his obligation to the people of the United States and of the world, he said, to get out the facts undiluted and uncolored "because of any prepossession on the one hand, or on the other any timidities or any unsocial leanings of any scientists." Not content, he went on to make uncomplimentary comments about Thurstone.[55]

This contretemps with May and Thurstone is revealing. Short had worked for four years with these social scientists. As the drafts of their reports came in he annotated them extensively, always seeking to get a more definite conclusion from the data than the author originally intended. He pushed his case at great length and in extraordinary detail, although persuasion was his only weapon. It was perhaps what this process revealed to May and Thurstone, certainly two of the leading academics in the group, that was all too vividly confirmed in the tone of Forman's original manuscript.[56]

In raising the stakes to nothing short of the future of U.S. civilization, Short was engaging in the same kind of rhetorical overkill that others were trying to clean out of Forman's manuscript. By dismissing dissenting scientists as dishonest, timid or antisocial he was exhibiting a streak of demagoguery not visible earlier in the project.

Some of the most penetrating internal commentary on the Forman manuscript came from the team at New York University, where Frederic Thrasher was extending his Boys' Club study to the movies with the aid of his assistant, Paul Cressey. Asked to read Forman's typescript, Cressey found fault not only with the tone, but with Forman's sociologically naive view of the movies as a socializing agency. Because of its oversimplification, Cressey argued that it would be an inappropriate introduction to the PFS series.[57] Expanding on these thoughts when faced with a revised manuscript, Cressey wrote:

It does not present at any time a unified perspective on our study. Mr. Forman does not indicate the essence even of the idea of the study of the theater and the movie in their social role in such a community. More important, except at the very end where he makes an inadequate reference to it, he does not develop the conception of the motion picture as an informal agency of education which contributes to a whole variety of behavior activities. We are seeing the movie as an informal agency for education which conditions activities ranging all the way from criminal exploits to solicitude for one's aged mother.[58]

This sums up one of the major intellectual achievements of the PFS research. Cressey and Thrasher had refuted their own earlier, rather simple ideas of how movies fit into the cause-and-effect chains of society. (Cressey's thinking continued to evolve toward his path-breaking article of 1938 which Ruth Inglis called "the best analysis of this complex subject.")[59] In passing on Cressey's ideas about Forman's manuscript, Thrasher told Charters bluntly that he would break solidarity:

Neither Mr. Cressey nor I can support the chapter as it stands and we cannot consider ourselves bound to agree with this chapter after it is published. We will necessarily make the proper qualifications in our own report and shall state our results without reference to the impression conveyed by Mr. Forman's chapter.

If Mr. Forman wishes to publish this material and take the responsibility for a later contradiction of his interpretations, there is no help for it. I believe, however, that this is poor strategy from the standpoint of educating the public as to the effects of motion pictures either from the point of view of science or propaganda, for the reason that, if we have to contradict Mr. Forman's interpretations later on, it seems to me it will not only weaken the effects of the use he has made of our materials but will weaken the whole volume, because people will say that if there have been misinterpretations in one chapter the chances are the whole effort is merely a biased presentation in the interest of anti-motion picture propaganda.[60]

This was less than two months before Forman's book appeared, and explains clearly why the studies were going to self-destruct. Those defending them would be labeled antimovie; those who wanted "proper qualification" would be ignored.

The researchers' doubts about Forman's manuscript worried those at Payne Fund headquarters enough that they solicited two independent reviews, one by James Rorty,[61] the other by Mabell S. C. Smith. The latter was detailed and supportive. The former was scathing and uncompromising. It found that Forman's manuscript violated scientific objectivity and was itself confused; it played into the hands of sectarians and crusaders; it played into the hands of the movie magnates. Forman's "capacity for moral indignation, and his personal Puritanism have mastered his better judgment." Rorty's anger was clear:

The trouble with Mr. Forman's treatment is not a matter of correctable details, but rather a definite and unfortunate limitation and bias in his point of view. The material is heavily editorialized and "interpreted" throughout: always, however, from the point of view of one who considers his personal system of moral and ethical values to be unchanging absolutes, believed in and adhered to by all decent people. It should be sufficient to point out that we have in America not a "culture" but a complex of conflicting cultures, variously determined by the economic and social pressures to which the individual and his particular class stratum are subjected. The social process is dynamic; any attempt to impose a particular traditional and class-limited set of values on this process is not only bad sociology but bad sense, and as such bound to be rejected not merely by sociologists but by intelligent laymen. . . .

In effect Mr. Forman's book is an emotional appeal to the public spirited middle class people of America to alarm themselves, and by implication at least, to take some action regarding the present state of the movies. . . . The language is much like that of a dry crusader; the attempt obviously is to marshal the crusading spirit of middle class evangelical America, with all its blindness, prejudice, and intolerance, for a new "noble experiment" of some sort. If the book is published and if it has the effects which I consider probable . . . the excellent and valuable work of the investigators will have been used merely to promote a new orgy of movie "reform" and censorship; that the indicated job of social engineering will not get done; that the Hollywood ex-pantsmakers will emerge for the most part triumphant from the melee; that something will probably be gained for the protection and education of children and adolescents, but very little and at a wholly dispro-portionate cost of social energy.[62]

As a result of this judgment, serious consideration was given to not publishing Forman's book.[63] The files do not tell us how Short overcame the distaste of Charters and the alarm Rorty's report caused at Payne Fund headquarters. A plausible inference, however, is that, as an inde-pendent writer contracted to Macmillan, there was no way to stop Forman, unless the MPRC was to seek an injunction – something Short would hardly have been persuaded to do, since he agreed with much of what Forman wrote and U.S. civilization was at stake.

The Eclipse of the Motion Picture Research Council

While these internal disputes over Forman's book had been going on, Short had been building up the MPRC into a body of "more than three hundred" august laypersons to lend weight to the plan of action eventually devised to respond to the facts the PFS disclosed.[64] And the Forman book did its job. In the words of the hostile *Motion Picture Herald:* "The immediate result [of the Forman book] has been to make the United States suddenly newly conscious of the motion picture in a critical sense and to stir up a storm of discussion that is likely to continue for many and many a week." It also wrote of "Reverend Mr. Short's publicity coup, with the city papers inclined to be a bit skeptical in the main, with the journals of the lesser towns tending to view and discuss the screen with new alarm."[65]

But the campaign was a little late in starting. By the time it began, some church-affiliated groups, in rather muted ways, as prescribed by the repeatedly expressed desire to avoid a conflict with the organized motion picture industry, had independently increased their agitation against the state of the movies, most notably in the founding of the Legion of Decency on or after 11 April 1934.[66] That campaign quickly eclipsed the efforts of the MPRC and the PFS.[67]

When Short died, in January 1935, he could not have helped but feel that progress was being made on the cause to which he had devoted his last eight years, but that the progress was not altogether the result of his efforts. The wave of public indignation he had hoped the PFS would provoke never materialized. Nonetheless, the movie industry was becoming more compliant. This was not wholly the Legion's doing either. Claims that specific pressure groups brought about the "cleanup" of the movies are too simple. Independently of these efforts, the motion picture industry was fragile. Objective economic factors were at work. With several of the major motion picture companies in receivership and the Depression worsening, the industry did not want to risk alienating influential elements of public opinion. Thus the industry made a great show of compliance, while quietly trying to find more ingenious ways of delivering to the public what it seemed willing to pay for. Had the industry been more robust, had it not been apprehensive about further government assaults on its trade practices, there might have been less compromise and stealthy evasion and more vigorous counterattack.

It is important to emphasize that the new and stricter Production Code, Catholic boycotts and threats of more, and the strength of the Legion and other pressures did not render the movies innocuous and uplifting. The cleanup was more superficial than real. While in the ensuing years the bulk of Hollywood movies became innocuous as far as sexual morality was concerned, they by no means became socially uplifting in the manner desired by pressure groups.[68] For example, when it was in a satirical and socially critical mode, Hollywood made movies that ridiculed or attacked established authorities and institutions, not always reinforcing the civics and moral lessons of schoolroom and pulpit. And in its continuing ability to glamorize and make attractive what was ostensibly being preached against, Hollywood remained peerless. From suggestive clothing on blameless heroines to excitingly staged orgies in moralizing religious films, "cleaned-up" Hollywood was far from delivering movies that unambiguously fulfilled the hopes of the MPRC or, for that matter, the Legion.

What this reveals is the flaw at the heart of the reformist attacks. Movies are complicated texts that can be read in multiple ways. The motion picture industry is in the business of pandering: of trying to find out what the public wants and then delivering it. In fact, what the public demanded was not so depraved: later sociologists have seen the popular Hollywood product as reinforcing and reproducing rather than undermining the status quo. But those who saw themselves as spokespersons for that status quo had a rather naive idea of its homogeneity. In a changing, immigrant society assumptions about mores and values are bound to be under constant question, as groups jockey for places of power. Insofar as the movies were implicated in change, they were responsive to wider social forces, not molders of them.

It remains to assess the effectiveness of pressure on the trade practices of the industry. In stating their aims, Short and the MPRC pamphlet had joined the chorus of those who thought that the movie industry insulated itself from pressure to reform by distribution practices that dictated to theaters what films they could get, rather than letting the theaters choose from what was available. The oligopolistic structure of the industry made these practices hard to subvert. Despite the fuss made by Forman, the Legion and many other pressure groups, there were no signs in 1933–1934 that the major distributing companies intended to bring an end to trade practices like block booking. In 1938 the federal government launched an antitrust suit against such practices. Only with the suit's resolution was a certain amount of restructuring forced on the distributing practices of the industry.[69]

The Academic Reception of the Payne Fund Studies

Our Movie Made Children was found by reviewers to have all of the shortcomings the researchers complained of, and, as already mentioned, it was an embarrassment to a number of them. Nevertheless, we must be careful not to hold the Forman book solely responsible for the academic neglect of the PFS. Those studies stemmed from a critical and reformist social conscience that thought it a simple matter to enlist fact-finding science in their cause. It had not been anticipated that social science might deconstruct the conceptual and rhetorical foundations of reform thinking about social problems. Those researchers whose work led them to question the way reformers conceptualized social causation and identified social problems were disparaged in private correspondence, and consideration was given to not publishing them (Thurstone and May were published only grudgingly, Thrasher and Cressey could not pull their manuscript together before the funds dried up).[70] Forman's book was responsible for coloring the PFS for much of the reading public and, just as seriously, helping discolor their academic reputation. Charters summed it up well in his "Ten Year Adventure":

From the point of view of the Research Committee this procedure [sponsoring Forman's book] was not a success because the writer, being consciously and deliberately opposed to the movies, did not present the case in good perspective.

    I am personally of the opinion that we would have been better off if we had rested the case without this attempt at popularization. It would have been wiser to publish the studies and thereby make them available for use by journalists and publicists without the implied sponsorship of the popularization of the Forman book.[71]

    The Forman book made it almost impossible for the PFS to escape being associated with antimovie advocacy. When the studies were reviewed in professional journals of sociology, psychology and education, the advocacy issue had to be carefully excused. Kimball Young, a sociologist at the University of Wisconsin, who had once been approached as a possible researcher, reviewed all but the Dale volumes in the *American Journal of Sociology*.[72] He insisted that they were an "excellent contribution to sociology and social psychology," but he also noted that Forman's summary was another matter. After summarizing the results and underscoring the care and caution of the authors, he indicted Forman for propaganda and mythmaking. Stressing that the movies were only one factor in a period of rapid social change, Young concluded that Forman's slanted presentation had done the authors and their fields of study a genuine disservice.

    Hadley Cantril, who would help inaugurate the new epoch of mass media research with his study of the panic engendered by Orson Welles's radio dramatization, *War of the Worlds*,[73] reviewed only the first volume, which contained Charters's summary. He noted Charters's criticism of movies and desire for uplifting films but commented that profit ensures that "if socially desirable pictures are ever to be made it appears that they will have to be produced by non-profit seeking organizations. This conclusion provides a further challenge to those who want better pictures." Yet he held back from the monocausal view: "The appeals common to racy movies, stories and conduct are no doubt due to personal maladjustments created by many factors in the social order itself and the popularity of undesirable movies might more realistically be regarded only as a reflection of underlying discontent."[74]

Malcolm M. Willey, a sociologist of the press and of education, who had worked on the President's Research Committee on Social Trends, reviewed Forman's book and four of the first seven volumes. He suggested that Forman's "over-dramatized" style would "actually detract from the true significance of the data that are involved." He praised Charters's summary as "academic and even tempered." He singled out Dale's *How to Appreciate Motion Pictures* as unique and eminently useful: "For the social scientists, these several studies will raise as many questions as they answer. For the lay reader, the summary volumes will unquestionably stimulate interest in the problem of youth and motion pictures. Both results are desirable."[75]

A long and careful review in the *Journal of Applied Psychology* by C. M. Louttit of Indiana University found the research "remarkably free from bias." Louttit suggested that Charters's summary conclusions were not adequate to the achievements of the research, which showed clearly that motion pictures, like coffee, can be bad for people in various ways, but that there is a strong individual factor in the reaction. Motion pictures did not influence *children,* he held; rather, they influenced this or that *child.* He concluded that with coffee the solution was not to frown on it, but to train the child to use elementary judgment. "Unfortunately, when it comes to matters of greater social import, as the movies, or books, or other interest, we leave the development of judgment to kind Fates, hoping for the best."[76]

By contrast, Abraham Krasker, a lecturer in visual education at Boston University, writing in *Education,* found that "all of these studies prove conclusively that children are being affected negatively by present motion pictures. Educators cannot neglect to combat the objectionable influence of the motion pictures. These studies by the Motion Picture Research Council are giving us the facts for a very vigorous campaign in the interests of children."[77]

Finally, H. Meltzer of the Psychological Service Center in St. Louis concluded his review in the *Journal of Educational Psychology* with what appears to be an allusion to Forman. He wrote that many making use of the PFS to justify their convictions should draw their attention to a qualifying paragraph in the Shuttleworth–May study: "Factors of age, intelligence, school grade, and home background are as important and possibly more important in influencing the conduct and attitudes of children as the movie. In the case of attitudes, the influence of the community far overshadows in importance the influence of the movie."[78]

In light of these reviews, we can now approach the question of what longer-term impact these scientific studies had on the community of psychologists and sociologists and the yet-to-emerge communications specialists. Only a small amount of this material had been acknowledged in scholarly journals.[79] Virtually nothing further was published from the program. Yet it had tackled some of the central problems of communications studies.

Under the later influence of the likes of Paul Lazarsfeld, Harold Lasswell, Hadley Cantril and others, the field into which most of the PFS fell came to be called "mass communications research." Lasswell was to formulate the basic questions of this research as "Who says what in which channel to whom and with what effect?"[80] The PFS, which pioneered the investigation of these questions, were narrowed by their focus on children as the "to whom," on "what" was said and "with what effect." The issue of "who says" (i.e., how the movies were owned and controlled) was supposed to have been included in the Payne Fund research program, but it was given a low priority in the early organizing meetings, in part because some of it was public information, but largely because research in this vein would inevitably involve contact with the movie industry, something the Fund and the Experimental Committee wished to avoid. Nevertheless, Seabury, Short and others were clear that the "who" was a monopoly controlled by persons born abroad and so not socialized to the right degree.[81]

"What" was said was by and large treated as unproblematic. The researchers did notice that goodness and virtue usually triumphed in the movies and villainy was usually condemned, but long before the PFS it was understood that such overt messages were only part of what was encoded in the movies. The gangster might end up dead, but for sixty minutes before that point his villainy might have been glamorized and his triumphs shown exultantly. A sexy lady might be condemned as a "bad girl" but still strike many moviegoers as attractive for all that. Beyond this, however, the analysis of movie content was rudimentary. Not only was Dale's *The Content of Motion Pictures* openly judgmental, it was based on literary summaries of plots, which were then fit into given classifications. Later generations of content analysts had to develop elaborate means to overcome such inadequacies.[82]

Even more rudimentary was the studies' attempt to research "with

what effect?" Children were shown a movie, then had their sleep moni-
tored. Children were shown a movie, then had their galvanic skin responses measured. Questionnaires that children filled out before and
after watching a movie were used to measure shifts in their attitudes
toward selected topics, which were then retested. Children were asked
to write movie autobiographies or were interviewed to the same effect,
and thus many cases of association between disapproved behavior and
movie memories were generated. Apart from the sense that some moviegoers were able to discount the effect of movies on them, these results
did much to confirm the suspicion that the movies were a social problem.
But all this inquiry took place in a vacuum: behind it was only a
commonsense view of society and its workings, even in the field of
child development.

Nevertheless, the Payne Fund researchers had at least begun to explore questions that would concern later generations of mass communications researchers. They have, then, been quite unjustly neglected. In
1947 Franklin Fearing, a major pioneer in the psychological study of
communication, tipped his hat to the volumes, and in 1950 Leo Handel
did the same, also pointing to some deficiencies. Little more was heard
until, in the mid-1970s, Sklar and Jowett gave them their due. Contemporary debate about their rehabilitation can be dated from then. Delia
stressed the contemporary relevance of the concerns and research techniques of the PFS and their continuity with methods used today.[83] The
most positive current estimate of the value of the PFS is that of Shearon
Lowery and Melvin De Fleur, the latter a leading communications
scholar, who declared:

Clearly, they were the great pioneering effort that established media research
as a serious scientific field. They brought together in one extraordinary
group of studies a major problem of public concern and the perspectives of
young sciences. The fact that various disciplines participated in the research
was a harbinger of things to come; the fact that a broad range of topics was
studied with many different techniques was also an indicator of future directions.[84]

Delia, as well as Lowery and De Fleur, choose to ignore the long period
of criticism and neglect of the PFS, including the odd fact that in his
definitive summary and discussion of research on mass communications
effects up to 1958, Klapper lists the studies in his bibliography but
scarcely bothers to mention them in his text.[85] By that time mass com-

munications research had turned decisively toward television, and while earlier radio research was seen as a precursor, the Payne Fund movie research was seemingly ignored. This was partly a personnel matter: not all members of the PFS group continued in the fields they had pioneered. Some went on to careers of academic influence, especially Thurstone and May in psychology, and Blumer in sociology. Thurstone continued with the study of attitudes, with which his name has been associated ever since, but without further reference to movies. May became interested in the use of movies in the classroom.[86] Thrasher became a Hollywood booster.[87] Blumer marginalized his early PFS works. He later become associated with "symbolic interactionism," a view of society as a symbolic mediating structure. He wrote relatively little, but had many students. His biographer, Kenneth Baugh, is unable to place Blumer's Payne Fund work in relation to his later theoretical work that interests him.[88] None of this augured well for the future prospects of PFS research.

What promised to be the most fruitful of all the studies, and which might well have provided continuity with the media research to come, was not published. That was Frederic Thrasher and Paul Cressey's "The Community – A Social Setting for the Motion Picture." Its authors came to the conclusion that the social model underlying much of the PFS research was inadequate, making the evidence gathered partial and to a degree difficult to interpret. Using a schedule devised by Blumer, Cressey and Thrasher's team collected motion picture autobiographies from 2,400 children. "It was felt that so far as this type of material was concerned the results obtained at New York University did not justify the continuation of the method or a further analysis of the materials already obtained at the present time." They then assembled questionnaires and found only 50 percent reliability in transcribing the diaries and questionnaires into statistically manageable form. Furthermore, cross-checking showed that the informants themselves were not reliable on the basic matter of frequency of attendance. Cressey and Thrasher's extra data were obtained from controlled interviews and were based on a deeper sense of how social institutions meshed with one another.[89]

This suggests another way in which the PFS were self-destructive. Although some of the best academics of the time did what they could with the tools available, and with some new methods especially developed for the project, their approach was guided by a naive or common-sense model of society and of social problems. That is to say, it was an approach that Katz and Lazarsfeld would characterize as hostage to a social model of atomized moviegoers, with every movie message a direct and powerful stimulus to action that would elicit an immediate response from viewers.[90] The question "What do the movies say to whom and with what effect?" was impossible to answer by looking only at the movies.[91]

With the researchers divided among themselves, their work publicly distorted and to a degree self-undermining, a further damaging blow was delivered to the academic prospects of the PFS by Mortimer J. Adler in *Art and Prudence* (1937).[92] Moley tells us that Adler was at work on a study of the influence of the movies when the PFS came out and so it was natural that he would look at them carefully. However, since Adler had already been critical of earlier claims of the crimogenic effects of the movies, he was directly encouraged by the movie industry.[93]

Adler's argument went to the heart of the matter, to the value of policy-oriented research, to Short's view that assembling the facts was a prerequisite for a program of action. Although conceding the paternalist and Platonic view that freedom of the arts might sometimes have to be curtailed for the common good, Adler argued that the Short approach systematically confused scientific, moral and political issues. Moral interpretation of the facts was beyond the competence of science. Any political assessment of what should and could be done must wait for that moral assessment. And political assessment had to take into account an unknown: the full consequences of any course of social action against an art form.

Not satisfied with this severe circumscription of the role of social science in policy making, Adler set about showing that the PFS had discovered little or no evidence of a harmful effect of movies on society and that all of their conclusions were highly qualified. Sometimes Adler merely corrected the misreadings of Forman rather than demonstrating that the scientists had not shown what they did not claim to show. Adler did not believe that social science provided the kind of information a prudent person required to make wise decisions about social welfare.[94] Will Hays of the MPPDA quoted with some trepidation Adler's summary statement:

In the matter of moral influence, the relevance of the scientific data is questionable. To whatever extent they are relevant can be considered as reliable, the findings are inconsistent and tend to be negative. . . . If all of this has any significance, after unreliability of methods and data have been taken into account and inconsistencies nullify each other, it tends to cast some doubt upon the popular concern about the moral influence of motion pictures upon the immature.

Hays commented, "That's a pretty strong statement and goes farther than I ever cared to go."[95]

Strong statement or not, the MPPDA was well pleased with Adler's blow to the theory that the movies were primarily or even largely responsible for juvenile delinquency and other social pathologies. But a heavy philosophical tome would hardly gain wide currency. So Raymond Moley was commissioned to do a Forman on Adler, so to speak, that is, to write a short, popularizing summary of Adler's philosophical treatise. The result was *Are We Movie Made?* of 1938.[96] MPPDA sponsorship of that volume was overt, and Adler himself became a paid consultant to the MPPDA around this time.[97]

The triumph of the industry was not solely a business one; its leader, Hays, espoused a view that approached the sociological perspective emerging from the most reflective of the PFS researchers and that would later characterize mass communications research. Hays noted rather ruefully that "the discussion of movies and morals, pro and con, went on endlessly in the press." He approved of this process and always took it as one of his jobs to send editors material for the debate.

As I look back on those middle years, I can't help wondering whether there were not factors involved that made it unusually hard to draw sound conclusions. Upsetting changes in home life followed World War I. Many family roots had been torn up. Schools were crowded. Cities were growing. Exciting commercial amusements were increasing. The depression brought phenomena we had never seen before. And in addition to everything else, I believe, an intensifying of sheer publicity, notoriety, and organized pressures tended to throw the truth out of focus and to turn opinion into violent attack.[98]

Conclusion

Gauging the impact of research is a tricky task. The PFS findings were meant to be utilized to shape public (i.e., elite) opinion in the direction favored by Short and the MPRC.[99] Yet the research itself had been conducted by respected social scientists on university campuses who were seemingly under no pressure to find things one way or the other (although the process by which the researchers were selected might be suspect, and Adler claimed their concepts sometimes muddled fact and value). Like the early social scientists Sidney and Beatrice Webb, Short and the Payne Fund sponsors believed that exposure of the facts would be enough to galvanize opinion. Facts were to be the effective rhetoric of reform. Unfortunately, the gathering of the facts had turned out to be a process heavily colored by the biases of the Payne Fund researchers themselves, more marked in the case of some than of others, and, still more deeply, by the uncritical attempt of the sponsors to isolate the movies as a social problem with a life of its own. This made it difficult to defend their work against the purposes that Forman made it serve, and it rendered it vulnerable to Adler's searching critique. But by the time Adler's book appeared, the only researchers still active in the motion picture field were Dale as part of the outreach program Charters was running at Ohio State, May, Thrasher and Cressey, who published articles in lieu of the promised volume *Boys, Movies and City Streets*. The next great infusion of talent and money into mass communications research came from advertising, radio and wartime government research. New personnel were involved, although they used refined versions of some of the PFS techniques. The debates about the inadequacies of the studies had clearly alerted researchers to the pitfalls of naive causal models, the artificialities of the laboratory and the questionnaire.

Most important, however, were the changes in the social sciences that were supervening. We might pick out three salient developments, each a response to the weaknesses Adler had exposed in PFS, including the philosophical commonplace that no amount of facts entails values; value conclusions require value premises. These were the critical response, the functionalist response and the depth-psychology response.

The critical response tries to rectify the lack of a general view of society animating the movie research and the consequent inability to put alleged social problems in an overall perspective. According to Lazarsfeld, administrative research can be distinguished from critical research.[100] "Administrative research" denotes such projects as the PFS, the president's Commission on Social Trends and market research (the latter almost completely lacking in the movie business).[101] This is applied research intended to serve stated goals (value premises). "Critical research," for Lazarsfeld, is research that theorizes about society and social trends first, expresses its social values second (value premises) and only then plunges into empirical study, paying much attention to unintended effects and the complexities of social meaning.[102]

If the PFS research had been critical in Lazarsfeld's sense, the moral panic among the sponsors of the studies would have been examined as part of current social trends in capitalist society, much more attention would have been given to the political economy of the movies, children would have been differentiated for research purposes by social class and family structure and the discussion of values and their embedding in movies would have been less complacent than was Peters's in *Motion Pictures and Standards of Morality* (1933). In other words, the assumption that American mores were being threatened by the movies would have been replaced by a much more critical view of the United States, and questions would have been raised about where the benefit flowed from deplorable but profitable movies. Lazarsfeld advocated critical research as a complement to administrative research, because it was able to "contribute much in terms of challenging problems and new concepts useful in the interpretation of known, and in the search for new, data."[103] He reported being stimulated by the ideas of T. W. Adorno and in retrospect worried that he did not devote enough time to trying to operationalize them.[104] Adorno's work on popular music, Herta Herzog's and Rudolph Arnheim's on daytime radio serials and Leo Lowenthal's on biographies in popular magazines illustrate this approach at its best in mass media research.[105] When the approach was revived in the 1960s under the title "critical media studies," it was more doctrinaire Marxist and often impenetrable.

A very different response, known as structural functionalism in sociology, was pioneered by Talcott Parsons and his student Robert K. Merton. It, too, addressed the treatment of the movies in isolation from the totality of the social structure. Structural functionalism recommended viewing society as an integrated system and explaining social phenomena by specifying how they were connected as functioning components of the system. Special emphasis was placed on the latent function of institutions. In face of the claim that movies created delinquency, the functionalist would want to know how it served functional integration to have a profitable industry that promoted delinquency, or what social function was served by elites' labeling the conduct of certain groups of youth "delinquent." Indeed, the function of movies and other forms of mass communication in society became a major research program for this school of thought. A critical sociologist might see the movies as serving and reproducing the dominant economic relations of society; the structural functionalist might see them as offering uses and gratifications to their consumers, or as socializing the audiences of children, immigrants and the general citizenry.

A third response was to the psychological insufficiencies of administrative research. Children and adults were to be envisaged not as stimulus–response machines but as having a complexly layered psychological makeup. The psychological effects of the movies were subtle. This kind of mass communications research was under the influence of depth psychology, especially Freudian and neo-Freudian. It could be and was grafted onto either critical research or functionalist research, even if the result was theoretically incoherent. The work of Wiese and Cole, Kracauer, Warner and of Wolfenstein and Leites exemplified this approach.[106]

The critical, functional and depth-psychology approaches to mass communications research did not converge; indeed, they were in theory rivals, the proponents of each assuming theirs to be the one correct approach to the study of society and hence to the mass media. But as the personal example of Lazarsfeld in his work with Merton shows, in practice the three approaches did converge on an aversion to the older style of administrative research.[107] They also converged in being much more rigorously sociological and less psychologistically reductionist than the PFS.[108] Whichever classics of "modern" communications studies we look at – those of Lasswell, Cantril, Herzog, Merton, Adorno, Warner and Henry, Hovland, Lumsdaine and Sheffield or Fearing – we find one or more of these approaches involved.[109]

The PFS are important, then, not for what they disclosed, but for their creative approach to research problems and the mistakes they made and hence illustrate. They were done at a time when the hypodermic model of social causation, especially of deviance, was still taken seriously by the public authorities and the guardians of morality. In this model society is envisaged as a system that tends to produce individuals in equilibrium with it and one another, unless some specific causal factor is inserted into the situation, like a needle into a patient. But some of the Payne Fund scientists were developing a more sophisticated understanding of society and of deviance, and were able to see that their own preliminary evidence refuted such earlier ideas. It is regrettable that refuted scientific ideas, which mark intellectual progress and learning, are all too often disdained by later generations. Indeed, the situation is a little worse than this. Succeeding generations in the academic world sometimes define their contribution by denigrating previous work as old-fashioned or worse. The PFS were victims of a process some would call a paradigm shift: abandoned by their makers, their approach superseded by a theoretically new and more professionalized social science and their ideas (attitude studies, adult discount) borrowed without proper acknowledgment, they took on a dusty and old-fashioned air. Close historical scrutiny reveals that impression to be a myth and a distortion.

The doubts and hesitations in the development of the social science of mass communication had little direct impact on the wider issue of the movies and social control. Influential, prudent individuals, as Adler would call them, continued to believe that control and regulation of the movies were imperative. Thus Hollywood maintains its self-censorship. From time to time further efforts were made to draw social science into the debate, but the results invariably disappointed those raising moral and hence political concerns. A good example from the past twenty-five years is the controversy over social science studies of the effects of pornography, beginning with the technical studies of the president's commission of 1970 and continuing without end in sight, perhaps with none possible.[110]

PART TWO

The Unpublished Payne Fund Material

CHAPTER FOUR

The Lost Manuscript

Why This Document Was Never Published

The author of "The Community – A Social Setting for the Motion Picture," Paul G. Cressey, is the unsung hero of the Payne Fund project. As explained in Chapters Two and Three, if he ever completed the project sketched in this chapter and the next one (which was to have been published as *Boys, Movies and City Streets*), the manuscript has not been found. To date the document we have reproduced here is the only known draft of this work and therefore is of some historical interest. Like many of the other Payne Fund studies (PFS), the document deserves to be better known in the history of American sociology as well as in the history of film studies. (This is true of Paul Cressey's work in general.) It is uncertain when this draft was written, but it seems to date from December 1932. As it stands, it is incomplete, repetitive, lacking analysis and radically different in style from the other published studies. Clearly, a great deal of rewriting and editing would have been necessary to bring it up to publishable standards.

The germ of the idea for this study was first voiced in 1928 by Herbert Blumer, then a young sociologist at the University of Chicago. Blumer outlined in a letter to the Rev. William Short a list of studies he would like to undertake as part of the PFS project.[1] Blumer did eventually undertake two studies, which were published as *Movies and Conduct* and (with Philip M. Hauser) *Movies, Delinquency and Crime*.[2] He was also eager to do another study examining the influence of movies under different living conditions and asked the Chicago-trained Frederic Thrasher, then at New York University, to consider undertaking such a study with the Broadway Temple Group, a settlement house group in the Harlem section of upper Broadway. Thrasher, busy at the time with his own projects, eventually enlisted the assistance of a University of Chicago doctoral student, Paul G. Cressey. The published version of Cressey's master's thesis, *The Taxi-Dance Hall* (which is still in print), had caused a minor sensation in Chicago. The study of movies and conduct in a low-income area was a natural extension of Thrasher and Cressey's current involvement in a large study funded by the Boys' Club in New York. For the projected *Boys, Movies and City Streets*, Cressey designed a multifaceted study of boys in their "total situations." He tried to avoid relying too heavily on one research approach, and therefore used twenty different data-gathering techniques, including personal documents, interviews, surveys, Hollerith punch cards, statistical correlations and health records.

Like many other researchers involved in the PFS, Cressey recognized the lack of validity of the "direct-influence" theories then generally accepted by the public.[3] His research was directed toward understanding the movies as one part of the total "social situation" or "configuration" in which they were experienced. Cressey articulated this concept in one of his academic articles and also took direct aim at the many fashionable books attacking the movies, particularly Henry James Forman's popular and influential summary of the PFS, *Our Movie Made Children*. Cressey noted:

This failure to include all the phases essential to the motion picture experience has misled not only ... critics of published studies, but also many "popular" writers and speakers. Disregarding the social background and personal interests of their subjects, they have made sweeping statements about the motion picture's "effect," even though their information pertained to but one phase of the cinema experience. Thus some have argued, solely from a sample of film content, that young people who see "undesirable," "immoral," or even criminal conduct upon the screen will go out and do likewise, or at least will tend inevitably to acquire corresponding attitudes and values. Others, merely from knowledge of instances of conduct and attitudes after specific screen action or values, have jumped to the conclusion that the cinema "caused" these changes in behaviour or attitudes. ... Social causation is entirely too complex a problem to be explained by any such simplistic interpretation of incomplete data.[4]

The draft of their study indicates that Thrasher and Cressey made a strong effort to place the moviegoing experience within the context of other influences in everyday life. The following document deals with the experiences associated with moviegoing in this interstitial neighborhood and serves as a reminder to motion picture and social historians that the movie house remained an important site for social interaction until the 1960s. While some of the behavior described may not be typical of most American youths at this time, the centrality of the movie house as a point of contact in this particular neighborhood becomes obvious.

While he was trying to complete the project, Cressey was visited by a series of disasters on what has been described in Chapter Three as a Wagnerian scale. The following letter, dated 15 January 1934, gives some feeling for these travails:[5]

My dear Mr. Short:

In response to your suggestion I am writing to state frankly the very difficult financial situation in which I find myself. May I ask that this statement be regarded as of the most confidential nature.

First, however, may I make quite clear my deep sense of endebtedness [sic] to you and the members of the Motion Picture Research Council, and to the Payne Fund, for the opportunity for my research work which has been made possible through this support. I feel such a deep sense of obligation and loyalty that I am using every means I know for staying with the study until its completion. I am at this time of academic unemployment and insecurity, definitely refusing and deferring, where possible, certain very attractive and remunerative positions which in the past weeks have come to me without solicitation on my part, because of my desire to "see this job through" at whatever personal expense to me. All I am seeking is some means by which I can remain to the completion of this research. It is regarding this personal problem that I have spoken to you and am now writing you.

You will remember that the work in the interpretation and classification of our material, which was going on during the first months of 1933, was suddenly interrupted by the very critical and prolonged illness of my wife. Following a period of protracted colds and illness Mrs. Cressey was operated upon for the removal of her tonsils on April 13, 1933. Subsequently she developed both lobar and bronchial pneumonia, and later bi-lateral phlebitis of the post-infectious type. This latter illness required her remaining in an immobile position for a period of eight weeks, attended both during day and night by trained nurses. It was not until November that she was able to get about the apartment herself. In fact, she is still quite poorly and will be unable to return to her employment until at least April of this year. We have been assured by many physicians that recovery from such a case of phlebitis is very slow and usually requires at least a year.

As you understand, my income was supplemented through the salary of my wife as an instructor in French at Montclair State Teachers' College, Montclair, NJ. This long and very expensive illness has played havoc with the usual resources with which we provide against emergencies. In round figures, our expenses were: Nurses $1,200; Medical services $500 (only partially paid to date); Medicines and Supplies $250; Hospital and Operation $115; additional household expenses occasioned through illness (estimated) $150. When it is remembered that my major object during these years was merely to meet expenses – not at all to atttempt to build up a surplus, even as a savings account – you can readily understand what this illness has done to our emergency resources. We, of course, borrowed up to the limit from our insurance companies, my wife sold her Carnegie old-age annuity policy, we borrowed at least $800 from our respective families and relatives. The normal resources to which one turns in emergencies have been exhausted, and now – with the inability of my wife to return to her teaching as early as it was at first hoped she could – we find no way practically of meeting the deficit in our family income.

Further financial stress has been occasioned by my own illness of the late summer and fall. Taken ill with what for a time was regarded by physicians as appendicitis I subsequently entered a hospital for clinical and x-ray examinations which apparently made possible fortunately another interpretation of the illness, making unnecessary an operation. While the costs for these examinations and the treatment are but a fraction of the cost occasioned by my wife's illness it has added appreciably to the financial burden at a time when we could least conveniently bear it.

May I say that, should there be any desire, I shall be very glad to furnish any information desired regarding these expenses or regarding the entirely untoward series of circumstances through which we have passed. I am happy to say that while Mrs. Cressey's present health leaves much to be desired we have every assurance now from medical men that, with the coming of spring and summer and the opportunity for rest and sunshine she will be restored eventually to perfect health. I personally am improving in health and for the past two months have been able to accomplish very nearly as much as before my illness.

Permit me to say, also, that we have attempted already in every way feasible to reduce our family budget to the very minimum commensurate with Mrs. Cressey's health. Even though we make no effort to retire the bills outstanding from my wife's illness – chiefly physician's bills, some of whom are quite insistent – my income for part-time instruction from New York University is not sufficient to meet our expenses. Now that a slight margin which we have had is exhausted we shall have no means for meeting this deficit after February 1. I am referring this matter to you because I have exhausted other possibilities and because I do not know anyone else to whom to turn in this emergency. I am very anxious to complete the study at whatever cost to myself and only covet a way by which I may be permitted to do this.

It would seem to me that my actual needs for emergency expenditures should not exceed $500. I plan *and fully expect,* given my health, to complete our study by September 1, 1934. Upon that basis these emergency expenditures should not exceed $500 and in all probability, I believe, should not be that much. This, it should be noted, is predicated upon the assumption that there will be no untoward developments, costly illnesses, etc., but, excepting that possibility, I am confident that it will meet all such emergency expenditures for our personal needs.

Permit me to say that while we do not have collateral to cover a loan of that amount our signatures will of course be backed by our own probity, by life insurance policies covering that largest amount. At this writing I have no contract for employment for next fall but have several opportunities where I have been assured positions paying from $3,500 to $4,500, these made uncertain only because of the desire that I begin work prior to next September. Mrs. Cressey has every reason to believe that she will be reappointed at her school. The radical retrenchment at New York University, made necessary by the drop in student enrollment, I have been informed, gives me no basis for expectation of employment here for the coming academic year.

May I report that the New York University motion picture study is being organized and written at this time. As I see it taking shape at this time I have more confidence than ever that it will be a most interesting and convincing account. Personally, I am convinced that if I am enabled to conclude this research, my own conviction that this study will be at least equal to, if not superior to any others of the series will be justified by the final product. For that reason I sincerely hope that a way will be found to make possible the completion of this work immediately.

Yours most sincerely,

Paul G. Cressey

On 5 August 1934, Cressey submitted a detailed chapter outline of the proposed book to Charters (see Chapter Five, this volume),[6] but there was no further correspondence until February 1935, when he indicated to Charters that he was still working on the first draft.[7] In February 1936, Thrasher wrote to Charters indicating that Cressey was still working full-time on the book and that it would be completed "within the next few months."[8] In November 1936, Cressey wrote to Charters that, since it appeared that the Payne Fund was not interested

in funding the completion of this study, he would apply to the Guggenheim Foundation.[9] Charters replied that he would be only too happy to
write to the Guggenheim on Cressey's behalf.[10] As far as we have been
able to ascertain, nothing ever came of this offer, and no Guggenheim
grant was ever awarded to further this important work.

It is uncertain whether Cressey ever completed the final draft. He
received a Ph.D. from New York University in 1942 for a dissertation
entitled "The Role of the Motion Picture in an Interstitial Area." Remarkably, it is not preserved at New York University Library.[11] Unless
it is found and examined, we cannot say for sure whether it represents
the culmination of the project.

The Boys' Club Study of "Intervale"

"Intervale" was the pseudonym given by the Boys' Club study researchers to the East Harlem tenement district of Manhattan, site of the
Jefferson Park branch of the Boys' Club of New York. Throughout
Cressey's manuscript there are references to the Boys' Club study and its
subsidiary research projects, of which Cressey's was one. The Boys' Club
study (1928–1935) was a massive program initiated by the Boys' Clubs
of America, which sought "an impartial scientific study" of the effectiveness of urban Boys' Clubs in preventing juvenile delinquency. The study
was sponsored by the Bureau of Social Hygiene (an arm of the Rockefeller Foundation), which granted $37,500 to the project, conducted by
members of the sociology department of New York University's School
of Education. Thrasher, author of *The Gang*, was hired by the university
to direct the study, and he envisioned an enormous sociological investigation of troubled boys in their "total situations" of home, school and
play lives. New York University graduate students, recent Ph.D.'s and
junior faculty members conducted the research.

In early 1929, Thrasher arranged with the PFS administrators and
researchers to append a study of boys' relationships with movies and
commercialized recreation to his already-huge program. Orville Crays
originally headed the movie project; Cressey became associate director
of the Motion Picture Project in the fall of 1931 (see Chapter Two).

The Boys' Club study faced highly ambitious research goals, general
disorganization, the withering effects of the Depression on researchers
and sponsors and the stress- and overwork-related illnesses of staff

members Thrasher, Cressey and Robert Whitley, followed by Whitley's suicide. Most of the final report of the Boys' Club study appears to have been written in 1932 and 1933, but the project was not complete. The Bureau of Social Hygiene withdrew funding for the study in 1934. Thrasher submitted "The Final Report of the Jefferson Park Branch of the Boys' Club of New York" on 21 October 1935. The main report was 1,150 pages long, with twenty-two appendixes listed, although much of the appended material, including Cressey's preliminary report of the Motion Picture Project (appendix 2), has not survived in the Bureau of Social Hygiene papers. It is unclear whether any of the primary research materials generated by this huge project exist, for little supporting material referenced in this Cressey report and in the final report was deposited at the time of their completion, and the documents have not been located in any archive.

Thrasher projected a series of publications stemming from the Boys' Club study, but little of the study's material on juvenile delinquency appeared in print. The tardiness of the Boys' Club project itself, financial limitations caused by the Depression, the discussion throughout the Boys' Club documents of the sexual practices of youth, prostitution and gang rape, taboo topics for academics in the 1930s, may all have contributed to the failure of the Boys' Club study to be published. Another reason for the study's undeserved obscurity may have been the researchers' strident conclusion that the rigidly organized Boys' Club, unable to perceive slum-area youth's real cultural, social or economic needs, had virtually no deterrent effect on juvenile delinquency.[12]

The Editing Process

The condition of the only known draft of what would have become *Boys, Movies and City Streets* is not ideal. It is a first carbon, consisting of 176 letter-sized, hastily typed, double-spaced pages, with long passages of single-spaced quotations and other extracted material. The whole amounts to about 100,000 words. There was no bibliography attached. Many of the numerous footnotes were incomplete, lacking text altogether or not always useful because of the lack of bibliography and the reference to lost primary Boys' Club study materials discussed in the preceding section.

For inclusion in this volume, it was first transcribed and its references completed to the extent possible. The often erratic spelling and punctuation were corrected and standardized, except that the original attempts to re-create the dialects of East Harlem were retained. For the purposes of this book, we decided that it needed to be shortened. Some of Cressey's descriptive passages were reduced, longer interviews that were adequately summarized in his commentary were removed and redundant extracts were eliminated when they did not advance the discussion. Some judgment was exercised regarding scholarly value and readability. Major omissions are marked by ellipses. As an aid to film scholars, an effort was made to track down and add the dates of all cited films, which appear in square brackets (interpolations in the original are in parentheses). Where explanatory notes have been added, they are identified as editorial notes. In the interest of clarity, we have deleted note references to the case studies, interviews and other research documents noted only by abbreviations or codes, as it is unclear whether any of the primary research materials still exist. They were not retained by the Bureau of Social Hygiene or the Motion Picture Research Council. Cressey himself considered this to be only a preliminary report; he hoped to revise it and add a more extensive conclusion.

This document, alternatively titled "The Social Role of Motion Pictures in the Boys' Club Area" and "The Preliminary Report of the Motion Picture Project of the Boys' Club Study," is located in the Motion Picture Research Council papers, Hoover Institution on War, Revolution and Peace, Stanford University.

We would welcome hearing from any person with clues to the whereabouts of a later and better typescript. It remains our hope that somewhere, sometime, a complete and final manuscript of *Boys, Movies and City Streets* (or some version thereof) will turn up and can be published in full.

The Community – A Social Setting for the Motion Picture

PAUL G. CRESSEY

Part One: Boy Life in Intervale

The street, the sidewalks swarm with people. Pushcarts range along the curb; the proprietors hawking their wares to all passersby. In the store windows bordering the street is a bizarre assortment of dry goods, cheeses, condiments and liquors, and from opened doorways and cellars issue a host of smells even more provocative. People elbow each other for passage along the sidewalk while others pause to bargain loudly with the pushcart peddlers. The shrill notes of a hurdy-gurdy are heard down the street and from somewhere overhead in the solid block of dingy six floor tenements comes the strident noise of a radio out of control.[1] A street car clangs its way along among the pushcart peddlers and their customers, and a moment later an elevated train roars by overhead. The traffic lights change and from another direction a heavy truck lumbers along spreading the dust and dirt of the street in its wake. The boys in the side street at their game of ball give way before it, but in the ensuing traffic are able in some way to continue their play. Through a nice judgment of distance and a dexterity in traffic born of long experience, they continue their game – even though at the risk of life and limb. Such is the street world with its hazards to which many of the underprivileged boys of America's largest city are exposed.

This is in part, no doubt, a description of many sections and communities in New York City; it is at the same time a picture of street life in a certain section in Manhattan which frequently has arrested public attention. From it has come many of New York's youthful gunmen and desperados of recent years. The most notorious of these have become known from coast to coast and their names have been associated with

133

organized crime of the worst forms. Murder, kidnapping, organized violence, holdups, burglary, racketeering, and wholesale bootlegging are but a part of their list of crimes. From this section of New York City have been developed several of the bootlegging organizations which at different times have sought to control the illicit business throughout the city. Up from the street-corner gangs and the racketeers' hangouts in this part of New York have graduated not only many of those who have met their end in gangland's one-way auto-rides, but also several of the more successful underworld chieftains who now live palatially on suburban estates, far from the scene of their early activities. One may well ask what are the characteristics of this community, and is it typical of many other American metropolitan communities which have made possible this unsavory record.

In some ways this section of New York City is to be differentiated from many other parts of the great metropolis in the fact that many familiar conditions are seen here in their more extreme forms. There are other sections in which poverty is found; in this community poverty and destitution appear to be nearly universal. In 1932 with a considerable portion of the heads of families unemployed, the resources of the many social agencies in the area drained, and the undernourishment of children reported to be increasing,[2] poverty and its ravages can be seen on every hand. A very large proportion of the people are unskilled workers: street cleaners, dock hands, truck drivers, milkmen, pushcart vendors and day laborers of every sort.[3] As unskilled workers they are often employed irregularly and their wages – even when employed – are small. Almost the only type of skilled labor represented among these people are the building trades, and these too are notably irregular in employment. Yet even with the larger earnings of this group sandwiched in, the average wage per week of adult males when employed was reported to be but $26.98.[4] This section has the doubtful distinction of having one of the highest infant mortality and morbidity rates[5] in the entire metropolis. Concerning it, Professor Haven Emerson of Columbia University, noted public health authority, recently said, "If New York City did not have a well operated sewage system this area . . . would be the most awful plague area in the United States."[6] In congestion and the "doubling-up" of families this part of the city also leads. Many instances can be cited in which entire families have been found living in one or two rooms and where the average number of people per room has been three and four. These people because of poverty are packed away in deteriorating "Old Law" tenements, in "railroad flats" shared by several families; and other larger and more expensive quarters in this area remain "for rent." Yet, with all the unrented property and the space devoted to small industries, foundries, and business houses, the United States Census reports a phenomenal concentration of people in these old buildings. In some of these individual city blocks over three thousand people are reported[7] to live – more people in some of these small city blocks than contained in the total population of some of the country's state capitals.

. . . The sobering records of the children's agencies and the children's court present another picture. Of all the "natural areas"[8] or communities into which Manhattan can naturally be divided this section is second only to Negro Harlem in the rate of juvenile delinquency.[9] Except for two natural areas in which the sparsity of the child population makes inconclusive any statistical calculation by individual years, the section of Manhattan upon which this report is focused can claim the doubtful honor of having the highest rate of male juvenile delinquency in any natural area with a dominantly white population. Several other sections rival it, and the other white districts may exceed it in the delinquency of girls. The community within Manhattan upon which this report is based still stands forth as an area of high delinquency challenging the best efforts of those interested in social reconstruction.

Many factors, no doubt, play a part in causing this high delinquency record. One important element certainly is the existence on every hand of conflicting and contradictory social patterns. Twenty or more nationalities or races are found among the people of this community. The largest proportion, over seventy percent, are of Italian stock while twenty-three percent of the remainder come from such countries as Russia, Poland, Austria, Hungary, and Germany.[10] Of these nationalities and races only the Finns, the Greeks, the Turks, the Negroes, and the Puerto Ricans have been increasing in number since 1910. But the largest increase between 1910 and 1920 was for those of native birth, an increase of 573 percent.[11] Nevertheless, the United States Census of 1920 reported that forty-six percent of the population were yet foreign-born and that only four percent of the people in the community were native-born of native-born parents.[12] This part of the city is clearly a "first-generation settlement" for immigrants and their families. The problems arising from the conflict of cultures, from contradictory mores and especially those involving the adjustment within the family of "Old

World" parents and "New World" children are potential difficulties in such situations.

The Boys' Club Study has already revealed that these conflicts really exist and that they are often very serious. Frequently the issue itself may seem quite trivial yet behind the immediate controversy between parents and children there exists a deep conflict in standards and practices, one which often seems impossible to alleviate. Parents, reared in the "Old World," have their own conception of the rights, duties, and filial obligations of children while their offspring, conceiving of themselves as "Americans," may look with disdain upon their old-fashioned parents with their queer "foreign" ideas. These basic differences are so universal that any number of petty situations may call forth a controversy.

. . . In such a situation a hangout and a club become a means not only for the avoidance of constant friction in the home but also a means for self-development in what may be thought of as "American."[13]

Certainly such a development is superior to some other possible adjustments. Complete alienation of members of the family and the breakup of the home often happen. If not that, a chronic state of distrust and mutual recrimination may exist within the family. The efforts of the father to bring about obedience by the time-honored method of the rod results only in more insubordinance.

. . . Out of the frequent situations of conflict and filial insubordinance in the community there apparently arises among the boys on the street an attitude of indifference toward family reproof and a feeling that their misconduct was inevitable. Possibly the exasperation of parents and the mutual inability of parents and children to see their problem objectively in the light of the non-material but very real forces of social causation may have contributed to the boys' feeling of fatalism. Certain it is that the prevalence of this type of filial insubordinance, as recounted by the boys to each other on the street, is a contributing factor to the feeling that insubordinance was somehow inevitable.

. . . A second possible factor explaining the high delinquency in this section of the city is the absence of any feeling of community consciousness or of a common bond which would cause all adults of the community to be mutually responsive to each other. Instead, we find members of each racial or nationality group in amicable relations only with each other. Adults of each group take no notice of those of other nationalities except when their interests conflict or when they wish to make sport of them. This situation in itself makes well-nigh impossible any effective community organization. In contrast to the nationality cleavages in the adult world the child on the street takes no notice of nationality heritages and racial origins. With their play contacts intensely localized to but one or two city blocks,[14] where nevertheless because of population congestion they may have thousands of possible playmates from whom to choose, children find in the social world of the streets an emancipation from the narrower nationalistic standards of their parents.

. . . The moral effect of this absence of community organization and this failure to provide collectively for the character-building and recreational facilities for childhood is nowhere seen more forcefully than in the struggle of the boy of this community for a place to play. School playgrounds are at best small and inadequate and the only other resource is a small park (without playground equipment or program) at one margin of the community and a large park some distance from the residence of most of the boys. Except for these and a recently established Boys' Club with excellent equipment, but of inadequate facilities for the needs of the entire community, there is no place except the streets for the boy to satisfy his natural and wholesome impulse to play. With a thousand or more children in many of the city blocks the competitive struggle for a chance to play becomes quite acute and many conflicts arise from the effort to take advantage of the facilities that do exist.

In K_____ Park they don't allow you in there unless you go on a baseball field. You can play on the field if you get there before somebody else. You can't play ball in the park because children are in there and if they catch you playing ball they throw you out. If you are rough – if you play ball – if you stand on the swings – they throw you out.[15]

Police officers often seem to be the only ones who are interested in the boys' efforts to play – and these interests unfortunately are negative, those of restraint or punishment. An antagonism for the police is often the result.

I hang around X street, play stickball and have some fun. I play stickball only once a week, because the cops chase us all. Donkey is the name of one of the cops. He got his head busted. Three Italian fellows threw him down the cellar. These fellows were about nineteen or twenty years old. Another cop . . . is around the block now. One night at one o'clock he chased us, but he couldn't catch us. When the cop chases us that way, the gang gets together and breaks up all the windows. They won't let us play stickball because they say we break the windows. The cop is too easy for us. He can't

catch me. When he starts after me I'll be at Y Street. Every place you play
the cop chases you away.[16]

. . . Failure to provide adequately for his recreational life results not
only in chance misconduct arising from the struggle for an opportunity
to play, but also provides an opportunity for the growth of vices and for
the invasion of commercialism into the play life of children. When
wholesome play is impossible or unsafe, gambling, smoking, narcotics,
and illicit sex activities are very often the substitute. When wholesome
play is found to be so dangerous or so regimented and restricted that it is
not immediately accessible to the boy in the community, commercialized
amusements may often be accepted as substitutes. Thus, the candy store,
the poolroom, the burlesque theater, the taxi-dance hall, and – most
significant of all – the movie may become a substitute for wholesome
play.

The relatively high frequency of attendance at the motion picture
theater, despite the poverty of most families, suggests that for many boys
in the community this is true. Significant also in this connection is the
fact that though most boys go to the movies at least once or twice a
week, only six out of a total of more than twelve thousand boys – but
one-twentieth of one percent – reported attendance at motion pictures
as a "hobby." Whitley reports that out of a group of two hundred and
seven truant and delinquent boys studied by him, whose movie attendance is in most cases once or twice a week or oftener, only six – 2.9
percent – reported motion picture attendance as "what they like to do
best."[17] His reports reveal also that of this group only forty-seven, or
22.2 percent, reported favorite activities which did not require special
space facilities. The other one hundred and sixty, or 77.8 percent of the
total group, "liked best" physical activities and games making a special
demand for space. It is clear that even though sedentary amusements
may be greatly indulged in by the boys of this community these are not
their preference and that much of the appeal which these may have
arises from the fact that congestion of population and the absence of
community organization and planning make it impossible for many to
enjoy their favorite physical activities and games.

A third factor contributing to this high rate of delinquency and crime
in the community is its long tradition of lawlessness, criminal gangs,
spectacular crime and criminals, and the intimidation of local people
who might have damaging information concerning criminal characters.

This condition also, in part, results from the indifference to community interests. But the longtime effect of a tradition of lawlessness extending back several generations contributes not only to an indifference toward community responsibilities but also toward the encouragement of crime. Where the traditions of the community include spectacular crimes and criminals, "unsolved mysteries," and on the part of the average citizen an acceptance of crime as inevitable and ineradicable it is much easier for the criminal to flourish. From a time but shortly after the community slipped out of the hands of the early Dutch burghers who settled it, the community has had a history of crime.

There used to be gangs on every block. They were the "Murphy Alleys" who came from X street between Y and Z streets and the "Black Hats" who hung around on W street between U and V streets. The World War did it for those gangs; it broke them up; and the gangs that there are now don't have any names. On U street between W and Y streets there used to be a place called the "murder stable." People walking by were in danger of being killed. It was there that one of C.W.'s (mentioning the name of one of the big racketeers and underworld chieftains in New York whose name is seldom in the newspapers) relatives was killed.[18]

. . . These patterns of crime, in some ways unique to this type of area, are nevertheless traditional in it. Yet with it all, nothing perhaps is so firmly embedded in the community pattern as the gang. In the following report by a motion picture proprietor, not a native of the community, he indicates that he too has discovered that the gang is a reality with which even the motion picture enterprise must reckon.

The children are as bad as the adults. From the time they are old enough to have friends they work in gangs. Hit one child and you have to deal with not five but fifty. We tried once to put one boy out of the theater but we had to deal with his whole gang and we now make no effort to control them. This gang rule is carried out throughout the entire strata of this society. We don't get gangs of mixed ages, ten-year-olds mix with ten-year-olds and a definite line of cleavage is noticeable between the different aged gangs.

Traditional also in this community are certain questionable institutions, illicit practices, rackets and quasi-legal ways of "getting by" to which the street boy is exposed on every hand. Among the dubious institutions are the "hangout" – sometimes a corner cigar store, a candy store, a restaurant, or a "private social club" – the speakeasy, the "fence," the taxi-dance hall and the houses of prostitution. For the younger gang the candy store or the cigar store may be a "hang out" in which some of the worst associations are established and in which many crimes are planned. Older boys may "hang out" at all-night "coffee pot" restaurants – of which there are many in the community, or, if they are more affluent at a "private" social club. For others the pool hall is the center of their social world. Here are to be found many criminal characters, many racketeers, who in this setting are in a position to transmit their philosophy of life and their ways of "getting by" to the younger and more impressionable young men.

... The "fence," an established means for disposing of stolen goods, is also an institution in the community. Whether it be a candy store which buys at a great discount cartons of cigarettes or other pilferings of young boys, or the junk shop which accepts stolen copper tubing and lead pipes, or the "fence" for jewelry or for "hot cars," the ways for disposing of stolen property abound in this community and are known to the underworld. Even the burlesque theater and the taxi-dance hall are not free from the racketeer and the gangster. Recently gangsters have been reported to be operating in the lobbies of the burlesque theaters, playing upon the gullibility of zealous patrons and pretending that they can establish for them liaisons with chorus girls for a consideration. Taxi-dance halls in recent years in New York City have become a source of revenue for the corrupt politician and for the gangster.[19] Within the past year it was revealed that a notorious gangster of this community has been receiving "a cut" from the earnings of one of the local taxi-dance halls. This establishment has been reported by investigators to tolerate the most sensual dancing of any place in the city; it is in reality a substitute for a house of prostitution. Recently through a street brawl resulting from an argument over the "cut" from this resort the community's "toughest" gangster was apprehended and convicted.

Speakeasies and bootlegging are to be found on every hand. A block by block survey of the entire district made in 1931 resulted in the location of establishments which could be identified as saloons, speakeasies, or questionable soft drink parlors. Bootlegging is such a common enterprise that it has been described as the "second industry" of the community. For many families it is admittedly the means for piecing-out an inadequate family income and for others it is no doubt the major source of income. In recent years the development of cooperative fruit growers associations on the Pacific coast, certain changes in the railroad rates for delivering grapes and other fruit to this part of New York and the increased demand for bootleggers' wine following the advent of Prohibition have made of the area a great grape-consuming and wine-producing center.

. . . Prostitution is also to be found in the community. Under some pressure and restrictions from the police it nevertheless flourishes openly on certain streets of the community. In an area in which there is so little civic pride and community organization it is to be expected that some illicit activities would be carried on openly. Actually, prostitution in recent years has been so openly practiced that the whole activity and its meaning cannot escape the attention of the boy on the street:

The special investigator and I walked along the city blocks which had been reported and found them to be almost entirely Negro. We stood for a while across the street from a tenement entrance where some eight or nine colored girls ranging in age from about 18 to 30 were openly soliciting men who passed by. The investigator had reported that when he saw this street before, these girls were soliciting boys from the school yard of a public school next door; their charge to public school clients was reported to be twenty-five cents. We saw several men accept their advances. Suddenly the girls looked down the street and disappeared hastily within the building. We looked and saw a policeman approaching. He was herding before him a half a dozen Negro boys whom the investigator said were pimps. As the officer came along he ordered people off the front stoops into their houses. When he came opposite us he asked, "What are you doing here?" We said, "We're social workers from downtown." "Well, you don't want to come around here. This is a tough neighborhood," he countered. We replied, "That's why we're here. We're watching things." "Well, you'll see plenty," he said. "This street is full of nothing but tramps and pimps." He turned then, to a rather seedy looking individual who was lounging beside us and asked, "Is this guy with you?" "No," we replied. Addressing him he said, "Well, get out of here and get out quick. We got orders to arrest any white people that we find hanging around here." The man moved on. We stayed. The men who had preceded the policeman all climbed into a car which was parked near us, but did not drive away. The policeman went on and the girls who in the meanwhile had been peering from second and third story windows, all returned to the doorway and continued as before.

Less apparent to the casual observer and yet just as much a part of the illicit activities going on in the area are the facilities for assignation. Hotel and rooming house facilities for assignation abound in the community:

The Hotel M____ [Minton] is nothing more than an open house for women of the streets to come with their pick-ups. The Hotel M____ has been on the same spot for a number of years and enjoys the reputation of being the only Hotel in the district. While it is not actually a brothel, arrangements are made by the management whereby young men who come to the hotel are introduced to "hostesses." The hotel is supervised by a youthful gentleman called Joe, but who is only a minor member in the organization. There is a very small lobby to this hotel. Directly opposite the main entrance is the stairway leading to the upper floors and to the right is a smaller room which is supposed to be the office of the manager. Before this room is a small table on which is a greasy mimeographed sheet which is supposed to be the hotel register. At the time I looked at this register there were four John Smiths and three Jones's registered. No other addresses or information were given.

While I was in the lobby several couples came in, the men signed their names to the mimeograph sheet, paid $2 to the clerk and were taken upstairs. I was in the Hotel lobby for about three-quarters of an hour and noted that of the three couples who had gone upstairs when I first came in, two couples came down shortly before I left. I was informed that these girls bring young men to the hotel, each have a definite post on Fifth Avenue somewhere, and when they are picked up by young men in cars, they bring them to the hotel. The price of the room is always $2 and the girls do whatever is mutually arranged. Since the depression, the fee has fallen from $5 to $3 to $2. In the late evening, many of the taxi-dancers bring young men to the hotel whom they have picked up in the dance hall. The girls prefer to use the hotel rather than to take the men to their own rooms or apartments. The girls usually have a system which they call $5 all around. That is, $2 for the Hotel and $3 for the girl.

Saturday nights and Monday nights are the busiest nights of the hotel. These are the nights on which a great many workers are paid off during the day. On Saturday nights, clerical workers make up the clientele and on Monday nights they are usually mechanics from neighboring plants or garages who are usually paid off on Monday. During the day there isn't much business but the hotel books as many as 200 "guests" a day and often has an income of about $3,000 a week. This may seem surprisingly large but I am assured that it is the truth. Huge sums are paid to the local police for protection as well as to the headquarters and federal men. There is no traffic in liquor or drugs, only in women. These women are free . . . and have no definite connections with the hotel. . . . The place is amply "protected."

Other facilities include the use of the "private" club or "joint," as it is sometimes called, the city parks, and even less auspicious situations. These uncontrolled activities, and the community attitudes with reference to them, have no doubt been a factor in the sex precocity of the boys and girls. Most of the boys of fifteen or sixteen who have roamed the streets for any length of time have had startling sex history. The following is not exceptional.

Case 55 suggested that he was introduced to sex by an older girl in his community. They used to meet together late at night on the stoop or go to the park. He engaged in a variety of practices with her. He also engaged in sodomy with other boys, in fellatio, in mutual masturbation and in a variety of practices of similar nature with girls.[20]

A typical experience of a young delinquent boy suggest the "unofficial" and yet traditional manner in this community in which boys of fourteen gain sex experience.

The next day we met and Steve said he knew three girls and that we could make a date with them. We said O.K. About two o'clock we went to Coney Island and first went in swimming; then about six o'clock we ate and went on the amusements and what fun we had. I did. I had some hot mama and what a shape! Her name was Clara. About 11 o'clock we came back and took them to Central Park. Tom said to his girl, "What do you say, Babe?" He took her behind the bush and started to make love. After a while we heard him say, "Come on, baby." She said no at first, but after a while she said yes and what happened is nobody's business. We then took our girls to different spots. When I was alone, I said, "Come on, what do you say?" She said "O.K." without hesitating and was I surprised. We stood in the park a half hour and then we took them home.

Another immoral pattern identified with this community is a form of rape involving more than one man. It is not only one of the most demoralizing experiences to which a young girl can be subjected but unquestionably has a deteriorating effect upon the boys and also contributes greatly to the increase of venereal disease. This practice, known in the vernacular as "the line-up," is another extra-legal institution to which many boys of the street are introduced at an early age.

I went to a show one night and I saw this older fellow Joe with a good-looking girl. He came over and said he wanted her to make believe the wrong name. He said, "Come here, I want to introduce you." So I said, "No," she was too much of a pretty girl. So he introduces me to her, he said, "I introduce you to my girl friend, Louise."

So I was shaking her hand, so she was holding my hand tight so as she would not let me loose. There was an empty seat next to her and she told me, "Come on, sit down," so I told her that I had to go some place. She was forcing me to sit down. Finally I sat down. So instead of talking to the friend of mine, she started talking to me. So he started giving me the eye, like to go away. He said, "You better go and look for your hat and coat or something. You better escape from here." So I told her, "I loaned my hat and coat to someone. I'm going to go and see if I can find it now."

So this girl called me over again and said, "You meet us later, we are going to another show. You meet us later." So I walked out after talking her into going with him and I would meet her later. So she said, "All right, make sure you be there."

So I met my friend of mine, Barney, so he said, "I got a date for to-morrow." So I said, "Give me my coat and hat, we have tonight maybe." So we saw where they went and we followed them all around and we saw them go in the show. So we went in there and me and my friend went in the place, too. They went out first and they went to X Street. The show was over, it was a quarter of twelve. So while we was looking around staying with that guy, we walked over. She saw us, she said, "Hello there." So this guy Harold was telling her, "Come on in the hall," he said. "Cops see out there, and they think something bad."

So she said, "That's all right, they won't see nothing bad." She must have been afraid, back of her mind, because the hallway was darkness, I was thinking. "What am I going to do to make her go in there." So I told her, "Hey, Louise, there's my father duck back in the hall."

So she fell for it, she ran in like she was afraid. So I said, "Come on, more in." I said my old man was coming. So while she was going in there, she was afraid to go in. She said, "What's this." I said, "Those empty rooms, stay in there."

So when she got in there, we mugged her. We put a hand around her mouth so she couldn't holler. She was, you know, like ready to holler but she couldn't holler. (The group of several men forced the girl to share relations with them.)

I went out to the hall, like, and she came out and said, "Who are you?" I said, "What do you want, I'm the janitor." I changed my voice like. So she went out and I stayed inside. I don't know what happened to her after. She went away. I felt sorry for that girl, I felt like, "Don't make no one touch her." There were nine who did it. The guy was telling me, "I know you framed her." But he was the one who wanted to have a line-up on this girl. I wouldn't do nothing. I was taking pity for the girl.[21]

Traditional patterns of crimes also exist in abundance in the community. From the filching of edibles from the pushcarts, "mugging," shop-lifting at the five and ten cent store, and "lush-diving" for the younger children, to burglary of delicatessen stores and the operation of many petty rackets for older boys, and to the more serious crimes of extortion, hold-ups and bank robberies, there exist on the streets of the community many conventional ways of "getting by" without work. For the little fellows of ten years or less there is the robbery of pushcarts. Most small urchins learn that it is possible to appropriate a handful of fruit and be gone before the peddler is aware of them. Others discover that it is possible for them to hide underneath the pushcart and manipulate the cash box without detection. Time after time cases have been revealed in which boys of ten years of age or less were introduced to petty shoplifting as an almost inevitable experience in a childhood career upon the streets. The use of a confederate to distract the attention of the clerk is early learned.

A favorite trick is to go into a candy or tobacco store, giving the impression that they intend to buy something. One of the boys curses at the owner of the store and runs out. The owner follows him. While the owner is pursuing this boy, the other boys in the group appropriate whatever articles are immediately available in the store and retreat before the owner returns.

"Mugging," as it is called in New York, is an early lesson in crime. This gang said they got their money for their street clothes by stealing market goods — today was to be tomato cans; with the money their parents had given them they went to the movies. While I was talking to a member of the group, one of their gang joined them and asked if they had seen anybody today they could mug. I asked them what that meant. One of the fellows demonstrated on another by getting a back strangle hold on him with one arm and robbing him with his free hand.[22]

Closely associated with "mugging" is "lush-diving," an art known in Chicago and other cities as "jack-rolling."[23]

I used to go after lushes (drunken fellows) and we used to take their money off them. We used to knock them cold. One guy would knock him in the chin and the other guys would hold him and then we go through him. . . . Every Saturday, we used to go out for lushes. I don't go out for them any more. I almost got caught once. This guy made out he was drunk and he was a bull. He held us. We tripped him and we started to run away and he blew his whistle. You get ten years if you get caught and I don't want to be sent up.

The young boy is also exposed to a seemingly endless variety of petty rackets which also contribute to his education upon the street. One of the most interesting forms of petty racketeering involved the "planting" of a runaway boy in a motion picture house by an older confederate who used it regularly as a means for supporting himself. After inciting the boy to become a truant, and after paying his way to a motion picture theater, where he was confident that the boy would remain, he would then approach the boy's worried family, offering to lead them to their runaway son for a consideration. Parental–child conflict and many other factors are indicated but it clearly shows also the possibilities for "childish rackets" in a street world such as this.

Q. How does he make the boy's parents give him money?
A. For catching the kids that play hookey.
Q. They don't have to pay him, do they?
A. I don't know. He used to gyp a lot of stuff and tell my mother I did it. My mother told him if you catch him you will get a lot of money.
Q. Your mother always believed him?
A. I told my mother not to believe him and not to give him any money but she went and believed him and gave him money just the same.
Q. Did your mother know what kind of a racket the colored boy was working on you?
A. I told her but she wouldn't believe me. He used to tell my mother a whole lot of lies about me and used to tell her that I was in shows and gypping in the show house and all kinds of lies. When he tells her that, she gives him money.
Q. Who told you to go away from home?
A. The colored boy. Then he went and got money for telling and so I got sore.
Q. How much did your mother give the colored boy?
A. She just took all the money she had and gave it to him.
Q. Your mother thought she should give it to him?
A. Yes, I guess so. He left me flat and snitched on me.
Q. The time he told your mother the first time, were you away from school then?
A. Yes, about two days. The first day he went home and he didn't have any money so he was sore and he went and told my mother and he got money from her for telling.
Q. How often does he work that trick?
A. Always with me.
Q. Do you know, I think you are a dope. Do you know what a dope is?
A. One that is nuts.
Q. What I mean is, you were a fool to let this boy lead you away and get you into trouble.

A. I told my mother not to give him the money, so she hit me.

Q. Why?

A. Because I told her not to give him the money. My friends were sore when they saw him bring my mother and after he left they ran after him.

Q. Why were they sore?

A. Because he snitched and made my mother pay him money. He always did that.

Q. So you got into trouble because of that?

A. Yes, and then they put me here (institution for delinquents).

From such childish escapades it is an easy transition to an older group of crime patterns, to which the boy is also exposed in this street world. The chance acquaintanceships made on the street with boys somewhat older or more experienced are enough to bring about the transition. At first these more serious crimes are engaged in chiefly for pleasure and excitement.

A week after we were with the girls we did a stick-up. Steve said he knew a fellow who used to work in an office and he was getting about $70 a week. He also said that the fellow did not know him. So Saturday night we waited for him. Finally about ten o'clock we saw this fellow come by and we followed him. When we got to a dark spot, Tommy put his hand in his pocket and said, "Stick 'em up." The guy was scared and put his hands up. Steve said, "Get against the wall with your face towards the wall." He did. I searched him and took his wallet and I took the money and put his wallet back. I also took a watch and ring. Then Steve said, "Do you see that guy on the corner, well if you make one funny move, he will blow your brains out." We then went away. I forgot to say that we stuck this guy up at XX street in the Bronx.

When we got back around the block, we counted the money. There was $70 there. We split it up. Steve started to laugh and said, "Boy! Did we fool that guy with no gun and that gag we pulled about the guy being on the corner."

Later, if persisted in, this way of "getting by" becomes so easy and satisfactory that it becomes habitual.

The following extended interview, stenographically recorded, reveals a criminal personality rather fully matured, though in this case only nineteen years old. He reveals the effect of many of these questionable institutions, patterns of crime and ways of "getting by," and much of the criminal's philosophy of life and his belief in fatality. In this instance the pool room, the local ways of burglary, the common practice of "playing" (exploiting) homosexuals and the maintenance of a mistress with the money gotten from crime are all clearly delineated.[24]

Q. How long were you up at the home (institution for delinquents)?
A. Three years.
Q. How many times were you there?
A. Twice.
Q. What was the matter the first time?
A. Robbing money.
Q. What kind of money did you steal?
A. Money and jewelry.
Q. Get away with anything today?
A. That is a secret.
Q. One can keep a secret better than two?
A. I can keep it myself.
Q. What is the great secret?
A. I won't tell you.
Q. Why?
A. Secrets are to be kept.
Q. I am not an officer. Whatever you say to me – my business is purely my own – I am interested in making a study in the area that you come from – it is a good job maybe?
A. It is all right. You don't think that you can stop that stuff, do you?
Q. Why not?
A. It is in the blood.
Q. Who do you hang out with?
A. In a pool room.
Q. What do you do – think up something new?
A. Go after fags (homosexuals).
Q. How do you shake them down?
A. They bring you to an apartment and you just clean it out.
Q. How often do you get a fag?
A. (No answer)
Q. That is interesting – what do you do with most of your spare time?
A. Hang around the pool room.
Q. What was the last pinch you were in?
A. Smacking a guy around.
Q. Assault?
A. Yes, he was disturbing my lady friends.
Q. Are you a ladies' man?
A. A couple.
Q. What a man?

A. I pick them up fast.

Q. How about the movies?

A. Once a month.

Q. Who is the actor you like to see?

A. James Cagney or Edward G. Robinson.

Q. What was the last picture you saw James Cagney in?

A. "Taxi" [1932] and "Blonde Crazy" [1931].[25]

Q. How about Edward G. Robinson?

A. I saw Robinson in "Little Caesar" [1930].

Q. Did you like it?

A. Sure, I liked it.

Q. What is your ambition in life?

A. A gentleman.

Q. Yet you hang around pool rooms?

A. That is not important. Where should I go? All my friends are there.

Q. Can't you get a new set of friends?

A. I don't want to. I can control myself.

Q. That is, you limit yourself to one job a month?

A. Maybe two.

Q. What was the last job you were on?

A. Fags and drunks – sometimes you catch a store.

Q. What kind of a store?

A. Any kind. Except jewelry stores, they are a little too dangerous. Candy stores and butcher stores. They got a cash register in the back. There's a safe in the back too.

Q. Do you crack the safe?

A. Work the dial. Knock it off and work it with your hand.

Q. You are a Jimmy Valentine (a safe-breaking motion picture character of several years ago)? ["Alias Jimmy Valentine," 1928].

A. Oh, we're pals.

Q. Where do you get those ideas?

A. From the section – I was born there.

Q. Are you working?

A. I am not working as a barber now for about eight months. I started working as an electrician.

Q. As a plumber?

A. Yes.

Q. Safe cracker?

A. That is not a trade.

Q. Do you ever use soup (nitro-glycerine)?

A. Just chisel the dial.

Q. Do you use a can opener?

A. All we use is a hammer and a chisel. All you have to do is put a rubber cap on the end of the chisel.

Q. Where did you learn that?

A. You naturally find that out for yourself.

Q. Did you ever get any of these ideas from the movies?

A. No. I was born on XX street (mentioning street in heart of community).

Q. What is up there?

A. Bunch of small gangs. When I lived there they used to have shootings every day.

Q. Do you remember the first job you were on – how old were you?

A. I was about ten.

Q. This fellow that did it was older than you?

A. He was about 15.

Q. Did he live on the same block?

A. Yes, on 107th.

Q. Did any of the crowd ever rob a store in the same neighborhood?

A. No.

Q. How did they get a line on the store?

A. Walk in the candy store. The other fellows did the work and I could collect and I would be out of danger.

Q. What did you do, tell them where it was?

A. Yes.

Q. Where did you get that idea?

A. Thought about it myself.

Q. Where do you get the fireworks (guns to use when engaging in the crime)?

A. I hire it from a racketeer. Get the bullets from home.

Q. How are we going to solve this problem?

A. I don't think you will ever straighten it out, it is in the blood. You can graft the cops as quick as anything.

Q. When did you first learn of this?

A. When I was a kid.

Q. How old were you?

A. When I started going to school. My mother let me free on the streets.

Q. Did you steal off pushcarts?

A. No.

Q. What did you start at?

A. I started out with the big fellows.

Q. What would they do?

A. They would grab hold of a guy and throw him into the cellar or in the hallway and frisk him.

Q. Do you remember the first time that you ever got mixed up in anything – where did you get the idea?

A. Hanging around with the fellows.

Q. Can you describe the situation?

A. When I was a kid I used to hang around with the fellows – we used to need money – the big fellows used to grab hold of somebody.

Q. Do you remember the guy that used to do that?

A. Yes, we all used to do that.

Q. Who was the guy?

A. One of the fellows.

Q. Was he older or younger than you?

A. Older.

Q. Did you hang around in his crowd?

A. Only when I was broke.

Q. Then you would hang around with them?

A. I used to use my head.

Q. What do you mean by that?

A. When I was broke I used to get money from them. I would go with them and I would stay outside and then when they got any, they would split with me.

Q. Got a girl?

A. Yes, I am keeping company.

Q. Does she know what you are doing?

A. Yes, she thinks I am a barber.

Q. What do you dream about?

A. Women.

Q. What kind of women do you dream about?

A. Women you pick up and lay.

Q. You are quite a lay artist?

A. Yes, three or four times a week.

Q. Did you ever get blown (fellatio)?

A. No, just let them get their head down, and then push them back.

Q. Are you keeping a woman?

A. Yes.

Q. Whom do you live with?

A. I live with the woman.

Q. Where did you meet this girl you are living with?

A. Walking along the street.

Q. Does her family live in _____ (mentioning name of community)?

A. She is married and divorced.

Q. Did she use to live there?

A. Yes.

Q. Is she working?

A. No.

Q. You are her support?

A. I am her sugar daddy.

Q. How many rooms has she?

A. Two rooms.

Q. Whose furniture?

A. It is a furnished room house.

Q. What do you pay for it?

A. Eight dollars a week.

Q. How do you manage to keep these two girls from knowing about each other?

A. One is steady company.

Q. You mean you take your steady company to the movies and then go and get the other one and lay her?

A. Sure, leave her and take it out on the other one.

Q. Do this girl's parents know you have a woman?

A. No, but the girl knows it.

Q. What does she think about it?

A. She doesn't say anything. She knows better.

Q. What would you do if she did?

A. I'd just tell her to be on her way. I told her if she saw me out with another woman to keep her mouth shut. "What I would do to another woman, I would not do to you." She knows what I mean.

Q. Suppose one of the other guys might force your girl sometime?

A. His mother would not recognize him after I got through with him.

Q. How long have you been going with her?

A. Quite a while.

Q. Are you going to marry her?

A. Yes, it is all set. I'm looking for a job.

Q. What do you do in these times of depression – if you roll a lush you won't find much?

A. If you are short, just go out again. No matter how much they got they never have enough. If you walk around with a thousand dollars in your pocket, that's not enough – it is in the blood, you can't get rid of it.

Q. Your father and mother are not living together?

A. No.

Q. You have a younger brother?

A. A younger brother and sister.

Q. What do they do?

A. One is working and the other goes to school.

Q. Have they gotten into any trouble?

A. No, I see to it that they don't. When my brother is working I know he is out on the street. I just watch the other one, she is only a little kid.

Q. Your mother was always pretty good to you?

A. Yes – if she was a little stricter, I would have been different.

Q. Does she think that she is strict?

A. No.

Q. You know that she isn't?

A. If my father lived with us I would not be that way. I watch that the others don't go wrong.

Q. How would you like to move away from _____ (mentioning name of community)?

A. I would only come back – I was in the country – I was only up there five days – I grabbed a car and came back.

Q. What was the matter?

A. Lonesome – if I had four or five fellows with me it would have been different.

Q. When you marry, how are you going to raise your family?

A. The right way.

Q. Where are you going to live?

A. In the Bronx – go to some place where it is country-like.

Finally, concerning the patterns and traditions which contribute to delinquency in this community, it may be suggested that there has existed for some time a community-wide fear of giving identifying information concerning local lawbreakers and their activities. Among some of these criminals there is the feeling that they have the right to intimidate and "punish" for "squealing" any in the community who cooperate with police and courts. In this way the common indifference toward community interests is abetted by an omnipresent fear of the consequences. These attitudes provide the delinquent and the criminal with a sense of virtual immunity for his offenses and at the same time impede seriously the work of officials in apprehending and convicting wrong doers.

. . . A fourth major factor contributing to juvenile delinquency in this community is the wide disparity between the standard of living and material ambitions of the younger generation in the community. . . . While possessing standards of living commensurate with those of all American youths, they are handicapped in the economic world by limited educational opportunities, a limited cultural heritage, and with few opportunities for ready entrance upon occupational careers which promise sufficient financial return. On every hand they often find themselves blocked by subtle yet very difficult barriers which they must surmount. The popular prejudice against those of Italian extraction, the natural selection of those who have "family connections" and the usual preference for those who seem "cultured" in the traditional American conception – all provide hurdles difficult for even the "bright" young man from this community to surmount.

On the other hand there are in the neighborhood many opportunities for immediate entrance upon illicit activities which promise an immediate reward which far exceeds anything which could be anticipated from legitimate employment. Bootlegging, racketeering, and several other forms of crime provide these. Further, virtually the only people of affluence seen in the community, to whom the youth can look for his stimulus to ambition, are the bootlegger, the racketeer, and the politician. They are the ones who have the "fine cars," the palatial homes in the suburbs, the beautifully gowned women, and the other conspicuous signs of wealth. Also, the reputed immunity of many gangsters and criminals from any serious difficulty with the law indicates to many a youngster that, after all, success as measured in our money-shaped society can most certainly be obtained by the road of the gangster and the racketeer.

The ease with which considerable money can be secured through crime is no doubt significant in inclining the young boy toward such activities. Where the boy has been bound on every hand by poverty which has made it impossible for his parents to provide him the spending money which they might have liked to have provided him, and when the boy is in a community in which everything which he may want – very nearly – can be gotten only through the possession of money the impulse to follow unlicensed channels in securing it is most strong.

. . . Finally, it is clear that another major cause of juvenile delinquency in this community is the unsupervised boy life on the streets, with the contacts and the experiences it is possible in this way for the boy to have.

Most families in the community are without adequate income, are crowded together into small quarters, and do not have the means or the opportunity for supervising their children's play. Hence it has often been impossible even for thoughtful parents to do anything but turn their boys out upon the street. Here the boy is exposed to the chance associations and experiences which may be his lot. Although parents may do their best to maintain some knowledge of the experiences their boy is having upon the street, other necessary adult interests and the evident inability of parents in this polyglot community to learn quickly the character and reputation of their son's playmates make this impossible. Even if the effort is made to enroll children in the activities and programs at present sponsored by non-sectarian character-building agencies – such as the social settlement houses and the Boys' Clubs – there is no great assurance that this will prevent the establishment of questionable associations. The limited time per week which these activities require and the rather superficial contact which these agencies and their staffs are able to have with individual boys limited greatly their value. And while these activities no doubt often serve to direct the interests of boys toward wholesome channels it is sometimes possible for the ties established by boys as incidental to a program of supervised recreation to result later in delinquency.[26] Adequate supervision of the boy's play life and his associations is seldom provided even in organized recreational programs and most certainly is never to be found upon the streets of this community.

In the street world of the boy are to be found "toughs," petty criminals, many individuals personifying an anti-social attitude toward life; but most important, perhaps, is the fact that in the street world of a community of this type is to be found the boys' gang in its natural habitat.[27] The street world provides the boy a social milieu in which "ganging" is encouraged and in which the patterns of crime can be most easily acquired. Says Thrasher:

Crime and delinquency never exist or develop in a social vacuum. They are always part and parcel of the delinquent community, which is extensively organized and characterized by a high degree of social contagion; and this in turn is organically and functionally related to the community in general. The child's life is group life and group life is a part of the juvenile community which is indigenous to the streets and alleys of these sections. It is in these areas that juvenile rackets flourish and a variety of mercenary types of juvenile delinquency are discoverable. Hold-ups of young children by older children, snatching pocket-books, purloining merchandise from trucks and railroad cars, "junking," and petty stealing of food is traditional. "Mugging" for money to go to the movies, robbing drunken men, and petty blackmailing abound. . . .

This juvenile community serves as a sort of social incubator for delinquency and criminality. We are not dealing with individuals in these areas, but with members of groups, with groups, and with a complex of social influences – a social milieu. Here there is a high degree of social contagion.

Attitudes of independence, cynicism, disrespect for law and authority are common. These are quickly propagated so that the whole juvenile community is more or less infected and certain types of personality patterns well adapted to the development of delinquent careers are inevitably the result. Here delinquency itself becomes traditional, and knowledge of the technique of crime is acquired from close contact with all the types of social demoralization and organized crime which flourishes in such areas. All children in these districts do not become contaminated, it is true, and many of them succeed in surviving these influences; yet the wholesome influences which are present are often thwarted and large numbers of boys succumb to this process of social contagion. . . . It is in such areas that the juvenile gang and the gang in general flourish. . . . For the child, it is the life on the street, experience in the gang, and the general background of the demoralized juvenile community which lead to the development of criminality and crime careers.[28]

. . . Another very significant aspect of the boy's street world contributing to his delinquency is the possibility for him at any time to move quickly from one social group to another and to become wholly different personalities in these different groups. Merely by moving from the play group in one city block to that on the next it is possible for the boy in this community to become, if he chooses, a different type of person. On his "home block" he may for a time be known as a wholesome, well-mannered boy, yet on another at the same time be a predatory young gangster, or even a major criminal. As long as the individual is not so unique in appearance or dress or manner as to focus attention upon himself, he dissolves into the crowd and becomes but one of the thousands of street arabs who obstruct the streets.[29]

In this situation of *anonymity,* as it is often termed,[30] is to be found a major factor explaining not only the unusually high rate of emotional instability among the boys of the area,[31] but also the community's record in delinquency and crime. From the earliest offenses the child is presented with the opportunities which anonymity presents. In an interview with a young delinquent, conducted as a part of this research, the boy was asked his reactions to his father's whippings for "robbing" from a pushcart in front of his home. He replied, "Oh, I was a dope (fool) before that, I didn't know better. But after my father licked me I just went around the corner to do my robbing. Around on XX street they didn't know where I belonged, so it was easy." More often this condition is not so clearly seen by the boy, but exists nevertheless.

Q. Didn't you ever gyp (steal from) the pushcarts after that?
A. No, I never gypped after that.
Q. Why not?
A. Because the pushcart guy saw me and I didn't want to go back.
Q. What did he do?
A. He couldn't do anything, he didn't know where I lived.

The condition of anonymity is also implicit in the almost universal tendency of street boys in the community to use aliases, even though they are in no way in fear of the police. It is reported[32] that boys often have a different alias for each of the several social worlds in which they may move. These practices and the opportunities for engaging in dubious activities with only a relatively small chance of detection seem also to create in the minds of the boys a "sportsman's attitude" toward misconduct. For them it comes to be that it is not the misconduct which is reprehensible, it is "getting caught" which is to be condemned. To most of these boys of the street the use of skill and astute planning makes of the avoidance of detection in misconduct a thrilling "game." Whether it be serious felonies or childish venality this same "practical" viewpoint of the "good sport," the risk-taker, seems to be the natural result of this condition of anonymity.

We all play hookey. Everybody plays hookey. There is not one guy in this school without playing hookey. Let me see a guy staying in school ten years without playing hookey. Sometimes I fool around and have some fun; sometimes I go out to see a show; sometimes I go up in the Park; most of the time I go to a show. If you play hookey every day you get a summons and get put away; that's impossible to play every day. . . . I would play it every day if I wouldn't get put away. Oh, once in a while I go with my friends. Sometimes I go alone; sometimes I make up my mind that I don't want to go to school. I sometimes go with my friends where they want to play. If my old man finds out I get a beating. If he don't find out I get away with it. He finds out because the truant officer comes over to the house. Then he comes down from work and I get a shellacking.

The preceding description of the community, with the emphasis upon five aspects which seem to contribute toward delinquency and crime, is but a partial account of the characteristics of areas of high delinquency. With it can be correlated the results of other social research upon delinquency areas, notably the work of Clifford R. Shaw and his associates of the Illinois Institute for Juvenile Research. Taking their key suggestions from the work of Burgess,[33] Park,[34] and McKenzie,[35] Shaw and his associates have made exhaustive studies of the delinquency areas of Chicago[36] and of some other cities and have developed the "delinquency gradient" as a measurement of delinquency rates in different sections of the city structure.

... Another effort of sociologists to explain the concentration of crime, gangster activities, and other social ills in certain sections of the city is found in the research work upon the "interstitial area," as these areas of deterioration have been called. This research takes its roots in the study of the gang and its habitat by Frederic M. Thrasher. It was in this project that the areas of crime and of gangs in the city were first seen as interstitial areas.

The most important conclusion suggested by a study of the location and distribution of the 1313 gangs investigated in Chicago is that gangland represents a geographically and socially interstitial area in the city. Probably the most significant concept of the study is the term *interstitial* – that is, pertaining to spaces that intervene between one thing and another. In nature foreign matter tends to collect and cake in every crack, crevice, and cranny – interstices. There are also fissures and breaks in the structure of social organization. The gang may be regarded as an interstitial element in the framework of society, and gangland as an interstitial region in the layout of the city.

The gang is almost invariably characteristic of regions that are interstitial to the more settled, more stable, and better organized portions of the city. The central tripartite empire of the gang occupies what is often called "the poverty belt" – a region characterized by deteriorating neighborhoods, shifting populations, and the mobility and disorganization of the slum. Abandoned by those seeking homes in the better residential districts, encroached upon by business and industry, this zone is a distinctly interstitial phase of the city's growth. It is to a large extent isolated from the wider culture of the larger community by the process of competition and conflict which have resulted in the selection of its population. Gangland is a phenomenon of human ecology. As better residential districts recede before the encroachments of business and industry, the gang develops as one manifestation of the economic, moral and cultural frontier which marks the interstice.

The city has been only vaguely aware of this great stir of activity in its poorly organized areas. Gang conflict and gang crime occasionally thrust themselves into the public consciousness, but the hidden sources from which they spring have not yet been understood or regulated. Although their importance in the life of the boy has sometimes been pointed out, the literature of the subject has been meager and general. This region of life is in a real sense an *underworld*, through whose exploration the sociologist may learn how the gang begins and how it develops, what it is and what it does, the conditions which produce it and the problems which it creates, and ultimately he may be able to suggest methods for dealing with it in a practical way.[37]

Thrasher, in a recent publication, explains further the importance of the "interstitial area" or "delinquency area" and indicates the importance of a crime prevention program in these communities.

While each individual case of delinquency may be dealt with through the study of the peculiar organization of factors responsible for its development, studies of numerous cases reveal . . . typical conditioning factors in the local environment of the delinquent which have significant causal relationships to the development of delinquent personalities and the commission of delinquent acts. . . . It is these factors of the environment to which the sociologist directs his attention in formulating the more fundamental and basic attacks upon the problem of mercenary crime at its roots. . . .

In whatever way we may account for the concentration of high delinquency rates and the beginning of delinquent careers in these typical areas, the fact of this concentration cannot be controverted. It is in these characteristic areas that crime breeds. They are moral lesions, so to speak, in the structure of the community and although they contain much that is good and wholesome, it is upon their conditions of criminal infection that attacks and programs for crime prevention must be focused. . . . Such programs tend to lie in the direction of crime prevention through dealing with criminal careers at their inception and in their early stages and through modifying social influences by programs of neighborhood planning and community organization.[38]

The challenge which this type of community condition presents suggests the rise of a new type of "frontier" – the urban frontier. With the disappearance from our western plains of the zone of inadequate or ineffectual social organization and control at the margins of our civilization – which made possible the "bad man" of a former era – Thrasher suggests that a new frontier – an area of ineffectual social control – has grown up in the interstitial areas of our cities.

Borderlands and boundary lines between residential and manufacturing or business areas, between immigrant or racial colonies, between city and country or city and suburb, and between contiguous towns – all tend to assume the character of the intramural frontier. County towns and industrial suburbs which escape the administrative control and protection of the city government and whose conditions of life are disorganized, as in the case of

West-Town, develop into appended ganglands. The roadhouses, fringing the city, and those occupying positions between its straggling suburbs, represent an escape from society and become important factors in maintaining the power and activities of the gang.[39]

In the careful, painstaking analysis of the forces and influences in these interstitial areas – these "urban frontiers" – and in systematic experimentation in programs of community organization and in crime prevention in these areas is the only way in which the problem of crime and juvenile delinquency can be effectively handled. Further, if we would seek to ascertain the influence and role of any one possible factor in delinquency in this community, such as the motion picture and the motion picture theater, the problem can only be handled by studying it in its relationship to all other contributing factors and influences in the community. If we would avoid the "social vacuum fallacy,"[40] so prevalent in much sociological and psychological research, it is necessary that we see the motion picture and the motion picture theater in the proper relationship to all the other forces and influences which bear in upon the delinquent boy in these areas of high delinquency.

Part Two: The Motion Picture Theater – A Community Institution

In the New York City community under study there are fifteen motion picture theaters. These range from a rather large and somewhat luxurious theater, built fifteen years ago, to several dilapidated store compartments which have been converted into cheap "movies." These the boys inconsiderately, though with a measure of veracity, label as "dumps." The attitude of the boys toward these "dumps" is such that a great many will not frequent them, or at least will not admit to others that they attend. In a preliminary study of motion picture theaters in this area a former graduate student writes:

Varying concomitantly with the cost (of admission) is the degree of comfort in seating, expense in lighting, lessening of noise and confusion by carpets, drapery, curtains, etc., and supervision and behavior of patrons, the type of ventilation, recency in release of picture, efficiency in sound or talking picture equipment, and additional features in program including acts. Although there is no scale set up in the boy's mind as to just what he can or will pay for any combination of these features there is a minimum standard below which he thinks he cannot fall and still keep his status in his group. The theaters in the area of study which do not possess these minimum requirements are known as "dumps." If a boy had only a dime, could not supplement it, and knew that a "good picture" was playing at one of "the dumps" he would probably go to see it, but would probably go alone rather than ask any of his friends to go with him.[41]

Only two of these fifteen theaters supplement their photoplay program with vaudeville acts. While several of the better theaters in the area have photoplays but a month or six weeks after they appear on Broadway, most of them are from six months or a year behind in their offerings.[42] Although there is some opportunity, no doubt, for selection of photoplays by the local exhibitors, a study of the offerings over a three year period gives the impression at least that the local movie diet is about the "mine run"[43] issued from Hollywood.

. . . Certainly the motion picture theater proprietors in this community, as well as elsewhere, have been greatly concerned in reaching as many potential patrons as possible. Nowhere else, perhaps, is the drive for maximum profit in a business seen more clearly than in the advertising and publicity concerning "coming attractions." The use of "trailers" of forthcoming photoplays as advertising in the theater program, the advertising and movie reviews in the local newspapers, and the special advertising in the theater lobby all reflect this extreme commercialization. Lobby displays are adapted to the type of photoplay being featured and to the type of community. A crime picture may be ballyhooed in part through the use of a stiletto, a hangman's noose or a replica of an electric chair established in the theater lobby. A dismantled airplane and an exhibit of guns and hand grenades may call attention to the public that the photoplay being exhibited is a "war picture." A lurid drinking scene painted over a large expanse of beaver board showing young girls in suggestive poses may be used to indicate to those outside that the photoplay is of a "sexy" nature. Even a loud-speaking amplifier attached to a revolving phonograph record may ballyhoo the merits of the current attraction to passersby.

In it all the motion picture proprietor is clearly studying his "box office" returns and his clientele and neighborhood to see what types of photoplays are the most profitable for him to exhibit. A series of interviews conducted with proprietors in the area of special study revealed that this interest was present to a striking degree. One proprietor was quoted as saying:

These people are a restless type; they go to the movies to see action, and plenty of it. Give them thrills and these boys will imagine themselves as actors.[44]

An investigator in summarizing his observations and his interviews with proprietors reported:

Most of the proprietors agreed that the gangland pictures drew the greatest number of juveniles. . . . It is the opinion of several managers that the young boys prefer this type of picture because the stories are recurrences of activities in their own environment. These youngsters hear of the doings of the local "big shots" but seldom see them at work. Therefore, the movie satisfies their wishes.

The second choice of the youngsters, in the opinion of some managers, is the sex picture. Advertisements are often "played up" in such a manner that the public gets the impression that a very bad and immoral picture is being shown, one that deserves to be censored. The natural tendency is to see it before the "cops" come along and close up the theater. Boys may be young in years but they are old in experience. They are frequently known to have illicit relations with the opposite sex. Immorality is quite popular and the boys prefer pictures that have a snappy sexy story.[45]

A poll among the proprietors of the photoplays of recent years which have proved to be of the greatest value, from the box office point of view, reveals the following as the exceptional productions.

"Little Caesar" [1930]
"Alias Jimmy Valentine" [1928]
"Underworld" [1927]
"Cimarron" [1931]
"Taxi" [1932]
"Skippy" [1931]
"All Quiet on the Western Front" [1930]
"Up for Murder" [1931][46]

To attract the passersby there are many "catch-lines" and illustrative colorful drawings placed in theater lobbies and in newspaper advertisements. The following "catch-lines" are but a listing of some of those which have actually been used in this community during the past three years.

"Gang War" [1928], Beware Gang War is sweeping nation. The story of the greatest drama ever told!
"Gun Runner" [1928], Romance! Thrills! Drama! Suspense!

"Why Girls Go Wrong" [1929], Who is to Blame? Is it the Girl? Is it the Boy? Is it the home?

What does the Traveling man do after he kisses his wife good-by?

One Wife against Six Blondes.

She Stopped at nothing – the shockingly real drama of a modern girl.

Promised a Palace – she wound up with two rooms and a baby.

She made herself a present of a past!

Married Just Enough to make her Interesting!

Hot Stuff.

A Shady Reputation was all this Wall-flower Needed to Blossom Out!

When she loses her heart, a man loses his head! Lock up your husband! Barricade your boyfriend! But don't miss her technique – its unique!

Its New! It's Original! It's Different! It starts with a bang as Madame loses her dress! It leaps into high as her lover hires a sin-thetic wife! It reaches an amazing climax amid the love gondolas of Venice! It's peppery in Paris! It's intimate in Italy! Which all means that it's Hot Cha in the Good old U.S.A. Snappy as a French Magazine.

"Naughty Baby" [1929], She's got this! She's got that! Oh Boy what a girl! She's got a million dollars worth of It!

"Private Life of Helen of Troy" [1927], You couldn't keep a gal like Helen under cover. She burned right thru the pages, etc.

"Marriage by Contract" [1928], When a companionate wedded wife finds her husband with another woman, what can she do????

"Black Butterflies" [1928], They're everywhere! Chasing life's gilded pleasures, burning up the nights, mocking at marriage rights, scorning the rules of the conventionals!

"Stolen Love" [1929], petting and forgetting, loving and living – chasing the mad Gods of pleasure thru a seething whirlpool of unrest – the youth of today, etc., etc.

"Nothing to Wear" [1928], drama of a woman who never had enough clothes to wear and had to start to a ball in her teddies.

"The House of Shame" [1928], Husbands, would you sell your wife for money. Wives, how far would you go to save your husband?

"Fighting the White Slave Traffic" [1929], Learn how to protect yourself from this great danger.

In addition to the ballyhooing devices which the proprietor himself or his employees can develop, most exhibitors are assisted by many free suggestions offered in "press sheets" ... as to how to "exploit" the picture in the local newspapers and by other means. Also, in instances where a chain of theaters is owned by one company, the advertising men of the company often send out confidential suggestions upon how to ballyhoo the coming attractions. The following are two such suggestions received by proprietors in the area of study and acted upon by them. These are not exceptional illustrations but serve merely to illustrate the type of suggestions being received constantly by individual proprietors.

Get over the hot-love flavor of this thrill-romance, and you'll be hitting in the right direction for the big grosses. And with Lupe Velez to sell as the principal exponent of this peppery brand of the kiss-business, your campaign should be a pleasure. . . . There are ample scenes of Lupe whose high position as a queen of scorching love is well known to all movie fans, in love poses with Melvyn Douglas, whose handsome and arresting masculinity were made apparent in Gloria Swanson's "Tonight or Never" [1931].

Use these displays as teasers, two or more a week in your program. Send me a copy of the program each week.
_____(Advertising adviser's name signed)

DO YOU FEAR SEX?
. . . You'll learn about the riddle of sex on our Screen TUESDAY, WEDNESDAY and THURSDAY, April 5th, 6th, and 7th.

Learn the real Dangers of Sex . . . that lead to the STREET OF SORROW [1927] . . . TUESDAY, WEDNESDAY and THURSDAY, April 5th, 6th and 7th!!!!!!!!!!!

The Octopus called Sex rears its grisly head . . . along the Street of Sorrow! . . . Watch for it TUESDAY, WEDNESDAY, and THURSDAY, April 5th, 6th, and 7th.

GRETA GARBO will be here soon! This time it will be a story of vice and poverty and redemption! You'll understand what folks see thru lust and gin-filled glasses. WATCH FOR THIS SENSATIONAL SEX DRAMATIC SMASH coming to the REGUN screen TUESDAY, WEDNESDAY, and THURSDAY, April 5th, 6th, and 7th!!!!!!!!!!!

LEARN THE TRUTH ABOUT
SEX
Take a trip through the STREET OF SORROW where the end of the lane is but a stone's throw away!

SEE GRETA GARBO
the idol of millions
In a tremendous
melodrama of

a beautiful
woman
DRIVEN
TO WALK THE
STREETS BY
POVERTY and WANT!
Here's the type of dramatic
Screen Drama that will hit
deep . . . and many times close
to home! Thru gin-filled
glasses promises of today
look rosy . . . but there is
that TOMORROW that trails
close behind . . . with the
menacing fingers of Destiny . . .
clutching . . . grasping . . . ever
reaching out to DESTROY . . .
to KILL . . . TO MAIM . . .

STREET OF SORROW . . . will be
offered on our screen
<u>TUESDAY, WEDNESDAY</u>
<u>and THURSDAY</u>
APRIL 5TH
6TH AND 7TH!

DON'T MISS THIS UNUSUAL SEX
PICTURE. It's SENSATIONAL!!!!!
IT'S THE TRUTH ABOUT SEX.
Children under 16
Will Positively
NOT
Be Admitted!!!

These catch-lines, these emphases in advertising, no doubt make profit for the movie interests. Inevitably they must stimulate also toward a sexual interpretation of motion pictures and toward a morbid interest in murder and crime on the part of young people. Such influences and conditionment are no doubt factors in contributing to the sexual precocity and the indifference to wrong-doing frequently observed among young people today. It is clear that for many of the young boys upon the streets, whose sex attitudes – even though unwholesome – are nevertheless quite common, the suggestive pictures and phrases found on lobby posters have a definite effect. Cases are on record in this research in which such lobby displays have served as a stimulus to masturbation and to mischievous sex play among boys and girls. However, the following instance, reported by Dr. Whitley in his study, is typical of the more immediate sexual stimulation which more certainly results and which *may* or *may not* result in sexual activity.

At X street there was a movie showing a picture entitled "Unguarded Girls" [1929]. A very suggestive scene was displayed in the photos in front of the show. Above the sidewalk hung a sign, reading to the effect that a professor would deliver a talk after every performance. Vito and his friend did not notice the poster at first, but suddenly it caught their eyes. Vito said, "What's this?" He and his friend walked over and examined the picture shown on the poster. They came back to me and did not say anything about the poster at that moment. Later Vito walked over to the picture again. Then he said to me, "Say, they are showing dirty things in those pictures, aren't they?" A few minutes later he said, "Those pictures get me hot."

That the boy is, in any case, greatly attracted to the motion picture theater is born out in the data upon frequency of attendance which have been collected. Second only to the time spent in the home, in the school, and on the street is the time the boy spends in the movie. Among the questions upon motion pictures submitted in various questionnaires to groups of boys in the community was one phrased, "How often do you go to the movies?" Their replies to this question were tabulated in such a way as to eliminate duplicate replies from the same boy on the several questionnaires[47] [see Table 1].

It will be noted in the table that the "normal" motion picture attendance of *once* or *twice a week* is reported by 79.7 percent of the Boys' Club group and by 74.6 percent of the non-Boys' Club members.[48] . . . The replies were tabulated with references to the active and past affiliation of each boy to a large non-sectarian Boys' Club active in the community. It will be observed that the great preponderance of the boys report that they attend the movies once or twice a week, that less than one percent report that they "never attend the movies," and that the Boys' Club members exceed the non-Boys' Club members in attendance of commercial movie houses.

In the program of this Boys' Club the question may well be asked whether these motion pictures, instead of preventing the boys' attendance at commercial movie houses, may not actually stimulate it. More

Table 1. Frequency of Attendance at Motion Picture Theaters by Boys' Club Members and Non-Boys' Club Members

	Number			Percentage		
	Boys' Club Members	Non-Boys' Club Members	Total	Boys' Club Members	Non-Boys' Club Members	Total
Four or more times per week	57	22	79	4.2%	4.5%	4.3%
Three times per week	137	26	163	10.1%	5.3%	8.8%
Two times per week	455	118	573	33.6%	24.2%	31.1%
Once a week	627	246	873	46.2%	50.4%	47.3%
Three times per month	8	4	12	0.6%	0.8%	0.7%
Once or twice per month	45	39	84	3.3%	8.0%	4.6%
"Seldom," "often" etc.	18	9	27	1.3%	1.8%	1.5%
"Never"	9	7	16	0.7%	1.4%	0.9%
Information not given	0	17	17	0.0%	3.5%	0.9%
Total	1356	488	1844	100.0%	100.0%	100.0%

important for this study is the fact that 78.4 percent of the whole group of 1844 boys report the "normal" motion picture attendance of *once* or *twice a week*; that as many as 13.1 percent report the excessive movie attendance of three, four or more times per week; and that but 16 out of these 1844 boys report that they "never attend the movies."

If these data for this large sampling of individuals are converted into the average frequency of motion picture attendance per year and into the total average time per year spent within the commercial motion picture house, the educational significance of the "movie" immediately becomes apparent. For the net group of 1784 boys who report some movie attendance and who give estimates which can be treated quantitatively[49] the *average* frequency is 83.4 times per year.

. . . Inasmuch as the typical motion picture program is at least two hours in length it may be said that the average boys in the community, according to their own testimony, spend a minimum of at least 166.8 hours a year in the commercial motion picture theaters. If it is remembered that boys very often remain to "see the show over" it is clear that this average is too low and that a more satisfactory figure could be at least 200 hours a year, more than 22.2 percent of the annual time spent by the boy in school.[50] Even a brief consideration of figures of this type make more obvious the fact that the commercial motion picture theater is of profound educational importance to the community. It certainly has an influence, either for weal or woe, which must be recognized and dealt with accordingly.

The educational importance of the motion picture theater is also suggested by a careful examination of other significant attributes of those who either go excessively or sparingly to the movies. While the results have always been negative when attempts were made in this study to relate statistically atypical motion picture attendance to such social factors as: occupation of head of family, occupation of boy, use of public library, hobby interests, participation in the physical activities in the Boys' Club, and the number of delinquency charges preferred against the boy, certain other tabulations have proved suggestive.

Contrary to popular supposition, it could seem to be true in this community that it is the exceptional boy – and not the dull boy, mentally – who in proportion to his numbers is found most frequently to have reported excessive motion picture attendance. Conversely, for those boys who are found by standard psychological tests to be as much as four or more years behind the mental development normal for their age, there would appear to be a tendency toward reduced motion picture attendance.

. . . The most significant suggestion derived from this material would seem to be that for this community, at least there is probably a tendency for the intellectually superior boys to go to the movies excessively and for those "very dull" to go at a frequency much below the average for the community.

To many this probable trend may seem to be very surprising. Most adults do not regard ordinarily the photoplays being turned out regularly from Hollywood as being sources of intellectual stimulus. If anything, the typical commercial photoplays seem very often to be a bit bromithic, but, in the absence of more complete statistical evidence, it would seem that for a community such as this there is a strong plausibility that the motion picture productions may have genuine intellectual appeal. Particularly for adolescent boys, growing up in homes in which the "old world patterns" even dominate the boys' efforts to become associated familiarly with American ways of acting and thinking may in part have a reflection in the appeal of the motion picture. Were it possible without a question to sustain this interpretation of the data, the tremendous educational significance of the motion picture in this connection could not be questioned.

However, with the data at hand, it should be noted that there are several additional explanations which present themselves and which may equally well contribute to this apparent trend. It is possible that the excessive attendance of the brighter boys may indicate merely that because they can with better facility "take care of themselves on the street" they are given more freedom by their parents, hence, have more opportunity to attend the movies and also to earn the money by which to frequent the cinema. It likewise is possible that the superior boys are able to do their school work more quickly, and hence have more leisure with which to attend the movies. At the same time it should also be noted that this trend may be in part a product of the tendency in this community for the more intelligent heads of the families, not only to have more intelligent children but also to hold the more lucrative jobs – hence, being able to provide more "movie money" for their families. In any event, however, it is clear that the implication of these statistical data – inadequate though they are at present – is that the motion picture theaters in this community, instead of attracting the duller more phlegmatic boys tend to appeal to the superior ones, providing a special social milieu for all those who in native endowment would seem to be most promising.[51]

... Those boys who in this community attend the movies most frequently are clearly individuals of intelligence above the average of the community[52] but who for reasons other than intelligence are very often retarded in school, are often truants and delinquents and, as far as the data reveal, are somewhat higher in emotional instability. Why these types of boys are the ones who go most frequently to the movies is not entirely clear. Their attendance is an individual phenomenon not primarily influenced by family relationship. It is interesting also that only a fraction of these same boys regard the attendance at motion pictures as a hobby.[53] Their attendance, however, is no doubt in part a reflection of certain school and social maladjustments and it is quite probable that in individual instances excessive motion picture attendance creates emotional conditions and attitudes which in turn contribute to more motion picture attendance.

That the boy in this community when attending the movies is very much restricted by the offerings shown in the local theaters is revealed in a study of the attendance habits of these boys. Nearly 96 percent of a fair sampling of over 700 boys in this community report that they go to the movie theaters within the community or immediately adjoining it. Though there are 14 theaters in the community to which the boys go, many of these are very cheap affairs showing inferior pictures. Ecological studies indicate that on the average when the boy sets out for his movie he goes further than he does when he attends church or to an elementary school. While some of the cheaper neighborhood theaters draw from only a radius apparently of 2 or 3 city blocks, the larger theaters draw from a distance of 12, 15, and even 18 city blocks. It is also interesting that the ecological configuration of the community seems to be such as to induce the boy when setting out upon his motion picture venture to go in an easterly or westerly direction rather than northward or southward. This condition arises apparently because of the fact, in the first place, that the boys are of necessity pedestrians; and secondly, because this community like much of the rest of Manhattan has been organized only for facilitating major traffic movements northward and southward. Thus the boy from poor quarters can achieve the greatest social ascendancy in his choice of theaters by moving latitudinally across Manhattan rather than in the opposite directions. The significance of the boy's motion picture visits is in part that he is often forced to go through sections of the community with which he is not at all familiar. As has already been indicated the street boy in this community is to an unusual degree localized to the social world of his own city block. Trips through other neighborhoods may mean contacts with other groups of boys, invasion of the "home territory" of rival gangs and the broadening of the boy's conception of the community and of the city. It is perhaps in part because of this that the typical boy in this community when he sets out for the motion picture theater desires especially to be accompanied by others. In these movie expeditions is to be found a basis for some of the most interesting and significant experiences which the boy of this community has. These excursions hold opportunities for weal or woe, but their significance cannot be entirely seen except by reference to the social world into which the boy is introduced when he enters the theater.

In and about the local theater is a social world of special interests and values which make of it a distinct and unique experience in the life of the boy. Within the theater special contacts, special activities, and certain practices are made possible or are facilitated. In fact, the variety of special uses to which an inexpensive motion picture theater may be put is quite surprising. Frequently it serves distraught mothers as a place to "check" their small children while they are busy about other cares. They can leave them at the cinema, confident that they will remain there, held by the spell of the picture. Sometimes a local criminal gang, when they are known by proprietor or attendants, may use attendance *en masse* at a motion picture theater as a means of establishing an alibi. During cold days of the winter the cheaper theaters may even be invaded by entire families who come in the morning carrying sandwiches and remain until evening when they can go immediately to bed, thus saving a coal bill at the expense of the local cinema. These are but illustrations, but a complete inventory of the activities in the local theaters in this community would have to include everything from the "spotting" and "planting" of victims for gangland bullets to clandestine sexual activity in the darkened movie house — and even to childbirth.

While such illustrations are exceptional and only serve to show the range of possibilities afforded by the local cinemas, there are also disconcerting sights and suggestions to which the boys in the community are certain to be exposed when they go to the movies. Many of these, contrary to supposition, are to be found not upon the screen but in the conduct of others seen in the movie house. The evidence at hand seems to indicate that in this community at least the questionable or precocious ideas and suggestions gotten from the observance of the conduct of others in the cinema is often greater than that acquired from the screen. Says Whitley:

In a number of cases, the motion picture house is much more important in relation to delinquency than is the material shown on the screen. The motion picture house is generally dimly lighted. Ordinarily there are some sections of the house where few people are sitting. The house in general is one of the most convenient spots in the community, for this reason, in which boys may engage in a variety of sexual practices. Especially during daylight, there are few spots in the community where boys may engage in sexual dalliance with girls without being apprehended and punished. Occasionally the boy is able to find a vacant apartment or a secluded spot in the park, but ordinarily the boy confines his sexual activities outside the movie house to the night. As a consequence, a variety of sexual practices are observed by the boy ordinarily in the movie house, and occasionally he engages in various forms of sex activity in the house himself.[54]

The following documents presented by Whitley indicate the type of suggestions which boys very often get when frequenting the motion picture theaters of this community. In the first excerpt the childish curiosity of the young boy is clearly seen.

This boy sees fellows "fooling around" with girls in the movies. They put their hands around them. They feel around them. . . . He has seen girls sitting on boys' laps in movies. He does not know what boys do to the girls after they get them outside of the movies. "Once in awhile I put my hand around a girl, that's all. I don't like to do any more, she may squeal. Maybe get me into trouble. I would do more to a girl if she would let me. You can't tell when they will doublecross you."

This boy says that he sees bad things going on in the movies. He says that he sees boys fooling around with girls. He says that the things they do make other boys hot. He said he sees this going on in cheap theaters and in dumps.

"In the pictures you see guys necking. . . . The _____ theater is a dirty place. All the girls cursing and the guys holler, 'Hey, any chances?' After the show is over they have a good time upstairs. They are drunk nearly every night up there. Those ushers are always drunk." The boy saw a man in _____ theater handling a girl intimately. He saw "guys fooling around" with girls in a number of ways.

In a community such as this one, proprietors find it profitable to permit much free play of the emotions. As a result such conditions as described below very frequently occur, to which the boys are witnesses.

This boy says that "muzzling" (kissing) is done all over. At the midnight shows there is petting. There is a lot in the _____ Theater, on X Street and Y Avenue. The same is true of other theaters. A friend of his took a girl to the movies. He did almost everything to her. Talking about "Chinatown Nights" [1929], the boy said, "A guy owned a cabaret and there was a whore-house upstairs and there was a lot of rooms and every time a fellow was stewed he used to go up to a room, and once the guy said, "Get that damn thing out of here." The boy reported that he saw a girl masturbating a man in the movies.

Two boys observed having seen women masturbating men in the movies.

Whitley summarizes his material on this point as follows:

Eleven boys indicate that they have seen men petting women or boys petting girls in the movies. Six boys have admitted engaging in sexual dalliance with girls themselves in the movies.[55]

In the darkened theater there is also an opportunity for the individual to make contacts and to engage in activities which he would not countenance were there any probability that he would be identified. The contacts and activities may vary greatly, but they are all products of these opportunities for clandestine contacts afforded in the unsupervised movie house. It will be remembered that a document previously cited[56] tells of a contact in a theater house which resulted in collective rape. Many such instances could be offered. Sometimes the theater serves as a means for making clandestine contacts which result in sexual misconduct.[57]

The girls used to whistle at me in the movies. I used to make a date, pick up a date and I used to go in the back. I fool around with the girls in the movies. I saw men hugging girls in the movies.

Four boys indicated that they met girls in the movies and engaged in the necessary courtship there to gain their consent to engage in sexual relationship outside the movies.[58]

One boy admitted that he had engaged in the sexual act with a girl in the motion picture house. This boy also admitted that he met a girl in a burlesque to engage in sexual relationships with her there.[59]

Whitley reports also the contacts of boys with homosexuals in the movie house:

One boy told about being approached by a homosexual in a theater. Three other boys indicated that they had observed homosexuals approaching boys in the motion picture house.

The interviews which have been conducted in the past year as a part of this study reveal strikingly the frequency with which the local theater is the initial point of contact. Typical of many is the following:

Q. Did you ever run across a fag?
A. Yes, in the show.
Q. Did you ever go out with them?
A. No, I changed my seat.
Q. Did you ever run up against a fag?
A. Plenty.
Q. How often?
A. I don't know.
Q. Did you ever have anything to do with them?
A. Sure, if I got paid for it.
Q. How much would you get?
A. Whatever they had, take it.
Q. What do they do, blow you?
A. That is all.
Q. How do you feel after that?
A. I feel all right.
Q. Would you still go with them if you had the opportunity?
A. I don't know.
Q. How much did you get?
A. One or two. The most I ever got was four dollars and seventy-five cents.

The theater is so much a place for such contacts that for some, chance associates desiring homosexual contacts make it a racket to prey upon homosexuals:

Milton is unusually good looking. He told me that as a kid he made at least ten "pansy" pickups in the various local theaters. For his services, he received from two to ten dollars. Last year he thought he'd go out for "bigger fish." He made a practice of standing in the lobbies of the Broadway Theaters where he came across a finer and wealthier type of "fag."

A few days ago Julius ... told a friend that a homosexual attempted to entice him to the mens' room of the _____ Theater at XY Street, between A and B Avenues. His friend asked him if the man had any jewelry. Upon Julius' response in the affirmative _____ also wanted to know if the man was about my size. I couldn't help laughing as the thought struck me that his plan was to hire the "fag" into the men's room, "mug him" and then take the man's personal belongings including his clothes.[60]

Out of the opportunities for contacts afforded in the motion picture theater has arisen certain established practices, accepted usually by the management and recognized by all. Chief of these is the institution called the "pick-up." As a means for making acquaintanceships the "pick-up" in the local movie house is known by all young people and is utilized by many, both by men and women. This practice may be facilitated by the fact that in a community such as this, in which the latin *mores* upon the parental surveillance of young women are accepted, the mere presence of unattended young women in the cinema is often accepted as an indication of their character. At any rate the "pick-up" is so much the vogue that local theater proprietors accept it as a part of the local situation and accommodate their standards of supervision to it.

Pick-ups and petting go on constantly, the manager said. But in relatively few cases does it happen to those who do not come for it, and except in these the manager said it was the policy of the theater to ignore it. Very little occurs immediately outside the theater; pick-ups generally occur while inside the theater. For example, girls often go along in a group and then come out with a group of fellows.

There are never any serious cases in which the police have to be called in, the manager says. Either the manager himself is notified or the person changes his seat. When the ushers notice a thing like that happening, he said, they usually try to ignore it. Occasionally women police come around in search of mashers, but they are not successful. Mr. W_____, the manager, said that he very seldom gets any complaints about "annoyances." In most cases they either come for the express purpose of petting, in which case they do not disturb any one, or else if they come unattended, they are willing enough to receive attention from a stranger. He said, "The type of girl who comes to the movie, in most cases, does not say 'no' and we do not bother with those cases in which both are willing."[61]

Actually the "pick-up" is a part of the common practices of the older boy on the street. He has his own code with regard to it and in a rudimentary way he has his own conception of the "techniques" by which it is accomplished in which "having a line" and "working your points," i.e., utilizing one's own advantages in physique, appearance and accomplishments for the greatest immediate profit, play an important part.

Mary and Jane are witnessing the "silent spectacle" from "standing room only." These seventeen year old girls work six days a week in one of the Woolworth's, go to the Church of Y_____ on Sunday morning, attend their pastime in the afternoon at the X Theater, and in the evening they eat at a Chinese Chop Suey joint – if they pick up two "suckers."

Standing directly back of them are two fairly good looking local "lady-killers," Jim and Jack. They are standing in their best $22.50 suits, slick shirts and $3.00 hats. These adolescents rest their eager optics on the girls' forms.

"Whadda ya say, Jim, pick 'em up?"

"Y' betcha life," whispers Jim.

Since he's the bolder of the two he chances a grin which he calls the "magnetic smile" at the better looking of the two, Mary. Girls are girls. She lifts up her left shoulder and points her nose to the heavens. Her face seemed to say, "The idea, trying to pick me up." This was not the first time Jim attempted to "pick-up a doll." He tries again. This time she does not incline toward astronomy. She smiles at her girl friend.

The ice breaks then and there. Half the battle is won.

"Kin we help youse get seats?" suggests the young masher. This is said to start a conversation which may continue favorably or otherwise. The wise, experienced "baloney" takes it up. "How can youse do that when youse ain't got a seat yourselves," coyly parries the sweet young thing.

"It's all right," says Jim confidently with a wave of his hand, "we got a drag wid de head usher."

"Ain't dat grand!" the artful little coquette exclaims with a look of admiration toward Jim, whose chest is expanding a few inches and his head even more. Both of them know that Jim doesn't know the head usher from Socrates. But then, conversations have to begin somewhere.

The two reeler is ended and the crowd rushes in for seats. The outgoing patrons of the theater mingle with them. There is an over-abundance of disorder and confusion. The four young people seat themselves in what seems to be the darkest and gloomiest spot in the movie house. The boys place their arms around the girls' shoulders with a view to "petting."

They exchange names, addresses and 'phone numbers. After two and a half hours of "petting" they get up, all tired out. They walk to a Chinese restaurant. Then the girls are taken to their houses where "another two hour milling takes place" – in the hallway.

"I only go to shows when I gotta go wid a girl. But I won't sit where dere's a lotta people. I go way in de back – dere ain't so many people and den I kin muzzle (kiss) in peace wid de girl an' I don't have to be ashamed. Sometimes I don't even know what de picture's all about."

When I asked how he managed to "pick-up" girls in the movies my interlocutor replied, "Aw, dat's easy; I did it so many times." I asked the methods he used.

"Well," he said as we lit up, "it's like dis. I go to de show an' I walk up an' down de aisle until I spot a girl dat looks passable. I sit next to her. Den I puts my arm here (he pointed to the elbow rest) and if she don't move her arm I ask her, "You don't mind if I keep my arm like dis, do you?" Den when de pitcher comes I laugh when she laughs at the funny parts. Sometimes I offer her a cigarette an if she has a watch I ask what time it is. Den I put my arms aroun' her shoulder and I start to muzzle (kiss) her, if she lets me. Sometimes a girl is bashful or she makes out she don't wanna, but I talk nice to her an' it works."

"Do the rest of the guys work it like you?" "Dey stink. A lotta o' dem just sit nex' to the girl and dey start fooling around with their hands widout working their points. Some o' dem mopes, dey ain't got no line an' de girl calls an usher if dey gets wise."[62]

The contacts that are made in this way in these theaters run the entire gauntlet of the approved and the disapproved forms. In some instances the contacts may ripen into marriage; in other instances these contacts grow into some of the most undesirable activities.

Rosie was everybody's girl a few years ago. Then she moved away. Last week Tony P_____ met her in a movie. He was sitting next to her but didn't know it was Rosie until she spoke to him, after he had made a few advances. They talked over old times. She told him she had moved back to the neighborhood. She was willing. He took her around to XXX street and six other boys joined him. She went up a roof and the seven kids "lined her up."[63]

Actually the boys and men are not the only ones who avail themselves of the "pick-up." It is utilized by women and girls and is used for many purposes.

There were two girls sitting in the center of the row, with no one in front of them to obstruct their view. The girls were about 13 years of age, but in the dark I could not give their exact nationality. No one sat near enough to them to cause their indignation. I noticed them looking around, then changing their seats to others beside two Italian boys somewhat older. As they sat there they continually looked over at the boys, but the latter left shortly afterward, and apparently were not at all interested in the girls.

A hard boiled individual, whom the management seemed to know, was standing at the rear of the right side. A man came along – she coolly looked him up and down, and sideways, seemed to approve, nodded to him to approach. Before he did, the manager, who walks the aisles continually hushing the crowd, spied her – he came rushing up the aisle and told her to sit down, she was in the way – the man sheepishly disappeared. She was well known to the Manager; he called her by name.

Finally, it should also be noted that the unsupervised motion picture theater also makes more easy contacts of younger boys with older more matured criminals. The motion picture theater is but one of the many forces and social situations in this community which facilitate these contacts and of these the motion picture theater is no doubt less important than several others.[64] But before a judgment is reached upon this point it is necessary to note certain factors in the situation. First, that although no special effort in this research was made to consider this possibility, several instances were revealed in which initial contacts were made with criminal characters or older, more hardened boys while in the motion picture theater.[65]

Secondly, some of the case material which has been amassed reveals the operation of a certain socio-psychic process of suggestion by which boys under the spell of a photoplay depicting especially criminal exploits may find in the society of each other a dynamic for the re-enactment of what was seen upon the screen. At present there are not sufficient case materials available to substantiate fully this hypothesis interesting though it is. However, those instances which are at hand seem to indicate that under the appropriate circumstances the stimulus derived from the screen may be sufficient not only to break down some of the inhibitions and restraints of associates, but also to turn their collective thinking and their activities toward very different channels. Thus, there is a case on record in this research of two boys, one a superior boy in high school and the other a boy of normal mental ability, who after an initial period of conventional acquaintanceship discovered in each other an appetite for crime narratives which, when once stimulated by the gangster pictures, led the two of them eventually to a career of crime which eventuated in the accidental killing of one of their victims.

The role of the photoplay in conditioning some members of the theater audience toward a tolerance for unsocial activities seen on the screen and toward the entertaining of suggestions concerning such conduct received from casual acquaintance seen in the theater is most clearly seen in the following case. Although the two boys had known each other for two months they had only been casually acquainted until the evening at which they attended the cinema together. It should be noted that the writer of the following document also has indicated that he did not know of the criminal activities of his chance acquaintance, nor even suspect these until after witnessing the gangster photoplay with him.

Only two months after I met Steve we were in a show looking at a gangster picture. I don't remember the name of it but it goes like this: They were bootleggers and the big shot liked this fellow's sister and this sister did not like him, so he told her, "I am going to get even with you if you don't go out with me." He got her little brother in his gang. One day they were holding up a truck of booze and the cops made a raid and the "big shot" shot one of the cops and stuck the gun in the kid's pocket, and then the other cops came over and said, "Who did it?" They searched everybody and found the gun in the kid's pocket and took him to jail. Then the young fellow told his sister that the big guy planted the gun in his pocket and framed him and he wouldn't squeal on him. The sister told the detectives that, but the detectives would not believe her. We will leave that part pass. Now, the "big shot" is talking to the other crook; he was standing next to him when the "big shot" shot the cop. They were splitting money and so the "big shot" said to the crook, "You are not going to get half, you are only going to get a part of it." The other crook got sore and said, "If you don't give me my right share I will squeal that you shot the cop." The "big shot" said, "O.K. I will give you half." While pulling the money out of his pocket, he pulled a gun also and shot the other crook and laid him out in the gutter. The cops came and picked him up. He didn't die yet. He told the whole story how it happened and died right after. They phoned to the penitentiary and told them to stop the execution. The kid was just going to get the electric chair – it was a matter of a few minutes. Then they found the other crook and it shows in the paper how he was executed and that was the end.

I am now talking with Steve again. Steve says to me, "Do you want to make some easy money?"

I said, "How?"

He said, "We will break in joints in the night and get money out."

I says, "No, do you see what happened in the picture to that guy. It will happen the same to us."

He said, "Ahhh, the pictures are a lot of baloney."

From one word to another he said "What are you, yellow?"

I said, "No, I don't want to take any chances, I don't want to be in jail."

He says, "Don't be afraid, the way we do it we won't get caught."

I said, "I don't want to do it."

He says, "O.K., you are afraid."

From one word to another, I agreed to being in his gang and going with him. Then we pulled our first job.[66]

In this instance, young fellows under the stimulus of a gangster picture which they happened to witness together experienced a breaking down – at least temporarily – of certain inhibitions and restraints which in this case was followed by a criminal career. Whether this socio-psychic process occurs frequently cannot be said authoritatively, with the paucity of data at hand upon the question, but it is at least an interesting hypothesis which merits further inquiry and research.

Part Three: Movies, "The Enchanted World of the Street Boy"

No one can conduct interviews with typical boys of this community of special study without being impressed over and over again with the vast amount of knowledge concerning actors and actresses which the boys have. When they are asked to name actors or actresses whom they have seen in photoplays, it is not uncommon to have the interlocutor give with very little hesitation thirty or forty names. The titles of photoplays are even remembered with almost as great facility. While the material upon this aspect of the study is not at this writing tabulated, it is certain that the typical boy of this community, when interviewed about his motion picture experiences, can give information concerning photoplays, actors, and actresses and concerning the private lives of actors and actresses which far out distances that which an average adult can furnish.

With this great amount of information there has grown up among the boys on the streets of this community a certain body of pseudo-information concerning actors and actresses which in itself is but a reflection of the intense interest and intellectual significance of these actors and actresses and their photoplays in the lives of these young men. Much of this pseudo-knowledge is obviously false and if publicly stated would be just ground for libel suits. Some of these conceptions of individual actors and actresses as reported by a special investigator who moved among groups of street boys in this community are as follows:

George O'Brien is such a good prize fighter in the movies that if he went into a ring he could make professional prize fighters look sick.

Tom Mix, Hoot Gibson, Jack Moxie, and Harry Carey were real cowboys before they became "real" cowpunchers.

Charlie Chaplin is a living example of Pagliacci.

Edward G. Robinson of "Little Caesar" and "Five Star Final" [1931] fame is of Italian extraction and grew up in this community. James Cagney, who also grew up in this community, used his "dukies" (fists) to scare Jewish movie magnates into giving him a chance. The boys in this community, because they have this erroneous belief that Cagney and Robinson both are products of it, have certain pride in this fact because they believe that "two of the local boys have made good in a big way in the movies." Their conviction that these two actors are products of the local community is abetted by the feeling that their acting is a perfect depiction of styles of conduct approved among the street boys of the community.

Female stars of the entire history of the movie industry have gained favor with movie magnates by serving for a time as their mistresses.

Rudolph Valentino was not only a great Italian, but the greatest of all movie actors, and he died as a result of having too many "affairs" with Hollywood beauties.

Many of the leading actors in the movies are inverts or have unnatural sex practices which make it impossible for them to continue a marriage for any length of time. Most of the so-called "bad men" in the movies are really good in private life and vice versa.

Every star except Douglas Fairbanks, Sr., has a double who receives a low salary for work which the star cannot do or is afraid to do.

Pola Negri served as Valentino's mistress and Marion Davies is the mother of William Randolph Hearst's natural children.

Fatty Arbuckle is so physically constructed that a normal sex life is impossible for him.

Janet Gaynor, married to Lydell Peck, loves Charles Farrell and in turn he loves her though he is married to Virginia Valli.[67]

To be sure most of the boys and young men in this community do not accept all or most of these ideas, but they do reflect correctly the ideas which a certain group of boys and young men met on the street corners of the community have. The following is an illustration of many conversations which go on every day concerning these movie actors and actresses:

"Look't Clark Gable!" he continued. "Dere's a guy for you. He claims to like them old, dey gotta be at least toity years old, he don't mess around wid the young chickens. He's toity-one himself and he's married twice to women more than ten years older than him. Whaddya think he married 'em for, love? Baloney, but he ain't getting stuck, de old dames are rich and dey give him de dough and I'm sure on the side he gets his young honey when he wants it."

I asked him if he did not think that the old dames could keep him tied down.

"Naw!" my wise guy friend replied. "Dey know his nature and he treats them nice now and den and he can do whatever he wants. Dey look good when he is out with the old ladies. . . . Whaddya tink got him in Hollywood, his good looks? Baloney, it was de wife's dough."[68]

If space and time permitted it would be possible to submit a great many pages of evidence as to the extent of the general information and pseudo-knowledge concerning movie actors and actresses which are to be found among the street boys in this community.

Not only does the cinema afford these boys a basis for much information concerning the actors and actresses themselves but it is an important basis for giving to the boys in this community many conceptions of the world and of America. Particularly with reference to those realms of life and social intercourse with which they have no immediate contact and about which they have no organized knowledge is the effect of motion picture representations most clearly seen. These conceptions of "stereotypes"[69] range all the way from certain rather naive conceptions of judges, courts, college life, and racial and nationality groups to some of the more personal problems which interest the individual boy. Thus, it is found that the younger boy whose urban provincialism restricts him to a first-hand knowledge of but a small part of New York City tends to accept the belief that "The West" is composed chiefly of cowboys who ride into town Saturday nights, shooting up saloons and bars. In the same way "college" is seen as a place where the playing of football is a major interest of all.

I like men who act in pictures like collegiate pictures. I like girls that take parts as co-eds in college, like Marion Davies and Nancy Carroll. You know why I like them? Because in college pictures they show you football games, baseball games and all kinds of sports. All the games I saw that they played in the movies I played already.

I think movies help because most of my experience is what things look like in the movies. Well, now I know exactly how they run colleges. They are like in the movies. Well, I have an idea of what other countries look like. There is a lot of pictures all about different countries. There is some pictures though that teach boys bad things. There are some pictures where they show scandalous thoughts and bad ideas. When they are getting married and they have a kid they sort of leave their kid and everything. . . . We see things that are good and bad, I think movies do boys more good than harm because it teaches you so many things.[70]

What are judges like? I don't know, I never was in a court. A judge is a judge, a man who takes a place in the court, he tries to find out who is guilty, some like to tell a lie when a man is guilty. . . . I don't read about it in books. I don't read about it in the newspapers. I saw them in the movies. Yeah, I saw "The Trial of Mary Dugan" [1929], that was pretty fair. The judge gave a square deal, I mean he let the lawyer talk first.

What are lawyers like? I don't know. If anything happens, though, lawyers are with you. They are like a witness to you. First, they take you to court, so this man went, so he gets the lawyer. How did I learn this? I don't know. Lawyers were in "The Trial of Mary Dugan," two district attorneys. One district attorney killed a man. He killed this man named John Wright, then they set out to prove this lady killed John Wright. At the end it gives out the truth. The man was left handed. He shot the man left handed. Norma Shearer had a brother by the name of Jim. And Jim was a lawyer from Pittsburgh or from Philadelphia or from Canada, I don't know where from. Then after he threw the knife to Lewis Stone and they called to the guy "left handed" so the wife of this man yelled, so the lawyer said, "There's the murderer" so they arrested him and that is the end.

Q. What are the judges like?
A. He tells the court and when he sits on the stand he dismisses them and everything. He tells the jurors to go into the jury room. He tells them if he is guilty or not guilty.
Q. How did you learn about this?
A. I saw it in the movies.

Certain very definite attitudes and racial prejudices also arise from the motion picture representations. Many people are aware of the extent to which people of other lands conceive of the American motion picture as representative of life in the United States. For boys and young men growing up in the restricted world of contacts in this community, the movies also serve as a means of strengthening certain racial prejudices.

In my childhood the movies developed in me a prejudice against Chinese, Mexicans, and Indians, as they were usually all "bad men." I recall that whenever my father would take me to Chinatown I would be afraid that we could be kidnapped. If I saw an Indian in one of the side shows, I would be afraid that he would pull out a tomahawk and scalp me.

There are many factors which probably account for the exceptionally vivid impression which the action on the screen makes upon impressionable young boys. The screen with the possibility of presenting scenes not technically possible upon the stage serves in part to give to it the vitality for the young boy which the stage, by contrast, lacks. Also certain photographic techniques which are possible in the motion picture facilitate the conveying of impressions not possible upon the stage. Thus, the "close up," the "trail back" and the possibility of injecting a brief explanatory scene – to mention only a few[71] – give the cinema certain special appeals to the boy. Now, with the introduction of the "talking picture," even the restriction upon the interpretation of the photoplay arising by the necessity of reading the script of the silent play is eliminated. Thus, boys with a very limited ability to read the English language and those of low general intelligence are now able to enjoy the cinema. These motion picture representations, therefore, are now being impressed upon youth with even less native ability to understand and interpret rightly the cinema representations of life.

These typical stereotypes of the movies, it should be noted, have their greatest influence with regard to those realms of life with which the boy in this community has had no immediate experience. Being to a considerable extent a product of the street he tends to assume a role of sophistication about movies and to be rather critical of them. As soon as the typical street boy of this community has available data from the "real" world outside the movie house which would seem to contradict the photoplay representation, there is a very strong tendency for the boy to discredit the photoplay.

Thus, the motion picture representation of "The West" populated by cowboys is quickly discredited as soon as the individual boy has any data whatever by which he can discredit the movie representation. In fact, in some cases he does not wait for real data but seizes upon anything which in his urban provincialism seems to him to be pertinent. Hence, in one amusing incident a twelve year old boy who had been born in New York City and had never been beyond the limits of the Metropolitan District, when asked whether "The West" was as shown in the movies, replied, "Naw, I went away out to Irvington and it is the same out there." The same tendency toward discounting the movie representation of racial groups seems also to exist. Thus, "Chinamen" are commonly thought of by boys who know none as "having yellow skin and funny eyes, wearing pig tails and carrying knives up their sleeve which are used without immediate provocation and as those who frequently poison their enemies." But it appears that as soon as the boy knows personally a member of this race, even though it be only the neighborhood laundryman, he very readily discredits the motion picture representation. One boy when interviewed upon this point replied, "Naw, Chinamen are not like Dr. Fu Manchu. I always go to get the laundry and he gives me back my change just right every time." Among the first fifty boys interviewed by the use of the "controlled Interview Technique,"[72] no instance was found in which the boys failed at least to question seriously the motion picture representation when they were known to have available data obviously contradicting it or when general information for this group might be expected to include a basis for questioning the motion picture representations.

To boys who for the most part do not have an opportunity to become acquainted with that which is traditional American in our culture, the movies along with the tabloid newspapers seem often to be the chief means for getting acquainted with that which they consider "American," or at least that which is felt to have prestige value. Thus, the movie representations of certain characters or types in American life are accepted as true representations. Cowboy pictures, the "bold bad man of the plains" type, the rural "hayseed," the "carefree" American Negro, the profligate living of people "of means," and the caricature of the "college professor" and even the "prohibitionist" are all a part of the "stereotypes" provided by the movies by which the boys in this community think out their own problems. Significant in this connection is the definition of American life in terms of monetary success. This is an easy way for the movies to represent social achievement, but it also serves to give to these boys of this community a misconception of the true valuations characteristic of the older America.

An interesting point with reference to these stereotypes is the conception of feminine beauty and morals which apparently develops under the persistent suggestions coming from the movies and press. For boys of the racial extraction coming from southern Europe the emphasis in the motion picture in recent years upon "blondes" has seemed to be to a considerable extent a contributing factor in their attitude toward the American girl. Almost invariably there is a conception of the "blonde" as more beautiful, dazzling, and provocative; but who while beautiful is nonetheless of often questionable morals. She is a seductive person who is to be enjoyed for all she is worth, but is often not regarded as a type to marry. The "brunette" on the other hand is thought to be more virtuous and to be a "home girl" such as the boys would like to marry. From the early cinema days when the vampire was pictured as a seductive "brunette," movies apparently have changed their characterizations. The full effect of this emphasis is seen in the attitude of south European people who regard "blondes" as beautiful but faithless and "brunettes" as possessing the potentialities for deeper affection and greater honor and loyalty.

Without question, for the great mass of people the greatest significance of the movies lies in their tremendous importance in imparting information and knowledge about aspects of life with which they are not immediately familiar. The influence of the movies in this connection arises in part from the fact that the commercial motion picture as presented to young people is so gripping and so aesthetically appealing that learning takes place without effort. This is true, in part, because of the conservatism of the school. Many of those things which are most vital to the lives of young people are not included within the curriculum. In this way the movies supplement and often provide ideas and patterns which to many young people seem much more important than most of the subjects with which they are burdened in the conventional school curriculum. Thus, questions of etiquette, social amenities, style of dress, carriage and posture of the body, techniques of gaining favor with the opposite sex, even though not a part of the curriculum, often seem far more significant to young people than the conjugation of a Latin verb or even Browning's poetry.[73] Out of this fact has arisen some interesting observations. First, while the so-called "educational" movie is often so unattractive or so obvious in its educational import that it does not achieve its purpose, the typical production from Hollywood provides a form of unconscious learning which is nevertheless more important than that accomplished by the so-called "educational" picture. In the following instance, the boy indicates clearly the ineffectiveness of a typical educational film in influencing his subsequent conduct.

Q. Did you learn anything in school about what to eat?
A. Yep.
Q. What did you learn.
A. Eat milk and bread. One day I seen a picture.
Q. What about the picture?
A. It was like this – about your health.
Q. What did it say about your health?

A. It showed you a man, a man he put coffee, candy, chewing gum in his mouth. That was not healthy for him. After he did that the devil came out and he broke out his teeth, broke out the man's teeth, so then the man comes out with milk, bread, cream, vegetables and all that, so the devil was trying to break his teeth so they said, "Never drink coffee." I like coffee.

Q. How long ago did you see this picture?

A. About four years.

Q. Did it influence you about eating?

A. Yep.

Q. How? How did this picture influence you about eating?

A. I think so.

Q. Did it make you quit drinking coffee?

A. No, I drink coffee every morning.

Q. Do you drink milk?

A. No.

On the other hand, pictures of activities in which the boy has a natural interest have a very significant appeal to him.

One day a man who had a son about my age asked me if I wanted to go to the show to keep his son company. His son was about my age (about 10½ or 11 years of age). I asked my father's permission and we went. I remember seeing a picture about submarines. Up to that time I had some queer ideas as to how submarines looked and how they traveled under water and how the crew was able to breathe and especially how to see where they were going. This picture answered my questions to such fine satisfaction that when I left the theater I felt as if I had learned a great deal.

Another boy indicates that the movies have been a means for learning acrobatic stunts from the movies, while still another indicates that movies have been used by him as a means for instruction in sports.

All my family like the movies except my father, who used to go to them. . . . My parents regard my favorite sport, which is basketball, as foolishness. They say that all I do is to run my brains out. But I like to play and to see a good basketball game or any sport. Any time a ball game of any kind is featured at a neighborhood theater I am almost sure to go and see it. From the movies I gather many useful points about that sport.

In the following case a boy interested in tap dancing used the vaudeville and the movie reviews as a means of self-instruction.

Paulie is a youth of seventeen, with only an elementary school education. His favorite type of motion picture is the musical comedy. He is very interested in acting and tap dancing. The greatest movie and stage man, in his opinion, is Bill Robinson, reputed to be the world's greatest tap dancer. When asked who he thought was the best actor on the screen or stage, he said "Bill Robinson" without hesitation. A second later he followed with "Gee, I wish I was his son!"

Q. Why?
A. Because then he could teach me all the steps he knows and he knows plenty.
Q. Did you ever see him in person?
A. Sure, every time he was at the place. I saved my money and I used to go early to get a front row seat.
Q. Did you ever see him on the screen?
A. Yeah, once, a friend of mine told me he was in a picture, "Follies of 1930," and I saw him there.
Q. Do you go alone to see him?
A. No, I like to take someone with me so that I can speak to him and show him how good Bill Robinson is.

Throughout the interview, Paulie never referred to Bill Robinson as Bill or Robinson. He seemed to have too much respect for the man to refer to him as merely Bill or Robinson.

Q. What good does it do you to see Bill Robinson?
A. I study some of the steps he does and then I go home and practice them.
Q. Why do you practice tap dancing?
A. I want to go on the stage some day and make a name for myself.
Q. How do you come to be interested in tap dancing?
A. A couple of years ago during the summer time, four guys from XX Avenue used to go on the platform in the park and they used to do a routine and practice new steps. One of the guys used to have money so he went to tap dancing school and the steps he learned he used to teach the other guys. There was only a bunch of kids watching. One night, it was raining hard. I got up nerve and asked him if he would teach me some steps. To my surprise he said he'd try. After a while he said I was very good and that I was a natural tap dancer. The next night the other guys came around and this guy told them about me. So that's how I started. This guy's name was Charlie Brown. Brown wasn't his real name. Then he began to call me Petie Brown. A couple of years ago he went on the stage at the X_____ Theater. Before I went there with Charlie he took me to a lot of weddings, so that I got used to the crowd. They threw

money on the floor when Charlie and I danced at the weddings and parties. Some times we danced at Block Parties and there we made lots of money. One time we made about $12 for about five minutes of dancing. With this money we bought our uniforms for the stage. Now Charlie is away dancing with a girl on the stage somewhere.[74]

No doubt if a complete record were available it would be clear that the motion pictures are the basis for a great deal of informal learning on the part of the children.

Though a great deal of the informal education gained at the cinema is, at least, not socially undesirable knowledge – and in fact in many cases very valuable – there are times in which the motion picture serves as an education in the techniques of crime, racketeering, and exploitation. Crime and gangster pictures, murder, mystery, and detective photoplays all seem to contribute to instruction in crime for those who so desire. Yet occasionally even the best of films may be used for purposes of instruction in petty theft. In an interview, a delinquent boy gave as his choice for "the best picture ever seen" the classic "All Quiet on the Western Front." When asked his reasons for this choice he told of an obscure scene in the play in which a soldier accidentally caught a piece of meat being thrown from a refrigerator car and made off with it. This, he explained, gave him an idea for intercepting some of the foodstuffs thrown off in a similar way from delivery trucks in his neighborhood. But for the most part, the films from which the boys seem to get ideas about crime are the gangster and underworld pictures and occasionally a photoplay revolving about the technique used by detectives in apprehending the offender. During the past year in the community of special study a detective serial was shown on Friday nights. Subsequent interviews with boys who saw this serial revealed that they had learned many things concerning the detective's art. One boy casually informed an investigator that he learned to wear gloves when carrying a revolver, thus avoiding the chance for identification through finger prints. Another reported that he learned to wipe off a knob of a door with his handkerchief before leaving the place of his crime. Another boy reported as follows:

Q. Didn't you say that you covered your hands with paper to hide your finger prints?
A. No, we didn't put nothing on our hands. I didn't see nobody put things on their hands.
Q. You don't know anything about that?

A. No.
Q. How do they hide finger prints?
A. Put gloves on.
Q. How do you know?
A. I saw it in a picture.
Q. What picture?
A. I don't know. They were opening a safe.
Q. Is that where they got the idea?
A. I don't know.

Many ideas concerning the way "jobs" are done are learned by boys seeing the gangster pictures of recent years. One of the most interesting cases discovered in this research was the use of a suggestion for concealing firearms seen in a gangster picture.[75] In this photoplay a violin case was used as a means of concealing a machine gun which was later used in a murder. A special investigator reported the use of this idea by a group of young men who were planning a burglary.

After considerable discussion as to how revolvers might be concealed on their persons, should a patrolman chance to search them while standing on the street awaiting the time for the actual burglary, it was suggested that an adaptation of the machine gun in a violin case might be valuable. The violin case for these boys who considered themselves "tough" was recognized to be a bit unsuitable, but since two of the three young men are known ostensibly to be bill collectors the small leather pouch used by collectors was thought to be a suitable substitute. Later report was to the effect that they were successful not only in their burglary but also in deluding in one instance a policeman who was suspicious of the actions of one of the trio.[76]

Another technique of crime was the racing of an automobile engine as a means to drown out the noise of possible revolver fire.[77] The following report of a special investigator indicates another instance in which criminal techniques were noted by delinquent boys.

Q. Did you ever go home and dream of how you could become a great racketeer and make lots of money with the ideas you get from the pictures?
A. Yeah, lots of times.
Q. Tell me about it?
A. That was some trick, they stole the whiskey with the gasoline truck by tying the rubber hose to the barrels upstairs. I saw this picture and this is what happened. Two men posing as telegraph repairmen climbed the pole and entered the warehouse where the whiskey was stored. With

them (the repairmen) they had a long rubber hose. In the meantime, a big gasoline truck backed up to the warehouse. The driver and his helper got out and pretended that they were repairing the motor. The telegraph men sent the hose down and the truck driver attached it to the gas tank. In this way they filled the gas truck and they pulled away.

Q. What other trick did you get from the movies – that you thought about in order to make quick money?

A. The machine gun in the violin case is a good way to carry it. Of course, everybody knows about it now, but you could carry it in a saxophone case.[78]

So much of these chance illustrations of criminal techniques become a part of the thought of some boys that the technique once understood is undisputed in their photoplays.

Another scene in the photoplay "Union Depot" [1932] shows Douglas Fairbanks, Jr., opening a violin case. When the lid was thrown back, packages of paper money were thrown into full view. The entire audience gasped, but my companion "Zip" did not move. "What's the matter?" I asked, "doesn't that money bother you?" "Naw, I expected a machine gun." "Why the machine gun?" I asked. "Tell me any picture that ain't got a machine gun in it. They all got typewriters (machine guns) in them."[79]

Though in many cases these ideas regarding criminal techniques may eventuate in some sort of attempted crime, it is significant that these films are recognized by the boys quite commonly as being a source of stimulation toward criminal interests.

"Who's your favorite actor?"

"Jim Cagney." His answer came as soon as my question ended.

"You like the way he acts?"

"I eat it. You get some ideas from his actin'. You learn how he pulls off a job, how he bumps off a guy, an' a lotta' tings."[80]

In an attempt to trace the source for criminal patterns in this community, seventy-five delinquents were interviewed and questioned upon the origin of their practices. In a large majority of the cases the criminal patterns were found to have been gained through instruction by older persons met on the streets. Occasionally, however, there was some evidence that definite ideas, later used in their own conduct, were obtained from the movies. In the following instance very clear evidence is apparent that these ideas were gained from the photoplay.

A very tall fellow of about 19 years, a high school boy, an only child, interested in radio broadcasting and building sets, saw "Raffles" [1930], "The Gentleman Burglar," in the movies. With a younger friend of 16, he decided that he would try to do that. He made cards with a "Hand" sign from a rubber stamp on them and printed "Compliments of Kid Gloves." He then started a series of robberies of small stores nearby. The police were foiled and didn't know who it would be who would take so little – only a few cents in change, some fishing tackle, queer things of that type. They realized that it wasn't a professional since so little was taken, but always the card would be found.

One day at a High School football game "Kid Gloves" cards were passed out. They were found to be genuine. Then a plain clothesman was assigned to the High School each day. This young man was seen exhibiting a gun and acting quite important and self-sufficient. It was not long before they had him before the police and he had confessed to his crimes. He had chosen a weaker 16 year old for an accomplice in some of the stunts, but most of the time he had done things alone.

In the following case a young man was interviewed, a negro who was apprehended for burglary and who was reported to have said that he got his idea for his crime from a photoplay. A stenographic record of those parts of the interview bearing upon motion pictures and crime is included below.

Q. We are making a study about moving pictures and what they have to do with crime – we are trying to find out if they inspired you –
A. (Interrupting) So you can put that in the newspapers, eh?
Q. No, we came here to find out if the movies are responsible for your present trouble. If they are, we want to know about it.
A. That don't help me none.
Q. The only reason I am doing this is to find out why you did it. What made you do it?
A. I wouldn't have done it if I wasn't drinking and broke. I would have gone into any place.
Q. Well, how did you get the idea of breaking in?
A. I saw that in the movies, I saw crooks taking the panels out of the door.
Q. Did you know about taking the panels out of the door?
A. Yes.
Q. Where did you get that idea?
A. I saw it in the movies.
Q. And that's where you got the idea?

A. I thought I would get in that way.

Q. What clothes did you have on?

A. I had on a grey suit, grey hat.

Q. Did you have a gun?

A. Naw.

Q. Any tools?

A. No.

Q. How did you get the panel off?

A. With a knife.

Q. What kind of a knife?

A. Just a plain pocket knife.

Q. You know how it was done – you took the panel off and reached in and unlocked the door?

A. You explained exactly how I done it.

Q. What time of day was it when you broke into the house?

A. I guess around 2:30 or a quarter of three.

Q. What picture do you remember seeing which showed the way to break in?

A. I can't remember exactly – I couldn't answer that. I see so many pictures – I go most all the time.

Q. What did you go in to take?

A. Anything valuable.

Q. For instance, what?

A. I don't know. I thought I could get a couple of good suits and pawn them.

Q. Don't you remember the name of the picture you saw taking the panels out of the door?

A. No, I don't think the name was Raffles. The picture I saw showed where they move panels and had fake looking doors, they pressed buttons and they open up, but what the name was I don't know – I think it was "Hole in the Wall" [1929] – some Chinese picture.

Q. Tell me, did you actually see that picture "Raffles"?

A. I don't believe I have, I saw so many I can't remember.

In this case the motion picture pattern is of sufficiently clear delineation to indicate with a fair degree of certainty that the motion picture in supplying a pattern was a factor in the crime. Other cases[81] suggest with almost equal clarity the incorporation of a cinema crime pattern into an overt behavior. In the following instance a little girl of nine, who lived in an interstitial area in an industrial city adjoining New York City, was found to have incorporated into her crime patterns – purse snatching and shop lifting – the vivid stimuli from motion picture scenes. It should be noted, first, that while the subject was a girl here, her role was that of a "tomboy" in a gang of little boys. Hence, the sex factor is in this case relatively unimportant. Secondly, it is interesting to observe that the chance instruction in crime she had on the streets from boys was strengthened and made more vivid by the scenes of the motion picture. Finally, the great significance of the motion picture in this case is shown in the fact that she remembers with great vividness a certain few photoplay scenes showing theft and when interviewed most exhaustively merely returns to the same story, telling it over and over again, each time varying but very little from the previous narration.

. . . The attempt was also made in this study to discover the possible causative relation between photoplay scenes and felonious assault by delinquent boys. Of three cases involving serious stabbings, two were found upon examination to reveal some rather tangible movie patterns. One of these, a superior boy in high school, tells of having seen a "Dr. Fu Manchu" picture in which one of the characters of the play stabbed an individual, jumping at him from the back and striking at him in a manner quite similar to that used by the subject in his own offenses. It should be noted here that the boy indicates that he had happened to have seen a stabbing in real life and that he had also read newspapers and books telling of the underworld and of crime. The report dictated by the interviewer shortly after studying the case is as follows:

He told of having seen the "Dr. Fu Manchu" picture and mentioned especially the one I believe he called "The Return of Dr. Fu Manchu's Daughter" [1930]. He said that in this picture one of the other characters in the play stabbed an individual by jumping at him, striking him in the back. He said that he had also seen gangster pictures which included gun killing and stabbing. He did not, however, cite a concrete incident in a gangster picture where stabbing had been shown.

Upon further inquiry he said that he had also seen stabbing in real life. This incident occurred a number of years ago in a congested section of the city near where he lived. He saw two men get into a fight over some goods at a stand. He said that at that time one of the men drew out a knife and stabbed the other in the side of his abdomen.

It is interesting in this connection to compare the way in which Joseph said that he held his knife when he did his stabbing, the way in which the knife was held and the motions of the stabber just before the stabbing. He said that in the stabbing by the man which he had witnessed at the goods stand, the man drew his knife from a belt, apparently, and that he used the knife in such a way to give a forward thrust. The knife was held with the blade end of the knife nearest his thumb and the stabbing was made by a forward and upward thrust.

The "Dr. Fu Manchu" pictures, however, were described by Joseph with certainty to represent the use of the knife in the opposite way; the blade end of the knife was held in the hand in such a way that the blade was nearest to the small finger of the hand and the stabbing was made by a backward thrust of the hand. Further, in the "Dr. Fu Manchu" pictures, the assailant leaped at the victim stabbing him from behind. Joseph said that he did not want to kill the boy and so was afraid of stabbing him in the back. However, Joseph says that he jumped at his victim, although from the side, rather than from the back as was represented in the "Dr. Fu Manchu" pictures.

Upon being questioned especially regarding his own judgment at this time, looking at his conduct in retrospect as to the influences of the movies and other influences which might have provided the stabbing pattern, he said that he does not believe that his stabbing the boy was because of the movies or those other experiences. He said that he was angry and wanted revenge, and that he did not think of "Dr. Fu Manchu" or anything at the time. He said that if he had never seen the stabbing at the goods stand nor seen the "Dr. Fu Manchu" picture or any other movie involving stabbing, he is assured that he would have acted in about the same way. He did suggest, however, that he also got some notions of stabbing from reading the newspapers and particularly gangster stories in the newspapers.

. . . The material which has been assembled in the preceding pages provides a basis for calling in question, at least, the frequently heard claim of defenders of the present types of motion pictures that the motion pictures as such do not contribute to delinquency and crime. Further, it has been the claim of these apologists that even the gangster and underworld films always show that in the end the offender meets his just dues and that therefore the movies instead of inciting to crime are really giving an eloquent sermon against it. In view of the fact that the area of special study was known for its crime, it was thought that careful interviewing of a sampling of the boys and young men upon their interpretation of the treatment of the underworld films would be in order. Frequently at the appropriate place in the interview when the gangster pictures were under discussion, it was a practice to seize upon the boy's reply to return the comment "But that only happens in the movies. Gangsters do not always get bumped off in real life." The replies of the boys to this comment have not as of this writing been tabulated, but there is no doubt a basis for the generalization that at least the younger more unsophisticated boys tend to accept the motion picture representations. Typical of these replies is the following excerpt of such an interview in which "Scarface" [1932], a recent photoplay which was regarded as "the gangster picture to end all gangster pictures," was the center of discussion.

Q. How about gangster pictures?
A. "Scarface."
Q. Did you like it?
A. Yes, it was nice.
Q. What did you like about it?
A. At the end when the detectives get him.
Q. Do you think the story is true?
A. Yes.
Q. Why?
A. It shows the baby shot on XX Street. Most of it is true.
Q. Would you like to be a gangster?
A. You get shot down and killed.
Q. That only happens in the movies?
A. It happens in real life.
Q. Suppose gangsters don't get shot down, would you like to be one?
A. No.
Q. Why?
A. You get put away for life.
Q. Who is your favorite actor?
A. James Cagney.

On the other hand the older boys, those who know underworld figures or who perhaps know of criminals who somehow manage to carry on without much interference with the law, tend to discredit these cinema preachments as but a part of the "baloney" of the pictures. Significant in this connection are the comments of some of the boys with regard to a gangster photoplay. "I like it when they make you laugh and when they shoot a guy, but that's a lot of baloney."

"Sure I like Little Caesar and Jim Cagney but dat's de baloney dey give you in de pitchers. Dey always die or get canned. Dat ain't true. Looka Joe Citro, Pedro Salami, and Tony Vendatta.[82] Looka de ol' man."

His father was in the recent Department of Street Cleaning scandal. It cost him 20 G's ($20,000) to beat the rap. At one time he owned a cafe and ran a string of brothels. Now he has interests in an undertaking establishment, a job with the city, a political boss, and runs a joint. He has a pistol permit.

"Dose guys in de pitchers oughta be able to get away. If my ol' man had de dough he'd run de city."

He prefers pictures "dat show lotta action wid gangsters, bootleggers, and high-jackers. I ain't going to get in Dutch wid de law 'cause I'm gonna get protection before I do anything. An' I ain't havin' no broads aroun' while dere's work to do. You can't trust 'em and dey get you in trouble. If it wasn't for a broad dey never woulda got Little Caesar."

He dresses Cagney style. Soft green hat, tight fitting suit, puff shoulder coat, leather heeled shoes.[83]

A superior boy in this community, attending high school, in giving his attitude toward gangster films reflects clearly a reaction to the lax enforcement of law in his own community.

"Most of the stuff you see in the movies is bunk anyway. I saw 'Scarface' the other day and at the end of the picture you see him getting bumped off, but out where I live we know it's a lot of baloney. On my block a couple of the big shots are always pulling off jobs, but they never get in trouble because they got too much pull. They ride around in limousines and have all the liquor and women they want, and you never seen them get in trouble the way they do in the movies."

The extent to which the preachment of the gangster pictures is accepted by the boys and young men of this community is not entirely clear but it is certain that especially with the older and more sophisticated street boys there is a very strong tendency toward the discounting of this feature of the underworld pictures. An interesting point may here be raised with reference to the wholly different responses of the boys and young men to various gangster films. While such photoplays as "Little Caesar," "Doorway to Hell" [1930], "Public Enemy" [1931], and even "Scarface" have been found frequently associated in the minds of delinquent boys with their own criminal career, other gangster pictures have apparently seemed to have a distinctly "good" influence upon a considerable number of street boys. Chief among these is the photoplay "Are These Our Children?" [1931]. Time after time in the interviews with delinquents and also in the reports of special investigators and in written life histories, this film was cited as one of the "best ever seen."[84] The following report by a special investigator is but one instance of the effect of this photoplay.

I found myself talking to Steve Colombo, 19 years of age, and turned the conversation toward the movies. He told me he saw a picture not so long ago which created a profound impression on his mind. "I'll never forget it. It was terrible. The name of it was "Are These Our Children?""

I told him I had seen it too. It starred Eric Linden. At the outset of the picture Eric Linden is a good high school boy. He is a candidate for regional honors in a nationwide contest sponsored by a certain newspaper. The subject which the contestants must deal with is the Constitution of the United States of America. Linden has great hopes of emerging a winner. His grandmother, brother, girl, and a friend of the family have great confidence in him. He fails. His school friends chide him. He becomes depressed.

Because of his good looks a flapper type school girl decides to lure him to her side. In order to make money with which to take out his new girl he mixes with bad company and the audience is given to understand that he is the new "baby-type" stick up man.

In trying to force a grocer to give him a bottle of gin the erstwhile model high school boy kills him. The act is kept under cover for a time but they finally get caught. Linden is all "puffed up" because his picture and name in the newspapers are in bold black type. But later his Buddy turns state's evidence and he is sentenced to the electric chair.

Steve told me it reminded him of his big brother Pete who is "up the river" doing time for assault and extortion and for attempted extortion. He told me that the night Pete was arrested the family got together and had a very serious family conference in which they all cried and the mother tearfully asked each of eight kids to promise not to be bad like poor Pete who was led from the straight and narrow path by evil associates.

Steve said Pete would not have gone wrong if it hadn't been for a number of bad breaks. He compared Pete to the central figure in "Are These Our Children?"

"Are These Our Children?":
"De guy was going to high school an' he looked like a smart kid."
Pete Colombo:
"Pete had a nice job driving an ice wagon."

"Are These Our Children?":
"Den he lost in some kind of a talkin' contest (debate) and began to feel lousy."
Pete Colombo:
"He lost his job and he felt bad because his friends had dough even if dey didn't woik an' he didn't wanna get lend of money because he knew he couldn't pay it back."

"Are These Our Children?":
"Get in wid bad company and started to go out on jobs."
Pete Colombo:
"Pete's friends *forced* him to get into de racket."

The only known photograph of Rev. William Short; it appeared in the *Sioux City* (Iowa) *Journal,* 15 January 1935.

The Payne Fund logo. This illustration was found in the Bolton papers collection; it is not known how widely the logo was used.

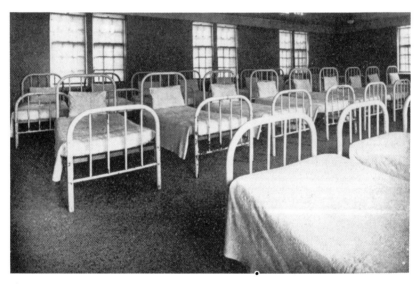

Upper: The Ohio Bureau of Juvenile Research; boys' quarters on right, girls' on left. *Lower:* The boys' dormitory; the beds near the wall are equipped with hypnographs.

Typical group of boys and girls used in the sleep experiments.

The hypnograph unit attached to a woven wire spring.

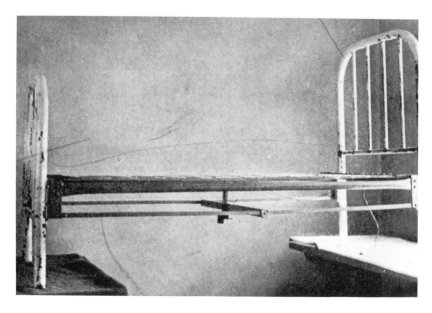

A bed with hypnograph mounted in center of springs for maximal sensitivity to postural movements.

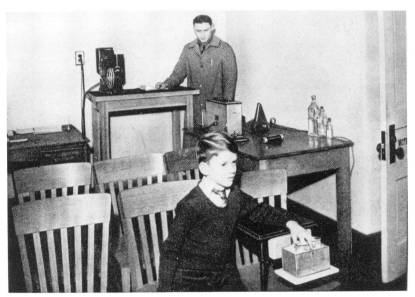

Upper: An experiment in a movie theater. Child is shown holding the fingers of his left hand in the electrodes. The wristband of the pneumocardiograph is seen around the right wrist. The control is operated by the experimenter, while the psychogalvanograph and other apparatus are under the control of the assistant. *Lower:* The laboratory theater. The psychogalvanograph is on the table, with the Kodascope on the stand at the back of the room.

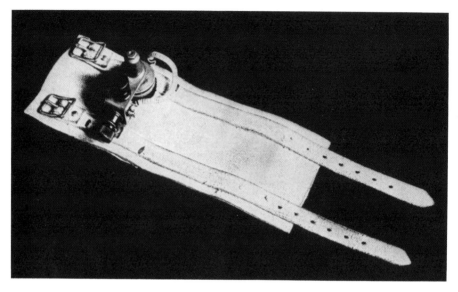

The leather arm strap of the pneumocardiograph.

what Are the Movies Doing to Us?
Lowell Heads Movement to Find Out

Former Harvard President
Heads Film Research
Council

By NRA Service

BOSTON, Aug. 24.—Dr. Abbott Lawrence Lowell, the blue-blooded 77-year-old educator whose long presidency at Harvard left indelible marks on America's richest and oldest university, is going to lend his influence to making the movies social-minded.

Dr. Lowell has accepted unanimous election to be chairman of the Motion Picture Research Council, a 5-year-old organization for making studies of the social influences of the movies. Following such studies, the council expects to make suggestions for more effective use of the movies as a social force.

The council already has produced a series of reports which Dr. Lowell has said "impressed me very much." Dr. Lowell succeeds his old friend, the late President John Grier Hibben of Princeton, in heading the council's work, which Dr. Lowell believes to be "most important."

Research Has Wide Scope

The movie researches being engineered by the council are in three parts:

The first is a study of the influence of pictures on the audience, especially in children.

The second will be the effect of movies on international understanding and world peace, and especially the ideas of America which are being given people all over the world by the present Hollywood output.

Third will come a study of the economic, financial, legal and administrative aspects of the movie industry with reference to whether these fit or unfit it to perform its social duty properly.

These second two phases of the council's study would have to be completed under the guidance of Dr. Lowell, recommendations made, and plans devised to get them adopted. The first, relating to the effects on youth, is largely complete.

New Field for Savant

Dr. Lowell, last of a long line of Boston bluebloods, only recently retired as president of Harvard. During his presidency he not only revolutionized the physical aspect of Harvard, building and putting in operation its famous "house units," but he increased its endowment nearly $100,000,000 and made it the richest university in the country.

Now from his retirement he essays to direct studies that will ultimately bring the movies to a greater sense of responsibility for what they are doing to, and for, America.

The original set of studies was made in collaboration with the Payne Fund, which is concerned

Dr. Abbott Lawrence Lowell.

with the informal education of youth thrugh all influences outside schools. he Payne Fund created a committee of scientists of high standing, nd studied various phases of the elect of movies on young people.

Such qestions were studied as these: Wat sort of ideas do children get from the movies? How deeply a they affected emotionally? Ho many children go to the movies, ad how often? Do the movies hpire criminal and delinquent tedencies? Do they affect children's sleep or nerves? And so on.

Four yars of studies, conducted in a moe careful manner, resulted

Effects on Children Revealed
in Long, Scientific
Studies

definitely that it did, not only on the night of the picture, but for as long as five nights afterward.

A general report on the studies of Dr. W. W. Charters, also of Ohio State, was approved by Dr. Hibben just before his death in an auto accident. Dr. Hibben commented that the research showed that many current films conflict with the teachings and standards of the training of home, church, and school. They "constitute a valid basis for apprehension about their influence on children," Dr. Hibben added.

Highly Impressionable

The studies included such interesting findings as these: Of 35,941 boys and girls between 8 and 19 years old, each girl went to the movies 46, and each boy 57 times a year. Another check showed that every week 28,259,000 youngsters between 5 and 20 years old go to the movies. The tremendous potential effect on youth is evident.

Other tests showed definitely that children take movies more seriously than grown-ups, that they are more real to them, and that their emotional reaction is sometimes as much as eight times as marked as that of grown-ups watching the same picture.

Not Censorship

The council does not aim at censorship, and is the first to admit that some movies may have a relaxing and even beneficial effect on children. It has no idea of preventing children from going to the movies, for it is first to admit that they will go anyway.

Nor has it any idea of demanding that all movies be reduced to a level where they will be suitable for 9-year-old children. Its work is largely fact-finding, in the belief that after the facts are disclosed it will be time enough to determine what changes, if any, are necessary.

Stage No Problem

The movies have never before been subjected to so careful a study regarding their social influence. It was never necessary to make such a study of the stage, because it has been definitely shown that stage plays in general have little effect on young children. Youngsters just don't "get them." But they understand the movies, and they remember what they see there in almost as great detail as do adults, the tests showed.

To the task of finishing these studies of the social effects of the movies now comes the man who has been for 24 years the presiding genius of America's world-famous Harvard. Dr. Lowell

in a series of reports which are now being published. The author of the first of these, for instance, Henry James Forman, concludes that the movies are as powerful an influence in American life as our whole costly educational system.

The investigation "has been thoroughly scientific," Dr. Lowell indicated in accepting the new post, and cated in the manner in which it was made seem to bear this out.

For more than a year, under direction of Prof. Samuel Renshaw of Ohio State, the sleep of 170 children was automatically recorded by instruments to determine whether going to the movies cost them lost or troubled sleep. The tests showed

---

Article in the *San Francisco News*, 24 August 1933.

LOVE CONFESSIONS of MOVIE FANS

Group of Scientists Makes a Serious Study of How the Flickering Films Affect the Minds and Behavior of Adolescent America--- Youngsters Write Startling Admissions of Ways They Imitate Their Screen Idols

BY JASON BRADON

HOW are young people affected by the love scenes they see in the movies?

Article in the *Boston Sunday Post,* 17 December 1933.

"Are These Our Children?":
"He had good times wid some broads."
Pete Colombo:
"Pete was havin' a lotta fun. He was gettin' clothes, he bought a Nash Coupe and he married a Jew (Jewess)."

"Are These Our Children?":
"He killed a guy."
Pete Colombo:
"Pete was 'shaking' down some dealers dey started to say but it ain't true. He was framed."
"De d_____ sheeny handed him marked money."

He expects his brother to come out soon, even though he was sentenced for a three year term. "Dat'll be fixed up," he said.

This I observed was inconsistent with his statement about his brother's innocence. Why should an important man "Kick in 2 Grand ($2,000)" to clear his name of a crime he hadn't committed?

He said he saw "Are These Our Children?" three times. "Now I'm gonna go straight. No foolin' around with me."[85]

The entire explanation for the exceptional appeal of this film and of its influences as contrasted with the frequent reaction to "Scarface," "Little Caesar," and others cannot be given. However, one very obvious difference is to be found in the absence in "Are These Our Children?" of the "tough" role played by the leading character. Eric Linden is here presented as an attractive high school youth who impulsively had "gotten off on the wrong track." His unfortunate end very probably seemed to many a possible outcome for even such boys as themselves and their friends; while the "tough" characters in "Scarface," "Little Caesar," and "Public Enemy," though fascinating, nevertheless did not seem sufficiently like themselves for the association to be made. This, of course, is but a hypothesis but this differentiation between the two groups of gangster films is basic and should be noted in any attempt to understand the educational significance – for good or ill – of underworld pictures.

Ambitions also seem sometimes to clearly reflect the influence of motion pictures. In the interviews with boys from this community they frequently indicated that even at that time and at a different time they had aspired to be movie actors. There is indicated that they emulated greatly certain of the movie actors, younger boys such actors as Tom Mix and Hoot Gibson, and the elder ones such actors as James Cagney and Edward G. Robinson.[86] Even for boys of superior native endowment who read extensively in books as well as attend the cinema, favorite motion picture actors fuse in their mind with authors and public figures whom they also emulate. The following list of men admired during adolescence by a thoughtful rather introspective boy growing up in this community suggests in the proximity of names, as well as in the number of photoplay heroes, the dignity with which the cinema actor was held. For this boy, who if anything might be regarded as superior in his community, there seems to be nothing incongruous in associating in the same galaxy of heroes such figures as Rudolph Valentino and Voltaire, and Buck Jones and Sabatini.

Some of the men that I have admired during the different stages of my life are: Tom Mix, Buck Jones, William S. Hart, Rossini, Ronald Colman, Jack Dempsey, Raphael Sabatini, Jules Verne, Rudolph Valentino, Voltaire, Lawrence Tibbet.

Other boys who do not seem to be ambitious to become a movie actor may nevertheless be interested in an occupation featured in a photoplay. One boy indicated that he was interested in becoming a detective and another that he was interested in a gangster career and another a doctor as a result in part at least of their seeing certain photoplays. Dr. Whitley reports in a summary of his interviews the following:

One boy expressed a desire to be a cowboy and also a desire to be a soldier. Case 52 expressed a desire to be an actor. Case 57 said that he would like to be like Ken Maynard. Cases 15 and 26 would like to be Johnny Hines. Case 2 indicated a dancing trick in which Harold Lloyd participated in "The Freshman." Case 63 said that he imitated Douglas Fairbanks. Case 16 expressed an interest in boxing pictures and said that he would like to be Jack Dempsey. Cases 48 and 62 also indicated an interest in boxing pictures.[87]

Another boy wrote that a movie entitled "The Big Broadcast" [1932] suggested to him the career of a radio crooner.

I have never yearned to become a movie star. I never wanted to go to Hollywood to seek a career. I never had any occupation or ambition to become a lawyer or a soldier. The movies only gave me one desire and that was in a picture that I saw lately, "The Big Broadcast." I saw Bing Crosby croon and he gave me the idea that I'd rather become a crooner instead of a movie actor. I'd rather become a star on the air, I mean the radio. College pictures have never given me the ambition to go to college, but the rest never gave me any ideas. My ambition is that I want to be a radio crooner. Some people don't like crooners, but that is my ambition and I got the idea from "The Big Broadcast." I saw Bing Crosby and, also, on my radio I heard him plenty times and also Russ Columbo.

Many professions and occupations are no doubt suggested by photoplays. In some cases the representation of the occupation is a fair and stimulating one but it should be noted that the evidence which is available in this study seems to indicate that at least occasionally, the suggestions gained from the movies are not in themselves assimilable.

When it came time to choose a profession I was stumped for whenever I attended a movie and the hero was a doctor I wanted to become a physician; if he was a lawyer I wanted to become a lawyer. I could picture myself in the Supreme Court defending a great client and winning my case through my ingenuity. I finally ended by becoming nothing, because I could not make up my mind.

A few self-conscious young men from this community, many of whom feel seriously social and cultural restrictions which bind them, unconsciously find in the movies a source of many of their efforts for gaining a certain type of social grace and refinement. For many, the talking picture now serves as a model for learning what is commonly called good English or a correct way to hold a conversation. For others a certain actor may provide, in part, an unconscious pattern for modeling their conduct and personality.

. . . For some young men in this community, the struggle to gain social advancement takes on often an objectiveness represented in a studied technique. In the following descriptive account of a certain individual in this community, the young man has almost consciously followed the patterns presented by his favorite movie actor.

Johnny Smith is not the he-man type of lover. Neither does he fall in the category of Casanovas and Don Juans who promise eternal love and nights of ecstasy to their inamoratas.

Take it from Johnny that "When you come across a 'dame' who is got the guys playing dead at her feet, leave her alone. Don't give her a tumble, see? Jus' say Hello and den pick out the worst looking dog (girl) in the crowd and make out you're trying to budge her. If dere's no funny looking "baloney's" in de crowd, den pick out some "frail" she don't like and budge her. Believe me, when she sees you doin' dat instead of being near her she'll get plenty steamed. She'll start wondering why you dont acks (ask) like the rest o' de guys who always chase after her. Den you'll see dat she begins to come after you. That you call technikew (technique)."

Johnny Smith's cinema idol is the incorrigible, impertinent and irresistible William Haines. His worship of the screen star has reached to an extreme, where we find Johnny imitating the smart sleeky mannerism. Johnny's a doorman for one of the snooty men's clubs in the fifties. During his off hours he goes through a complete transformation and becomes Mr. William (Billy) O'Shay. His clothes remind me of a study in brown. He heard that Bill Haines wears his clothing in accordance with his figure, complexion and color of hair. Billy, as we shall now call him, is tall, has brown hair and eyes of the same color.

In his pictures Bill Haines is rarely humble in the presence of the fair sex. He laughs at a girl when he is supposed to be making love to her. Billy's version of this type of technique comes forth at neighborhood dances, when he asks a girl for a dance. (Usually the shy drooping violet type of a girl.) As the girl is preparing to dance with him, he tells her, "In your hat, baby, leave me alone. Go home and wash your dishes." Before saying this he assures himself that he has a large enough audience. To him, it's a joke. Too bad for these shy wallflower girls.

William Haines, Jr., of _____ has visions of a big break which will bring him the luxuries he sincerely believes he deserves, because the gods favored him with a collar-ad "pan" and a strong desire to enjoy what he considers "de best tings in life."[88]

... Several instances are on record in this research in which the efforts of the boy to make satisfactory social adjustments find definite stimulus of an incontrovertible sort from the movies. In such matters as dress and posture, the movie suggestions are utilized.

I also became passionately fond of the movies. . . . When I got home from a show I would imitate a character and make my whole family laugh. Many times I was surprised by one of the family making motions in front of the mirror.

These efforts to imitate the dress and manners as seen in the movies seem sometimes to be more frequently failures than successes.

Of all the pictures that I have seen I have adopted few manners. I have tried to form my hair like Will Rogers but it has been a failure at every attempt. From my first experiences with the movies I have learned from an extra how I should dress. I wear a blue-black pants, blue sweater with an overlapping white collar, making my face dominant.

Interesting also is a definite use of the suggestions gained from a movie plot in the solution of the young man's personal problems. His account of the episodes in his life, as told to the special investigator reporting it, gives a definite suggestion as to the way in which motion picture plots may sometimes be utilized.

When I came back from the West I saw a girl I liked. She lived on XX Street. I ain't one o' dese sheiks but she tol' me I was O.K. I liked her too. We wanted to get married. I asked her ol' man an' he called me a tramp and a bum. He said, "Get outa my house an' don't see my daughter again." The old greaseball wanted her to marry some Zulu (a middle-aged Italian) wid plenty o' cush (money).

An den I remembered that in a pitcher I saw one time de good guy had relations with his girl because then he thought her folks would have to let them marry, but he was shot instead. But I knew her ol' man wouldn't shoot me. I'd a broke his neck.

We hired a furnished room an' she went home cryin', but even after that her father wouldn't let her get married. But I fixed it up wid my mother and father an' they went to her house an' we fixed it to get married. Pretty soon I'll be a daddy. . . . Lucky I saw that picture!

At this writing all of the evidence upon this point is not available but the trend as revealed in the returns upon the first fifty "controlled interviews"[89] seems to indicate quite clearly that the superior and "nondelinquent" boys frequently seize upon the suggestions from the motion picture as a means for dealing more satisfactorily with their immediate social problems. The extent to which the motion picture may influence the boy in his thinking and in his plan for his own life is also suggested in some of the interesting documents gathered in this study. For many of the boys of somewhat superior mental caliber the movies are closely associated with books and with their sources for ideas and gaining personal aspiration.

I feel towards the movies the same way that I feel towards books. The only difference is that the book takes a longer time to unfold the story, while the movies acts out the story with definite characters flashing before you on the screen. I like books better, because I like the characters that form in my mind better than those picked by the movies. Chances are that I might dislike the picture because of the rotten acting of the cast. Books are different, they give wonderful descriptions, philosophy of life and experience that you would not meet in your own life.

Significant also is the way in which the boy in his account of his life and in his account of books read and photoplays seen are fused together. This very probably suggests that the ideas gained from movies are not so clearly distinguished in his mind from those gained from other sources. The following is but an illustration of that apparent tendency.

As a child the books that impressed me most were historical novels, histories and books on travel to far and mysterious lands. Today they still have a great hold on me, although I have added biographies and sciences to my reading. If I read a book on the sea – my ambition was to be a sea captain. If I read a book such as "The Three Musketeers" then I would curse society for having adopted modern ways of personal defense. How much more magnificent would it be to challenge the villain to a sword duel and run him through his vile body with your rapier.

Just as some of the characters in books had been worshipped by me, so were many actors of the screen. The special ones, the heroes of serials. There was a particular actor whose name was Eddie Polo and he was starring in a serial by the title of "Do or Die" [1921]. That title was used quite often by our "Gang." Everything we did was either do or die. The youngest and weakest one in the gang would jump over the fire hydrant in a do or die spirit because our leader and other fellows had been able to do it.

In the conjury of ideas which the boy may possess probably there are none which are more frequently associated with reverie than those gained from motion pictures. The following instance could be duplicated many times in the records of this study.

When I outgrew this yearning for exciting pictures I usually day dreamed when I had nothing to do or before going to bed. I usually dream about a picture that I have seen which strikes me for its emotional qualities. I believe that the world isn't such a bad place to live in after seeing a picture like "Reaching for the Moon" [1931]. It makes me wish that I was the hero of the picture. I day dream and see myself in my dreams. I, of course, catch the plot against me before the hero in the picture did. I also punish the offenders more severely. I imagine myself outwitting every villain, any enemy of mine and coming out of every battle victorious and unscratched.

Whether the suggestions be those gained in early childhood or those acquired in adolescence the same deep impression of motion picture imagery is to be noted.

It was during these days that I saw my first moving picture. I remember a certain scene very well. There was a young man who because of some reason was thrown into prison. A day or so later a young lady entered his cell (she probably was his sweetheart), and brought him some food including a loaf of bread. After the jailer and the young lady had left, this young man began to eat. He took the loaf of bread in his hands and broke it in half. No sooner had he done so than he saw a black object which on closer investigation proved to be a file. That scene as I have said impressed me very much, and it took me many months to get over the fact that files did not come in loaves of bread. Whenever my mother would cut a loaf of bread, I would always expect the knife to strike against the file that I thought would be there.

Not long after that my father took me to the moving pictures again. The second picture that I saw had a scene that would impress me far more than the prison scene. There were two men in a room. One was a young man and the other an elderly man, probably his father. The young man seemed to be in great mental agony. The older man took him aside and tried to soothe him, finally ending by telling him what his brain was like when he worried. While he was speaking the young man's head became bigger and bigger until it occupied the whole screen. Then the upper part of his head faded a little and there was a river flowing between two embankments of earth. As the water flowed it slowly ate away the earth. The old man was telling him that something on a similar basis was happening to his brain. That is a scene that really frightened me for many years. Whenever my parents worried that scene would immediately come to me for many years and I would fear for their brains. Today I am over twenty-three years of age and whenever I am alone thinking, that scene of a river flowing between the two embankments comes before my eyes. Of course, I do not have the fear that I had for it when a child, but I mention it to show the deep hold that that scene has on me.

Another striking phenomenon frequently observed in the interviews with boys and in the life histories written by them is a frequency with which the boy in his imagination projects himself into the role of the hero in the motion picture. Though the information upon this phenomenon is at present meager, the presumption is that the extent and nature of this transference is conditioned by the past experiences of the subject, the extent to which these experiences make it possible for him to project himself into such a role. In the following instance the individual in projecting himself into a role in a photoplay selects one who is somewhat like himself, both in appearance and nationality.

My first yearning to become a movie star was when Valentino passed away. That was because my folks and friends were saying that I looked very much like him. I had a scar on myself as he had and combed my hair in the same style. Then I did not think of the fact that I lacked eight or nine inches to be as tall as he was. I could already picture myself taking Vilma Banky in my arms and kissing her. Flashing my eyes here and there. And whenever I would reach the Grand Central Station young ladies would beg for my autograph or attempt to kiss me and probably swoon away. The idea of running away to Hollywood began to gnaw on my brain but thank heavens I got over it after a few years.

More frequently the documents in this study reveal this tendency toward projection of one's self into the picture but not as obviously and perfectly as is indicated above. However, in the interviews it was quite common to have the child indicate that he did not like a certain gangster picture because "he died." This, if one is willing to admit the interpretation at least, gives some basis for the belief that this tendency on the part of the boy or young man to project himself into a role in the picture is relatively common. Further, there would seem to be a tendency for this projection of one's self into a role of a motion picture actor and the emulation of him results sometimes in a changed demeanor in his everyday activities. The following is but an illustration of this tendency toward projection and emulation.

I also recall that I saw a picture entitled "The Ghost Breaker" [1922] starring Wallace Reid. That picture was gone over by the gang for many many nights. In fact that picture helped in a way to break my fear of the dark. Whenever my mother would tell me to go upstairs, I would go with a pounding heart – but I would keep on telling myself that Wallace Reid was not afraid of ghosts so why should I be.

The extent of this tendency to carry over into one's personality in life's activities the role into which one has projected himself in the photoplay is indicated by, at least, phenomena noted in this study: (1) the plays and games of children, and (2) the tendency sometimes observed in this community for boys to take over in rather "whole cloth" a personality pattern seen and admired in a photoplay. Countless instances can be found in the play of children to indicate the "carry over" of movie patterns.[90] Whether the boys' interests in western plays or in films dealing with "cops and robbers" is cause or effect for the spontaneous play activities, it is not necessary here to discuss. Clearly there is an obvious relationship between these play patterns and the films.

. . . Sometimes the intensity of the play activity exceeds normal bounds and serious consequences occasionally result.

I went to the theater almost every day and when I came out I would try some of the things I had seen done on the screen on some other boy. After seeing the first chapter of the "Green Archer" [1925] all the kids in my block made bows and arrows out of old umbrellas. Shooting these at each other we had great fun, not realizing that the points of these might stick one of us in the eye and blind him. We used to make darts out of a match stick and needle and paper. Splitting the match stick at one end, we put the paper into the slit. This acts as feathers. Then we push the eye of the needle into the other end of the match stick. We now have our dart. I once threw one of these just as my brother was passing and it stuck in his nose just below his eyes. I was afraid but glad that it did not stick him in his eyes. I never threw one of these darts again.

Several instances are on record in this study in which the "acting out" of a vivid scene in a photoplay resulted in such intense portrayal that the lives of some of the participants were endangered.

In response to information secured through a social agency a call was made at the home of a very bright, active and euphoric little boy of seven, whose conduct was reported to be seriously influenced by motion picture imagery. Among other instances of the child's behavior, the mother mentioned particularly the frequency with which he and his playmates "act out" what he has seen in a recent "Western" photoplay. To illustrate the extent to which his imagery seems to be dominated by what he sees in these pictures the mother asked the boy to tell us what he had seen in the last "Hoot Gibson" picture.

Immediately his eyes began to flash and he began very rapidly to spin off a seemingly endless line of talk, illustrating his description by hopping about the room, using his hands to represent guns, etc., such as: "Then Hoot Gibson sees the bad guy and he takes a shot at the bad guy and the bad guy runs out around the cliff and then the other good guy sees him and he shoots at him but the other bad guys came up from behind and shot the good guy and then Hoot Gibson comes around and he goes 'boom, boom' and three bad guys fall dead but Hoot Gibson gets away," etc.

The boy apparently upon the slightest provocation is ready to go through the whole scene over again, acting it out a second or third time with as much enthusiasm as the first.

The mother told of an incident which happened but a week before which caused her a great deal of worry. A somewhat older and larger boy in the neighborhood who nevertheless was not liked very well, and was reported to be mentally slow, had somehow been induced to play the part of a victim when the three others – her own little boy among them – were with entirely too much realism acting out a hanging. The boy when rescued was blind folded, his feet upon the ground, his hands tied securely behind him and a noose around his neck was suspended from an eyelet fixed upon a pole in a neighbor's yard. The mother reports that it was only because of the interference of a neighbor who fortunately saw the incident that the boy's life was spared. When the neighbor interfered they were pulling at the rope to lift him from the ground. In a subsequent interview with the boy it was ascertained that it was their interpretation of a Hoot Gibson picture which they had recently seen.

Occasionally this type of play activity results in serious injury or a fatality. Recently in a New York suburb, such play of children was reported to have been responsible for the accidental killing of one of the participants.

... The most significant cases of this tendency to imitate actors however are the instances in which young men have been found to adopt the personality patterns shown in Edward G. Robinson's portrayal of "Little Caesar." Three striking situations of this have been recorded.

"Call me Little Caesar," Ernie Rico, 23, of XX Street told his friends several months ago after witnessing a current movie of that name. . . . "Gee, I'd like to be a guy like that!" But a short time after he was found in a dying condition on the streets near his home. He had been stabbed twice, once under the heart and once near the abdomen, in an altercation which was found later to have resulted from an argument over a division of profits from hauling a truck load of bootleg beer.

Inquiry at the home of the young man following his funeral revealed that this young man had served for over a year and one half as a taxi driver getting into no trouble whatever. But finding business more uncertain he lost some of his enthusiasm and turned to the attendance of motion pictures. His parents, while quite reluctant to give any information, indicated that his attendance at motion pictures had been quite casual and apparently without any great significance until but a few months before his death when he chanced to attend the photoplay "Little Caesar." His father said that after seeing this photoplay he came home from the theater very enthusiastic saying that "it was a great picture" and insisting that his father should see it. The father further states that in the next two days his son attended two other showings of this film, each time coming home with renewed enthusiasm for the picture. The father said that following his son's renewed efforts to tell of this photoplay, he became angry and ordered the son to refrain from any more comments regarding it. The father reported also that shortly after his son became associated with a group of petty racketeers and bootleggers with whom he had been acquainted but had never had, to his knowledge, any regular associations with.

In an investigation into the home and the reported personality of the young man, it was indicated that while the home and psychological make up of the boy were not ideal, there was nothing exceptionally unusual or atypical. There was a step mother in the home toward whom the son was reported to be, at least, cordial. The young man himself was reported by several informers to be somewhat "temperamental" and "easily led." However, police reports indicate that they had no previous record upon him and that he had not been reported even as a juvenile delinquent.

The extent to which the chance fact that the "Little Caesar" in the photoplay was represented as having the name "Rico," the same surname of this young man, has a bearing upon this young man's adoption of the "Little Caesar" role, could not be established. Newspaper accounts and the report of the father and mother to indicate that he made frequent reference to the "Little Caesar" picture and desired to be called "Little Caesar" make it seem, at least, plausible that this chance association of names also contributed in this case.[91]

. . . Any attempt to seek to understand this very great appeal which the gangster and underworld pictures make to street boys of this type of necessity must include many factors. One of the chief appeals is, no doubt, the romantic and attractive life enjoyed for a time by the gangster heroes. For boys who have been restricted on all sides by poverty, the appeal of expensive apartments, costly automobiles, and "flashy" clothes seems in itself to be an invitation toward that type of activity and aspiration. Even though the boy may not consciously and deliberately plan for a criminal career, the constant association in the photoplay of opulence and the underworld career may in the end have its effect. Whether – as is sometimes claimed – such photoplays serve as a vicarious expression for repressed impulses, it is apparent that these appeals coupled with the typical human tendency to project oneself into the photoplay in itself sometimes lead toward an interest in criminal exploits. In the following case a young man of good family and background and training, who was allowed considerable unsupervised leisure, eventually became involved with a petty racketeer and his assistant, all three of whom were apprehended while attempting to burglarize. Although making no claim that the photoplays in themselves were cause for his crime, he suggested that the attraction of the large automobile, flashy clothes, attractive women with which the gangster life in the movies had been associated, was a background of impression by which the racketeer was able to interest him in this type of career. He was quite ready to admit that if immediate sufficient income had been available to him through legitimate work, he would not have succumbed to these appeals, but with these impressions gained from gangster movies and from the concrete attractiveness of the gangster car and his big roll of bills, he was induced to enter into crime.

... From a sympathetic interpretation of the plot and emotional stress of the criminal in the photoplay, it is quite possible for one of normal or even superior intelligence under the stress of circumstances to succumb, at least, temporarily to some of the suggestions toward crime included in the photoplay. Although the evidence on this point is far from adequate for thorough generalization, there are individual instances[92] to suggest that this is an hypothesis which justifies further research.

Not only are the emotions of the spectators of films stirred to sympathy for the gangster and criminal; they are also aroused to sympathy for their mother, their kid brother, and often for their dog. Of all the films mentioned, "Over the Hill" [1931] was given the most frequently as that which influenced them most. This film apparently retold the old story of the sons who forget the devotion of their aged mother and in their ambition for themselves allowed her eventually to be sent to the poor house. One young man reports, "There was a certain picture that made me think a great deal about my mother; that was 'Over the Hill.' When I saw that picture I decided that whatever the knocks or profits I would be able to get out of this life, my mother would always share in them." Another writes, "One picture that remained in my mind very vividly was 'Over the Hill' with Jimmie Walker. I enjoyed the scene when he drags his brother all the way to the old woman's home. It was a scene that I shall never forget as long as I have my mother. I remember how much I tried to make her happy after seeing that picture."

Among the interviews with the young boys many references were made to this picture. In most instances the boys told of going home from the theater and doing some act to show their affection for their mother. One boy said, "After seeing that picture I went home and kissed my mother and then I brought up the wood for a week without her having to tell me." Sympathy for unfortunate people has also been evoked by the motion pictures. One boy writing his experiences on motion pictures tells of the effect of a filming of "Uncle Tom's Cabin" [1927] upon him.

As far as I can remember "Uncle Tom's Cabin" made me react to its scenes of agony with tears. When Simon Legree beat Uncle Tom with his whip, the agony Uncle Tom underwent was too much for me to stand and I burst into tears and felt like going up to the picture and tearing Simon Legree apart.

Another striking emotional effect of the motion pictures seems to have been the stimulation of fear reactions. Especially to young boys who have already been shown to be higher in emotional instability, the mystery pictures and the portrayals of weird phenomena have seemed to have their effect. In the following excerpts certain boys in the community tell of their experiences in witnessing such films:

After seeing pictures like "The Terror" and "Frankenstein" [1931], I feel horrified and frightened especially when coming home at night alone. I am not afraid outside but in my mind I realize and measure the horror of it all. It disappears after a day. While seeing "Frankenstein" I became horrified when Frankenstein was digging for dead bodies and when he was making the monster. During that time I felt a tinge of fear creep through the sides of my body. It started from my hand and swiftly went down to my feet. When it reached my feet my mouth watered and my cheeks felt like they went in a little bit. This fear only stood for a moment. When I jumped into bed late that night with everybody asleep the picture unwound in my mind and I thought that any moment my great imagination would cause me to see that monster but as soon as I laid my head on the pillow the fear disappeared and I thought of this picture without any fear whatsoever. The next day I related this picture to a friend without the slightest bit of fear. I get my greatest fear when I see a person on the screen imagining that he sees someone. This image scares me until it leaves. Why I feel scared for this I don't know.

I was once frightened by a motion picture when I saw "The Phantom of the Opera" [1925]. I once had to go down through the cellar to the back yard to pick up a pair of underwear. In this picture the man had the face of a skeleton. While passing through the cellar I heard somebody walk. I stood motionless. My heart began to beat furiously, my blood began to run cold in my veins, all of a sudden. I let out a yell, "mama!" and to my surprise there stood the janitor before me asking what was the matter. Even to this day I hate to go alone in a dark place without anybody with me, when I recall that experience when I was in the cellar.

The picture that horrified me the most was "The Phantom of the Opera." I was at the age of 10 or 11 years. The scene was when the opera singer took the mask off the phantom, disclosing the hideous monster. The monster began coming nearer and nearer. I got up and walked out. The fact haunted me so much that I dreamed of it. The fright lasted for two or three days but as each day passed the fright lessened. Scenes of agony never seemed to remain in my mind, because I tried to dismiss them by saying "it's only a picture." But I remember a scene in "The Cossacks" [1928] when John Gilbert was being tortured by the Turks. I began to become restless, I chewed my nails and felt a lump in my throat. Some scenes did make me cry but when it became too sad I went home very gloomy. I judge a picture by the acting; a sad picture might be a very good one but it doesn't appeal to me.

The following report by Dr. Whitley is but typical of much material which he obtained in his research. It should be noted in some of these cases that while excessive attendance at the motion pictures does aid and abet emotional instability, some of the following cases indicate an emotional instability which is almost abnormal:

Three boys indicated that they dream about pictures that they have seen. Case 16 reports that he dreams that somebody is getting shot. Case 41 said, "When I seen 'The Phantom of the Opera' I dreamed that I seen something white. I was scared. He was in the room. I waked up and I went like this and I went to sleep again."

This boy's problems consist of stealing, gambling, truancy and malingering. The boy occasionally has a fainting spell and apparently goes into unconsciousness. He gives evidence of a trend toward paranoia.

He said that he likes to play by himself better than to play with other boys, that other boys don't let him play with them; that he has run away from homes; that it makes him uneasy to cross a bridge over water; that he is afraid of water; that he is afraid during a thunder storm; that he is afraid of the dark; that he is frightened in the middle of the night; that he talks in his sleep; that he dreams about play; that he cries himself to sleep; that he sometimes stutters; that he gets cross over small things; that he cannot stand pain as quietly as other boys; that he has a harder time in school than other boys; that his eyes pain him often; that he has headaches often; that he has fainted; that he has a feeling that things are not real; that he feels somebody is following him; that he is afraid of fire; that he does not make friends easily; that he gets tired of people easily; that he has superstitions; that he thinks that he sees something when he doesn't and that he is a bad boy.

Q. Are you troubled with dreams about your play?
A. Yeah, sometimes I go to shows and see mystery pictures and after at night I dream about them, and everything like that. They come nearer and nearer and after I feel like they are on top of me. I holler when they are on top of me.
Q. And then what happens?
A. My mother gets up and my father and they say, "What's the matter, what's the matter?"

Q. Do you ever have the same dream over and over?
A. Yeah, the dreams about that man.
Q. Do you dream the same thing about him every time?
A. Every time.[93]

There is considerable reason to believe that in some cases the strong preference of certain boys for the weird and mystery pictures itself reflects a natural emotional instability or the influences of a home or community situation which stimulates fantastic fear reactions. In these cases, it seems to be apparent, the boys genuinely "enjoy" being frightened.

. . . In any case, however, it should be noted that excessive attendance at mystery pictures for the pre-adolescent serves only to aggravate further the emotional instability which no doubt contributes appreciably to sleeplessness and nervousness as well.

As the boy becomes older, however, the Western pictures and mystery pictures or even the gangster pictures very often come to have less appeal. With it there seems to come gradually an increase in the interest in love and romance photoplays.

. . . But with the coming of these interests new problems in adjustment present themselves. He is beset by the interests arising from a maturing of sex and at the same time is most curious of this veiled but apparently very interesting world of sex and romance. In the boy's adjustment to this whole problem the theaters play a part. On the one hand he finds in the theater many instances for defining his random sexual interests in wholesome terms of love and romance. On the other hand he also finds there an opportunity for overt sexual stimulation as well.[94] One characteristic reaction is the conception of "dirty pictures," "dirty writing," etc. It is interesting that the younger boy in his selection of his movie very seldom seems voluntarily to choose the film strongly charged with sex stimuli. His first reaction to so-called "love pictures," that of indifference or dislike, reflects this inability to understand and to participate in such a photoplay, but toward the more obvious evidence of the world of sex such as scenes showing young women in dishabille he does understand and respond. Whitley reports as follows:

Sixteen boys indicated that they were stimulated in some way sexually by what they saw on the screen or by the behavior which they observed in the movie house. This boy reported that in one movie a girl was undressed behind the screen and the leading man in the movie "went over there and was talking with the girl right in her face."

But in such a community as this and with the definitions of sex which are at hand on every side, the boy quickly gains a certain type of sex sophistication which serves in part only to intensify the moral struggle against that which for him has come to be defined as "dirty."

This boy likes sound pictures better than the others. He goes almost every Saturday night after work. He goes to see Broadway midnight shows. He liked the "The Singing Fool" [1928] best. "When Al Jolson sang the song to his boy when he was dying he didn't know it." He felt sympathetic when he saw this picture. He likes a nice picture that is interesting. He doesn't like western pictures. He sometimes likes the comedies, the Fox Movietone Comedies. He goes with some friends to the shows when he goes. In speaking of a picture which he saw he said, "A guy owned a cabaret and there was a house of assignation upstairs and there was a lot of rooms and every time a fellow was stewed he used to go to the room and the guy said 'Get that darn thing out of here.' "

The possibility for this definition to be intensified through experiences with motion pictures and the reaction of the spectator to them is seen in the accounts given by institutionalized boys of their experiences with "dirty moving pictures." In one institution with which some of the boys interviewed had had some experience, it apparently had been the practice of those in charge to exhibit the general run of photoplays without previewing them carefully. As a result photoplays presented occasionally showed scenes which called forth responses from the boys when viewing them at the institution. It is interesting that in this way for some of the younger boys in this institution the definition of what was a "dirty picture" was most effectively made.

Q. Which picture do you like best?
A. Everything but love pictures. I don't go for them at all.
Q. Why?
A. Sometimes they show dirty parts of them though, and at the home (institution) they cut them off.
Q. What are the dirty parts you didn't like?
A. They show you legs and they all start hollering so they take the picture off.
Q. Who starts hollering?
A. All the guys. They say, "Come on, put it on again," so they take the picture off.
Q. Do you like the dirty parts?
A. No.

Q. How about at the "home"?

A. Yeh, sure, I did there. When we saw a picture about bad girls they shut the pictures off and then I got hot.

Nowhere is the emotional association between movie actors and characters and the emotional organization of their movie patrons seen more clearly than in the emotional reactions to actors as seen in the autoneurotic practices of boys. While it is to be expected that practically all boys in this community will engage in onanism at some time, it is surprising that as large a proportion that do tell of emotional responses to certain actresses on the screen which results either in autoeroticism in the theater or elsewhere later. At least nine-tenths of the boys questioned admitted masturbation in some form. Of these nearly half indicated that they have at some time engaged in autoeroticism either with a picture of their favorite actress before them or have it very definitely in their "mind's eye" at the time. Interesting in this connection is the fact that a considerable number of these boys and young men stated definitely that one actress, Jean Harlow by name, has in their mind played this role. Typical of these responses is the following stenographically recorded interview.

Q. Do you ever sit in the movies and get excited?

A. It don't bother me much now.

Q. You did?

A. I used to.

Q. Do you dream?

A. Yes.

Q. What kind?

A. Things you see in the movies. What I like to do, what I like to be, being rich, all kinds of funny dreams.

Q. Do you get wet dreams?

A. Once in a while.

Q. What kind of women do you dream about?

A. Any kind.

Q. Who?

A. For instance, Jean Harlow.

Q. Dream about her, once in a while?

A. Sure.

Q. Who do you think of when you masturbate?

A. Anybody, anybody that comes to my head.

Q. For instance?

A. Jean Harlow.

For others the emotional preachment to the screen may take channels which reflect an incorporation within the boy's conception of "nice girls" of the appearance and personality traits of a favorite movie actress. Thus the type of young woman the boy may select for his "best girl" may occasionally be influenced by his previous response to a movie actress. Such is apparently the type of adjustment found in the following case.

Q. Would you like to have a girl like that? Is your best girl like any actress you know?
A. No, well, she reminds me a little of Mary Astor.
Q. Well, what is Mary Astor like?
A. She is a kind of doll. Got a good line.
Q. What is there about your girl that reminds you of Mary Astor?
A. Do we have to go into that?
Q. Not if you don't want to.
A. Well, she looks like her.
Q. Tall, slender girl with brown eyes – dimples or something like that? Did you ever tell your girl that she looked like Mary Astor? Why didn't you tell her she looked like a movie actress? When did you have your last date with your girl?
A. Sunday last.
Q. Did you go to the movies?
A. Yes.
Q. What kind of movies does she like?
A. Love pictures.

CHAPTER FIVE

The Intervale Study

"New York University Motion Picture Study – Outline of Chapters," the manuscript reproduced in this chapter, is a model for *Boys, Movies and City Streets*. According to the cover letter accompanying it,[1] the manuscript was completed by 5 August 1934 and sent to W. W. Charters in advance of a conference between them about the prospects for Cressey's completing and publishing the overdue manuscript. It was written not long after Cressey had experienced his "epiphany" that the sociological premises on which he and the other Payne Fund researchers had been trying to study the movies as a social phenomenon were far too restricted.

Cressey's realization had led him to scrap much of the previous research done for the project he took over, reinterpret what was left and begin collecting more data. It also led him to redesign and retitle the project. The fact that the long manuscript reprinted in Chapter Four does not have the title "Boys, Movies and City Streets" but "The Community – A Social Setting for the Motion Picture" shows that he was shifting from an emphasis on what movies did to boys on city streets to an attempt to place the movies in a wider social context where they are merely one link in the complex chain of social causation. We know that Cressey was awarded his Ph.D. for a dissertation entitled "The Social Role of the Motion Picture in an Interstitial Area" (a manuscript that he continued to list as unpublished in 1947),[2] which may have been as much as he was prepared to concede to the expectations aroused by the dramatic original title.

In the absence of that dissertation we have to look elsewhere for more information on the direction his thought was taking. We have the two major journal articles of the late 1930s, as well as his review of Adler's attack on the Payne Fund series.³ Fortunately, some other, intermediate evidence turned up. This is the "New York University Motion Picture Study – Outline of Chapters," which contains the nearest thing we have to a synopsis of the dissertation.

The reader will see how Cressey, who had been financed to concentrate on delinquent boys, intended to shift the perspective from how they were affected by movies to general questions about the presence of movie theaters on city streets. In Part One the motion picture theater is presented as part of the social world. Cressey sketches "Intervale" itself, its general social setup and the character and failures of the major institutions of the family and the school. He brings out what researchers of that era referred to as the "social disorganization"⁴ in which the youth of such areas lived.

In Part Two Cressey brilliantly reverses the angle of view: now the motion picture theater is a social world in itself, providing special opportunities for socializing in its lobby and dark auditorium. It is an institution in the community – moviegoing is an established "folkway."⁵ In Part Three he goes deeper, into what we would now label "reception theory" (fifty years before that term became fashionable). He wanted to explore the "meaning and value of the photoplay in the life and thought of patrons," utilizing sophisticated psychological notions of the time. He looked at how movies were integrated into children's play. Only when more than halfway through the outline did he finally turn to delinquency and offer his considered view that "the photoplay, upon the basis of data available upon Intervale, cannot be said, strictly speaking, to be a 'causative factor' in delinquency" (Short's reactions can be imagined).

In another bold leap, Cressey in Part Four looks at how "youth measures itself against the world," the world seen primarily through the cinema. Cressey wanted to show how the young viewer incorporated material learned informally at the movies into the formation of ideals, standards and schemes of life, for the movie theater was "a second school house" – a school house that took over where formal schooling failed, and that utilized motion pictures, a potent method for certain kinds of education. Cressey ended with a set of recommendations that we may find startling in their prescience, since a good many of them were in due time implemented.

Emblematic of the quality of Cressey's thinking, even in these notes for a project, is the following:

The ultimate factor to be noted in all the controversy regarding the movie is that the cinema is really an agency in "speeding up" communication. . . . Thus the cinema is bringing to remote centers with more facility "foreign" (i.e. locally unapproved) patterns of life which before were not presented.[6] Significantly, its contribution is not merely to facilitate the contact of local citizens with those elsewhere (as with the telephone) but whole patterns of life as unities are presented. "Psychological mobility" rather than spatial mobility is here involved but it is nevertheless very real mobility.

Cressey's thinking was wide-ranging and deep. He developed ideas that were unfortunately lost but that, before communications studies could advance, would have to be rediscovered by others. Cressey succeeded in moving well beyond a position that is still taken for granted in public thinking about the role of electronic mass media in society.

We have edited the document slightly, correcting errors of grammar and punctuation, completing bibliographic references and, for clarity's sake, eliminating a few lists of the case study documents Cressey wished to use. It can be located in the Charters papers, Cressey file, Ohio State University.

New York University Motion Picture Study – Outline of Chapters

PAUL G. CRESSEY

Part One: Hollywood Comes to Intervale

INTRODUCTION: BOY LIFE IN INTERVALE

A picture of boy-life on the streets of Intervale, with an emphasis upon those aspects of street play which are especially influenced by congestion and poverty, i.e., health and auto-accident and manslaughter records; also baseball converted into stick-ball and stoop-ball, marbles to flipping coins and block checkers, and lawn tennis converted into sidewalk box-ball. Practical difficulties in reaching what limited park facilities as are available – and the alternatives in sedentary games – cards, dice, "numbers," "odds and even" and the game of license numbers.

The history of the area seen from point of view of invasion and succession as is viable today in institutional vestiges: old Dutch buildings and churches, German turn-vereins, Russian churches, Czarist consul service, Jewish synagogues and schools, markets, Italian stores, Spanish. Ending with emphasis upon high mobility, cosmopolitanism, economic penury as is experienced by the boy in the street world's requirements in spending money, Catholicity in standards and conduct, "front," "promptness" of action, individual resourcefulness, "toughness" and the only tangible and immediate requirement – that of "getting by." This street life is an interesting, thrilling, fascinating world to which children, to feel themselves a part, must be introduced when quite young.

Then follow several paragraphs telling very simply of our methods and approach to these problems – with a brief justification of these.

CHAPTER I: HOLLYWOOD COMES TO INTERVALE

The local movie graphically shows – and presented as a "way out" – a possible and practical escape from the conflict, strife and hazards of this street world. A documentary picture of child behavior in a movie theater – response of children to screen portrayals.

Questions which the presence of the movie theater in such an area raises. Is it an opiate which releases from the restraints and inadequacies of life? Does it stimulate to envy, unrest, or to imitation or ambition? Does it educate or merely entertain? Does it stimulate toward crime; and if it does educate – in what direction and how extensively does it educate?

How Hollywood Invades Intervale: newspaper advertising, billboards, window cards, store tie-ups, endorsed merchandise, use of prizes and gifts; radio and newspaper copy and street play indicating indirect impact of Hollywood upon Intervale. Special reference to ballyhoo – documentary material on "Flying Down to Rio" [1933] and "The Carioca" (a popular dance step).

The Intervale movie diet itself – statistical tables upon the East Harlem movie diet and comparison statistically with Dale's findings, using the same scheme of classification. Interpretations of these findings. Possibly some reference in certain current photoplays indicating some of the commendable and questionable aspects of content of these and the nature of educational content by types of photoplays.

CHAPTER II: INTERVALE AS AN INTERSTITIAL AREA

Early movie theaters and present theaters in Intervale. Number of the latter, their distribution, seating capacity and estimated attendance. History of area and ecological succession presented from the standpoint of theater history.

Definition of an interstitial area (quoting Thrasher, *The Gang*); citing characteristics of areas of deterioration (as given by Shaw, *Causes of Crime*, volume II), citing evidence from Intervale upon these points. Much of this chapter taken from Cressey's Preliminary Report, Division I.[1]

CHAPTER III: THE BOY, HIS FAMILY AND HIS SCHOOL

The typical Intervale family, its structure, the roles of its members (patriarchal pattern); basic mores and cultural values. Essential differences which affect the problem.

The boy of foreign parents and his experiences in a typical American school system. Definitions of situation, acquiring of social roles, instances of interaction to logical extremes, truancy and delinquency. . . . Only outstanding factors in school conflicts will be cited and these will be discussed only as situations which *sometimes* arise.

CHAPTER IV: THE YOUTH'S STREET WORLD AND
DISORGANIZATION

The world of the street as a major socializing force in the boy's life. The influence of the gang, the hang out, the pool hall, the stoops, roofs, backyards, vacant lots, docks, water front. Certain sociological forces such as mobility, anonymity and the opportunity for promiscuity. The gang and hang-out seen as agencies which seem temporarily to resolve the conflicts in the boy's life but which in turn contribute ultimately to further disorganization. . . .

Part Two: The Motion Picture Theater, a Social World

CHAPTER V: THE BOY GOES TO THE THEATER

The attendance habits of Intervale youth. . . . Frequency of attendance, by days of the week, by hours in day, with whom attended. How he chooses his movies. What he says he selects. What he actually sees. . . .

Ecological and economic factors in the choice of theater. (Spot map of residence of patrons of each theater related to location of theater and to ecological configuration of area.) Special roles of theaters in the lives of boys in the area ("Dump," "Wop House"). Prestige values in attending theaters and devices for "keeping face" despite inadequate funds for attending preferred theaters. Gangs in attendance and activities and interests in attending theater.

Methods of Entrance: Youth's experience with evasion of the law –
begging an adult to "take him in" – use of "Professional Buyer" –

"Stealing" one's way in. Women and girls soliciting to be taken into theater. Special ways for earning admission. Gang intimidation of proprietor to gain admission and special privileges. Effects of constant violation of child attendance law; reproduce New York law and show how it puts New York City police "on the spot."

CHAPTER VI: THE THEATER HOUSE, AN ADVENTURE IN CONTACTS

The Theater House as a social world. Special vocabulary and practices. Many different distinct types of personality, each treated with certain special considerations by the ushers. . . . The code and policy of the theater house as enforced by ushers. . . . Boy's recognition of differential standards of supervision among theaters in Intervale. These differences in turn conditioned by ecological position in area, racial groups served, and appropriate adjustments in conduct. Documents upon some theaters as places to "raise Cain" and others as "high class."

What goes on in a movie house. Wide variety: from child birth to auctioning of automobile. Under a cloak of anonymity, many theaters in Intervale (except for midsummer) are a sexual hunting ground: heterosexual interests, homosexuals, prostitutes soliciting, married women seeking diversion. The technique and the code of the "pick-up." Petting, courtship, and occasional use of the theater as a house of assignation. Theater as a place for the truant and criminal to "hide out" (also to "forget" his troubles) and for criminal or gangs of racketeers by attendance at certain times to establish a satisfactory alibi. Stealing, lush diving (jack-rolling), rackets for exploiting homosexuals and for "placing" runaways and others sought by parents or police.

The theater proprietor's conception of his problem and of his responsibilities. The policy and the code of Intervale theaters (somewhat differentiated among theaters): the seat hopper (one seeking pick up), the masher, soliciting, homosexuals in theater, uses of reputed gangsters in theaters to "keep order." The ticket taker's conception of his patrons and of his job. The candy butcher and the bouncer's conception of his role and his community.

Some results of contacts made in the theater: line ups, contact with criminals (Fagans), contact with homosexuals, prostitutes, but indicate that these are experiences which follow cinema attendance only occasionally.

CHAPTER VII: THE MOTION PICTURE THEATER AS AN
INSTITUTION IN THE COMMUNITY

"Going to the movies" as an established folkway in our society. Youth's
acceptance of his "right" to go to the movies. Even though family
undernourished and being cared for through public relief, they somehow
reserve some money to "go to the movies." Use of movies as common
subject for conversation, getting acquainted and for maintaining status.
To have seen the "latest movies" is a matter of social status among those
of high school age. The necessity in certain other circles (delinquents and
idlers) for seeing certain movies once the "local board of review" (fellows who see shows first on Broadway and later report upon them to
crowd at pool room) has approved them.

The prestige and omnipresence of the screen world and movie stars
in the lives of children and youth. Added data: the children's extraordinary knowledge of actors and actresses and photoplays. . . . Also, importance of movies in the program of a large boys' club in the area and
in other social settlements and churches. The purchase of endorsed
merchandise, of movie magazines, the joining of fan clubs, the use of
cinema stars as models for hair dress and costume design, Cinema
Shops[2] and in the use of popular songs introduced through recent musical pictures. . . .

The theater in its social, economic and political inter-relationship to
the community: accommodating itself to standards and practices of the
community and patrons (documents contrasting tolerance of institutionalized lobby soliciting at midnight shows at Spanish theater with stricter
supervision during hours for family patronage, and contrast between
policy of Mt. Morris and Cosmo [theaters] re: homosexuals; contributions to local charity by managers, free benefits shows; advertising tie-
ups with local stores selling merchandise endorsed by stars being featured at that time in photoplay at the theater; practice of employing all
help through local Tammany organization and in turn getting certain
privileges in building and fire regulations. Christmas remembrances to
police and politicians.

Function of the theater in the lives of patrons. Many incidental functions as well as main functions: place to "check" the children (document
on baby carriage row and doorman serving as nursemaid, calling mothers when needed); retreat from noise and turmoil of overcrowded apartment; place to keep warm and save on coal bill in winter; substitute for

courtship parlor of other days; place for clandestine sex adventure; place to sleep; for pastime for these unemployed (document of uses of movies by the unemployed). Main functions of movies in the lives of certain boys and young people of interstitial area.

Part Three: The Photoplay's Appeal and the Patron's Interests and Activities

CHAPTER VIII: MEANING AND VALUE OF THE PHOTOPLAY IN THE LIFE AND THOUGHT OF PATRONS

A discussion of the question of whether the photoplay is for children and youth a "vicarious experience" and release of repressed impulses and unsatisfied wishes, or whether it is for them a "broadening" of their world. Some criticism of psychoanalytical assumptions and inferences and citation of case material. . . . Probable conclusion: that while instances can be found where the screen world was a retreat from unpleasant and dissatisfying experiences in the play world, the photoplay is for children and youth (perhaps to a higher degree than is true for adults) an adding of additional experiences and interests – in short, an "education" (in truest sense of the term). (Note: special exceptions will be made for emotionally atypical and psychopathic viewers.)

The hypothesis will be offered that the significant responses of patrons to photoplays can, if enough is known, be related to the subject's social background, his emotional dynamics and to his axiological world. If enough is known it is suggested that such a relationship can be seen in that content of the photoplay which in some way is thought by the subject to be specifically related to his own interests, his personal problems and his own conceptions of life. Further, it is suggested that what will be perceived in the photoplay, what will be remembered longest and most vividly, and what possibly will in some way be used subsequently by the individual in his own thinking and his conduct can be found to be so related. . . .

The questionnaires which include data upon movie preferences in films and stars which have been obtained from several outlying suburbs . . . will provide a basis for an interesting comparison with our data for the same age and sex groupings in East Harlem. Similarly, the findings upon the drawing study could, in this connection, be made very valuable through a comparison with a small sampling of drawings from a similar assignment in the public schools of Montclair (to which I am confident I can gain access). Visual imagery will in this way be given some consideration. Small samplings of drawings in other suburbs made by my students in former years seem to support the above hypothesis. . . .

Another very interesting aspect is the study of the preferences in photoplays in terms of the age (and where possible, the mental age) of the boys and young men. Special tabulations of preferences, both by individual "best pictures" and by "types of pictures," are now being made. It is anticipated that certain general cycles in movie preferences and interest can be discovered. Hypothetically it is hoped that these preferences can be linked with what is known of the interests and activities of boys and youth of different ages. In this way it is hoped that a second suggestion – really to be incorporated as a part of the same basic hypothesis – can be offered; to wit, that responses to the motion picture can also be related to the socio-biologic process of "growing up."

It is also suggested that a detailed analysis of the immediate settings in the photoplays which, according to the data available, apparently elicited very definite responses from the subjects would be a very productive line of effort. These immediate photoplay "settings" could of course be related in each instance to the nature of the response the photoplay setting was recorded as having elicited in the subject and, also, to pertinent aspects of the subject's known social background, his emotional dynamics, axiological world, and life-organization.[3]

At this time the process by which the subject "projects" himself into the photoplay and responds to it is being explored using as a point of reference the suggestion from Max Scheler as given by Howard Becker in the *Journal of Abnormal and Social Psychology*.[4] Here Scheler is quoted as defining six definite "forms," or "stages" or "degrees," in this basic process, and which, possibly, may be found on occasion to result in differentiated responses on the part of subjects themselves. These "forms" or "stages" as defined include: mimpathy, compathy, transpathy, empathy, sympathy (a restricted definition), and unipathy (or "identification"). As yet only two or three of these have been noted in our materials and much of our case material is not sufficiently penetrating to make possible finer distinctions. However, tentatively a hypothesis may be offered, for instance, that the subject's response may tend more frequently to be restricted to intellectual or attitudinal qualities – "impressions," "general information" or "stereotypes" – when the situation is that of empathy, than when it can more accurately be defined as "sympathy" (strictly defined) or "unipathy." Other similar hypotheses may of course develop. Editorially, Becker in this article suggests that the small child at a theatrical performance may actually experience "unipathy" (i.e. momentarily a complete identification with the character being portrayed or with the situation); that the child's responses may be very different and of a different quality from those of adults. Also, studies by anthropologists of cultural transmission and selection should be of assistance, notably the work of Margaret Mead, Lowie, and others. Special inquiry in this regard remains to be done.

CHAPTER IX: THE SCREEN WORLD AND THE BOY'S PLAY WORLD

Here, the implications of principles stated in the previous chapter are restated in terms of considerable case material upon dramatic play. Presentation of striking parallels between the boy's interests, activities, and standards of value at the time and his preferences as to actors, photoplays, types of photoplays, his "best pictures ever seen," and the photoplays which he remembers most vividly and can retell with the greatest wealth of detail. Similarly a citation of the ways in which what is seen upon the screen is later incorporated into the boy's behavior, his vocabulary and conversation, his play and games. Hypothesis is here restated more specifically: that which is seen upon the screen which is felt to be most fascinating and compelling is that very often which is related to the interests, values, and behavior patterns which the boy experiences in his play life, and in his gangs. (Other factors, such as family and cultural background, socio-biologic process of growing up, will of course be cited to qualify this generalization.) That which is seen upon the screen which subsequently eventuates in the spontaneous behavior of the child in his social activities with his play groups is that which, it is felt, can somehow "fit into" the texture of his play world, enlarging and enriching it. This contributes both to building up and breaking down existing behavior patterns and standards. . . .

Special attention will also be given to the child's play world and this integrated screen world as primary factors in the process of socialization by which the young child gradually attains a world for itself, by which its patterns of behavior are conditioned and its personality and character are in part formed. Professor George Mead's brilliant insights and suggestions are especially applicable from this point of view. Possible other suggestions from Cooley, James Mark Baldwin, Dewey and Faris may be applicable. Special attention must be given, however, to the place of dramatic play in the development of the child's personality, and to the role of the motion picture as one important source for behavior patterns. A special bibliography upon dramatic play has been assembled and it is believed that a critical analysis of dramatic play and of the game (suggestions from Mead and Thomas) as revealed in our materials will assist in making it possible to see the role of the screen in relationship to the child's process of "growing up."

CHAPTER X: DELINQUENCY AND THE MOVIES

The photoplay, upon the basis of data available upon Intervale, cannot be said, strictly speaking, to be a "causative factor" in delinquency. With boys and young men who are not definitely psychopathic or obviously emotionally or mentally atypical, the cinema, even at its worst, can be seen to be a purveyor of countless and variegated patterns of behavior, fascinatingly presented, from which the individual is free to select for personal utilization whatever may seem to him to be valuable. This, it is clear, is the basic influence indicated in Chapter VIII and revealed more fully in Chapter IX. The cinema does not "cause" delinquency, but with the content of some of the photoplays exhibited today it is possible for the cinema to be used by those so disposed as a means for self-instruction in crime. Other ways in which the screen may in individual cases be contributory to crime are also to be noted.

Thus techniques of crime, techniques for evading detection, and techniques for escape which may be but an incident in a photoplay may be carefully noted by those criminally disposed and, upon occasion, may later be attempted by them in their own criminal exploits. Thus, in our materials there is ample evidence that special attention was given by East Harlem boys and young men – whether they were among those described technically as "delinquent" or "non-delinquent" appeared to make little difference – to techniques of crime employed in popular gangster pictures. They remembered these techniques long after other apparently more significant parts of the photoplay had become hazy in memory. In several instances, techniques of crime first seen in photoplays were definitely used in their own crimes. . . . Yet, as important as are these instances, it is perhaps more significant that in 57 extended interviews with delinquent boys in institutions (or on parole from these) not more than one case (this one debatable) was found where a technique of crime first seen in a movie was later attempted by this individual.

The photoplay showing criminal and other forms of proscribed conduct may also serve occasionally as an incidental stimulus for the release of mechanisms, habits, associations which are already a part of the personality, i.e. suggestion. Thus, a delinquent boy in clandestine association at gangster films with an older criminal youth may find therein a stimulus to the commission of a crime immediately after leaving the theater. In the field of the appetites, even more clearly, a scene in a photoplay may serve incidentally as a stimulus to subsequent activity. This is especially true in the realm of sex behavior. Yet in these cases it is clear that the patron's response is primarily in terms of habits and associations already established.

It can also be stated as a hypothesis, deserving of further study, that the repeated presentation and association of a type of photoplay which portrays a fascinating activity possessing for the spectators definite prestige value, and which represents wishes they are unable to satisfy, with the criminal's and the racketeer's methods of gaining these desired objectives may, on occasion, pave the way for criminal activity. Constant repetition of a typical setting or photoplay milieu may not only inure the individual to shock and resistance to this type of life, but also may condition the person to a response in terms of the attractive objectives presented. Thus, it is possible that the presentation of the apparent affluence and luxury of the successful gangster or criminal, his penthouse, his expensive roadster and his attractive "blonde" may not only checkmate the salutary effect of the "ignominious end" of the gangster, but may ultimately condition the individual to acceptance – at least at a time of crisis – of the suggestion that the gangster's methods may after all be the most desirable means to the attainment of these desired objectives.

Finally, it would seem to be a tenable hypothesis, also, that gripping portrayals of gangster characters, of criminal personalities, may provide a basis for both unconscious imitation and conscious copying of personality characteristics and mannerisms of the screen characters. With all the glamour conferred upon the cinema actor through the arts and techniques of film production, through the prestige attaching to one who seems upon the screen to deal so effectively with every unforeseen situation in which he finds himself, the movie star may in his acting provide personality patterns for conscious copying or for slow and unwitting imitation. The actor's portrayal of a gangster character may on occasion serve to afford more definiteness to the personality attributes of the successful gangster. Boys and youths predisposed toward crime find here models for imitation. With those who are mentally and emotionally "normal" (that is, definitely not atypical) this patterning never goes beyond the experimental adoption of individual gestures, expressions, postures, styles in dressing – soon sloughed off if they are not found to be helpful or applicable. However, for the psychopathic or the emotionally atypical, more complete re-orientation of personality may result. (Cf. the "Little Caesar" cases.)

Yet, with all of these generalizations and hypotheses, it is very important to note that they cannot be entirely understood except in terms of the social backgrounds, the personal dynamics of the subjects themselves, and in terms of the characteristic conditions of life in the interstitial area. The potency of gangster films in disseminating techniques of crime takes on its real meaning when it is seen that in the interstitial area is found the greatest concentration of delinquents and criminals – those predisposed toward noting and availing themselves of criminal techniques. With the ineffectiveness of the family, the school, and other institutions characteristic of the interstitial area, the possibility for establishing within the individual mechanisms, habits, and activities of an anti-social or proscribed nature needing only the stimulus of a photoplay to "set them off" is presumably greater. Likewise, in the interstitial area it is much more difficult for the youth to find an entree to lawful employment of a type stimulating to his ambition, but avenues to crime and racketeering are everywhere at hand. These factors and the economic penury of life in the interstitial area may serve only to make the road of the gangster seem more attractive. Finally, the underworld photoplay, the gangster character, and the movie actor frequently associated with the gangster roles he plays possess an especial appeal in the interstitial area because these represent vital issues, "life choices," to those living here.

Nor does the inglorious end of the gangster hero, uniformly portrayed in the series of gangster pictures of several years ago, serve uniformly in the interstitial area as a deterrent. While, for a large number of the younger delinquents, the gangster's ignominious end does seem to serve as a deterrent, many of the older delinquents discredit this as "the baloney of the picture," yet do not fail to note critically the criminal devices and strategy portrayed. Others find in the gangster hero's fall object lessons in the mistakes to be avoided if one is to succeed in what they uniformly concede is at best a "tough racket.". . .

Part Four: Youth Measures Itself Against the World

CHAPTER XI: YOUTH SEES THE WORLD THROUGH THE CINEMA

Though during childhood and early adolescence the movies may provide a body of fascinating patterns for play and games, and though on occasion certain movies may be used by those interested in delinquency and crime as a means of self-instruction in crime, the major "contribution" of the movie to youth is as an agency, presenting patterns of life and personal conduct of which children of all types may avail themselves, which conveys to all types and ages of children and youth impressions of the larger world beyond their immediate personal experience. In the commercial cinema, the child and youth are made acquainted with certain facts of history, geography, literature, and social science, but these are all interpreted for them by "Hollywood."

During earlier years the child getting acquainted with the "world" is exposed to hosts of stimuli and social forces which impinge upon its world. While the motion picture is but one of these, instances are on record of very young children upon whom very definite impressions and associations were left. This probably is due in part to absences of adult discount and to the fact that "unipathy" is such a characteristic experience of childhood. Where the photoplays are of a highly exciting type, mysteries, especially the "abnormal mysteries" – or where some association in the child's experience serves to condition it, a serious emotional disturbance arises which may on occasion serve to make more lasting the impressions and attitudes arising at the time. . . .

The earliest impressions are often of this chance sort (here referring to "impressions" which can be recalled years after, in life histories). But at an early age the child's world (according to our data) is enriched with characters and activities shown in "animal pictures," "comedies" (especially of the slapstick variety), the mystery thrillers, and very shortly by the classic "westerns" and the "episode" (serial) pictures.

Herein is the origin of the first of the "stereotypes" (discussion of the role of stereotype in present-day life will of course be included) – the stereotype of the "West," the Western "Cowboy," the "Chinaman," the "Indian," (American), "detective," "police," "judges," and "murderers." Later to these concepts are added "gangsters," "underworld," "war," "aeroplanes," "spy," "college" (college and student life). . . .

It is significant to note that out of the experiences from which arise these earlier stereotypes especially have in part arisen certain derived conceptions. This age-old lore of the conflict of good and evil takes on a special personalized form in the "Western." Interesting also in our interpretations of the conception of life for boys of foreign parentage growing up in the interstitial area is their conception of those of earlier American stock. . . . "Blondes" also take on a special meaning, in part incidental to the gangster and underworld films.

Later stereotypes include: stereotype of the dance hall or night club girl, stereotype of marriage and divorce, stereotype of love and romance. Especially pertinent here, perhaps, is youthful adolescents' conception of "love," "romance," and "sex."

It is important to note that often the motion picture is but one of several sources for these stereotypes. Further, the effectiveness is roughly, perhaps, in inverse ratio to the degree of acquaintance of the child with the world and to his own maturity. Yet these stereotypes are unquestionably a significant part of what is retained by the child.

Equally significant is the familiarity of the child with a host of subjects, activities, interests, human problems, and human foibles characteristic of the social milieu presented by Hollywood. . . . The educational and informational value of photoplays picturing scenes in other countries and in other parts of the United States, travelogues and newsreels are all attested to in the materials. . . . The phenomenal knowledge of cinema actors, actresses, the photoplays in which they have been seen, the general character of an exceptional number of plots, and their ability to offer readily examples of "kinds of photoplays" indicate also the extent of informational knowledge about Hollywood in the possession of the boys of Intervale.

CHAPTER XII: THE SCREEN AND YOUTH'S IDEALS, STANDARDS AND SCHEMES OF LIFE

Motion pictures are recorded in the materials as having been significant aids to young people in many of their personal adjustments to life, in assisting them in their attempts to meet the problems which they believe they are facing. These are apparently in many forms, but in outline the major aspects can be included below:

A. Fashions, Styles of Dress, Hair-dress (Standards of Feminine Beauty). Experimental attempt to adapt the style of dress, hair-dress, etc. for oneself.

B. Mannerisms, Gestures, Posture, Vocal Inflections, Expressions. Experimental adaptation (conscious) of self to these patterns. "Unconscious" modification of one's own behavior in certain recognizable ways. Deliberate use of certain techniques for interesting the opposite sex in self as exhibited in acting of Star. Techniques of courtship.

C. Etiquette, Manners, Pronunciation, Diction – use for self-instruction. Table manners. How to meet members of the opposite sex. How to dance. How to converse with the other sex. Subjects to talk about socially, repartee. Pronunciation and diction.

D. Occupation: Personal Interest and Ambition Reported Stimulated through Movie Portrayals. Aviator, detective, doctor, lawyer, singer (both crooner and opera).

E. Occupational Ambitions Associated with Cinema. Actor, camera man, scenario writer, assistant on sets, run a theater.

F. Use of Screen for Self-Instruction in an Occupation. Tap dancer, singer, radio crooner.

G. Solution of Special Personal Problems, Attempted from Ideas and Information Gained through Movies. How to circumvent prospective father-in-law's objection to marriage. Building up one's own scheme of life and philosophy of life on the basis of data from movies. Note: inadequacy of most parents (foreign born) in Intervale for preparing young people for "American Life."

CHAPTER XIII: THE CINEMA THEATER, A SECOND SCHOOL HOUSE

The cinema as an incidental educational force, having influence in relationship to the individual's own background, interests and needs. But, in more general aspects, the cinema may be said to be an incidental educational force for the following considerations:

A. Failure of School (and other institutions and agencies) to meet certain of the basic interests and needs of growing youth. It is in such fields that the vitality of movie patterns will be found. From data on Intervale note: high frequency of attendance at movies for truants and delinquents; High attendance (relatively) for those intellectually superior ("bright") and for those accelerated in age-grade.

B. Demonstrated, Pedagogical Superiority (in certain fields) of talking cinema. . . . In case of commercial photoplays add: attention-compelling plot; artistic and production skill represented in feature films today.

C. Special Pedagogical Advantages of the Screen.

1. Presents subject matter which is vitally related to immediate interests and spontaneous activities of the child. . . . In contrast to the formalized, disjunctive subject matter offered in school, the result of adult imposition, and which cannot have meaning for the child, contrast the presentation of what seems to the child to be unified segments of life, and situations thrillingly portrayed.

2. The immediacy of the appeal of the commercial photoplay is insured by the necessity that it must "sell" its "curriculum" each day to its patrons – no attendance officer to support it.

3. Opportunity of the child in the theater for more freedom of movement and expression, opportunity to come and go as he pleases is not permitted in the school.

Yet it is significant that the cinema's incidental informational role is not more effective. The patterns of conduct and standards it presents are often contradictory; and, while there is a great potency inherent in the screen portrayal, producers (except when in times of a national emergency – note the propaganda films during the war and recent N.R.A. films) have apparently sought in every way to reduce the educational potency of the film without reducing its entertainment value. Today these films contribute educationally to youth partly because producers have not discovered a way to avoid it, and because of social and individual maladjustments which augment the potency of the film.

CHAPTER XIV: THE CINEMA AND THE COMMUNITY

A. Special Problems in Reorganization Found in the Interstitial Area.

1. Elimination of blind and block booking. Probably results in more gangster and crime pictures being shown in the interstitial area. Limited possibilities of family programs and children's week-end programs in the interstitial area.

2. Parental supervision of child attendance. Parents may both work – too busy to supervise child. Parents not able to gain ready access to information beforehand re: photoplays being shown. Children cannot be restrained from going by the refusal of show money. They will find own ways of getting money to go, or of stealing it, and parents will have no way of learning. . . .

3. Non-enforceability of present child attendance law.

B. Much of the problem and controversy regarding the acceptability of patterns presented in the cinema arises because of heterogeneity in social milieux within supposedly homogenous America. . . . Cf. Record of that which is censored in various states having censorship boards as reflecting local differences, local codes, standards. Also the important fact of social change – that our culture is in rapid flux.

Actually, in the last analysis, the ultimate factor to be noted in all the controversy regarding the movie is that the cinema is really an agency in "speeding up" communication (note its fitting place in the recent book by Willey and Rice).[5] Thus the cinema is bringing to remote centers with more facility "foreign" (i.e. locally unapproved) patterns of life which before were not presented. Significantly, its contribution is not merely to facilitate the contact of local citizens with these elsewhere (as with the telephone) but whole patterns of life as unities are presented. "Psychological mobility" rather than spatial mobility is here involved but it is nevertheless very real mobility. Cf. Statistics of the National Song Writers Protective Association on the shortened life time of popular songs as affected by radio and movies.

C. With all of this there is the legitimate desire of parents to protect their children against exposure to patterns of life which generations of parental experience before have seemed to indicate were "unwholesome." But this problem is complicated by the following:

1. Inability of ascertaining or predicting beforehand what children of every social milieu and age will "perceive," what they will not perceive, how they will respond. Hence, the lack of wisdom and intelligence in attempted censorship.

2. Difference among adults as to what is "good for children."

3. Contradictory ratings on films by different reviewing agencies.

4. Problems arising from distortion of facts of life, history and literature by Hollywood.

D. Recommendations.

1. Special organization or agency necessary for supervision of child attendance in the interstitial area.

2. Adequate and free publicity of ratings upon films by reviewing agencies.

3. Provision for greater freedom for exhibitor in affording special family programs for weekends.

4. Cultivation of study in schools — possibly by the English departments of high schools —in the field of motion picture appreciation and criticism.

5. Integration of a program for motion picture control with the entire program for community organization within the community.

6. More intelligent efforts, experimentally, to predict beforehand the response of types of children. This would be a substitute for "censorship" of the "Young Reviewer's League" of the National Board of Review.

7. Necessity for some sort of Children's Theater under public control and supervision.

Suggestions from Mr. Short and others.

CHAPTER SIX

Student Movie Autobiographies and "Movies and Sex"

Herbert Blumer's *Movies and Conduct* (1933) has been the Payne Fund study most often quoted by historians and media studies scholars. Academics illustrating the impact of new forms of mass media on American society have been drawn to the book's vivid autobiographical accounts of the movies' influence on the attitudes, ambitions and behavior of children and adolescents. Blumer claimed to have collected statements from 1,115 college undergraduates and 583 high school students; his book presented 326 excerpts leavened with some explanatory material. While the bulk of the original autobiographies apparently no longer exist, a small cache of Blumer's student essays and an unpublished manuscript have been located in the files of the Motion Picture Research Council. These documents reveal new insights into middle-class adolescent attitudes and behavior of the late 1920s, but they also raise questions about Blumer's research methods and his basic assumptions about media influence.

Beginning research on his Payne Fund study in early 1929, Blumer solicited between 80 and 100 essays from University of Chicago undergraduates, assigning his sociology students to write "life histories" describing the movies' impact on their developing emotional, social and intellectual lives during childhood and adolescence. (While scholars have used *Movies and Conduct* as evidence of working-class children's film experiences in the 1930s because the book was published in 1933, its quotes in large part illustrate the relationship between urban and suburban middle-class youth and the movies from 1915 to 1929.)[1]

In April 1929, Blumer sent Short sixteen of the undergraduate autobiographies (ten from women, six from men), plus four gathered from female high school students and a fifth from a female office worker.

Blumer would use these twenty-one autobiographies extensively in his
Payne Fund reports. He excerpted ten essays twenty-six times in *Movies
and Conduct* and included two more in their entirety in the book's
appendix, while five others would be quoted from extensively in "Private
Monograph on Movies and Sex."[2]

It is disturbing that, in almost every case where Blumer used multiple
excerpts from the ten autobiographies in *Movies and Conduct,* the identifying biographical data were altered. In material drawn from "Autobiography of My Motion Picture Experiences," a young woman was at
one point identified as "19, white college junior," while an excerpt
found two paragraphs later in the original essay was noted as "20,
Jewish college sophomore." That the student author wrote of the outrage she felt at the treatment of blacks in *The Birth of a Nation* might
have motivated Blumer to change her ethnicity in order not to "offend"
conservative readers. In "Autobiography of Number 30," the author
(internal evidence suggests a young Jewish woman) was first presented
as a 20-year-old white (Protestant) female; elsewhere she was labeled a
20-year-old Jewish man, when she wrote of how viewing *The Ten
Commandments* strengthened her religious faith.[3]

It is unclear how deliberately Blumer made these misidentifications.
He was sensitive to the unwanted publicity that knowledge of their
authorship could cause students on the Chicago campus and in the press,
so he might have attempted to conceal the authors' identities further in
this way. The mistakes may have been the result of carelessness, confusion or sloppy editing on Blumer's part. They may also have been due to
an effort to make a small pool of research data appear larger. Since
Blumer went on to fame with the study of symbolic interaction and
rarely returned to the topic of movies' influence during the rest of his
career, the intent of this mislabeling remains a mystery.[4]

The area of film's impact that most concerned Blumer was, ironically,
absent from *Movies and Conduct.* "No treatment is given in this volume
to the influence of motion pictures on sex conduct and life," he stated in
the preface. "Materials collected in the course of the study show this
influence to be considerable, but their inclusion has been found inadvis-
able. The omission is not to be construed as implying the absence of the
influence." One of Short's major goals for the Payne Fund Studies (PFS)
had been to examine the impact of movies on the erotic lives of adolescents, and at one point or another Shuttleworth, May, Thrasher, Cressey, Peters and Blumer each proposed a research plan for a sex attitudes

study. The topic remained tantalizing, but a fear of hysterical public reaction scuttled most projects in the initial stages (see Chapter Two). Blumer's document "Movies and Sex," even though brief and underanalyzed, came the closest to being published, but it too succumbed to concerns about conservative public tastes.[5]

Initially, Blumer had been frustrated while gathering student autobiographies because Chicago undergraduates seemed so reluctant to write about the impact of movies on their sexual conduct. His students may have been more reticent than other youth of that era, for the University of Chicago was an elite college affiliated with the Baptist church. Nevertheless, Blumer found that when he assured students of anonymity, the unsigned papers were "fuller, more frank and more intimate."[6] Spurred to investigate further, Blumer conducted personal interviews with a number of the students. He also went "into the field" to speak with male Chicago undergraduates in fraternity houses and locker rooms. To gain the students' trust, Blumer regaled them with stories of his latest gridiron triumphs as a professional football player with the Chicago Cardinals. He transcribed the conversations he overheard about young men's erotic fantasies about female movie stars and combined them with excerpts from the written autobiographies into a twenty-nine page manuscript.[7]

When Blumer mailed final drafts of his two PFS volumes (*Movies and Conduct* and *Movies, Delinquency and Crime*) to Short in December 1931, he coyly mentioned that he had also "included in the package . . . a separate statement which I have called 'Movies and Sex.' I have written this account merely for the purpose of your information and without the intention of having it published. I thought perhaps you would like to get a glimpse of the kind of materials which happened to crop out in our study reflecting the influence of motion pictures on sex disposition and attitude." Short gleefully reported to Charters that, even though Blumer's sex manuscript was "hastily thrown together" and was "not necessarily for publication, although he is not adverse to its being included if we wish to do so," "I am more than satisfied with the total results of Dr. Blumer's work."[8]

Short was indeed pleased to have what he considered explosive evidence of the movies' corrosive impact on adolescents; he immediately forwarded Blumer's three manuscripts to Henry James Forman, who devoted Chapter 13 of the first draft of *Our Movie Made Children* to "Movies and Sex." However willing Blumer was to further Short's goals, when Blumer saw Forman's draft in March 1933, he got cold feet. "I have been thinking for some time concerning the other matter which you have raised," Blumer wrote to Short,

> namely inclusion of the material which I have presented in the private monograph on sex. Even though this be presented in Forman's manuscript in a completely anonymous form, I feel that identification may still occur and accordingly I find myself distinctly reluctant to have it published. You of course have the material on file in your office for confidential and private use, and I suppose that this will in some sense serve your chief purpose. In the event that a separate study of the influence of movies on sex is undertaken, this confidential material might help to orient the investigator.[9]

Concerned about the damage its inclusion might inflict on his academic career, Blumer insisted that the "Movies and Sex" material be deleted from all PFS publications.

Today's readers will find "Movies and Sex" more quaint than offending, and it is a shame that Blumer so underanalyzed his material here and in his two other volumes. Possibly he felt that film's influence on adolescent sexuality and emotions was so self-evident that he need not elaborate, but Blumer's dearth of evaluations gives the impression that he was terrified of the topic of sexuality (particularly of female sexuality). He did not discuss what "normal" levels of erotic interest might be for college-age young people, nor did he attempt to compare movies with other sources of sexual education and stimulation. Blumer's basic assumption here, as in the two published volumes, was that any influence on young people's attitudes and behavior stemming from the movies, an information source not controlled by traditional providers of values like school, church and home, was alien and therefore must be harmful. It was the exact opposite of Paul Cressey's theory of media influence.

Obviously, having only a limited sample of original documents, we must be careful not to critique *Movies and Conduct* and "Movies and Sex" too harshly, for Blumer's overall conclusions might be justified if the full measure of his sources were available. Given how thoroughly Blumer drew on these sample documents and the disturbing discrepancies found between the documents and Blumer's published reports, however, the recently surfaced "Movies and Sex" manuscript and student autobiographies raise important issues. As with any scientific study, the existence of at least some of the source materials provides a basis for others to draw their own conclusions from the data and a road map for understanding the biases of Blumer's methodologies and beliefs. Furthermore, on a historical level, the rediscovery of these documents allows us to reposition the students' rich and varied film experiences within the contexts of their complete movie life histories and to acquire fresh perspectives on the popular culture of middle-class youth of the late 1920s.

In both of the Blumer documents that follow, all of the footnotes are ours. We have corrected the simple spelling errors (in many cases merely to conform to shifts in spelling conventions from the 1920s to the 1990s), but left the more egregious mistakes alone. We have also left the neologisms and other attempts at creative self-expression in place rather than correct grammar and malapropisms. We trust that the reader will appreciate the flavor of these original autobiographies.

The student material can be found in Herbert Blumer, Autobiographies, MPRC, Box 4, Blumer file. "Movies and Sex" is located in Herbert Blumer, "Private Monograph on Movies and Sex," n.d. (c. 1930), MPRC, Box 4, Blumer file.

The Motion Picture Autobiographies

COMPILED BY HERBERT BLUMER

Case 1: Autobiography of Motion Pictures

It is rather difficult for me to distinguish between the influence of the motion pictures and the influence of books on my life. I cannot even remember my first movie; I attended so many between the age of eight and eleven that there is a regular jumble in my mind. I believe I was allowed to attend too many movies in this stage of my life. I often went three or four nights a week because I was following up some serial which to my way of thinking at the time, if I missed one episode – nothing could be done to right the matter. The children next door to us were given their dimes practically every night in the week and when they went I cried and pouted around until my parents consented to my going.

I remember a serial star by the name of Arthur. He was my hero in those early days. He was a large man and very good looking thus he won my childish heart. Oh! The hand of iron that used to grip my heart when I saw my hero go into some fresh danger so willingly and so courageously to save the heroine whom I often thought was not good looking enough for my handsome hero.

There is one picture which I can remember the title of, it was "The Octopus." I recall that the story was centered around a sea disaster. It opened with the wrecking of a ship and on this boat there are some papers, which are valuable to a beautiful girl. Her father lost his life in the disaster. The papers are in a steel box and in the safe of the ship. The girl's lover aids her in the search for these papers and on the occasion of one of his dives he encounters this huge octopus. Of course, there was a violent struggle but the hero finally got the best of the huge monster.

Then there came a time when I enjoyed seeing comedies. The two comedians whom I liked best were Fatty Arbuckle and Charlie Chaplin. My favorite actresses at this time were Mary Pickford and Pearl White, a serial star. Mary, who often took the part of an orphan, was my idol. I started, I believe, to suffer as much as the girl of the story did. When any misfortune fell upon this beautiful girl of the picture I would cry very readily. I admired Miss White for her daring and courage.

The first love picture which attracted my attention, was I believe Rudolph Valentino in "The Sheik" [1921].[1] Up to this time I had detested these pictures where people do so much for love, etc., but here was a picture which struck my fancy. To begin with I can recall distinctly saying to myself, "Oh, what a Lucky Girl to have enough money to take a trip like that – a trip across the wild desert with only Arab guides in her company. Oh, how daring! If it were only I! I really lost myself in the character of the heroine in that picture. I responded to her moods just as if I were acting out the part instead of she. I resented and despised the youthful sheik when she did and in turn I loved him as much as did she. I had a couple of opportunities to go and see this picture over and I went, not telling anyone that I had previously seen the picture. The more I saw the picture the more I fell in love with the handsome hero – I resented him for his abrupt and brutal manners but still I used to care for him despite his cave man tactics.

We used to play show on the sidewalk every evening and we had a dreadful time picking out the characters for we generally all wanted to play the same part. I always wanted to take the part of the heroine. How wonderful it must be to be loved by a handsome man and of course I was beautiful enough to be the heroine of any play. Alas! When I look upon myself now, how unfit I was to take the part of the beautiful lady of the film – I, the lanky and freckle-faced child.

At about this time, I became interested in mystery and detective stories and I also began to be interested in films of the same nature. Evelyn Brent became my heroine. I did admire her daring ways, if I only could do things like she did. She often led the police to some notorious gang. No matter how hard-boiled or treacherous she was, I always found some good reason which justified her leading such a life.

I was a student at a parochial school and the church gave a movie one afternoon. What an impression that picture has left on me! It has only been within the last few years that I have been able to cast it entirely off. The picture was to emphasize the seal of the confessional. It opened with a murderer making a confession to a priest and while confessing he managed to get some of the blood of his victim on the hands of the priest. After the man has gone the priest calls the police and they accuse him of the crime and his knife is found alongside of the body of the victim stained with blood. Because he will not break the seal of the confessional, the priest is doomed to the electric chair. Before the electro-cution the murderer confesses on his deathbed and thus the priest is saved. I realize now that this was to impress the seal of the confessional on our young minds. For some time after this I held the ecclesiastes in awe. What a wonderful and yet in some respect how terrible a life they must lead. I resolved that I would do anything possible to make life happier and easier for them. I did try helping the nuns after this but after a short time the novelty of it wore off and I drifted back into my old ways.

I now developed a strong disliking for any of the childish comedies, which the small moving picture houses showed. I liked pictures with regal settings, especially those that had their settings in Russia. Those huge castles so sumptuously furnished had to be in the setting to make some arch plot attract my attention. I just doted on pictures displaying the ousting of the nobles from their beautiful home but how I longed to help the beautiful maid, who was too honest to fall below the standards, which she set for herself and would rather face death than fall short of her ideals.

At about the age of fourteen the movie craze left me, and I did not seem to care whether I saw a movie or not. My interest was soon aroused again and it developed along the line of college life. I often wondered what life at college would be like. I often sat dreaming, planning what I'd do when I got to go away to college. Oh, what a life! To be a popular co-ed, the member of a spiffy sorority! My first formal! What a hit I would be! When I saw these college romances develop before my eyes I wondered what my beau would be like. Of course, he would have to be a tall dark, handsome boy; an athlete of repute. What would his first kiss be like? Would it send me to a world unknown as some authors express it? Then of a sudden, I would snap out of these dreams and tell myself not to be such an insipid fool. Of course, nothing like this happens in real life, it only happens to people in books and in pictures. It never entered my mind that there wouldn't be a beau. Such a thing would be impossible.[2]

Now, I often sit and wonder – does it pay a girl to play a perfectly square game? Does it? If so, what is the secret of these girls who are so popular? When you compare them with girls whom you know are playing a square game, what a contrast. It seems that the girl who does not indulge in the so-called popular pastime of petting is out of the picture. They are more often better sports and are better looking and have better personalities than the popular girl but yet they cannot get a date or attract the male sex. What is it that is lacking? As Joan Crawford says in "Our Dancing Daughters" [1928], does it pay to be frank, honest, and a regular sport with the fellows and yet keep yourself for the one man? Of course, I am not saying that I approve of the conduct of the heroine in this picture, but I wonder if it does pay and if so the debt is certainly heavy. If only the problems of life were ensured the happy endings which they have in the movies. I suppose in this debatable question a lot depends on what you mean by playing square and by being a good sport.

At present, I am in a restless state of mind. I don't care whether I see a movie or not. I think that they are a lot of rubbish. I am in a period in which my general attitude seems to be one of indifference. I say to myself, what's the use? I just can't explain; I'm even uneasy and dissatisfied with things which I do myself.

[The writer appended the following comment to her essay.]

I found the paper rather difficult because I am naturally reserved. It took a great deal of effort to be perfectly frank. I accepted the task of writing the paper as somewhat of a burden before I started it but in spite of the difficulties I found myself interested and it took little effort to finish the paper. I wrote the main part of my paper on January 27th. I had been reflecting on my different experiences ever since the assignment was made and I had occasionally jotted down a few notes. On this Sunday afternoon, being alone, I sat down and wrote on the paper. I spent about six hours drafting it up. It really took me as long to start the paper as it took me to write it. After doing this, I abandoned the paper but recalled it to my mind occasionally trying to remember things which I might have put in. I did not change the paper; just revised it in order to correct a few grammatical errors. On February 10th, I took the paper out and made these revisions. I spent about two hours trying to correct these mistakes because I am naturally poor in grammar. I typed the paper, reread it and decided it would serve the purpose but I was rather reticent about handing it in. I thought that probably it was not just what you wanted, after all.

Case 2: Autobiography of My Motion Picture Experiences[3]

In this modern age there are many things which tend to make us feel the gap between the time of our youth and that of our parents. Possibly one of the biggest factors expressing this gap is the motion picture, for it in itself shows the novelty, speed and finesse which are characteristics of our age. I cannot remember ever having been without a movie house, so that this enterprise can be called a guiding factor in my life.

I do not know the name of the first film I ever saw, but I recall that every Sunday afternoon my sister and I received a quarter with which to go to a movie and buy popcorn or a taffy apple. I remember that to us the spice of the program was the serial, the film in which the villain had stolen some valuable plans which the hero must recover for the heroine before a certain date or she would lose her inheritance and have to marry the villain. How we "hissed" the villain!! How we gasped when we saw the heroine imprisoned in an out-of-the-way shack which was set on fire by one of the villain's hench-men. Then, just as we all began to get interested and hope that the hero would come on the scene, the announcement came on the screen that "the serial would be continued next Sunday afternoon." What ah's! What oh's followed! The favorites of the serial world were Pearl White, William Duncan, Ruth Roland, Art Acord, etc.

I remember too, the slap-stick comedy. What pie-throwing! I kept thinking of the many pies that were spoiled at each showing of the film, thus proving that I knew nothing of the technique of the motion picture. What rolling-pin throws and bathing beauties! Snub Pollard with his drooping mustache, Bebe Daniels with her Al Christie personality, Larry Semon with his wide pantaloons, and Ben Turpin with his "east is west" eyes were the comedy stars that I now recall.

The feature pictures that I remember were long drawn-out affairs. Only a few of them remain with me because of the way we played the parts later. "The Poison Letter" with Ethel Clayton, "The Woman's Secret" with Theda Bara, and Francis X. Bushman's "Relations" come to my mind as examples of the early movies. The day after I saw "The Poison Letter," I wrote weird notes to my friends using smears of catsup instead of blood as the heroine was supposed to have used. As I wrote these, I sat with a shawl over my head just as Miss Clayton had in the movie.[4]

When a few years later I saw "Broken Blossoms" [1919] with Richard Barthelmess and Lillian Gish I could not rid myself of the idea that the Chinese laundryman was a crook and the contents in his bag a person he had kidnapped. I could not sleep that night and remember that my parents thought I was ill.

In "The Birth of A Nation" [1915] I felt my first feeling of rebellion over a racial question. I remember coming home and crying because the poor colored people were so mistreated. I expressed my views of the "terrible" white people, saying, "How would they feel if they were colored?" For weeks, I looked with sympathy at every colored person and got eleven cents together within two weeks and gave it to a little negro boy.[5]

The films which I most wanted to see were those advertised by the sign – "No Children Admitted." I couldn't understand why I couldn't go in. I could not begin to tell what I thought was in that film, but thought that perhaps the film was so good that there was no room in the house for children.

As I grew older I began to like the "love" pictures. Only those which were full of tender love scenes appealed to my adolescent nature. I would come home and act and imagine I was Norma Talmadge in the arms of Eugene O'Brien. I would sit for hours dreaming that I sprained my ankle on Michigan Avenue and some great movie actor carried me to his car, told me I was fit for his picture, etc. When I saw Rudolph Valentino in "The Sheik" [1921], I could do nothing but think of him for days to follow. Several of my girl friends and I sent to Hollywood for the star's picture.

Now I enjoy the historical drama because it connects itself with my background in history. I dislike the movie which deals with the idle rich because I find that the conception given by it is false. It exaggerates the customs and habits of the rich and I believe it is very misleading.

Often-times when I see a movie which has a situation similar to mine in it, I enjoy comparing myself with the heroine, even perhaps using her tactics on my hero. Sometimes I go out of a movie determined that only wealth is necessary for love; other times, I feel love over-rides wealth. The film tends to influence my thoughts.

On the whole, I believe the films emphasize class distinction simply by the lavishness of the scenery and costumes. Suffice it to say that I feel the movies are a great factor in the intellectual movements of our day for just as they have affected me, they have affected others.

Case 3: Autobiography of Number 30

My earliest recollection of movies is the fact that as a young child, going to a movie was not a habit of mine but rather an adventure for me, and a rare one at that; my Mother didn't approve of movies for children unless the picture happened to be one particularly for children, such as ones taken from Children's books as "Little Lord Fauntleroy" [1921], a comedy featuring Charlie Chaplin, or the like, or a serial picture of particular merit. Perhaps this early training accounts for the fact that even now I do not usually go to a movie unless I know that it will be worthwhile. But I can distinctly remember asking Mother if I could go to the movies on Saturday afternoons with the "kids," and invariably receiving the answer that "movies were no place for children," and that "it was much better for me to play out-of-doors." It seemed to one then that Mother was unreasonable, and many were the times when I used to say that when I had children I would let them go to the movies anytime they wished so they wouldn't have to play out-of-doors all alone when all the others had gone to the movies. But I suppose that when I was allowed to see a picture, I enjoyed it more than I would have had it been a habit of mine.

But I did see all the children's pictures that ever came to town. Mother used to tell me days before that such and such a picture would soon be here, and I would look forward with much eagerness to the day when I could see it; it was a big event in my life.

I remember that I saw all of Charlie Chaplin's pictures and after the show I used to go home and imitate him, as every child probably has done.

Wild west shows were, are, and always shall be something to be avoided. I saw one when I was very young that made such a horrible impression on me that I dreamt about it for weeks afterward.

As I grew older, Mother became more lenient with me and I was allowed to go to the movies more often. When I was about twelve years old, college pictures had a particular fascination for me. I had a beautiful mental picture of college life and an ambition to be allowed some day to attend one. I used to get the biggest thrill when I saw pictures of young people having such glorious times at college, entering into athletics, being in dramatics, going to "proms," and having midnight escapades. After these shows I used to go home and study with renewed vigor so that I might get to college all the sooner. Alas, college is not all that I saw it to be on the screen or even imagined it to be in my wildest dreams. But that only proves that my imagination and my emotions overshadow my sense of reality,[6] and often, I have relived the experiences of the actors and actresses with them.

From the time I can remember I took aesthetic dancing lessons and I was very much interested in the art. I often thought of continuing it as a profession and this idea was certainly enhanced when I saw the beautiful actresses dancing on the screen. Unfortunately for me, my physical make-up turned out to be such that I was not the type for the work, but every now and then, when I see Joan Crawford, for instance, dancing across the screen, I envy her.

Love pictures played no vital part in my childhood. It took me a long time to reach the stage where men were important to me, and the only impression that remains with me now is that I used to think them "awfully silly" and well can I remember how we girls would get together and mimic, by way of ridicule, the technique which we saw on the screen.

I am very emotional by nature, and perhaps no pictures have played on them quite as much as some of these modern pictures which portray, with exaggeration, the modern generation. I remember seeing "Our Dancing Daughters" [1928] and "Dancing Mothers" [1926] not so long ago, both of which influenced me a great deal. These pictures emphasized the harm that can result when daughters do not confide in their mothers. Now Mother and I had never been each other's confidants; I couldn't seem to confide in her as other girls did in their mothers, although I knew that she longed for me to do so, so that we might be pals; it just didn't seem to be my nature but I realized that I was wrong and that I was making Mother unhappy. During the performance of each of these pictures, I seemed to live the whole story myself, oblivious of all around me. And when I saw how happy a Mother was made when her daughter finally confided in her, and how so many misfortunes resulted from not doing so, I immediately decided to change my tactics, even if I had to force myself. Ever since, Mother and I have been the closest pals.[7]

Probably no other single factor influenced the spiritual side of my life as did the picture "The Ten Commandments" [1923]. I am Jewish but no one in our family is orthodox and we do not make much of religion in our home. I can remember how I hated to go to Sunday School –

"What was the use?" I always asked. When I was sixteen years old, I saw the picture mentioned above, and from that time on, I never asked that question again, and furthermore, I never doubted the value of religion. The many, many hardships which my people went through for the sake of preserving our race, were portrayed so vividly and so realistically that the feeling of reverence and respect for my religion was instilled in me, too.[8]

War pictures, too, have played on my emotions. I distinctly recall seeing "Wings" [1927] last year. It was so realistic that I completely forgot that I was seeing only a picture, and I, myself went through every experience in the picture. I became so oblivious of my surroundings that I shouted out in a time of distress, and finally, became so hysterical that my escort took me out. The rest of the day I was in a hysterical condition, and that night I dreamt about aeroplanes and war; it took me several days to recover my equilibrium and now I hesitate before I consent to see pictures of such caliber.[9]

I suppose every girl hates to admit that she is sentimental and being so, nevertheless, likes to see a love picture now and then. However, I must admit that such pictures now-a-days are more or less alike, and they do get monotonous, but occasionally I do enjoy one that is a little different from the general run of them. And I'll go further to admit that I often place myself in the position of the heroine and wish that I actually could play her role in real life; the after affect often causes me to day dream, arranging some event or planning something that was suggested by the picture.

In summarizing my life in reference to the influence of movies on it, I think I can safely say that it has been the idea, the moral, the point of the picture that has been the influencing factor in my life rather than the idea of a movie in itself, or the actual movie actors and actresses. I cannot remember even wishing to be a movie star, or wishing myself in the "shoes" of any one of them, or even imitating them for any length of time. Furthermore, I never got the "craze" of writing for pictures or autographs of the stars; I guess I never went through the stage of hero-worship of the movie actors. Now that I think of it all this does not seem natural to me, according to the views and experiences of others but still I do not feel as though I have missed anything of vital importance, but perhaps I have – in such a case, then "ignorance is bliss."

Case 4: Autobiography Concerning the Effect of Moving Pictures on My Life

Note: In trying to be sincere I have more or less disregarded the term paper style of writing.

All my life I have lived in a good residential district in the city's south side, and have had ready access to good theaters here. The first fourteen years of my life were spent in the Hyde Park district; specifically at 51st and Michigan Avenue. Around this neighborhood were a great number of shows, such as the Michigan theater, the President, the Metropolitan, the Willard, the Calumet, and others.

Consequently I had ready access to many theaters. But, on the other hand, while I was young my eyesight bothered me and as a result kept me from attending movies too often.

The first show I attended I was accompanied by my parents. From them I have gathered information as to my reactions. They say I spent most of my time watching the drummer in the orchestra; the orchestra then consisted of a piano and a drum. Finally I became restless and spent the rest of the time running up and down the aisles, talking to and annoying people.

I didn't start to go to shows very often until I was ten years old. Seldom was I allowed to go in the evening. Most of my movie attending was in the afternoon, particularly Saturday matinees. (I recall an incident when I attended a movie in the evening with my uncle and cousin. After we had seen one show we decided to see another and so walked to another theater. When I got home it was around eleven thirty o'clock and mother, although she knew I was with my uncle, became frantically worried and I got hail columbia when I got home.) I often went to the show on Sunday afternoon with my older cousins, too. But Saturday was THE movie day for me. While I was still a youngster a nurse would take my brother and me to the matinee. I used to get to the show as early as possible for apparently no good reason at all. Comedies and serials were my favorites. The show was usually packed with children on Saturday afternoon and they all seemed to have tastes like mine, as, when the feature picture was over and the comedy flashed on the screen, we would cheer wildly. I could enjoy a light feature picture, such as "Treasure Island" [1918] or "Jack, the Giant Killer" ["Jack and the Beanstalk," 1917], but seldom saw any sense in the heavy feature picture. Consequently, I went to the show that had the most promising comedy or serial picture. (Once in a while the manager of the show would provide for light feature pictures merely to interest children, and would advertise them around grammar school as being shown Saturday afternoon.)

Often, too, the school would have an interest in a certain picture on Saturday afternoon. The teachers created interest by holding contests to see which student could sell the most tickets. (Consequently, many of the parents and relatives got "stuck.") All this I believe was usually sponsored by the parent teachers' association and the benefits derived usually went to some unknown source, and for some unknown thing.

My favorite actors around this time were such as Charlie Chaplin, Fatty Arbuckle, Douglas Fairbanks, William S. Hart, William Duncan, Francis X. Bushman, and many others. I used to enjoy Mary Pickford, Pearl White (a serial actress), and other actresses, too.

From the time I became ten years old 'till I was twelve or thirteen I went to the movies quite often. During this time they had certain effects on my life. To some extent they affected my actions to my fellow playmates. I was influenced to a domineering spirit and requested much while ceding little. I took the roles of the heroes in our playing and was satisfied with none other. Often it was that we re-acted what we had seen that afternoon during the show. (I recall how we would imagine we were cowboys and would gallop on imaginary horses all the way home.) Playing cowboy and Indian, cop and robber, and the like, was not infrequent among us. (Strange as it may seem the role of the robber was not always the one sought after.) Thus in our playing, in our dealings with one another, and in many other ways I was influenced to act according to what I had seen on the screen, during, of course, my early life.

Later on, during my last two years in grammar school, I became more interested in athletics and sort of lost interest in movies, particularly Saturday matinees. I, of course, went to the movies some and my attitude toward the feature picture changed due to age. I still didn't, however, care for the deep stuff but preferred young actors and funny, sport, and action pictures. By this I mean I liked racing pictures, western pictures with cowboys, and funny pictures with simple plots. Douglas Fairbanks was still one of my favorite actors.

After I entered high school I got to going out with girls and often

took them to the movies. It was then that I became interested in passionate love scenes and deep, soulful pictures. After I had one unsuccessful
love I became aware of the basis for so many of the pictures. Often I
would actually live the picture out. My favorite actors and actresses then
changed to the type that was young and good-looking. In acting and
talking to a girl I would often use the knowledge I gained from the
screen and the actors. During my puppy loves this was especially true.

During my last few years in high school I went to the movies for
various reasons. One of these was – it was a good place to go for a
cheap date, and I thought that if the girl I took saw a real passionate
scene it would make it easier for me to neck and kiss her after the show.
Another of the reasons was that I enjoyed the stage shows. Often we
would choose a show on the strength of its stage show rather than the
picture. I enjoyed orchestras a great deal and particularly Benny
Krueger, Waring's Pennsylvanians, and the like. The third reason I went
to shows was to learn to imitate the actors insofar as my actions with
girls was concerned. Then again I often went to see a particular show
because I had been told it was "dirty." (Why fellows go to see shows
that are filthy I don't know, but they do nevertheless.) Then, too, a
couple of us fellows would go to the show and take dates and sit in the
back rows where we could "neck" and "pet." Last and probably least I
went to the movies for sheer enjoyment or constructive instruction. It
was seldom that I did this. (It would be proper to say here that during
this time I lived in a new neighborhood where there were few shows –
67th and Crandon Avenue – and as a consequence, attended such shows
as the Tivoli, Woodlawn, Piccadilly, and the loop shows.)

From that time 'till the present I have gone to shows at many different
places and at any time I felt like it. The shows I see have different affects
on me depending on the show and the particular mood that I'm in at the
time. Sometimes I live with the pictures and often leave a show with the
desire to find a girl and engage in sexual intercourse. (I have never
satisfied this desire, however, as I never seem to have the courage that I
have when I am watching the picture.) Sometimes I see a certain picture
and decide to reform and do and act according to the moral of the
picture. This sometimes lasts as long as a day or two and I forget it. (An
illustration of the previous experience is certain of Lew Cody's and
Clara Bow's pictures. An illustration of the latter is the picture "Over
the Hill to the Poor House" [1928] and Al Jolson's "Singing Fool"

[1928].) Then again if the picture is mediocre and I am in an indifferent mood I rather disregard the picture and watch and occupy my attention with the audience or the showhouse.

I believe that watching the actions of people in the movies (the actors I mean) have led me to take up drinking and smoking. I sort of got the desire to smoke from watching some actor inhale a cigarette and since then I took up smoking. Incidentally, I have never been able to break myself of the habit. Watching the actors sip wine and the like on screen, and seeing young fellows and girls my age do the same in real life has tended to make me want to do the same thing and I have also satisfied this desire.

Most every young high school and college man had automobiles according to and in moving pictures and this gave me a desire to own one. This desire was fulfilled to some extent when I got a "collegiate Ford" but dad made me get rid of the thing and he bought me a car. It wasn't, however, a roadster like the sports use in the movies.

At the present I don't go to the movies very often as I prefer dancing and anyway girls think that a movie date is too cheap. It was, however, during my college career that I went to the movies with some other fellows to learn how to do a very disgusting act. This act was to French kiss where you put your tongue in the girl's mouth and slobber around, saliva dripping from both your's and the girl's mouth, as you try to see how far you can get your tongue down her throat and she her tongue down your throat. We were told that this was the next thing to sexual intercourse and that actors and actresses did this when they kissed in order to create passion. After seeing it done I used the same means in attempting to get a girl "hot" enough that I could engage in sexual intercourse with her but it didn't work.[10]

Thus movies have had certain influences over me throughout my life. From the very first 'till now I sort of regulate my actions in regard to society from what I see or have seen in the movies. I have never had any particular heroes or heroines insofar as keeping their pictures or reading their lives in movie magazines or actually idolizing or worshipping them. I did and do, though, pick out those I like best and act like my favorite actors, and choose my girl friends on the basis on my favorite actresses.

The coming of the "talkies" has to a certain extend lessened my interest in movies, too. Until the actors accomplish the art of talking or until the Vitaphone is perfected so that the actors can be understood by the audience I will continue to dislike talking pictures. The only good

Vitaphone picture that I've seen was Emil Jannings in "The Patriot" [1928].

Because I have spoken frankly I hope that you will not regard me as one of moron mentality or actions – as you know I speak merely of the effect of motion pictures.

Case 5: My Movie Autobiography

A logical autobiography would begin, I believe, with one's first impressions or recollections. A movie autobiography would surely have this in common with a life story, hence, in order to be logical, I have followed my tumbling thoughts back to my very first remembrance of moving pictures. That memory looms distinctly from the haze surrounding childhood.

There was frost in the air that night, and a high white moon followed us most strangely as we hurried along the darkened streets. I skipped ahead in elfish delight, for the joy that coursed through me was too much to be borne in stolidity. Daddy and I were out on a lark – Daddy and I were going to the show. He had whispered in my ear after supper, and we had slipped away, while the younger brothers and sisters were being put to bed, while I, who was ten, was on my way to see "Peter Pan"!

To this day I remember some of the scenes of "Peter Pan." The large nursery, and Wendy in her white night-gown, a scene in the woods, where there was a cunning little house built for Wendy. All of them are vivid. Especially do I remember the tense moment when the pirate put his hook-hand through a window and put poison in a glass of medicine. Above all, there stands out Peter Pan, adorable in his costume, with his soft dark curls rumpled a bit, and his lovely eyes all shining. My heart swelled as I looked upon Peter Pan, swelled with love and a longing that was half of envy, half of admiration. I wanted to be like Peter Pan – I wanted to fly – I wanted to have soft dark curls.

There must have been an interval between Peter Pan and my next real experience, of perhaps a year. In between times I saw a few shows, but they had not affected me. In counting the pictures that count, I go from "Peter Pan" to "Little Lord Fauntleroy" [1921], played by Mary Pickford. That picture was of intense interest to me. I was impressed by the mother's love for her little boy, and by the sunny disposition of the little Lord. Aside from leaving those two recollections, and influencing a newly acquired admiration for yellow curls, "Little Lord Fauntleroy" did little but entertain me.

In searching my memory, I have found that I was not influenced in any particular way by the movies I saw during my childhood. I had, it is true, a deep admiration for some, the popular actresses, and I loved to see them but I did not see enough to influence my play activity. It was in a later period, when I was reaching out to comprehend the mystery of a world made more fascinating by the strange new thoughts and desires which come to the sixteen year old, that I felt the real influence of the movie.

I began my high school days as an almost unconscious child, so far as anything but study was concerned. All week long, I hunched myself over my books, delving into them with an impassioned interest. Then came Friday night, the gala night of the week. I laid aside Caesar's Gallic Wars and the little blue geometry book, and I went to the show. There I lost myself in the realms of the mysterious, there I visited Treasure Island, and strange countries. A distinct change in my attitude towards myself, often looking into the glass with newly opened eyes, and was surprised to see myself looking back with a level, green-eyed stare. How ugly, I thought. But on Friday night I was beautiful, for I sat bolt upright at the show, watching the beautiful women of the picture, and I was drawn out of the shell that was myself and became the equal of any of the heroines in loveliness. I always walked home with haughty mien, but when I arrived I was confronted by the hall mirror which dispelled the pleasant illusion.

The desire for beauty was not the only greed which assailed me at this time. I wanted to be rich, to wear sparkling evening dresses, to travel, to visit the mysteries of Egypt, the grandeur of London, the intrigues of Paris. Dimly, these desires were sensed, formulated as they were from the fragile fabric of day dreams, reinforced by Friday night movies.

After a time a new sensation was added to those contributed by the picture shows. This was not so pleasant, but, fortunately, not of long duration. It happened that I went to see a mystery play one night, in the course of which were several blood curdling scenes – one of a girl locked in a room where she saw long bony fingers creeping over the back of a chair, and who found behind the chair a man who died as she bent over him; one of a dim room with a pile of rags in the corner, and, as I looked, the rags moved, crawled forward and became a person, an odious, horribly maimed, hideously bound creature which sent cold chills running over me. I was horrified. That night I dreamed of those horrid scenes, and was so frightened that I dared not pull the spread higher. The next night was not so bad, and gradually the memory faded, so I again became a movie enthusiast. Yet, there was an effect, and as I think of the scene which frightened me so, a half horror creeps upon me.[11]

The next year I found that my pleasure and my attitudes were somehow changed. My period of seclusion and intense study was destroyed by forces which I did not attempt to control. I had become associated with a group of girls who were just my age, for it seemed necessary for us to band ourselves together to attain that indefinite something which it was our desire to attain. We became "The Famous Five," eager young girls, intimate, filled with an understanding of each other and an instinctive realization of the things we must do for the common good. Without discussion, we accepted the inevitable and began to attend the picture show in a body, being always there on Friday night, seated in our special row. Often we were there Monday night, and sometimes, if a special attraction were offered we came on Thursday night. We never stopped to reason why we went – we knew it was a form of amusement – we loved the pictures – and besides, there were always the high school boys there, too, a row or two behind us, and aware of us.

The sensations of those nights were so intense and powerful that I can recall them in their pristine vividness. After the thrilling march down the aisle, during which we were exquisitely aware of the eyes that followed, and the whispers that circulated as we passed, we found our row and settled ourselves. Blessed emotion! The picture began. An electric fan lifted my hair with soft and wandering touch, a faint gleam from the wall lights played over me: I sat up straight and looked ahead, my heart poised to follow into the intricate mazes of the story; there were beautiful ladies, so lovely that I gripped the seat in front as they showered their starry glances upon some male creature. I noticed how rounded, how strangely pretty were my little white hands!

Remembrance swoops upon me! I can never forget Norma Talmadge, who seemed the perfection of the beautiful. The lure of Corinne Griffith was even more potent, for it was after I watched the breathless mysteries of "Three Weeks" [1924] in which she played, that I allowed her to reign supreme. Clara Bow and Colleen Moore had prominent places, but their girlishness could never compete with the languid lasciviousness

of Greta Garbo. The men I seem not to remember, except Conway
Tearle, whom I adored with a worshipful passion. He might have been
the leading man in all the plays I saw, and I would never have wearied
of him. I did like to see Monte Blue once in a while, especially when he
played with Marie Prevost. These two ranked next to Corinne and
Conway.

Favorites though they were, this selection was made not so much
from the personality of the actors as from the type of picture they played
in. I had a decided tendency to prefer romance, especially of the kind
which had its setting in an old castle, or, in some beautiful woodland; or
perhaps, in the mysterious beauty of a far away city. I despised wild
west shows and silly comedies. Next to romance, I liked mystery stories,
or adventure with mystery and love thrown in. Comedies had little
appeal, for they were silly – except for some of Harold Lloyd's best
ones, which really amused me.

A year of concentrated movie going naturally had results. Having
looked frankly back into the past, I am now aware that many of my
attitudes were directly changed because of the shows I saw. To make
this evident, I shall recall a particular night which was typical in many
ways of the nights that followed.

In the gloom of the Fox theater, I sat with my gang, and I gasped in
pleasurable anticipation as the tense moment approached. The hero
placed his hands about the heroine's divinely small waist, and pulled her
half fiercely toward him. Her beautiful lips parted slightly, he looked
into her heavenly eyes with infinite adoration – and their kiss was
perfect. My response was inevitable. My hand clutched Vera's. We
thrilled in ecstasy.

Short-lived – this bliss which passed all understanding. From behind,
where a group of boys sat, there came a rude burst of laughter, of
smacks and hisses. A furious wave of anger engulfed me. How revolting
and vulgar they were! I wanted to knock their heads together, to destroy
them, to tramp upon them – for they had hurt my sensitive soul without
a thought. They had ruined the sacred beauty of that moment with their
vulgarity. I had experienced that moment because I had put myself in
the heroine's place, I had felt the sweeping silk of her garment against
me, I had been as beautiful as she, in surroundings as glamorous, and
the hero had been replaced by a certain boy a few rows away, who, I
felt, was watching me at that moment. It was a personal insult to me,

that they had laughed. I turned, haughty scorn in my glance, to look at those insufferable creatures – and I caught his eye. He smiled – a warmth suffused me. In that moment I knew. . . .

The minutes hurried by. There came the close up, the flare of lights, the noise of the stamping crowd, anxious to gain the entrance. I walked in a dream, feeling a spell and a magic touch upon me. I had scarcely left my friends at the corner when the well known lines of his roadster loomed before me, and the headlights cut gaudy streaks across the pavement. Came the creaking of brakes, a subdued question, my mute assent, the opening of the car door, and the purr of the engine as we slid into the mystery of a vaguely fragranced night. I had known it all along, from the moment I had seen that perfect embrace in the movies; I had felt that this would happen. He had parked in lover's land, his arms were about me, persuading. To my bewildered mind there came two thoughts, one, "Mama said, 'Don't kiss the boys,' " the other, "What harm can it be? It is beautiful." So, I struggled no longer, and I learned the charm which before I had only dreamed of.[12]

Time, an infinite mystery, flees before one can accomplish that which he wishes to do. In the fleeting moments of those remaining high school days I seemed to drift, and to procrastinate when I thought of my life's work. I was going to be a writer who moved people to tears and laughter by my flow of vivid words, and I felt that I should begin writing soon. This desire to begin my work became especially intense at times when I was stimulated by some good book, some aspiring speaker, or some noble movie. The night that I saw "Ben Hur" [1926] I came away tense, and eager, so thrilled with the moral of the picture I had seen, that I felt as if I must surely write something equally stirring before morning. "Orphans of the Storm" [1922] and "The Hunchback of Notre Dame" [1923] created the same emotion, the same ecstatic wonder, which kept me silent and starry eyed for a day or two. Strangely enough, I find that the remembrance of those pictures is a shell, in which is packed a line or two, a single scene, or perhaps one impression. There were many good shows, and they supplied to me a kind of inspiration which caused a lump in my throat, and a resolution in my heart, but now they are dimmed to a recollection. Yet, there is power in the memory. I can still see the first picture of "Black Oxen" [1924], the long procession of oxen which mounted a hill, plodded into the foreground, turned a curve and plodded out of sight. They were followed by these words upon the screen. "The years like great black oxen tread the world, and God, the herdsman, girds them on." I cannot explain how that single sentence has influenced me, but I know that it has, and that the effect has been good.

Now that I have written my memories of the movies I have seen, and have traced their influence upon me, I wonder if, after all, they counted for so much. Could not my actions and ideas have been perfectly natural ones, hastened, possibly, by the inspiration of the movie? Perhaps. It is true that after several years of love, adventure, success, and other such qualities that make life so utterly pleasing. So, I shall render tribute to the movie, and consider myself unharmed by it, and shall go again when the opportunity presents itself.

These remembrances belong to other days. The present claims my attention, a present which is almost devoid of moving picture experiences, which has no thoughts due to the reading of movie magazines, which finds its inspiration in other things. As far as I can judge, I am but little affected by the picture shows, I have seen. Yet, there is this to consider. . . .

I long for a figure of the willowy slimness of Greta Garbo, and I want my hair to grow to the length of hers, so I can curl my locks and wear them as she does. I flirt when the proper occasion arises, and though I flatter myself that there is something of originality in my manner, I suspect that my actions are something akin to the wiles of Clara Bow, made over to correspond with my conception of what would suit me. I cannot force myself to believe that a kiss should almost never be, for though my theories about the matter are solid and somewhat old fashioned, they do not dominate the standards of this age, first shown to me in the moving pictures. And, of course, I would like to be a movie star, for a time, and I have the usual conception of my abilities, that is, I am sure I would be a great success – if only I were beautiful!

Here endeth my contribution to science in the form of this intimate autobiography. My story is told, and I will leave off telling – I wish I could see a show tonight.

Case 6: The Effects the Movies Have Had on Me

"Wendell, c'mon out to the show and see Charlie Chaplin." That little request heralded my movie experiences. I obtained the consent of the parents and the necessary dime or nickel and started to see a movie for the first time. The feature was a north woods picture of logs, bad men and women, a beautiful innocent girl and a dashing just-in-time hero. He coupled a superhuman strength, used to advantage against the villains, with a human kindness and love towards the girl. Young and impressionable, I entered into the spirit of the picture. I cheered the hero and hissed the villain and wept with the heroine. In fact I wept so hard that I beat it for home and mother. My tender nature couldn't see these hardened crooks lock up such a sweet young thing and beat her at every turn. I forgot all about Charlie Chaplin and his part of the picture and made a vow that if movies were like that it would be a long time before I would see another. I worried about the cruelty of these heartless loggers for days and days and fretted to think that such acts could go unpunished. If I had stayed until the end of the picture I would probably have seen the situations cleared up and everybody the receiver of his or her just desserts. My introduction to the movies was far from the rosy reception I had expected. I got off to a bad start.

I feel sure that I must have gone to the movies after that I have forgotten and the past is rather vague for some time. I remember being attracted by the title of "Little Women" [1919] – I thought it would be a picture of pygmies or fairies at least and was quite disappointed to find that it was only a story of ordinary people. I didn't enjoy the show at all for it was way beyond my years. I again had a reversion and wondered how people could spend their money so freely on such trash.

The next few years were a little more fortunate in their effects on me. I got my first taste of a real thriller. The cowboy hero rode a horse with the ease of the saddle and did unheard of things in escaping the claws of the desperado band. He received only a few beatings this time and I stayed to see him pay them back three fold after a desperate hand to hand fight with the main villain. I felt a little better. I enjoyed his calm braggadocio, his easy handling of his six-shooters. I believe that was my first introduction to firearms. I had always played with a bow and arrow and had a vague unanswered urge in my being. The sight of the guns aroused that slumbering emotion and gave voice to another desire. I thrilled to see them shoot the spots out of playing cards and light their trusty partners' cigarettes with their guns. I began then and there a continuous playing of questions about guns and a ceaseless crying after a gun of my own. At the age of eight or nine I was the proud possessor of a BB gun. I did as many tricks with that gun as accuracy would permit and with a maximum of practice and a minimum of training I got so that I could hit the target fairly often. Of course the target was large and close but that didn't take away from the feeling of pride and man-nishness that those few bulls eyes created. I was on the road to bigger and better things. I have never gotten over my desires for firearms and I feel that it was due a great deal to the influence of the movies that I became so rabid on the question of guns. I still have a gun, a little higher powered than the old BB, and I still take pride in hitting the bulls eyes. A little smaller and a little farther away. The feeling of latent power in a gun is a thrill that I shall always experience when I pick up a good gun. I might have had that feeling without the effect of the movies, but I'm not sure. I have enjoyed a gun and whether it is a good effect or not I can't say either. I have never hurt anybody and I have developed an appreciation of wild life that I might never have noticed without those hunting experiences.

Hand in hand with the cowboy thriller went the serial. They always left the hero in an impossible situation that kept me worrying all week and coming back to see ended. I was a whole hearted sucker and came to see the story to a finish. A long story of a pirate treasure that had been buried, mapped and left on a desert island, drew me. The map was cut into six pieces and divided among the members of the crew so that no one member could get it without sharing with the rest. Scarface Bender was the crook and his attempts to get the other five pieces of the map formed the basis of the plot. Acting against him was William Duncan who had come in from the outside to help the girl whose father had been killed by Scarface in an attempt to get his piece of the map. It ran along in a very interesting fashion and left the girl being burned at the stake, under a falling rock, in a closed room with a time bomb, or some similar impossible situation that kept my inquiring mind busy all week trying to solve. I followed the adventures of Pearl White in a thriller just as long and just as impossible, Ruth Roland in "The Adven-tures of Ruth" [1919] kept me in suspense for a whole season. An adventure where she was given a key every Saturday and initiated into some new mystery cult that her father had died for. Marie Walcamp starred in a picture, "The Red Glove" that took my weekly tribute and Tom Mix, William S. Hart, Elmo Lincoln and Charles Ray all were friends of the screen. The comedy roles were generally taken by Fatty Arbuckle, Larry Semon, or Charlie Chaplin. I cared little about the people in the pictures as a rule and only went when the title was sufficiently gory or otherwise attractive, and when I was in the good graces of the family. They have never been highly in favor of the movies, arguing that I could find much better ways of spending my time and in amusing myself, but they have always been lenient in letting me go. For a school teacher to have the movie habit was bad and for his family to have it would have been worse so we were limited quite a bit compared to other children.

I recall how easily I was impressed at that time. If the title labeled a picture as a comedy I laughed until I was in a dangerous mood, whether it was funny or not. I was easily excited and cheered and whistled with the best of them when the sheriff arrived just as the fuse was nearing the bomb. I had always heard that the movie actors were a bum lot and that they were a low class of people so I got a morbid kick out of the movies that I never told the family about at all. I think that the superior attitude I took was bad but unavoidable. I felt that I knew something that the family didn't and I gloried in the fact. The beauty of Mary Pickford, the alluring roles of Theda Bara, the heroine parts of the serial thrillers I have mentioned, were always a secret longing. Oh for a girl that could ride a horse like Pearl White, or for one with the face of Mary Pickford or the body of Theda Bara. Then life would have been complete. My imaginary trips to Hollywood were numerous, and triumphant. I always gypped the famous heroes and brought back their beauties to my lair, forever. Whew! The Gish girls were just coming into their prime and I remember their propaganda film "Hearts of the World" [1918] as one of the most realistic pictures I have ever seen. I remember seeing a trench full of soldiers buried by an enemy shell and one leg that had not been buried twitched convulsively. It turned itself into my memory. I can draw the picture perfectly. Many of the pictures were taken at the front and I hoped that each one was real. I recall when Lillian Gish was being put to work in the fields by the conquering Hun. She couldn't lift a basket of potatoes and was whipped until the blood ran out of her mouth. I never will forget that either. Blanche Sweet played in another war propaganda film that was based on a story by Rupert Hughes, "The Unpardonable Sin" [1919]. The population of the town was lined up across the street and shot down by a machine gun *en-masse*. This story gave me plenty of opportunity to glut my war-distorted soul. I broke out in a cold sweat to see this crowd of people shot down; I raged and fretted that I was powerless to help these unfortunates. I enclosed another secret in my innermost self when the German soldier found the sister of Blanche asleep in her bedroom. He jumped with a fiendish light in his eye, cautiously looked around the corners and then came back to carry out his desires. He left with a rather excited gleam in his eye and a rather fearsome jump in his step. The girl was bruised and her clothes torn in a suggestive manner and even at my immature age it made certain impressions on my sexual self that I had not noticed a great deal before. I used to think about being a German soldier just so I could go out and procure this forbidden fruit, this universal urge was so strong.[13] The girl died and that made me feel like going out and killing half the female population of Germany in the same way. My reaction to the propaganda film was quite in keeping with the frantic and insane attitude that everyone showed at that time so I guess it was nothing to worry about. I can still recall those pictures with remarkable accuracy and I have a hard time getting over the thrill I first felt when I saw the machine gun sweep down the mob or saw the torn and bruised body of the girl lying twisted and dead. I recall plainly one apparently meaningless incident. Wesley Barry was telling of the story of the massacre and stirring a cauldron of stew at the same time. He was touched with the remembrance of his mother and broke off with tears in his eyes to remark "Aw hell, let's eat." I have no particular reason for remembering that passage but like many others it has remained in an obscure place waiting for an occasion like this to bring it out. I must have seen it when I was only nine or ten at the most.

At about that time I began to get that sophisticated air that all boys get with the first knowledge of girls and boys and their differences. I began to feel that it was a weakness to show any kind of emotion at a movie and looked with scorn upon any one who let his feelings get away with him to such an extent. I spoiled a good many pictures that way because I would continually harden myself to any point and fail to get the reaction that would have made the picture of interest. I kept reminding myself during any touching scenes that I was seeing only a picture and that it was nothing to cry about. I generally covered my real feeling with laughter for those who were really enjoying the picture. I still found myself interested in the same films but I got a different reaction I think. I began to go to see the actor now instead of the picture. I recall one season where one actor was in two pictures. He took the part of the dashing hero in one serial and the part of a German spy in the other. I was in a quandary and found it hard to enjoy either film. I remember him taking a leap after a moving boat in which his lady friend was being carried away in his hero picture and I recall a scene in the war picture. He was painting, holding the brush close to the bristles (bad technique), and some American spies were admiring his work, supposedly, while their eyes took in every detail. In the midst of the scrutiny a side door opened and a young man with his chest perforated with bullets, his shirt and coat a mass of blood, his face a mess, broke in and gasped in his dying breath, "There are a million more." The scene remained fixed in my mind. The shock and perhaps the picture of the man himself burned it into my memory.

Love stories were still quite beyond my years and I never went unless I was misled by the title. I couldn't enjoy watching a gent kiss and fondle a girl that I would have given an eye tooth to know and touch. I couldn't put myself in his place enough to enjoy it at all. It made me all the more conscious of my youth and inexperience and I may add made me more daring in my relations with girls. I imitated the blasé attitude of all the Handsome Harry's that I had seen captivate the screen girls, but to no avail. I seemed to use the wrong technique somewhere and I never was successful in kissing a girl until my senior year in high school. I probably could have gratified that desire before then if I had not been too particular. In the meantime I began to appreciate the love scenes and worked marvels with my desires. I put myself in the old boy's place with great gusto and heaved and sighed with every kiss or contact. I went to many movies just for that unsatiated desire that was given a little outlet in the imaginary nearness of a female companion. I was never very socially inclined and never cared a great deal for the company of girls. Consequently I never had any and had to content myself with imaginary companions. I always felt a restraint when I got out with a real article and in my dreams and fantasy I never limited myself at all. The movie queen with all the atmosphere and the music was quite a factor in determining my present attitude towards women in general. I began to realize that women were quite as human as men and that they had just as many reactions to certain stimuli as we did. It helped break down the reserve that I had always felt and I soon learned to thrill at the proper time and that the thrill comes in thinking about the act, not in doing it. The thrill of expectation. My imagination played all kinds of tricks with cut scenes and I'm not so good inside as I am outside.

I grew out of the idea that it was a sin to show emotion and began to see that to enjoy the film it was necessary to let one's self go with the picture from beginning to end, sway with the crowd and really let the picture work its will. I go now with the feeling that I am to be the plaything of the picture and try to make the scenes belong to me. I really enjoy the picture much more fully. Before I had been killing the central requirements for the enjoyment of the picture.

I have heard lots of comment on the fact that people get criminal ideas from the movies. I am sure that such is the case. I remember in the distant past a crook using a long wooden curtain rod as a fish pole with which he reached out of his window and into a neighboring one swiping a pair of trousers from the radiator in that room. I can still see him carefully empty the pockets and replace the trou. The scenario writers suggest many criminal ideas and the history of many crimes can be traced to a movie where the scene was originally enacted. Another idea that remained with me was the use of a cigarette paper for spy's notes. I had heard of Nathan Hale and his false soled shoes but this was a new one. I recall the rival spies on the porch watching a few zeppelins drop their calling cards. The famous spy that could "unscramble eggs" asked the other if he had any rice paper. I forget how they finally settled the fight and how they got away with the "papers" but I remember the idea. I tried to write on some papers myself but was disgusted to find that I tore them to pieces with every attempt.

My more recent movie experiences have been of a more varied type, and the fixed reactions that I labeled my efforts with are not suitable now. I am affected by the mood I am in myself, by the attitude of the crowd, by the type of picture. If I am in a dreamy mood I want to see something like "Camille" or any rather dreamy love story. After a football game I want a comedy and nothing else. In a restless crowd I want a mystery story because the restless, breathless, silent motions in the crowd are more at home in a picture that continually scares one. I like to study the methods employed now in order to produce a certain resultant effect on the audience. I get a few ideas now and then about the morals and lack of morals of our age. The people seem to be interested in movies that depict the present conditions and in that respect [the motion picture] is the mirror of our lives. It is an exaggerated mirror no doubt but it shows the crowd mind. A historical novel or a famous story of any kind will generally find me a spectator. I go for the rest and relaxation that comes from the effortless amusement that can be had from a movie. I find it a pleasant way to take it easy after a hard week of work and studies and activity.

Case 7: [Untitled]

"You're a bold, brazen hussy," rasped my younger but infinitely wiser brother. I had just confessed with seemingly incredible naiveté that I was pursuing a man, that I had told the man I was pursuing him, and that I needed some fraternal assistance.

"My dear egg, what you mean is that I'm a damned nuisance," I corrected him. He snorted.

"You're plain crazy. I told Puppy you'd get funny notions hanging out at that dinky picture house every Friday night and seeing the impossible impossibly achieved. Who do you think you are anyway – Clara Bow in 'Get Your Man' " [1927]?

"Well, yes and no," I murmured, and that however ambiguous it may seem, answers the question of the effect of the movies on me. I didn't see a movie until I was nine; the country town we lived in didn't have any. For a year or so, a motion picture was starkly a series of moving pictures, stripped of all coherence and connotation. I preferred them to my uncle's stereopticon set because they were "alive" and because nobody told me to "pick them up and put them back in the box." From the first pictures to which my father took me I have vague recollections of sinister Chinese faces; terrified women fleeing from luring, staggering men; angry men standing over cowering women; and train wrecks that were my idea of "lovely messes."

When I was about eleven, my father allowed me to visit the "houses of iniquity" somewhat more often, but confined my diet to Mary Pickford, Marguerite Clark, Charlie Chaplin, Harold Lloyd, and other staples. I never conceived any great fondness for any of them except Charlie Chaplin, and to this day he has been a constant source of delight to my weary heart. I liked none of them well enough to care if Puppy saw fit to restrain my attendance.

Then I sinned. Puppy packed me off to see Mary Pickford in "Little Lord Fauntleroy" [1921], but neglected to go along and steer me in the right direction. With an innate tendency for coming out at the wrong place, I emerged two hours later from having seen Anita Stewart in "The Yellow Typhoon" [1920]. She had played a dual role assisted by a blonde wig, and she had done exciting things the like of which I had never dreamed. She became my idol. Gradually, sometimes with and sometimes without my father's permission, I became devoted to Priscilla

Dean, Wallace Reid, Tom Mix, Bill Hart, Betty Compson, and Olive Thomas. By this time I was quite capable of following a plot, but I was still so untutored in the ways of the movies, that I actually suffered in my fear that the villain would finish chewing up the table between him and the heroine before the hero arrived. O height of innocence!

Most pictures are comedies to me now, but then, when I was in grammar school, pictures of the type that I have mentioned were the only outlet for a sense of adventure that was no longer dormant but that was necessarily "playing dead." I would never have considered running away from home; I was far too passive a youngster for that, but my desire to attend any kind of movie disturbed my father greatly. Only once in my life have I seen him too amazed to punish me for my misdemeanors. I wanted to see Anita Stewart; he ordered me to stay home and practice on the violin. I remember ripping all the strings off my violin, snatching the hair out of my bow, and scattering everything in the middle of the floor. That incident marked the crisis in my desire for escape. I realized sulkily that it was futile for me to consider emulating Anita Stewart's escapades. With a stubbornness that amazed even me, I decided never to see another picture show. It seems that I was fool enough to insist upon making some sort of a melodramatic gesture; and, strangely, I alluded to my theatrical resolution for a year.

When I was fourteen I began again, with a gang of boys ranging from eight to fifteen years of age. Every Friday night we supplied ourselves with chewing gum, popcorn, and peanuts and stampeded the nearest movie house, familiarly known as the Dinky. We followed the serials regularly, but now I was much too blasé to find them other than amusing. We never failed to see a "Western," but I found myself incapable of taking them seriously. Fred Thomson and Tom Mix were the favorites. Lon Chaney supplanted Anita Stewart. I can laugh at him now, but I couldn't then.

Alberta Vaughn was our favorite serial star. She gave me an inkling of what I could do with that sense of adventure of mine. Alberta had a good time in her own back yard. I confess with infinite amusement that the good Catholic Germans in the neighborhood were relieved when I came to college. All summer this long-legged girl in her teens, who should have been learning to bake and sew for her future husband, ran wild, climbing fences and trees and telephone poles, and riding on the gasoline tank of a yellow puddle-jumper. I discovered that garter snakes were harmless, and the members of the gang strutted around with snakes folded up in their pockets when they weren't tying them in knots, around their necks. When I came away to college instead of getting married (of course there was not hope for one as insane as me, but I might have decently become an old maid) I definitely proved that I had no sense.

Naturally, I couldn't exist indefinitely without living affected by the low element in the movies. The first impression that I conceived was an extraordinarily simple-minded one. The girl's part was extreme haughtiness toward the man. It would never do to give him the idea that she might be so unmaidenly as to waste a second thought on him. The hero, however, knew better, and persevered in all manner of bravery. Finally, by rescuing her from some danger that two grains of forethought would have kept her out of, he rejoiced in having her subside in his masterful arms. There was a boy in the Gang just about my age. We had a sentimental hallucination after this fashion. My role of haughtiness was easy; his "brave deeds" consisted of bossing the smaller brats, playing mumblety-peg with amazing dexterity, climbing out of the second story window of his barn, and walking the back fence as skillfully as a cat. I never got to the point of subsiding in his arms, although I used to lie awake nights planning situations that would justify my doing so. Until I was seventeen, I firmly believed that I would be a ruined woman if I ever let a man kiss me, and all the desires that the movies aroused were counterbalanced by my father's lectures.

Having recovered from my first impression of love, I became interested in the sexual aspects of it. I had seen "The Sheik" [1921] earlier and found only the desert warfare interesting. The next time I saw Rudolph Valentino, I was interested in his technique. Again I changed my favorites. John Gilbert, Ramon Novarro, Gloria Swanson, Richard Barthelmess, Norma Shearer, and Ronald Colman were the stars of the pictures I preferred to see. I was never able to imagine myself in love with any of the male leads, but I was in the habit of picturing boys that I knew playing the roles of certain stars while I took the female lead. There's no sense denying that I was tremendously curious about this kissing business. I stubbornly set out to find where the attraction lay. I tried putting myself in the place of the heroine while the picture was going on, but still I was unsatisfied. I'd inveigle my boyfriends into the time, the place, and the mood only to remember my father's countless admonitions.[14] Then I gave the pesky thing up, but by this time I was beginning to find myself rather amusing.

Now, I can go for weeks without feeling the urge. My sense of adventure is not so blatant as formerly. I have filed it down to braggadocio and usually content myself with avoiding doing consistently what is expected of me. Occasionally I "go on a tear;" the incident of pursuing the man quite brazenly was one. He never blinked an eyelash or misunderstood. If I'm eating peppermints on the elevated, I toss the conductor one if I feel so inclined. He makes a hundred if he catches it and doesn't ask me for my telephone number. I still frequent the movies in a more or less desultory fashion, and sometimes I find beautiful photography, or a fine bit of interpretation, or genuinely clever funniness. Their infinite capacities for molding and crystallizing the thoughts and ideals of the people will find intelligent direction in time.

Case 8: The Movies and I

It was a curious experiment to look back over the years and trace the role that the movies have played in my life. I was in fact quite startled to find that I remember scarcely more than the titles of a small number of movies, had forgotten the plot of most of them, and the actors were but a dim recollection with a haze existing between their faces and names. However, I suppose the motion pictures have exerted a stronger influence over me than I realize, and as I recollect for a longer time, I do become aware that I have cultivated many little mannerisms manifested by different actors, thought many thoughts, dreamed many dreams, and read many books as a result of patronizing the motion picture theater.

Having lived for a number of years on a ranch fifty miles from the nearest town, it was quite an event to attend a movie when I was a child. The first one I ever saw was one in which Tom Mix played. The entire community attended that show, for Tom Mix was a product of the cattle country in which the town lies. Of course, he played only a minor part, but the idea that I knew some one in the movies was enough to assure me that some day, too, I would be an actress. I was stage crazy before I knew the least bit about it. And upon our return to the ranch I re-enacted for days the part of the heroine in the story and every stray cowpuncher that happened along I assigned a role to, the ones I liked best being given parts in the posse under the command of the beautiful virtuous heroine, myself! Indeed I shall never forget how I was completely lost in the assumption of the part and how temperamentally crestfallen I was when I was heartlessly told to "Be yourself."

My first movie thrill was succeeded by many pictures of the same type – all of which were so ordinary, so far-fetched, and so similar that I remember no names. The result of these pictures was the inspiration for my brother and me to attempt fancy riding, as for example, sweeping the ground with our hats, turning in our saddles, crawling under the horse's belly; attempts which, I must confess, resulted more frequently in injury than in success. Another action upon which we focused our attention for several weeks was the rolling of a cigarette with one hand; also the old gambling trick, the thumb shuffle. Yes, the "wild west" shows surely did influence me. Even while realizing their absurdity and their unlikeness to real western life, I enjoyed them to the utmost and they at least served to fill my thoughts and provide ideas for execution between our infrequent trips to town.

Then my first "wild west" epoch came to an abrupt close by the moving of my family to a large town where there were "more and better" movies. Among my first ones there were "Tom Sawyer" [1917] and "Little Lord Fauntleroy" [1921]. After having witnessed "Tom Sawyer" I was quite humiliated that I had ever imitated any of the heroines of western pictures. How unlady-like and boisterous I had been! My utmost desire was now to become the sweet, pretty dainty type of girl (I can't recall her name) that "Tom" so enthusiastically endorsed. So for a short time I gave up all active life; even went so far as to play with a doll for one day, the only time in my life – so you can see how greatly I was affected.

"Little Lord Fauntleroy" acquainted me for the first time, as far as I can ascertain, with Mary Pickford. I was quite impressed by the fact that in this picture she played two roles, that of the Little Lord, and that of his mother. I was perhaps more interested in the technique of such filming than in the story. Nor was I particularly impressed with the actions of the characters, but believe me, I vowed with great fervor to be as sweet to my mother as the Little Lord was to his! For who could tell, maybe I, too, would be taken from my mother some day, and I didn't wish to have done anything which I would regret the rest of my life. And so, again for several days I was a pattern little girl, insofar as my actions were associated with my mother. The reason I remember how good I was is because I was allowed to go to another show, a reward for my A-1 behavior – a movie which broke the spell!

This was the initiation of a new type of picture in my career, the Saturday afternoon two cent serial. I think that at this time I was in the sixth grade, at the age where one has "beaux" and scribbles two names on every billboard and draws a heart around them, and thinks one's self madly in love. You know the age, Mr. Blumer. This serial was [the] most gruesome, exciting, and sensational tale of men and women who had been lost in the deep African jungle. At every turn they were mocked by the monkeys, terrified by the lions, and imperiled by electric storms. Naturally the protection of the women by the men was superb and the love scenes following some particularly valiant deed were – well, simply fascinating and very illuminating to one not yet educated in the art of love-making. So, as Saturday after Saturday, my "Heart-Mate" and I secretly met at the show, we absorbed much of the sentimentality expressed on the screen. No, never can I forget the thrill I experienced when the lad put his arms around me as we watched a similar scene on the white sheet. It really disgusts me now as I recall how my heart throbbed at some such scene; and I am ashamed of the way I practiced so religiously before the mirror in the hope of attaining attractive facial expressions and movements. But eventually the serial ended and so did some of my foolishness.

The next era of pictures I remember well was that of Jackie Coogan and Baby Peggy. I do not remember the names of any of the pictures they played in but it seems to me most of them were concerned with the life of some poor little tot, whose parents were dead, and who, in the due course of time was adopted by some rich person and "lived happily ever after." Of these pictures I was particularly fond and I realize now that I developed an attitude of sincere [sympathy] toward those less fortunate than myself. It was impossible for one not to notice some little waif and long to do something for him after seeing Jackie Coogan in his characteristic garb and role. Oh, I did love those pictures! I wish that Jackie were still on the screen that again I might laugh and cry with him.

Chronologically these plays were succeeded by those in which Harold Lloyd, Syd Chaplin, and Charlie Chaplin were the ring-leaders. Before them, however, had come Fatty Arbuckle in whom I could never see anything funny, but, instead, a repulsive piece of humanity. Charlie Chaplin I always enjoyed seeing. This was perhaps due to the fact that I knew him quite well personally. Harold Lloyd in "Grandma's Boy" [1922] and Syd Chaplin in "Charlie's Aunt" [1925] I liked immensely. Many times I made mental note of the captions such as "She's the aunt from Brazil where the nuts come from" in order that I might appear original and witty at some future date. In the vicinity of my home it was the vogue to copy the various dance steps seen on the screen, also many little flourishes; for example we all accepted the hand shake exhibited by Harold Lloyd in "The Freshman" [1925].

But as I grew older and saw more movies I was not so profoundly impressed by them, and considered them more as an amusement for only a few hours. For a time my taste centered on pictures such as Mary Pickford in "Dorothy Vernon of Haddon Hall" [1924], Douglas Fairbanks in "Robin Hood" [1922], and various ones based on the "Graustark" books. These were all the same general type of production, the phase of which I was most interested being the historical background, costumes, etc.

Intermingled with these pictures were those in which Gloria Swanson, Pola Negri, and the Talmadges starred. Whenever I witnessed one of their plays I was with them body and soul. Gloria Swanson may be termed a clothes horse, but one of the things most alluring about her to me was the striking clothes she could wear so admirably. Even now I have images of some of her dresses and frequently when shopping I select my clothes along the lines of those dresses. Pola Negri fascinated me by her strong, individual, dark type of beauty. After seeing her, I would go home and persistently attempt to assemble my hair in the strange and attractive way that had become Pola so well. For several months the height of my ambition was to dress like Gloria Swanson and look like Pola Negri!

During the last three or four years the "Collegiate" type of picture has been created and gained great favor. Alternating with this type have been those of the Pioneer Days, War Pictures, the gruesome ones enacted by Lon Chaney, and the Historical Dramas exemplified by "Ben Hur" [1926]. Each of these has exerted an influence over me, as they have served as a stimulant for thought.

After having seen the "Covered Wagon" [1923] and "The Vanishing American" [1925] I realized more than ever before our great indebtedness to the pioneers; a sympathetic attitude was aroused in me toward the Indian by these productions, also. The War Pictures have forced me to feel more strongly than ever the utter futility and overwhelming horribleness resultant from war; while pictures of the early Christian period such as "Ben Hur" revived much of history for me and at the same time gloriously depicted the true meaning of Christianity, enough food for thought to last me forever!

Just as these pictures have influenced my thoughts, they have influenced my dreams, if I may be permitted to draw a distinction between the two. The collegiate movies played an important part in my dreams. From them I gained an enthusiasm to come to college, to enter into all the "pranks" and social life. I longed to come, and I dreamed of being one of the most collegiate, the girl to be the football captain's friend. Just as I have feasted on the thoughts of school I have dwelled hardily in the days of the settling of the west. Many times I have crossed the desolate desert wastes, encountering the Indians, loved some hero of the trail. After having seen a movie of pioneer days I am very unreconciled to the fact that I live today instead of the romantic days of fifty years ago. But to offset this poignant and useless longing I have dreamed of going to war. I stated previously that through the movies I have become aware of the awfulness, the futility, etc., of it; but as this side has been impressed upon me, there has been awakened in me, at the same time, the desire to go to the "front" during the next war. The excitement, shall I say glamour of the war has always appealed to me from the screen. Often I have pictured myself as a truck driver, nurse, HERO-INE![15] I honestly feel that when the next war comes nothing can prevent me from going, and indeed I shall blame such an action on the movies.

The pictures of Lon Chaney have caused me more misery than any pictures I have ever seen. For days after I have seen him I am nervous, and carry about with me the gruesome images of Mr. Chaney.

In my first paragraph I said that I had thought many thoughts, dreamed many dreams, and had read many books because of screen productions. I have disposed briefly of how my actions, thoughts, and dreams were the results of the movies, and my last point is to show how my literary taste has been molded to some extent by them.

As a child I was not particularly interested in books, but after seeing "Little Lord Fauntleroy" I wished to read the book, which I did. From that time on I have read most of the books that have been produced on the screen. Therefore, I am quite indebted to the movies for the reading of many interesting and worthwhile books, as well as many popular novels typified by those of Zane Grey. I have the motion pictures to thank for the reading of "Ben Hur," "The Hunchback of Notre Dame," "Beau Geste," "By the Order of the King," "The Resurrection" and many more.

I do not feel that the movies have caused me to slip a "moral cog" at any time. Perhaps this is because I have seen a rather high class of picture. The desperate love pictures I have seen have tended rather to disgust me or amuse me rather than arouse within me a desire to

experience the same emotions. Some of the movies today are very beneficial, others merely amusing, and others very degrading; it depends
entirely upon the class of picture one is in the habit of attending what
the outcome will be.

Case 9: My Life as Affected by the Screen

The motion pictures have been a big influence in my life because I have
always been a special "devotee" of them. When I was very small, I liked
nothing better than to spend as much time as possible in a darkened
theater and see men and women enact the every day phases of life.

I have a very vivid imagination and I think that it is probably due to
my extensive journeys to the motion picture houses. My views of life are
on a whole "rosy" or rather delightful because I have never experienced
hardships and in the motion pictures I have always seen the "sun shine
from behind darkened clouds." In other words most motion pictures
end happily and this constant repetition of happy sequences has made
every day life somehow seem very happy. It doesn't seem possible for
instance that a villain wouldn't get punished in the end for all his wrong
doings. Yet there are many villains who never feel punishment for their
wrongs. In the movies he is also made to pay. This creates a feeling of
safety if you know that your enemies will get their dues – at least it did
when I was younger.

Then too I have always liked pretty women. When I'd see them in the
movies I positively would try to act like them. People used to say that I
was too old for my age – they used to "kid" me and call me "Grandma"
because I liked to read and to go to the movies instead of playing "Hop
Scotch" or "rope." They didn't know and don't know to this day that it
was because of the movies. In the movies the girls were always beautiful
and lady-like and so I tried to be, too. When I was ten or twelve years
old I had already decided to join a "bathing beauty" contest when I was
old enough. I'd pose for long whiles sometimes before the big mirror
trying to get "effects." The reason I was such a conceited person is
because I had been told I resembled a movie actress and I tried to look
like her as much as possible. She has a beautiful face and figure and I
determined to be like her. At night in bed I would lay awake and day
dream about the big hit I would make if I were to go to California.[16] (I
know better now.)

Even today I get new ideas of dress and personality from the screen favorites.

Kathryn McDonald, called the most beautiful woman in the world, was my first real favorite and I certainly loved her. I had a "case" on her and she was my ideal for along time.

I think perhaps that my ideas about different people have been influenced by the same types in the movies. A dark squinty eyed person is to be avoided as a plague. I instinctively like innocent looking girls, but I know now that sometimes they are the most deceitful.

I am rather particular as to the looks and general appearances of the boys and girls I go with and this I know is due to the movies. The fellows I am seen with often must be "sheiky." That's silly I know but I can't get away from it. I have been in the habit of thinking of big good-looking boys for so long that I'm sure I couldn't get along with a homely one. I think my viewpoint is changing now, though, as I grow older because I have come in contact with both kinds and I find them a great deal different than before.

Love in the movies as portrayed by the stars always made me squirm because I knew nothing about it. Now I think it's all "applesauce." When I was younger though these scenes always stayed longest in my mind. I'd put myself in the girl's place and try to make believe. But after all the feeling was second hand.

No wonder girls of older days before the movies were so modest and bashful. They never saw Clara Bow and William Haines. They didn't know anything else but being modest and sweet. I think the movies have a great deal to do with present day so-called "wildness." If we didn't see such examples in the movies where would we get the idea of being "hot"? We wouldn't.[17]

I know a fellow that (every time I'm with him) wants to neck. He wants to practice I guess, but I have a sneaking suspicion that he got his method from the screen. It's so absolutely absurd. I get a kick out of watching him work up a passion – just like John Gilbert, but it doesn't mean a thing. Now that fellow is absolutely getting an education from the films but what good does it do him? It makes him appear silly. He's a nice fellow though but he has his "weakness."[18]

The first pictures I was most fond of were serial pictures. One, called "Tarzan of the Apes" was the most thrilling thing I've ever seen. I can remember being terrorized to death by some of the scenes, but I always came back the following Saturday for more. Now I like "college pictures" or pictures featuring Clara Bow or Vilma Banky. They are my favorites.

The movies play a big part in my everyday life even now. Once a week and sometimes twice my girl friends and I trot down town to see a big show by ourselves. I'd rather see a good movie than any play or opera in town and I go to see them all.

Case 10: My Movie Experiences

The earliest memories I have of my movie experiences are not at all distinct, but as I look back I feel that I reveled in the hair-raising serials and the wild and woolly cowboy type of entertainment. I started attending the movies with regularity when I was about seven or eight years old. Every Saturday with the utmost inevitability a gang of us fellows would attend the matinee; it became an accepted and looked forward to routine in our lives. At that time my parents very seldom allowed me to go to the movies with them on account of the fact that I generally was bored to the point of extreme restlessness by most of the movies they attended. But the Saturday afternoons were different, it would have been a tragedy to me to miss an installment of a serial I was following up. Those serials were very real things to us fellows, we accepted all that was in them with a perfect faith and never doubted the reasonableness of any of the incidents for a second. The serial we saw one week would stock us up with plenty of conversational material to hold us over for the next installment. We discussed pro and con all the probabilities of the manner in which the hero would escape the terrible predicament the villain plunged him into just before the "To Be Continued Next Week" caption was flashed on the screen. We conjectured upon the identity of the "mysterious rider" and prophesied the downfall of the villains in language heated with the illusion of reality. Our play was always influenced by the current type of serial we were inhaling. If it had to do with cowboys and Indians we played cowboy and Indian, if it had to do with cops and robbers then we played cop and robber. I can't remember that I ever quibbled very much over the part I was to play in the re-enactment just so long as I got variety, one part today and another tomorrow. Whether I was the hero or the villain I always played the part with a gusto that was exemplary from the point of intenseness, at least. There is but one movie star of those days that I can remember at all clearly, and that is Pearl White. My memory of her is vividly linked up with a serial in which she appeared that centered around Iron Man, an automaton, and which is responsible for the suggestion of the other I don't know. I can't say that this vivid recollection ever had any effect on me, however, or that any movie I ever saw had a lasting influence on my conduct. In those days I viewed my movies as I view a good basketball or football game now. I clapped at the least excuse, I yelled at the last minute rescue. I was almost continually in a high tension of emotion that absolutely forbade my seeing any movie plumped complacently in my seat. I certainly had a whole hearted ability for relishing the pie throwing comedies of those days, often laughing, really laughing, to the point of satisfaction.

Roughly speaking, this period of my movie reactions lasted until I was about twelve or thirteen years old. Then I began to get a little romantic in my tastes and found myself actually enjoying some of the "love pictures" which a short time ago I would summarily have relegated to the ash can. Not that I gave up the action pictures entirely, I still enjoyed them, especially anything that Douglas Fairbanks appeared in, he was my crowning favorite by far. But I began to become aware of the leading ladies, to notice them for themselves and not as mere incidental conveniences of the plot. If I chanced upon a movie in which the action was not very strong and I was not carried away by the plot, I would console myself with an aesthetic appreciation of the beauties of the heroine, but this appreciation never took in more than the features of the face. At this time also I occasionally saw pictures in company with girls, but for the most part I was more conscious of the fact that I was sitting next to a girl than I was as to what was taking place on the screen. One incident, though, I will never forget. I happened to meet a girl I was particularly partial to on her way to the show one afternoon and I went along with her. What the movie was I can't remember, but it was a slow moving affair with plenty of idyllic love scenes in it. We were sitting off to the side in a more or less deserted portion of the theater, and under the influence of the hero's amour I slipped my arm about her waist and left it there with her permission the rest of the picture. Such a long interval separated the next time that I went to a movie with her, however, that when we did go again I was afraid to repeat the experiment.

As I got into high school and into my sixteenth and seventeenth year

I began to use the movies as a school of etiquette. I began to observe the table manners of the actors in the eating scenes. I watched for the proper way in which to conduct oneself at a night club, because I began to have ideas that way. The number of buttons the leading man's coat had, the fact that it was single breasted or double breasted, and the cut of its lapel all influenced me in the choice of my own suits. The technique of making love to a girl received considerable of my attention, and it was directly through the movies that I learned to kiss a girl on her ears, neck and cheeks, as well as on the mouth, in a close huddle. My reaction to all cowboy movies in those days had already become rather flat, and I took more and more to the sophisticated society stuff. I also became more worldly wise and understood what the more suggestive movies were all about. I began to make it a special point to see all movies labeled "Adults Only." In fact, I began to consider myself quite a wise man about town. I didn't content myself with merely contemplating the heroine's face anymore. I began to notice the swell of her bosom and watched it rise and fall as she breathed a little harder in passionate scenes. I had my eyes out for the shape of her legs, too, and the more I saw of them the better I liked it. More and more my whole attention focused on the women in the movie, not to the exclusion of the men, of course, but to a quite great extent compared with my earlier days.[19]

Sometime in my eighteenth year I began to lose my former contact with the movies. I gradually began to despise them, to see them altogether too critically to permit enjoyment. I can account for this only in a growing taste and appreciation I began to cultivate for literature. I always had been an avid reader but at that time I began to get on the right track. Courses in literature at school laid a foundation which my natural interest in that field built up into a quite widespread acquaintance with the better books. My eighteenth year marks a turning point in my life; then I consciously began to seek "culture." I not only read better novelists, I discovered that rich field of poetry. I began to visit the Art Institute and found a new field of enjoyment in pictures that weren't movies. None of this was forced, I took to it very easily, and with it my former tastes in movies began to be so undermined that today I rarely ever attend a movie and thoroughly enjoy it. Five years ago I went to the movies on the average of two or three times a week; now I go to the movies on the average of two or three times a month. I see most movies now, by far, as insipid asinine things that produce mental weariness and irritation in me. But still they are useful as cheap places to take a date. I have one use for the movies in this respect that I flatter myself I have performed some research and experimentation in.

A good movie plays upon the emotions of all of us, but many people are moved by any sort of movie. It has been my experience that nine people out of ten are so played upon in their emotions by a movie as to find themselves in a particularly sensitive and weakened mood in relation to that emotion which the movie most strained. Let me make myself clear. For instance, after seeing a movie stressing the pathetic case of a white-haired and sweet faced mother sent to the poorhouse by the cruel neglect of her children, most people react tenderly to their own mother in their thoughts. A movie featuring the torture of a noble white man by fiendish Chinamen works people up against the Chinese. And so a highly charged sex movie puts many girls in an emotional state that weakens, let us say, resistance. I took a girl I became acquainted with not so long ago out for the first time to a very racy sex movie. It had the usual lingerie scenes, complications, etc. That night when I took her home she was, in vernacular, quite warm. The next time I dated her she wanted to see some gruesome thing with Lon Chaney in it. That night she certainly was not responsive to the same degree as the first, yet I knew her better. It merely means that her emotions weren't aroused in the same way by the second picture as by the first, her visceral tension and activities were controlled more or less, and therefore, with most girls, I generally pick the movies we attend with that point in mind. Remember, it is more or less a physical and natural phenomenon, and nine times out of ten with intelligent interpretation the girl's emotional state can be regulated and used to what may be either advantage or disadvantage.

Private Monograph on Movies and Sex

HERBERT BLUMER

This report is being written mainly to present some material showing the influence of motion pictures on sex life rather than that of interpreting this influence. The material will consist almost entirely of autobiographical accounts and of group conversations about sexual phases of motion pictures. The organization of the material merely serves the interest of convenient presentation rather than that of telling explanation.

The first set of autobiographical statements which are given will serve to show something of the milder forms of sexual agitation resulting from the witnessing of passionate or suggestive pictures. It may be remarked, incidentally, that the autobiographical material comes entirely from university and high school students. It may be taken as typical in some sense of this portion of our population (of all high school and college people). Without further explanation we may present the following series of accounts serving to show the less intense forms of sexual disturbance.

(Female, 19, White, College Sophomore) John Gilbert and Greta Garbo are another famous pair of screen lovers. They go in for sensational love scenes, and much sex stuff. I must admit that one of these scenes does thrill me and leave me with a rather goose-fleshy feeling.

(Female, 20, White, College Sophomore) I have been to the movies with other girls and had them grab my hand or tighten up at some of the more emotional love scenes. I used to pretend that I felt that way because it seemed the thing to do. But I do not remember that I ever really did. I once saw John Gilbert in "Flesh and the Devil" [1927] and I felt a bit excited by certain scenes of that. I was then in a rather restless mood which might have accounted for it.

(Female, 20, White, College Junior) The next year after finals, I went with a group of girls to see John Gilbert and Greta Garbo in "Flesh and the

Devil." I have never seen an entire audience so wrought up as that one. We vicariously enjoyed with Greta Garbo the thrill of every flash of Gilbert's eyes.

(Male, 16, White, High School Junior) No movie would ever move me to temptations, but I guess one feels "funny" when one sees a "hot" picture. I guess you know what I mean.

(Female, 21, White, College Junior) Having recovered from my first impression of love, I became interested in the sexual aspects of it. I had seen "The Sheik" [1921] earlier and found only the desert warfare interesting. The next time I saw Rudolph Valentino, I was interested in his technique. Again I changed my favorites. John Gilbert, Ramon Novarro, Gloria Swanson, Richard Barthelmess, Norma Shearer, and Ronald Colman were the stars of the pictures I preferred to see. I was never able to imagine myself in love with any of the male leads, but I was in the habit of picturing boys that I knew playing the roles of certain stars while I took the female lead. There's no sense denying that I was tremendously curious about this kissing business. I stubbornly set out to find where the attraction lay. I tried putting myself in the place of the heroine while the picture was going on, but still I was unsatisfied. I'd inveigle my boy friends into the time, the place, and the mood only to remember my father's countless admonitions.[1]

(Male, 20, White, College Sophomore) I have seen a great many movies and many with suggestive sexual relation scenes, such as "The Way of All Flesh" [1927] and the last one, "The River" [1928]. I am afraid my imagination always interprets the sexual relation scene in the worst way. If I am with a girl I am embarrassed at a suggestive film. If I am by myself or with some other boys I enjoy it. These films cannot but arouse some passion in those who view them. They do in me and in all my friends whom I have discussed them with. These pictures do me more harm than any others that I see.

(Female, 18, Negro, High School Senior) I remember the picture "Resurrection" [1927], taken from the story by Tolstoy, of a wronged Russian peasant girl. Its sensuousness played havoc upon my emotions.

(Female, 20, White, College Junior) I didn't care for love and sex pictures until I was about sixteen. I never imagined myself in love with a movie actor, but there was one I surely loved to see. He disgusts me now, and his love scenes are nauseating to me. John Gilbert played in "His Hour" [1924], "Three Weeks" [1924], "The Wife of the Centaur" [1925] and "Flesh and the Devil." This last picture seemed to appeal to me for I saw it twice, and I would have gone the third time but I didn't have the money. The love scenes were so amorous and during them I throbbed all over. I will have to admit that I wanted someone so bad to make love to me that way. I didn't go with any boy then, steady; but I went away from that picture craving to be loved. I thought him a perfect lover. Their long drawn-out kisses thrilled me beyond words, but now he is disgusting to me.

I pity the young folks who have not had the proper training at home. Some of the pictures that are shown today certainly put one's sexual desires into action. One who had had little teaching about morals gets the wrong thing from these pictures. In one of John Gilbert's pictures he went to his sweetheart's room at night; and it showed him climbing up the trellis to her window. They made the scene very beautiful; the moon was shining, and the orchestra was playing a haunting love song. The next scene showed him coming out of the window, and it was morning. These things do leave a dark brown taste in my mouth, but I find myself wanting to see a picture when I hear it is kind of fast.

(Male, 21, White, College Senior) I think there was only one picture that gave me a worked-up feeling – a bunch of fellows and I took in "The Plastic Age" [1925] and really when I left the theatre I had a desire for a good necking party, and I think I would have taken anything up if I had had the chance.

These accounts which have been given and those which follow may be allowed to speak for themselves. They do suggest something about the way in which motion pictures may be productive of the stirring of sex passion. Some further indication of this type of influence is suggested by the next series of autobiographical statements which point to the distracting effect of what are construed to be "sexy" pictures.

(Male, 21, White, University Junior) Although I never go out of my way to see a "hot" movie, I will say that they do not have an exactly good effect on me. If I am studying intensively or trying to train for some kind of an athletic contest and by any chance see an extremely emotional picture, the result is not a help. There is nearly always a strong tendency to go out and have a "party." I can nearly always overcome this temptation, but some- times it isn't so easy.

(Male, 21, White, Jewish, University Junior) The movies, with their super- sexual scenes and depictions of such enjoyment of life, have influenced me. They have not caused me to follow the paths of the movies, but I have been sorely tempted. When one witnesses an extremely "hot" scene where the allurement is very clear, it is very difficult to keep yourself from wishing a similar experience. If I hear from some of my friends that a particular picture is exceptionally torrid, I prefer it to one of more lukewarm atmosphere. But these scenes are merely enjoyed while being witnessed and vary rarely give rise to any day-dreams. The movies give one the impression that there are innumerable girls just waiting on corners for fellows to pick them up, but although I have tried out this, I have never had any success.

(Female, 20, White, University Sophomore) The usual movie shows a number of suggestive sex scenes, especially those pictures dealing with the high life of society people. Almost every picture with a triangle situation has suggestive scenes, unless a real artist is directing it. Personally I don't like them; it always worries me when a woman is losing her dress in a warm love scene. Such scenes make me feel quite excited and tingly, emotions which people describe as "animal sensations" and brand as unhealthy – since I am from this group I too must say such emotions should be kept under, although I wonder if I'm honest with myself; I'm afraid I'd like to be seductive too.

(Female, 21, White, University Senior) There was still another reason why I saw fewer pictures. As the industry developed, the "vamp" came into vogue. I soon discovered that I did not like to see this type of picture, as the melodrama, the "triangle" plots, the highly emotional pictures brought out the elements in me which I desired to keep under restraint. I have a deep repugnance toward things of the flesh. I have felt that this feeling should be tempered, and often feel that this maladjustment to life is childish. Nevertheless, it is there and anything which stirs me physically seems to bring out the grossest in me. This is never affected in actions, but in my mind. I soon learned this, and have consciously shunned the pictures which would have this effect. I had then and still have the habit of reviewing the picture in my mind after seeing it, and I certainly do not enjoy reviewing the lustful scene. This sort of picture places me in a very unhappy state of mind and at high tension, while a light comedy is really recreation for me.

Rather frequently the display of suggestive action in the movies may be received with disgust. Such a reaction, of course, indicates that in the eyes of the observer the display of sex is too brazen. A single instance will suffice to represent this kind of experience.

(Female, 21, White, University Senior) Only one experience thoroughly disgusted me with a movie. It was an episode from "The Man Who Laughs" [1928], a Dumas story which otherwise was exceptionally well done, and there was no excuse for the episode I am about to relate. A countess, a degenerate of the aristocracy, had just stepped from her bath, wrapped in a towel which reached her knees, when the court jester, the villain, who had great influence with the king, entered her room. In encouraging him to get her a favor, she deliberately lifted the bottom of the towel, lifted a leg, and invited her caller to have a look. He stopped and looked. It was the limit in suggestiveness. I saw the picture in a very small theatre, and I am quite sure this part was censored in larger theatres. My companion agreed with me that he had never seen the movies go quite that far. I do not think I am easily shocked, but on this occasion I was stunned. My nerves were shaken, and I was almost sick with disgust by the time I left the theatre. The experience did not bother me afterwards, but it disgusts me thoroughly to remember it.

In our materials there is a large number of autobiographical accounts treating of the fantasy which may be induced by motion pictures of a sexual nature. These accounts serve further to show the rather pervasive sexual attraction of motion pictures. They also indicate one of the major forms of experience through which sexual impulses aroused by motion pictures may express themselves.

(Male, 21, White, Jewish, University Junior) Often in my day-dreams I imagined myself in the handsome hero's place. How I kissed these beautiful women! How my lips burned against theirs! What wonderful bliss was ours in our secret rendezvous! Alice Terry was my ideal. With her at my side I could have conquered all the world. At times I felt that I would gladly give ten years of my life to kiss her once. Toward other actresses I felt a strong sex attraction. I felt a strong desire to fondle them, their hair, their breasts. But toward her my feelings were different. To merely kiss her tenderly on the cheek would have been enough.

(Male, 20, White, University Junior) In entering upon puberty, the cinema took on a different contour for me. Hitherto sex had played no part in my experiences with the movies. But gradually I began to sit up and take acute notice of the female stars. I became conscious of their face and body, and their physical attractions appealed to me. I experienced orgasms when close-ups of them were made, and I enjoyed physical titillations when the lover clasped his trembling loved-one in passionate embrace and "voila!" the blood rushed to my membrane virilis when their lips met. A new sensation took possession of me: my sex-life was launched! I took their images to bed with me, indulging in "wet dreams," as the colloquial would have it. Just as Bebe Daniels, Mae Murray, Norma Talmadge, Gloria Swanson and their girl friends now reacted to me in a different manner, so in my daily life, my associations of the opposite sex assumed a change of pose. The movie stars set a criterion of the beautiful, the desirous for me. I had reached manhood.

(Male, 20, White, University Junior) Blanche Sweet played in another war propaganda film that was based on a story by Rupert Hughes, "The Unpardonable Sin" [1919]. The population of the town was lined up across the street and shot down by a machine-gun *en masse*. This story gave me plenty of opportunity to glut my war-distorted soul. I broke out in a cold sweat to see this crowd of people shot down; I raged and fretted that I was powerless to help these unfortunates. I enclosed another secret in my innermost self when the German soldier found the sister of Blanche asleep in her bedroom. He jumped with a fiendish light in his eye, cautiously looked around the corners and them came back to carry out his desires. He left with a rather excited gleam in his eye and a rather fearsome jump in his step. The girl was bruised and her clothes torn in a suggestive manner and even at my immature age it made certain impressions on my sexual self that I had not noticed a great deal before. I used to think about being a German soldier just so I could go out and procure this forbidden fruit, this universal urge was so strong.[2]

(Male, 21, White, University Junior) About this time I had a reaction to all the strict discipline to which I had been subjected as a child and I went to a show almost daily, and the filthier and more appealing to the sex impulses they were, the better I liked them. I seemed to get an enormous kick out of any picture which had sex appeal and my imagination, which always has been very active, seemed to lend itself to such pictures as a stimulation.

(Male, 20, White, University Sophomore) I never did develop any absorbing interest in love pictures. They always seemed kind of silly to me. When I became sixteen or seventeen, however, certain love scenes seen on the screen would have a certain reaction within me. I was undergoing my first sexual cravings, and when I saw anything like "petting" or "necking" going on on the screen, I wanted to taste the same experiences myself. This craving sometimes rose to a very high pitch.

I didn't know exactly what I wanted, but certain things seen at the movies would start a train of thoughts in my mind which were not exactly respectable. The movies went far to urge and develop an instinct which would have appeared sooner or later anyway. The movies merely made me sex conscious a little earlier than I would have become normally. That is what I think. I know that I got my first sexual impulse from seeing some "dirty dancing" in a show about the Montmartre district in Paris. That started a train of thoughts in my mind that was new and sensually pleasant. For a while I was in danger of becoming a moron. Luckily, my lewd thoughts were submerged by most of my daily tasks and interests. It was usually at night and in bed that I gave way to my own "Decameron." I would think of an especially appealing, suggestive scene from a movie and would proceed to develop a big "hard on." This all sounds vulgar, but it's true.

(Male, 20, White, University Sophomore) I remember a picture in which Clara Bow, I think it was, took the part of a vain and indolent young vamp who stole her older sister's lover as well as her money. I can still remember vividly her lying on a couch and enticing the man with her expression and a little wriggle of her body. I can remember that I felt as hopelessly lost as the young man who gave in and kissed her passionately. After the picture I often day-dreamed of myself in the same scene with her, and thought how I would be forced to give in against my will.

(Male, 21, White, College Senior) I am afraid I would be too much of a hypocrite if I failed to mention that I have imagined myself parking my shoes under [Olga] Baclanova's bed. This, of course, in all seriousness – not that it will ever happen.

(Male, 19, White, Jewish, University Sophomore) Strange as it may seem, my sex reactions have always been most strong in scenes where the hero is being "vamped" by the villainess, and it is only in recent years that ordinary "good" love-making in pictures has ever aroused me. Sex desire, to my knowledge, has almost always been directed towards the villainess in the picture rather than toward the heroine, but the girls with whom I have imagined myself in love have almost always been of the movie heroine type. This phenomenon occurred, I believe, not because the villainess in the movies is more beautiful, as a rule, than the heroine, but probably because sex desire and wickedness became associated in my mind through unfortunate conditioning in early childhood, which I have only partially outgrown.

It seems most probable to presume that the sexual excitement occasioned by motion pictures would express itself in the realm of phantasy. It may also, however, take expressions in some form of overt conduct or at least in the experiencing of strong desire for such conduct. The following accounts typify this mode of expression.

(Male, 20, White, University Sophomore) After this more or less indeterminate period, my reactions became more physical. My first recollection of this was my falling in love with Carol Dempster. I say falling in love because I did so with all the force that a fifteen or sixteen year old boy is capable. I would go to her pictures two or three times, and sit with torturing desires to have her close to me. I dreamed of her and had her in my mind constantly. I was unconscious of everything else when she was on the screen before me. This was climaxed in her great picture, "The Mystery House." I was so taken with her that for weeks I planned to run away to California and marry her. It did not occur to me that possibly she might not be willing! The great blow came when I discovered that she was already married.

(Male, 21, White, College Senior) Sometimes love scenes arouse my passion; however, it depends upon how I am feeling. Sometimes a scene showing a fellow loving a girl and they are both getting pretty well worked up about it; and then the next picture showing them both panting arouses a passion in me. Of course, this doesn't bother me anymore. I don't think it does anyone who is past the adolescent period.

(Male, 20, White, University Sophomore) The temptations furnished by this type of movie have been to get drunk and to engage in sexual intercourse. However, these temptations are experienced only while watching the picture and do not exist after leaving the theatre.

(Male, 17, White, High School Senior) I do not remember when I first became interested in love pictures, only that it must have been quite a while ago – probably several years. Motion pictures did tend to increase my interest in the opposite sex. I never became amorous toward my movie idols, nor ever imagined myself playing opposite them. My friends, some of them and I, often would wish that we would be able to "do things" to some of the movie stars – opposite sex, of course. I never, of course, did these things, but one's passions are aroused in watching a pretty girl with a nice form being fondled and loved by someone. I often practiced love scenes with girl friends. As I related before, my passions were aroused by watching "hot" love scenes; and as I also related before, I wished I would be able to love the stars myself. Seeing these scenes has surely made me more receptive to love-making. At parties I have attended in the last couple of years (I am now sixteen) the main diversion was taking turns going into the bedroom with *your girl* and kissing, squeezing, loving, making absurd vows, and *often quite a bit more* [emphasis his]. I shall be perfectly frank, as is desired; many of my friends and myself stop only at sexual intercourse. The various other diversions I know were prompted and encouraged by passionate love scenes. Where would one learn to love, but at the movies, at our age?

(Female, 16, White, High School Junior) Passionate love pictures have al- ways made me feel good and wish I were in the girl's place and the man was the boy I happened to be in love with at the time. I became first interested in love pictures when I first fell in love. "The Love Parade" [1929] is the most outstanding love picture I can remember seeing. Maurice Chevalier and Ramon Novarro. After I see a love picture it just leaves me rather dopey. I always try to imagine myself in a like situation. Instead of making me feel like going out on a party with some men, I generally feel like going to bed with them. I always feel more ready to be loved. After such pictures I generally go to sleep or else doze no matter where I am at the time; it takes all the energy out of me to see a passionate love picture as I just live and work right with the picture. Books and movies have got it all over anything else when it comes to passionate stimulation.

The only benefit I ever got from the movies was in learning to love and the knowledge of sex; when I was about twelve years old I first started browsing around and I remember I used to advantage my knowledge of how to love, be loved, and how to respond.

(Male, 20, White, Jewish, University Sophomore) I often put myself into the hero's place. Pictured myself as in earlier youth, embracing the heroine, kissing and making love to her in the same manner. I was growing up now and immoral thoughts were springing up in my mind in connection with the movie heroines. Often as I sat in the school-room I would day-dream of what I would do to this actress or that one were I to have them alone.

As far as night dreams are concerned, only very rarely would a nocturnal emission occur in connection with my favorite or any other movie actress. It was in my day-dreaming that my sexual sense was aroused most. I often undressed my favorite actress many times, always imagining that we cared for each other. Heated love scenes like those that took place between John Gilbert and Greta Garbo led indirectly in my association with my own sexual cravings to my first visits to a "sport woman."

As it may be expected, members of both sexes frequently become aware of the powerful influence of motion pictures in arousing sex passion. Once this knowledge is attained, motion pictures may be used as a means of inducing a desired state or disposition in one of the opposite sex. This is particularly true in the case of certain males who may deliberately employ motion pictures as an advantageous aid to the fulfillment of sex desires. Something of this sort is suggested by the following accounts.

(Male, 20, White, University Junior) My first heavy necking party was brought on mainly through a picture which showed a harem with several beautiful girls, lightly clad, dancing while a man and woman were lying in each other's arms on a couch-like affair. I and a girl friend duplicated the scene in the living room in her home. We were about fifteen or possibly sixteen. I think that the movies show too many suggestive sex scenes. I know that whenever I want to neck a girl in order to get her hot all I have to do is take her to an especially hot love picture.

(Male, 18, White, College Freshman) Love pictures sort of turn my gizzard upside down, but I do not hesitate to re-enact them on the trip home with my date. After a hot love scene I feel safe to approach the date when before I was a little bit doubtful.

Some of the things I have done after seeing one of these pictures is not for publication.

(Male, 21, White, University Senior) At present I don't go to the movies very often as I prefer dancing, and anyway girls think that a movie date is too cheap. It was, however, during my college career that I went to the movies with some other fellows to learn how to do a very disgusting act. This act was a french kiss where you put your tongue in the girl's mouth and slobber around, saliva dripping from both your mouth and the girl's, as you try to see how far you can get your tongue down her throat and she her tongue down your throat. We were told that this was the next thing to sexual intercourse and that actors and actresses did it when they kissed in order to create passion. After seeing it done I used the same means in attempting to get a girl "hot" enough that I could engage in sexual intercourse with her; but it didn't work.[3]

(Male, 21, White, University Senior) I also became more worldly wise and understood what the more suggestive movies were all about. I began to make it a special point to see all movies labeled "Adults Only." In fact, I began to consider myself quite a wise man about town. I didn't content myself with merely contemplating the heroine's face anymore. I began to notice the swell of her bosom, and I watched it rise and fall as she breathed a little harder in passionate scenes. I had my eyes out for the shape of her legs, too, and the more I saw of them the better I liked it. More and more my whole attention focused on the woman in the movie, not to the exclusion of the men, of course, but to a quite great extent compared with my earlier days.[4]

From the accounts which have been given it is clear that in the experience of some young men and some young women motion pictures may become a source of distinct sexual agitation. One must recognize, of course, that the spectator or observer must become sensitized in some sense along a certain direction in order to be stimulated by the motion pictures. Such sexual stimulation, however, is a product, of course, of both the sensitization of the individual and the content of what is shown on the screen. One must be sensitized in order to be stimulated sexually, yet apparently after one is sensitized he has little difficulty in finding in motion pictures the behavior requisite for sexual stimulation. Some conception of these dual factors in sensitization and content is yielded by the following statements. It is to be noticed in these accounts the importance of the physical attributes of the actress as a source of sexual stimulation.

(Male, 19, White, Jewish, University Sophomore) My "movie-taste" since the age of thirteen was largely an expression of my sexual development. First, my imagination was stimulated to chivalrous fantasies. Chivalry gave way to an interest in the love-story that is part of every movie, with the result that I developed a taste for love comedies. The romantic tendency gave way to a sensual one, though it was not completely superseded by it; and for the last two or three years I began to enjoy and even to seek the displays of feminine beauty which are so abundant on the screen.

(Male, 21, White, College Senior) The sexual element had never entered our minds until an unfortunate thing happened in our school. We were freshmen in high school and one of the girls in our class had freely indulged in her sexual appetites until she had to quit school. This incident brought the sexual side to our attention, and knowledge of it spread like wild-fire. From this time on we looked for sex relationships in the movies and found plenty.

(Male, 20, White, College Junior) I will say the movies did play a big part in shaping my behavior toward the opposite sex. As this is a confidential paper I can say that the movies have done much to influence my behavior toward the opposite sex at the present. The hot love scenes in the pictures now get under my skin and I have the urge to re-enact them.

Clara Bow is extremely attractive. Expressing my sentiments in Anglo-Saxon, "She could put her shoes under my bed any time and be welcome." Her pep and life seems to overwhelm me and I have a desire to be with her even though I know that is impossible.

(Male, 21, White, Jewish, University Senior) When I attended the University of Illinois, I often got the urge to see a hot picture. My favorites then were the two "hottest" actresses I've ever seen. These two were Greta Garbo and Dolores Del Rio.

Pictures such as "Flesh and the Devil," "What Price Glory?" [1926] and "The Loves of Carmen" [1927] affected me quite a bit. There were some suggestive sex scenes that used to get me pretty hot. We often discussed these scenes in our "bull sessions." We talked about the seemingly passionate nature of these two women and of how much we would give to love them.

(Male, 19, White, University Sophomore) Today my favorites are the so-called "hot" types. Clara Bow, Sue Carol, and Billie Dove are idols more or less. The feminine actress has come into her own. But she must have plenty of "it" and sex appeal before she makes much of an impression. The plot means nothing if I have a good figure to watch.

(Male, 19, White, University Sophomore) In the last couple of years there have been three actresses that "I'd give my half interest in hell" for a date with either of them. They are Greta Garbo, Billie Dove and Mary Brian.

Greta Garbo isn't pretty and she may have odd-shaped eyebrows, but to me she is about the most alluring, enticing and fascinating woman I have ever seen. In slang, she has so much "it" that she calls it "them." In her picture "Flesh and the Devil" and "Two Lovers" [1928] I could hardly hold myself in my seat. I have often imagined myself in John Gilbert's place and I have been very jealous of him. In fact, she arouses my sexual emotions more than anyone else I've ever seen. To me her actions and expression are something I've never seen equalled.

As for beauty, *build*, etc., Billie Dove takes the prize in my mind. One night after having seen her at the Chicago Theater I had such a deep phantasy of her that I almost didn't get off the I.C. train at 57th Street. But Billie does not get me "all hot and bothered" as Greta does.[5]

At this point it may be worthwhile to state a few statistical findings, although the samples to which they apply are too few to warrant any confident generalization. Out of 42 male college students interviewed by the writer, during which interviews many intimate experiences were revealed, 19 admitted that at one or more passionate sex pictures they had experienced erections. Seven (7) spoke of having sex images derived from motion pictures on one occasion or another at the time of night emissions. Out of a group of 27 high school boys – juniors and seniors – who were interviewed, 8 declared that they had on occasion purposely taken girls to passionate love pictures as a means of inducing hoped-for responses from them. Three (3) spoke of having had sexual intercourse with girls following upon the witnessing of passionate love pictures.

No interview material was secured by the writer from university or high school girls. Some indication of the role of sex pictures in the lives of girls may be secured, however, by referring to the work, *Movies, Delinquency and Crime,* Chapter Five, "Female Delinquency and Crime." The chapter to which reference is made deals, of course, with delinquent girls who have been committed to a state training school because of sexual delinquency. Because of the selective character of this group their experiences are likely not to be representative of those who are high school and college girls.

A more embracing understanding of the role of motion pictures as a sexual excitement is yielded by the conversations among different groups wherein this phase of motion pictures is discussed. We are giving a series of typical conversations which have been written down as they took place chiefly among groups of university students.

One night a half dozen of the fellows went to see Greta Garbo in "Wild Orchids." The following morning this conversation took place in the washroom.

A. "Well, Greta Garbo worked last night."

I. "What do you mean?"

A. "Take a look at my bed-sheets and you'll see."

"A" went back to his room and then returned in a few minutes triumphantly swinging a large mug that had once been used as a beer stein. A coin jingled in it.

I. "What's that for?"

A. "That's my contribution to Greta Garbo. Oh may she give us the old penis erectus."

That evening one of the boys drew a picture of a sensuously formed woman and it was fastened to the mug. On it was written "Greta Garbo Fund." In this way a new institution was started in the House. Whenever a fellow has a wet dream he contributes a coin to the fund. The Greta Garbo Fund has become a tradition in our fraternity.

I. "Have you seen any movies lately?"

J. "Yes. I saw 'His Captive Woman' [1929] last night. I liked it very much because it was shown in an original way. Then, I was very tired and so appreciated something to rest my nerves."

I. "Well, what do you think of modern movies?"

J. "All they are good for is to give you an erection. The trouble with modern movies is that they lead you to a certain point and then stop. They should go farther. I do not care for movies because I feel that I could do better myself."

I. "What do you mean by that? Do you mean that you apply things you see in the movies to your own sex actions?"

J. "Certainly. When I see John Gilbert making love to Greta Garbo I observe, and when I have a girl of my own there is no doubt that I make use of his technique in playing with her. What is more, I think girls copy movie actresses in the same manner."

In a fraternity:

"Whew! I just saw 'Ingagi.' What a show! It's worth seventy-five cents of anybody's money just to see the naked nigger [sic] women. You see everything on them. There are lots of good animal pictures in it too. You see a gorilla attacking (and killing, I guess) the camera-man and a bunch of natives. Those women got me. One of them's sitting on a rock and an ape picks her up and carries her off into the jungle. It's a hot picture and you'll need cold towels to keep your passions down."

"Go see 'Ingagi' if you want to see a good show but I'm telling you not to take your girl or you'll be embarrassed to death. You can see hair all over those cannibal women. I never had a moving picture 'bother' me like this one did."

In a fraternity:

"Let's go see 'Ladies of Leisure' [1930]. It's for adults only, so it must be pretty hot."

"Aw, I don't go for these hot pictures so much like you morons around here do. They're all right once in a while, but all the time – bunk."

"Well, if you'd have seen the advertisement in this morning's *Tribune* you'd go for it. It had a hot illustration of a practically nude babe. I'm going to see it alone if you guys don't come with me."

In a fraternity, "Sally" [1929]:

"Jeez, what a hot woman she is! I burn up for that woman, and what legs and breasts she has! Damn near gives me chills."

"Why, Marilyn Miller is as old as the hills. If you could see her on the street without any make-up you would think she was an old hag. The way these movies fool the people gives me a pain."

"Just the same, I wouldn't kick her out of bed."

In a fraternity, "Anna Christie" [1930]:

"Boy, is that girl Garbo ever an actress! She impresses me as about the cleverest woman in the world. The way that she can sit and look into space reminds me of the old wise men or something. Kinda makes me feel small."

"For God's sake, Louis, why do you have to take your pictures so seriously. For my part, I think that she is just a keen 'bim,' and would I like to have been the guy playing opposite her, only in real life.". . .

"Janet Gaynor is my idea of about the perfect woman. Shape, looks, personality, everything. I wish I could meet a 'jane' like her some place."

"Yea, she is hot. But the pictures they play! My God, from the plots you'd think that all anyone lives for is to have a good time dancing, singing, and making love. Makes the rest of us poor devils discontented. At least it makes me feel that way."

"Hell, no, it doesn't. It makes me feel happy and carefree to see one of her pictures where she makes whoopee and has fun."

In a fraternity:

"Jesus, did you see Ann Pennington's latest. Boy, that woman's legs are perfect. And can she dance! She is one wicked woman and I would give half of my acre in hell to get next to her."

"I saw the picture, but it was too lavish, too extravagant. Then, too, I want to see my women in the flesh, not on some cold screen. There's no kick in that."

"Say, listen, punk. I could get hot and bothered about that wench any place. Did you ever see any curves like those around this campus? The women around here are a gripe to my soul."

A group of office girls:
"Gee, that's a cute dress you've got, Clara! Boy, it's hot! Where'd you get it?"

"Oh, Alberta Vaughn had one like it in one of the weekly installments of that college serial she's been playing in. Don't you think it's swell lookin'?"

"It sure is. Say – have you seen John Gilbert and Greta Garbo in 'Love' [1927]? Girls, it's great. Why when he kissed her I was so thrilled I almost passed out of the picture. If my boy friend ever kissed me like that I think I'd faint. Oh! for a man like that."

"Oh, John Gilbert's cute all right, but I don't think he can compare with Rudolph Valentino. Rudy knew how to make love, and I don't mean perhaps! I wish my boy friend was only half as good as that."

"Do you remember that one long kiss in 'Love'? I thought they never would break apart."

"Well, I'd like to be kissed by one of the movie stars at least once, but I don't s'pose I ever will be. That's out of the question. C'mon, Clara, let's dance. I'll show you that cute 'hop' I saw in a movie not so long ago."

Two girls in a sorority; one practical, intelligent and level-headed; the other one wildly romantic and collegiate.

Janet: "My God! I won't be the same for at least a year after that. Wouldn't it just thrill the pants off of you, the way he kissed that babe! Oh boy, can John Gilbert ever have a rival – in sensuousness and passion? I felt all through that show as if he was necking hell out of me instead of Greta Garbo. His kiss should last two weeks."

Mary: "Ha ha! You would. You're the chewing-gum type! I never realized you were such a damn fool until this minute. How in the name of the lord can you get any kick out of that old open face job with the ambush on his lip. He might have been good in 'The Big Parade' [1925], but he certainly has deteriorated since then."

A group of sorority girls:
"Wasn't the count the cutest thing in the show? ('The Love Parade' [1929]). I sure was crazy about him. That smile would lure any girl."

"Without him even saying a word, you could tell by the expression on his face what he thought. Boy, he certainly could love. I would like to have him for a fellow for just one night. Any girl would fall for him even if he was a devil. Ha!"

"I don't blame the queen for falling in love with him. He was such a passionate lover that she couldn't resist the temptation."

"And when he would kiss her hand in his passionate way I had little thrills going up and down my back."

"He got in some pretty scandalous affairs but that is just like a Frenchman. I sure would like to have a date with that man for a night. C. acted crazy during the show; he tried to hold my hand and act funny like the count. I suppose C. will be trying some of that kind of loving now."

A group of sorority girls:

"Did you see 'The Woman of Affairs' [1929]?"

"Yes."

"When she [Greta Garbo] went to his house to prove to him that he really didn't love his wife, the scene was over too soon for me. Just as the situation was getting interesting they shift the scene – a chance for some technique and then they don't let us have it."

"When she approached him, I was right with her, when her throat throbbed, mine throbbed, too. You know you can see a rise and fall in the pulse in her throat when she is luring and being lured. At least I think I can see it, and that is just as good. Each gesture of hers has a subtle effect on me. When she sighed, I sighed too – sounds crazy, doesn't it?"

"I suppose it's the suggestion idea. You respond to her gestures with gestures of your own. Ultimately your emotional state is the one the actress is re-creating or attempting to – in your case she seems to be successful. Do you always respond sympathetically to passionate love in the movies?"

"Well, I have an idea what you're getting at. I've already told you that it is a very poor movie that I don't react to in some way. I do respond to a sensual situation with sensual feelings of my own. I've caught myself going through gestures similar to those the actresses are making. It's really funny. I must be a very responsive person and I always go back for more. The stimulation I experience – sensory stimulation I suppose you'd call it – seems to be confined to my lips, throat, arms, and breasts. In other words, I never get really aroused or what you call excited by a movie. Is that being sufficiently frank?"

"I'm listening. Go on."

"I'm interested in analyzing myself. I've never done it before. Now that I think of it, I believe I have always been jealous of these seductive actresses. I identify myself almost completely with the woman; so much so that I'm jealous of her. That sounds contradictory, doesn't it?"

Discussion on "The Cock-Eyed World" [1929] by three boys at a fraternity house:

"That joke reminds me of the one we heard in the show we saw last week, 'The Cock-Eyed World.' Remember just before Flagg leads the marines against the rebels in Nicaragua, his orderly comes up leading a pretty

Spanish girl with one hand holding a map in the other. He says, 'Captain, I brought you the lay of the land.' Gosh, for the next few minutes the audience laughed so loud I thought the roof was going to be blown off."

"You know where I first heard that story? I heard it in the old house, with a different setting entirely. A college boy had just graduated from his college, as they do every so often, and was applying for a job to a New York real estate firm. They told him to go out and get the lay of the land before they hired him. The guy went out and came back with Peggy Joyce."

"The funniest thing about that gag in the show happened when S. took his girl to see it. After the line was pulled the girl turned to S. and asked him what all the people were laughing at. He turned to her in disgust and told her to use her imagination."

"Who was the girl?"

"B. L. You know, the one he goes out with so much."

"Did her imagination work?"

"No. In a few minutes she turned to him again and told him that she still couldn't figure out what the joke was. S., at a loss for what to tell her, told her that it meant a woman who slept with a lot of fellows. She got red and didn't ask any questions after that; she just sat back in her seat as meek as a mouse."

"Another part in the picture that must have caused her some embarrassment was the scene when Flagg and Quirt went to visit Olga. Remember, Flagg goes to see this Russian girl who is supposed to be so beautiful, and when he gets there he finds Quirt waiting there with Olga. He gets sore and says, 'I hope you're sorry you came here when you're through.' But I guess she wouldn't understand what it meant, so her feelings were spared."

"What a show to take a girl to!"

"Oh, I don't know about that; to me it seemed that most of the girls around me were enjoying it as much or more than I was. They seemed to take special delight in the dirty parts."

"Lily Damita was certainly hot, wasn't she? I'd like to have her for just about eight minutes."

"She's from France. I'll bet she knows the twenty-seven ways of making love. And what a pair of legs!"

"She ought to have a good build, being a dancer. She used to be in the Folies Bergere, however that's pronounced. She wanted some of Hollywood's gold and so came to America to dip her fingers into the golden stream. She must have let a couple of big shots finger her figure, for she got a big part as soon as she arrived."

"She certainly was screwed enough in the picture. Flagg and Quirt must have been taking turns with her."

"Don't forget El Brendel. When he wasn't horse-laughing or laying those other Spanish babies, he must have sailed into her once or twice. Ah, for the life of a marine."

"What is that poem, 'A ship sailed in and a ship sailed out and never a hair was touched.' I'll bet you couldn't cover her hole with a man-hole cover. I'll bet it's almost as big as X's."

"Nobody could have one that big. Pulling it out of there is like pulling it out of an open window. I wouldn't go within hailing distance of her now. But I certainly wouldn't shoo Lily away."

"There's the bell. Let's eat."

Discussion on "The Untamed" [1929] by roommates at a fraternity house:

"How did you like the show we saw tonight?"

"Pretty good. I liked the two theme songs. I liked her [Joan Crawford's] dancing, and I liked the way Robert Montgomery acted."

"You know, I used to like her a hell of a lot when she was a leading lady, but now that she's become a star I can't see her for dust. She can't act; all she does is exude sensuality and sexiness from every possible angle."

"I like it. When I see her on the screen I can't help thinking what an enjoyable wedded life Doug Fairbanks, Junior, must be having. As far as I'm concerned I like the ways she acts very much."

"There are quite a few people like you. That's the trouble with most of our movies today; the producers are giving the public just what it goes for – the hidden subject – sex. We don't dare talk about it right out in the open, but how we snicker and strain when we see things on the stage and screen that would be forbidden in everyday contacts. You saw how all the fellows at the house went for those dirty books of L.'s; I don't blame them. I went for them myself. But what I object to is the getting to the peak of success of young bags like Joan Crawford, who is swept upward in spite of the fact that she has no ability as an actress. She developed nicely underneath a couple of directors, and they pushed her up. My brother knows a doctor in Detroit for whom she was working before she went to Hollywood. She used to let boys take her out and screw her; about a month later she'd tell the guys she was pregnant and would give them this doctor's card as an abortionist. I imagine she got a pretty good rake-off. She goes to Hollywood, flops for a couple of directors and zing! she's a star."

"Well spoken and all that, but after all you demand too much. All of the people cannot have college educations and few that do can go to Chicago. After all, sex is the foundation for everything in life and we demand it in one way or another. It's true that better actresses than Joan Crawford don't get a break in the movies, but I don't think she's a bad actress. She's vivacious, and is young. I admit she's oversexed, but I like it. And there's a hundred million others like me."

"I thought Ernest Torrence should have been given the lead. Now, there's a real actor. He gave twice as good a characterization as that p.t. could ever give. He had a definite role and played it perfectly."

"I thought he was awfully good, too; he and Robert Montgomery were instrumental in putting Joan across; but Joan is still the star. I for one will see her and also like her."

Discussion on "The Love Parade" by four members of the basketball team:

"That was certainly a putrid picture we saw at the McVickers last week. I didn't think there was anything to the goddamned thing except a song, 'Dream Lover.' "

"I didn't think it was so bad; in fact, I thought it was pretty good. I liked both Jeannette MacDonald and Maurice Chevalier a helluva lot."

"I thought so too. It's really one of the dirtiest pictures I've seen for a long time, especially that scene in her bedroom when they're speaking close to each other and he's practicing the breast stroke on her, when she ways to him, 'If you do all this the first time, what is there left?' and he comes back with 'Plenty.' "

"Such big blue eyes."

"And she showed them off plenty too; I can't remember a single scene where she wasn't wearing some negligee or a low necked dress so you could see everything. Once there, when she stooped over I thought A.'s eyes would pop out."

"I'll bet you were looking at me when she stooped over."

"You know it seems that the motto for most of the pictures we get now is 'America is becoming breast conscious.' It's funny how few heroines these days wear brassieres."

"And I'll bet you see as many movies now as you used to see; you aren't kicking about that, are you?"

"Seriously though, I did like Maurice Chevalier. I think that of all those who have recently come to this country to make their fortunes in the movies he's the best. His accent, his actions, and his whole personality are pretty good as far as I'm concerned. In his last picture, 'Innocents of Paris' [1929] I liked him a lot better because it gave him a chance to sing his own French songs."

"Did you see the picture of him and his wife in the paper and what it said beneath it: 'Maurice says he has found his dream pal at last, and will not look at another woman.' From the picture of his wife I'll bet he enjoys his night's rest."

"Did you say rest or unrest?"

"Remember 'The Vagabond King' about two years ago in Chicago? Well, it's in a movie now [1930], and Jeannette MacDonald has the feminine lead opposite to Dennis King. I'm going to see it; both of them have swell voices."

"If it's anything like the show it's bound to be a knock-out. I think that was the best operetta I've ever seen. Let's go together as soon as we get back from Purdue."

"O.K. I guess we'll need something to cheer us up."

"The only guy I liked in the picture was Lupino Lane. I don't see how the hell he can do those splits. I should think he'd de-nut himself. He and his girl friend provided the only good stuff in the show. There's N.; let's eat."

Discussion on "Forward Pass" [1929] by two roommates at a fraternity house:

"Well, I just spent the evening in college . . ."

"How's that?"

"I saw another one of these 'college movies' – 'The Forward Pass' at the Tower."

"How was it?"

"Oh hell, it was just another collection of pure unblemished hooey about college life in America."

"Can you imagine anyone believing that college is like that? My god, those of us who go to school and know about classes as well as football games could certainly tell those producers a few things about college."

"Yeah, imagine the boys walking around the Chicago campus with an armful of ukuleles and forming into quartets to sing 'Hello Baby' to all of the girls they meet."

"Some of the music wasn't so bad, though, that football song was good compared to some of the stuff they get for college songs and I liked 'I've Got to Have You.' "

"Sure, but can you imagine how they can put in all this stuff about football. The boys fight in the locker room, but in the last half with two minutes to play, they go out and do their damnedest for old Siwash, score a couple of touchdowns, and always win the game by one or two points."

"I didn't think so much of Douglas Fairbanks, Jr., as an actor, either; he looked and acted more like the boy poet than a football player."

"The only thing I like about him is his taste in wives."

"I'll bet he spends all his evenings home since he married a hot broad like Joan Crawford. I'd spend my evenings in bed, too. But speaking of classy bims, Loretta Young comes right up to the head of the class. She has everything. Boy, how I'd like to have a girl like that in my arms for a while."

"Rave on – 'you tell me your dreams, I'll tell you mine.' "

"No, not that. I mean she's my idea of a swell dame. She has luscious lips, and I'll bet the boys in Hollywood find it a pleasure to finger that figure."

"Say, do you believe everything anyone tells you, or don't you think it's humanly possible for her to live in Hollywood and still not be a cheap pushover."

"Oh, I wouldn't say cheap, but you know what they say about movie stars . . ."

"Yeah, yeah, I know. 'I heard on good authority that Joan Crawford was kicked out of a school in Missouri because she decided to put out for the boys' and all that, but didn't it ever occur to you that some of that talk may be just as crappy as these pictures?"

"I'll bet you think Joan Crawford is a virgin. But at least we agree on these college pictures. I have never seen one that was honest about college life yet. It isn't fair to the college student because people think that college is nothing but what is shown in pictures like 'The Forward Pass.' "

"Well you ought to be a little more optimistic about actors and actresses – it wouldn't hurt you – and maybe some day we'll see a picture that tells as much about classes as it does about football."

APPENDIX A

The Payne Fund and Radio Broadcasting, 1928–1935

ROBERT W. McCHESNEY

The Payne Fund took an interest in the educational potential of radio broadcasting from its very beginning. In 1926 then-president H. M. Clymer visited the British Broadcasting Corporation (BBC) to inspect its educational program. He returned to the United States convinced that the "B.B.C. points the way" for Americans.[1] Immediately thereafter the Payne Fund hired Armstrong Perry, a free-lance journalist who had followed broadcasting closely since 1921, to serve as its full-time radio counsel. In addition, the Payne Fund provided annual funding of $10,000 to Dr. W. W. Charters at Ohio State University to conduct research in radio education. The Payne Fund was instrumental in assisting Charters form the Institute for Education in Radio (IER) in 1930. The IER held annual conferences in Columbus and published its proceedings. Eventually the IER incorporated television into its activities; the rechristened Institute for Education in Radio and Television remained active and prominent for decades.[2]

Had the Payne Fund's interest in radio broadcasting been limited

Robert W. McChesney is an Associate Professor in the School of Journalism and Mass Communication at the University of Wisconsin-Madison. A communication historian and political economist with more than sixty scholarly publications and conference presentations to his credit, McChesney recently authored the award-winning *Telecommunications, Mass Media, and Democracy: The Battle for the Control of U.S. Broadcasting, 1928–1935.* He is presently writing a history of the United States and international broadcasting from 1927 to 1953, and he is co-authoring an examination of the current global media situation with Edward S. Herman.

The author thanks Thomas Rosenbaum at the Rockefeller Archive Center, as well as his colleagues James Baughman, Steven Vaughn and Dan Schiller at the University of Wisconsin. He extends special thanks to Garth Jowett for alerting him to the role of the Payne Fund in the history of American radio.

to Charters's research and the IER, its contribution would be fairly unremarkable, at least in comparison with its other activities at the time. As it developed, however, the Payne Fund quickly found that, in pursuing its aim of promoting the educational usage of radio, it was thrust into the center of the political debate over how the United States might best organize its broadcasting system. As Perry wrote to Clymer, the "Payne Fund happened to be organized at a critical moment" in the development of U.S. broadcasting.[3] Thus, despite its reticence to become associated with political controversy, the Payne Fund spent some $300,000 in the early 1930s to subsidize two campaigns to reform U.S. broadcasting. These campaigns, the National Committee on Education by Radio (NCER) and the *Ventura Free Press* radio campaign, argued that a network-dominated, advertising-supported broadcasting system was inimical to the communication needs of a democratic society. They attempted to rouse congressional and public support for legislation that would create a significant nonprofit and noncommercial broadcasting sector, while many of their officers were sympathetic to the out-and-out nationalization of broadcasting. In this battle, the Payne Fund and the campaigns it supported were in direct conflict with the two networks that had come to dominate U.S. broadcasting in short order – the National Broadcasting Company (NBC) and the Columbia Broadcasting System (CBS).

In this appendix I chronicle these Payne Fund activities to reform U.S. broadcasting. Although the movement for broadcast reform failed, it left an important legacy for future generations of media critics. In many respects, the broadcast reform movement generated the first wave of sophisticated U.S. media criticism, anticipating much of the best contemporary criticism.[4] Moreover, to the extent that the Payne Fund was responsible for launching, funding and, at times, even directing much of this reform activity, the Fund played an important role in the development of U.S. communications policy. In short, with its campaign to reconstruct U.S. broadcasting, the Payne Fund went far outside the traditional activities associated with foundations and left a deep imprint on U.S. communications and political history.

The Founding of the NCER

U.S. radio broadcasting was about to undergo a dramatic transformation as the Payne Fund made its first forays into the field. Before 1927, broadcasting had been a haphazard, albeit bustling, industry. Most of the six hundred or so stations were operated either by nonprofit groups, especially colleges and universities, or by business concerns such as newspapers, car dealerships and public utilities to shed favorable publicity on the owner's primary enterprise. The industry was uniformly unprofitable, which is not surprising since there was almost no direct advertising over the air until the last two or three years of the decade. The passage of the Radio Act of 1927, which created the Federal Radio Commission (FRC) to bring order to the airwaves, brought some stability to the industry, although the regulation it authorized was only temporary. Legislation to establish a permanent basis for communications regulation would be before Congress at every session until the passage of the Communications Act of 1934, which remains the law to this day. With scarcely any congressional or public oversight, the pro–commercial broadcasting FRC instituted a general reallocation in 1928 that effectively assigned all the stations to new frequencies and provided them with new power allowances. For all intents and purposes, this largely unpublicized reallocation determined the shape of AM radio for the remainder of the century.[5]

NBC and CBS were the big winners. Whereas they barely existed in 1927, by 1931 their affiliated stations accounted for nearly 70 percent of U.S. wattage. By 1935 only 4 of the 62 stations that broadcast at 5,000 watts or more did not have a network affiliation; fully 97 percent of total nighttime broadcasting, when the smaller stations were off the air, was controlled by NBC or CBS.[6] Moreover, advertising rushed to the air in landslide proportions between 1928 and 1933, despite the economic depression. From virtual nonexistence in 1927, radio advertising expenditures rose to more than $100 million in 1929. Over 80 percent of these expenditures went to 20 percent of the stations, all network owned or affiliated.[7] As one commentator noted in 1930, "Nothing in American history has paralleled this mushroom growth." This has since become a standard observation of U.S. broadcasting history.[8]

In 1927 and 1928 the goal of the Payne Fund was to assist in creating a "school of the air," whereby educational programs for both children and adults would be broadcast by educators over the commercial stations. The Payne Fund had no qualms about working through the auspices of the two networks; however, it was insistent that all educational programming be determined by professional educators without commercial interference. Both NBC and CBS informed Perry in 1928 that they would be willing to provide the necessary airtime and facilities "without charge" for a national school of the air "supervised by educational authorities."[9] Perry spent much of 1928 attempting to find a philanthropist or educational group willing to subsidize a school of the air, without success. "I see no evidence," he concluded in 1929, "that any educational organization will do so on a national basis."[10] By the spring of 1929 Perry and Clymer were convinced that the prospects for educational broadcasting were dismal and that "schools will be flooded" with "radio programs prepared for advertising purposes rather than educational value." Using contacts in the National Education Association (NEA), they convinced Secretary of the Interior Ray Lyman Wilbur, whose department housed the Office of Education, to convene a meeting in May 1929 to address the crisis in educational broadcasting. The Payne Fund provided $5,000 to pay for the meeting and any subsequent activities.[11]

The 24 May meeting led to the formation of the Advisory Committee on Education by Radio, soon dubbed the "Wilbur Committee," to study the crisis in educational broadcasting and report back to Wilbur with recommendations. The Payne Fund helped subsidize the expenses of the committee, and it assigned Perry to work for the group until it filed its report. Perry spent the balance of 1929 traveling across the United States interviewing broadcasters and educators to determine possible solutions. In the course of his investigation, he became radicalized. He concluded that the commitment of NBC and CBS to provide free airtime and facilities was evaporating because the networks were able to sell their time to advertisers. There was the stark possibility, he concluded, that "all the time available on stations covering any considerable territory will be sold for advertising purposes."[12] In addition, Perry finally located a group of educators who seemed to grasp the importance of radio for education: the college and university broadcasters. These stations had been decimated by the FRC's reallocation of 1928 and their inability to raise sufficient funds. The number of college stations had fallen from more than a hundred in 1925 to half that figure by 1929.[13] Perry became convinced that the only hope for education on radio was to protect these stations and, moreover, to create a viable nonprofit and noncommercial sector in U.S. broadcasting.

Perry's influence on the Wilbur Committee was unmistakable. The report of the fact-finding subcommittee concluded that "it is clear that the basic purposes of the two groups [broadcasters and educators] are widely divergent" and that the commercial broadcasters seemed intent upon occupying all the frequencies. "Apparently, the only thing that could prevent this would be an early and united effort on the part of broadcasters to have radio channels permanently reserved for the use of educational stations." The NBC and CBS representatives on the Wilbur Committee filed "minority reports" to protest the alleged unwillingness of the networks to provide airtime for educational broadcasts.[14] When the final report was submitted to Wilbur in February 1930, it elected not to antagonize the commercial broadcasters, accepting at face value their declarations of interest in educational broadcasting. To the delight of NBC and CBS, the report merely recommended that the Office of Education establish a section to coordinate educational broadcasting and to "attempt to prevent conflicts between various broadcasting interests."[15]

This was not a thorough defeat, however, for the proponents of independent educational stations. Wilbur immediately authorized the creation of the new radio section, but since there could be no funding for another year, the Payne Fund "lent" Perry to Commissioner of Education William John Cooper to oversee the new office. Cooper instructed Perry to take charge of all radio correspondence and to keep him "up to date on radio." "This places me in a very satisfactory position," Perry wrote to Ella Phillips Crandall, secretary of the Payne Fund. "It apparently means that we can go right on with the investigations that the Payne Fund would like to make independently if they were not made under the auspices of the Office of Education."[16] Perry used his position to convince both Wilbur and Cooper that the existing situation was unsatisfactory and that the FRC was uninterested in protecting educational stations. His argument was buttressed by the collapse of twenty-three more college stations in the first seven months of 1930.[17] By the end of the summer, Cooper accepted Perry's contention that educators needed to organize in order to have protective legislation passed by Congress. Perry also used his position in the Office of Education to mobilize virtually unanimous support by national educational organizations for broadcast reform.

The most important battle for Perry came with the officers of the Payne Fund, who until that point had revealed no desire to engage in a political battle with the commercial broadcasters. Crandall wrote Perry that the Payne Fund did not wish to encourage "prolonged and obstinate opposition among educators to safe and sane co-operation with commercial companies."[18] Perry repeatedly wrote to Crandall on the need to directly challenge in Washington, D.C., the domination of broadcasting by the networks if there was to be any hope for adequate educational or cultural fare. Eventually Crandall and Frances Payne Bolton, president of the Payne Fund, accepted Perry's position. Crandall wrote Perry in July 1930 that there was "no opposition within the Executive Committee of the Fund" to the direction his work was taking and she urged him to formally "lay out a new plan of action more valuable than the original project." Crandall acknowledged that the Payne Fund's primary mission now was "to see facilities and time reserved for educational purposes free from all other considerations" and that the campaign would "be a direct blow against the monopolistic intentions and efforts of the commercial broadcasters."[19] In September Perry was informed that the Payne Fund had set aside $200,000 for a five-year grant to support an educator activist group. To no avail, the networks and the Radio Corporation of America (RCA), NBC's parent company, attempted furtively to undercut Perry's credibility with Wilbur, Cooper and Bolton.[20]

After meeting with Bolton and Crandall, Perry convinced Cooper to convene a meeting of educators to form a group to lobby for broadcast reform. Perry prepared the list of invitees and the meeting was called for Chicago so as to be closer to the Midwest land-grant universities that housed the largest educational stations.[21] In Cooper's opening address to the 13 October meeting, he stated that the conference was called to address "the fear that before education knows what it wants to do commercial stations will have practically monopolized the channels open for radio broadcasting."[22] Unlike the Wilbur Committee, this group made no pretense of trying to work with the commercial broadcasters; that strategy was presupposed as bankrupt. By the end of the one-day conference, the NCER had been established. It would be an umbrella organization of nine leading national education organizations, including the NEA.[23] The Chicago conference also resolved that the first order of business for the new NCER would be to lobby Congress for legislation that would set aside 15 percent of the channels for educational use. Joy Elmer Morgan, the editor of the NEA *Journal,* was appointed by Cooper to chair the NCER; thereafter, Cooper had nothing formal to do with the group, stating that it would be inappropriate for a government official to work with a group chartered to lobby Congress on a specific issue. No great thought had gone into determining the 15 percent proposal; as Morgan noted, it was merely "an emergency and not a final measure."[24]

Throughout November and December, the Payne Fund negotiated with Morgan and educators to determine the nature of the relationship between the Fund and the NCER. Given the Payne Fund's distaste for publicity, it had little interest in playing more than a secondary role in the operations of the new group. As Crandall put it, the Fund wanted to avoid "the untenable position of undertaking to do for educators what educators are now prepared to do for themselves."[25] The Payne Fund Executive Committee formally approved the five-year $200,000 grant to the NCER on 20 January 1931. Over the next few years, Bolton and Crandall would meet with Morgan once or twice each year to discuss the general status of the group. Bolton was very sensitive about appearing intrusive; in 1932 she would "emphatically" disavow to Morgan "the least intention or desire to influence the policies of your Committee when our judgments may be at variance." Nevertheless, Bolton added that "we are not like other groups, we of the Payne Fund. We are keenly interested in every possible angle of the activities which we sponsor and we like to be known for our ideas as well as our money."[26] Over the years, as the Payne Fund became increasingly dissatisfied with the performance of the NCER, it was tempted to play a somewhat larger role, a temptation it mostly resisted.

At the outset, at least, the Payne Fund regarded the establishment of the NCER as the culmination of its work in radio, "the fulfillment of the Payne Fund's objectives and efforts over a period of approximately three and one half years," as one memo put it. One educator noted to the Fund that its funding of the NCER "will go down as one of the milestones of educational achievement."[27] Perry could not help but see the irony in the Payne Fund's turn to supporting a group like the NCER from its original desire to work with the commercial networks. As he wrote to an executive at CBS in March 1931:

I certainly am aware that your company holds a very vigorous opinion against the setting aside of certain channels for educational broadcasting. The opinion has helped to turn hundreds of thousands of dollars of philanthropic money, which was appropriated for the purpose of developing public interest in your educational programs and those of other companies into other channels where it is developing a nationwide reaction against commercial broadcasting.[28]

The NCER: Personnel, Programs and Problems

The NCER was chartered so that each of the nine member organizations would appoint a representative to the NCER, all of whom would meet at quarterly meetings to determine basic policy decisions. Joy Elmer Morgan, the NEA representative, was formally elected the NCER's chair. He maintained his paid position at the NEA throughout his tenure. The full-time staff throughout the early 1930s was composed of Tracy Tyler and Armstrong Perry, although Perry's salary was paid for independently by the Payne Fund. Tyler, who earned a Ph.D. in education at Columbia University in 1931, ran the office and edited the NCER's four-page newsletter, *Education by Radio*. Tyler also coordinated the distribution of educational programs among the college stations, and he directed the research activities of the NCER, which the Payne Fund insisted should be a component of its program. *Education by Radio* was the NCER's most visible project; with a controlled circulation that reached more than 10,000 by 1934, this twice-monthly publication consisted mostly of reprints of speeches and articles from other publications, plus brief news items. Morgan characterized *Education by Radio* as necessary to counteract the "misinformation" that "has been spread so deliberately by selfish and greedy interests that even public officials have found it difficult to get the facts."[29]

Perry left his position at the Office of Education to join the NCER early in 1931. His primary function was to serve as director of the NCER's Service Bureau, the purpose of which was to represent educational stations in hearings before the FRC. Since station licenses were valid for only three months, and since commercial stations increasingly attempted to usurp the channels held by educators as the profit potential of the airwaves became apparent, this was a vital service. "Ever since the new broadcast structure was put in effect in the fall of 1928," the director of the University of Illinois station wrote to a member of Congress in 1930, "we wasted practically all of the money that our university has put into our broadcasting efforts" defending ourselves before the FRC, so that "it has been impossible for the people of the state . . . to benefit from the educational features which we have attempted to give them."[30] At Perry's insistence, the NCER hired Horace Lohnes as the Service Bureau's counsel to represent college stations at no cost in FRC hearings. Perry and Lohnes had their work cut out for them; between 1

February 1932 and 26 September 1934 there were 1,426 applications by commercial interests before the FRC for the use of frequencies at least partially occupied by educational broadcasters. The Service Bureau was credited with helping to stabilize the number of university stations by the end of 1932.[31]

Perry remained active on several other fronts as well. He was the NCER's official expert on international broadcasting, traveling abroad, studying other systems and representing the NCER at international radio conferences in 1932 and 1933. Perry also served as the liaison between the NCER headquarters in Washington, D.C., and the Payne Fund offices in New York City. He filed periodic confidential reports to Crandall regarding the NCER. Although candid, Perry's memos rarely engaged in political infighting. Because the NCER was largely the product of his labors, he wanted to see it succeed and to be held in high regard by Crandall and Bolton.

Between 1931 and 1934, Tyler, Perry and Morgan made hundreds of speeches and wrote scores of articles promoting the cause of broadcast reform. It was Morgan, however, more than anyone else, who gave the NCER its public identity. Strongly influenced by the Midwest populist tradition, Morgan had been active in the public utilities movement during the Progressive Era.[32] In his capacity with the NEA he had become convinced that it was absurd to think that commercial broadcasters would provide adequate educational programming. "That practice has been tried for nearly a decade and has proved unworkable," Morgan stated in 1931. "It is no longer open to discussion."[33] Nor was education merely a matter of classroom pedagogy to Morgan. "When we talk about education's rights on the air, we are not talking about the needs and wishes of some special group. We are talking about the needs of the people themselves."[34]

Morgan regarded the fight for broadcast reform as central to the general battle for political democracy. He cast the struggle in almost apocalyptic terms:

As a result of radio broadcasting, there will probably develop during the twentieth century either chaos or a world-order of civilization. Whether it shall be one or the other will depend largely upon whether broadcasting be used as a tool of education or as an instrument of selfish greed. So far, our American radio interests have thrown their major influence on the side of greed. . . . There has never been in the entire history of the United States an example of mismanagement and lack of vision so colossal and far-reaching in its consequences as our turning of the radio channels almost exclusively into commercial hands.[35]

"I believe we are dealing here," Morgan informed a meeting of educators in 1932, "with one of the most crucial issues that was ever presented to civilization at any time in its entire history." In the depths of the Depression, Morgan wrote that the United States cannot "solve any of its major political problems without first solving the radio problem."[36]

Given this type of rhetoric and the NCER's formal positions, relations between the group and the commercial broadcasters were hostile from the outset. Tyler summed up the feelings of all associated with the NCER when he stated that "the commercial broadcasters . . . are doing all they can to wreck the educational stations." The commercial broadcasters' trade organization, the National Association of Broadcasters (NAB), formally resolved against the 15 percent measure at its November 1930 convention, even before the measure had been introduced in Congress.[37] The commercial trade publication *Broadcasting* constantly disparaged the NCER in its pages, characterizing the group as "misguided pedagogues" with "silly demands." Morgan, in particular, was loathed. *Broadcasting* dismissed him as "coming from the ranks of primary school men," who "had to be fighting something all the time" with an "unreasoning sort of crusading."[38]

A primary problem the NCER faced, and, indeed, never overcame, was its inability to unite all the national educational organizations and major educators in the cause of broadcast reform. At a formal level, they were mostly successful in this regard. Virtually every major national educational group did officially support the aims of the NCER during this period. Some non-NCER organizations were even more radical. For example, the National Congress of Parents and Teachers (NCPT) passed resolutions calling for the complete nationalization of broadcasting. Moreover, a 1933 NCER survey of 631 college administrators found that only 4.4 percent expressed themselves as "being satisfied with the system of radio now in use."[39] Nonetheless, these figures and endorsements overstate the degree of support that broadcast reform had among educators. Even a director of the NCER-member Association of College and University Broadcasting Stations confided his distaste for the NCER's approach since it would precipitate a long and bitter fight and alienate the friendship of the commercial stations. In his mind, "we can get more by being friendly to the big commercial broadcasters."[40]

The educators' inability to unite was apparent even among those radio projects subsidized by the Payne Fund. Perry, Morgan and Tyler were mostly contemptuous of Charters and the IER, regarding them as unwilling to risk antagonizing the commercial networks and the NAB.[41] "At each of the past institutes we have had only one side presented and we have heard only of the 'wonderful showmanship' of the big station broadcasts," wrote one frustrated NCER activist about the annual IER conferences in 1931.

I would like to have the merits of the average commercial programs and the big chain programs discussed by some persons who do not assume it to be axiomatic that these programs are the acme of perfection and superior in every way to any thing that ever existed before or that can ever be produced again in the future.[42]

The antagonism between Charters and the NCER came to a head just weeks after the NCER was launched when the Payne Fund sought to have the Ohio State radio research and the NCER research conducted jointly. The Fund regarded this "coalition" as "greatly desired," going so far as offering to double the research budget for both programs if they agreed to the marriage.[43] The union never came about, mostly due to NCER resistance. As one memo critical of Charters stated, his research bureau "must stop doing those things which are a part of the commercial set-up and which the commercial people will gladly pay for themselves."[44] The two sides had minimal contact thereafter.

In addition to whatever natural suspicion of the NCER program among educators existed, two other factors played a large role in keeping the NCER from guiding a united front into battle on Capitol Hill. First, the commercial broadcasters did not sit idly by as the NCER challenged the legitimacy of their control of the airwaves. As Morgan put it, the radio lobby sought to "interpenetrate and paralyze all the groups working for radio reform."[45] "Every one of the educational organizations connected with his [Morgan's] Committee is being besieged by the radio trust outfit," one Payne Fund memo stated in 1932, "and Brother Morgan knows it well." The primary means the networks employed to divide the educators was to offer some of them free airtime. Morgan finally called an emergency meeting with Crandall to discuss, with little effect, the "attempts of the radio interests to interpenetrate their organization." Ironically, the commercial broadcasters enjoyed their greatest success with Morgan's own NEA, which developed a regular program of broadcasting over NBC under NEA official Florence Hale. As Perry noted, this left Morgan "constantly in a somewhat ridiculous position, not being supported by his own organization."[46]

Second, the NCER was not the only national organization dedicated to education by radio. In 1930, working closely with NBC executives, the Carnegie Corporation established the National Advisory Council on Radio in Education (NACRE). Directed by Columbia University adult educator Levering Tyson, the NACRE took an explicitly sympathetic stance toward commercial broadcasting, regarding it as entrenched and beyond challenge, and dismissing reform efforts as "fruitless and unwarranted."[47] The NACRE's function was to provide educational programs to be broadcast over CBS and NBC, though the connection with the latter network was so strong that the NACRE was considered NBC's de facto educational branch.[48] Although the NACRE had little formal support among national educational organizations, it included many prominent educators and public figures on its board of directors, including President Robert M. Hutchins of the University of Chicago, Elihu Root, Charles Evans Hughes and Walter Dill Scott, president of Northwestern University. Tyson was effusive in his praise of commercial broadcasting in his public statements and equally critical of the reformers, especially the NCER. The NCER, he noted, was "a belligerent and propagandistic organization" that had "attempted in every way to throw sand in our machinery."[49]

Tyson was no shill for the NBC or CBS, however; he acknowledged that they "are not interested" in the NACRE "from any educational motive."[50] Tyson realized that his leverage over the networks was the threat of reform. "Broadcasting's position in this country is not overly secure," Tyson wrote to one NBC executive in 1932 to convince NBC not to cancel a NACRE series when NBC had sold the scheduled time to advertisers. "I have no hesitation in stating to you that many influential members of the Council were supporters of the theory of government broadcasting until the success of our programs convinced them that the American system is and can be workable." Thus Tyson warned that if the NACRE series was canceled, "it will be perfectly apparent to these individuals that American radio will always be relegated to the pure commercial, and that all the public service for which the medium itself gave such promise is mere bunk."[51] Tyson won this particular skirmish, but it portended the fate of noncommercial cultural fare over the networks as advertisers were increasingly willing to pay for all the desirable time slots.

The NCER detested the NACRE, regarding it as "a smokescreen to further the efforts of radio monopolies in gobbling up broadcasting."[52] More broadly, the tension between the NCER and the NACRE reflected the conflict between the Carnegie Corporation and the Payne Fund over which organization, and which approach, would direct education by radio. Bolton agreed to support the founding of the NCER only after her inquiries determined that the NACRE's approach "is not particularly popular with the educators of this country."[53] Both sides realized that, by launching the NCER, the Payne Fund was effectively repudiating the NACRE's cooperative stance toward the networks. "If Payne Fund money was not available," Tyson observed, "this whole agitation would die from lack of nourishment." Accordingly, Tyson worked assiduously between 1931 and 1935 to "shut off this source of Payne Fund money," by attempting "the possibility of bringing Mrs. Bolton into our camp."[54] Bolton politely resisted all these overtures. Crandall, on the other hand, had no patience or sympathy for Tyson or the NACRE whatsoever. "Tyson's pandering to the commercial interests" is blatant, she wrote to Bolton in 1932, "and his intellectual dishonesty toward the educational cause" is "clear."[55]

In any case, the existence of the NACRE gave the strong impression of an educational community divided, even confused, with regard to broadcasting. With a lavish budget, the NACRE was far more visible than the NCER, and, with its rhetoric extolling education by radio, differences between the two groups were sometimes difficult to glean, even to those active in educational radio. As the radio committee of the NCER-member National University Extension Association noted, the two groups "presumably represent the same faction, and yet the two are quite far apart in so far as any cooperation is concerned."[56] Broadcasting historian Erik Barnouw has noted that among the public and educators there existed a "glorious confusion" about what each of the groups stood for. Even some of the scholarship on this period has failed to differentiate between the two groups.[57]

The *Ventura Free Press* Radio Campaign

The Payne Fund's sponsorship of broadcast reform did not end with the NCER. In 1931 it launched an eighteen-month radio campaign, costing some $50,000, under the auspices of the *Ventura Free Press*, a small daily newspaper in Ventura, California, just north of Los Angeles. The radio campaign had a three-pronged mission: (1) to mobilize newspaper opposition to commercial broadcasting, concentrating on the American Newspaper Publishers Association (ANPA), the trade organization of the newspaper industry; (2) to attempt to encourage extensive and sympathetic coverage of the broadcast reform fight in the nation's newspapers; and (3) to lobby on Capitol Hill for the passage of broadcast reform legislation. With the Payne Fund's commitment to the bold *Ventura Free Press* radio campaign, the Fund's blossoming opposition to commercial broadcasting had reached full flower. In short, it wanted to marshal more resources to the cause it had almost stumbled upon in its desire to promote the educational application of radio.

The campaign was the brainchild of H. O. Davis, a wealthy retired magazine and movie studio executive who had come to the Payne Fund's attention in 1930 with a plan to launch a monthly magazine for young working-class women. Although Davis's plan never got off the ground, he impressed Bolton and Crandall enough to get himself elected to the Payne Fund Board of Directors in July 1930.[58] Davis quickly realized that the radio project was becoming a consuming passion for Bolton and Crandall, "the most impressive example" of what the Payne Fund could accomplish, as Crandall explained to him.[59] Davis then put together his radio proposal. It called for the campaign to be directed out of the offices of the *Free Press,* a newspaper he had recently purchased, to give it legitimacy among newspaper publishers and editors. The Payne Fund not only approved Davis's plan, but also donated to Davis the services of S. Howard Evans, who had come to the Fund to serve as an assistant to the president in 1930. A "Bull Moose" Republican, Evans was held in the highest regard by Bolton and Crandall. His task for the *Ventura Free Press* campaign was to "handle the political side of the radio fight," in Washington, D.C., and with the ANPA.[60] Davis then hired two veteran journalists, Walter Woehlke and Harold Carew, to direct the publicity side of the operation from southern California.

The Payne Fund made the grant to Davis under the one condition that the Fund's involvement be kept strictly confidential. This was non-negotiable, the Fund insisted, because it would be highly embarrassing for Bolton's husband, U.S. Representative Chester Bolton, Republican of Ohio, if it were public knowledge that his wife's organization was funding such a controversy-laden enterprise. The secret was kept rigorously; Representative Bolton and the NCER, aside from Perry, were unaware of the Payne Fund role in the *Ventura Free Press* radio campaign. Evans moved out of the Payne Fund offices and worked out of his home on Long Island for the next two years; he was now officially the special editorial representative of the *Ventura Free Press,* although he remained on the Payne Fund payroll.[61]

The *Free Press* campaign was launched with much fanfare in July 1931. "The objective of the campaign, as I understand it," Woehlke wrote, "is the complete overthrow of the present system."[62] Davis's first general mailing to publishers was unequivocal. The campaign was a "national attack on the radio combine" with the goal of the "removal of advertising from the air," along with the elimination of the "exploitation" of radio for "private profit."[63]

Two problems plagued the campaign from the outset, particularly as it attempted to gain the endorsement of the ANPA, which Davis logically thought would be highly sympathetic due to its fear of radio advertising. First, many publishers were suspicious of Davis's motives, thinking "that anyone endeavoring to solve the radio problem without asking them to cough up, must have some ulterior motive." Similarly, publishers could not understand how any west coast newspaper, let alone the *Ventura Free Press,* "could afford an eastern representative."[64] Davis pleaded with Bolton and Crandall to let him tell the truth about the Payne Fund's involvement, but they budged only to the extent that they would let Davis confide to a few select publishers that Evans was a Payne Fund employee. This was far from satisfactory.[65] Second, many newspaper publishers insisted that the *Ventura Free Press* provide an acceptable alternative before they would support a campaign to smash the existing system. Although Evans and Davis both considered fully nationalized broadcasting as "distinctly preferable to a private monopoly," they realized that such a proposal would never fly among the conservative publishers, or even the public at large. Despite much effort, Davis never could determine a suitable reform model that could satisfy the publishers.[66]

The *Ventura Free Press* efforts collapsed in 1932 when major newspapers with network radio affiliations were able to overwhelm the reform movement. Then, in December 1933, with the Biltmore agreement that ended a nine-month press–radio "war" over how competitive broadcast news was becoming to the press, the ANPA committed itself to opposing broadcast reform legislation in Congress in return for the networks and the NAB agreeing to limit sharply their broadcasting of news.[67]

The *Ventura Free Press* campaign was not much more successful in its attempt to generate favorable press coverage of the reform movement. This was recognized as essential for the reformers if they were to generate the public support necessary to force Congress to confront an entrenched and profitable industry. The *Free Press* campaign certainly did its part; it sent out monthly newsletters, called "anti-commercialism radio bulletins," to some two thousand publishers as well as providing a free new service on broadcast reform to some five hundred newspapers. Consequently, the *Ventura Free Press* dubbed itself the "most widely quoted newspaper west of the Rockies."[68] The commercial broadcasters were well aware of the *Free Press* publicity; *Broadcasting* termed it "probably the most vicious campaign ever leveled against American radio."[69]

Nevertheless, the *Free Press* campaign barely made a ripple in the public consciousness. NBC's sizable press department alone easily overwhelmed the *Free Press* output.[70] Moreover, radio news was rarely covered in the news sections; it was generally the province of a distinct radio section that provided daily program listings and notes about the programs. Radio editors, in particular, quickly developed a shamelessly dependent relationship to the networks, which provided them with the material they used to fill their pages. In 1931, for example, a survey of two hundred leading radio editors found that they overwhelmingly favored the "American plan of private enterprise in broadcasting."[71] Perhaps the extent to which the press downplayed or ignored the reform movement is revealed by the lack of criticism the generally sensitive broadcasters made regarding the press coverage.

In both of these areas and even more so in its congressional lobbying, the *Free Press* campaign was handicapped by its inability to develop a satisfactory working relationship with the NCER. Certainly the secret basis of the Payne Fund's role did not help matters. Davis insisted that Crandall see to it that the NCER "openly endorse the Free Press campaign and aggressively work with it."[72] Crandall tried to comply, bringing Davis, Evans and Morgan together for a meeting in June 1931. The meeting failed to accomplish its mission. As Crandall noted, "It soon became evident . . . that there was no possibility of a meeting of the minds." Morgan insisted that reform was a long-term project in which each of the groups should be allowed to pursue separate courses, while Davis and Evans argued that "an immediate emergency program" was the only hope for defeating the commercial broadcasters.[73] Thereafter, the *Free Press* campaign personnel continually disparaged the NCER in their internal correspondence and in their memos to the Payne Fund, characterizing the educators as politically incompetent. "The whole educational crowd," Woehlke wrote to Evans after the NCER's Tyler had failed to mail him a report as he had promised, "is a bunch of theorists with no idea of how to run a publicity campaign. Tell them to jump off the North end of a ferry boat going South."[74]

Although the Payne Fund never intervened in this conflict between its two broadcast reform projects, Bolton's sympathies seemed to lie with the *Free Press*. Bolton informed Davis that the *Free Press* campaign "gives such evidence of activity that I am breathless!"[75] She followed the campaign with a singular devotion, in contrast to her more distant stance toward the NCER, reading copies of all the considerable correspondence exchanged between Crandall and Evans and Woehlke and clipping all the *Ventura Free Press* editorials for a scrapbook. Bolton probably did not clip anything else from the *Free Press*, however. In her enthusiasm for Woehlke's and Carew's editorials, she requested that the entire newspaper be mailed to her. Bolton was "quite shocked at the character of the paper itself," regarding it as "a sensational sheet" with a "quite unnecessary emphasis on crime."[76] Therefore, Bolton could probably see why major newspaper publishers had difficulty taking the *Free Press* seriously as a selfless national advocate of public service broadcasting.

The Broadcast Reform Movement: Critique, Proposals and Problems

Had the Payne Fund not subsidized the NCER and the *Ventura Free Press* radio campaign, there still would have been a broadcast reform movement in the early 1930s. Organized labor, progressive religious groups, the American Civil Liberties Union (ACLU) and a few other groups actively lobbied in Washington, D.C., for reform legislation.[77] Nonetheless, the Payne Fund bankrolled the efforts to mobilize the educators and the newspapers, and, along with labor, these were the constituencies that most concerned the commercial broadcasters. Moreover, the Payne Fund's grants to the NCER and the *Free Press* radio campaign dwarfed all the other reform group budgets. In this sense, it is clear that the broadcast reform movement would have been but a shadow of what it was had the Payne Fund not taken part. In addition to the organized reform efforts, the cause of broadcast reform received the nearly unconditional support of the U.S. intelligentsia. As the NCER's Morgan observed, it was impossible to find *any* intellectual in favor of commercial broadcasting unless that person was receiving money or airtime from a commercial station or network.[78]

Nor was discontent with commercial broadcasting limited to activists and intellectuals in the early 1930s. The initial public response to commercialized broadcasting was far more negative than it would be subsequently; radio advertising in particular was generally detested as an unwelcome intrusion into people's homes. As the *Free Press*'s Woehlke noted upon joining the radio campaign, "I know that dissatisfaction with the present broadcasting system and its results is well nigh universal. Out of one hundred persons you will not find more than five who are satisfied; of the other 95%, more than one-half are ready to support any kind of movement for a drastic change."[79] This assessment was accepted to various degrees by the industry, the FRC and radio editors as well. "Radio broadcasting," *Business Week* informed its readers in 1932, "is threatened with a revolt of the listeners. . . . Newspaper radio editors report more and more letters of protest against irritating sales ballyhoo." One pro–status quo radio editor even cautioned that "due to too much advertising and to too much mediocre program material," public sympathies were moving toward "Government control."[80]

In short, especially in 1931 and 1932, the broadcast reformers regarded themselves as the legitimate representatives of the vast majority of Americans; there was no sense of their being an elite attempting to force their own agenda onto a popularly embraced commercial system. In this context, the task for the reform movement was to convert this dissatisfaction into support for structural reform.

Although from a fairly wide range of backgrounds, these broadcast reformers along with the NCER and the *Free Press* radio campaign were in general agreement in their criticism of commercial broadcasting. If the Payne Fund had initially become involved in broadcast reform due to its concern about education, those affiliated with the NCER and *Free Press* campaign soon adopted a broad-based critique of the status quo in which the limited role of education was but one brick, perhaps a cornerstone, in a larger edifice.

Three themes dominated the reform movement's critique of commercial broadcasting. First, all the reformers emphasized that the system was flawed on grounds of free expression: it would be inherently biased against broadcasting programming that was critical of big business and the status quo. Morgan argued that "genuine freedom of thought" over U.S. radio was impossible: "The very points at which facts are most needed if people are to govern themselves wisely are the points at which freedom of speech is most certain to be denied."[81] When combined with an appreciation of the enormous role radio was playing in U.S. politics and culture, the reformers' concern reached fever pitch. As Davis put it, "This inevitable monopoly constitutes the greatest danger American democracy has ever been exposed to."[82]

Second, the reform movement was uniformly critical of the influence of advertising over programming. Most commercial programs were regarded as trivial and inane, and it was seen as inevitable that advertisers would downplay educational, cultural or controversial fare to favor inexpensive, unoriginal entertainment programs. One NCER member stated that "it is unavoidable that a commercial concern catering to the public will present a service as low in standard as the public will tolerate and will produce the most profit." "In order to get large audiences," Morgan observed, "they cultivate the lower appeals." It would be difficult to exaggerate the NCER's contempt for radio advertising. On another occasion, Morgan noted that "commercialized broadcasting as it is now unregulated in America may threaten the very life of civilization by subjecting the human mind to all sorts of new pressures and selfish exploitations."[83]

Third, the reformers regarded the commercial system as the product of a mostly secretive process in which the public and even Congress had played almost no role. This was grossly offensive to the reformers' democratic sensibilities. "So the question really is," Perry noted, "do we want to submit to the regulation of radio by the people whom we elect to rule over us, or do we want to leave our radio channels in the hands of private concerns and private individuals who wish to use these public radio channels for their own profit?"[84] In total, this was explicitly radical criticism. To the reformers, the experience of the FRC had made it clear that it was absurd to think that a government agency could possibly make private broadcasters act in the public interest. It is a "fact that the radio channels belong to the people," stated an NCER organizer, "and should not be placed in the hands of private capital."[85]

Given this critique, it should be no surprise that most reformers were hearty in their praise of the BBC, which was a noncommercial, nonprofit corporation with a monopoly over British broadcasting. Morgan, like

Evans and Davis, had gone on record as regarding the BBC model as the best option for the United States.[86] To Perry, the BBC provided the "ideal" example of a "broadcasting service maintained primarily for the benefit of all radio listeners" and was the solution to "the whole world problem of broadcasting."[87] The NCER even tried to get the BBC to formally endorse its activities, but the BBC demurred, informing Perry that "it does not wish to meddle in American affairs."[88] These sentiments notwithstanding, the reform movement never advocated the complete nationalization and decommercialization of U.S. broadcasting. For the NCER and the *Free Press* this was due mostly to the belief that it would be impossible to accomplish such a measure politically, since the public would not support it. Others, like the ACLU, were concerned that the government would play too large a role in the nation's communication system.

This left the reform movement in a conundrum. As Woehlke acknowledged, the reformers could never expect public support unless they could indicate "a new road leading to better things."[89] Given the economic depression and the decision of the major foundations either to support the status quo or to remain out of broadcasting, the question of how to fund nonprofit broadcasting if not by the government hung like a noose around the reformers' necks. As Perry acknowledged to Crandall upon the founding of the NCER with its mandate to lobby for 15 percent of the channels, "Our problem still is unsolved: the finding of financial support for college and university stations."[90] For that reason alone, the 15 percent scheme was almost dead in the water before it reached Congress. The reform movement never did agree on a uniform alternative and then coalesce to work on its behalf. In Washington, D.C., this meant that the reform groups generally worked in isolation. After a few months on Capitol Hill, a frustrated Evans wrote to Woehlke that "every son-of-a-gun and his brother has a definite idea about the way it should be handled."[91] To some extent, this inability to unite also revealed the lack of political savvy of many of the reformers, who, though well intentioned, seemed clueless about how to win a fierce political struggle.

Nor were these the only problems that plagued the reform movement. If its critique of the status quo on the grounds of a pro–big business bias might generate mass support in a decade of intense labor activism, the reform movement's critique of advertising at times harbored a profound elitism, which dismissed entertainment programming categorically and could only repel mass support. "Even the so-called entertainment aspects of the programs are such that no civilized person can listen to them without nausea," one critic wrote. "This is often the result of a deliberate policy on the part of the advertiser, who finds that people of low intelligence respond most readily to his commercial appeal, and therefore baits his trap with material intentionally designed to reach those that are not quite bright." Another reformer confessed that his "ideal broadcasting station" would make no "hypocritical pretense" of attempting "to present something for everyone." Rather, all the programming would "be aimed at and above a frankly upper-middle class" audience.[92]

The NCER and the *Ventura Free Press* radio campaign tended to eschew this tendency to blame the audience for commercial fare in the early 1930s, although these sentiments were not entirely absent from their correspondence. They argued instead that commercial fare was intended to please advertisers, not listeners. As the system became entrenched, however, the educators gradually accepted the notion that the commercial broadcasters "gave the people what they want," whereas the educational stations were chartered for a higher calling, for which there was an admittedly limited audience.

Moreover, the *Ventura Free Press*'s efforts notwithstanding, the reformers were ineffectual in their attempts to communicate their existence, let alone their position on broadcast reform, to the bulk of the populace through the mass media. Most Americans, no matter how dissatisfied with radio advertising and programming, probably had no idea that there was a movement afoot to address these concerns in Congress, or that it was the public's right to do so.[93]

These problems paled, however, in contrast to the largest barrier that impeded the progress of the reform movement: the strength of the radio lobby of NBC, CBS, RCA and the NAB, which the NCER soon realized was "one of the most powerful here in Washington."[94] Besides having the sort of political leverage that traditionally accompanies great wealth in U.S. politics, the radio lobby had two other advantages. First, it was well positioned to publicize its own version of U.S. broadcasting, one in which it was an innately American and democratic system that responded directly to listener desires through the marketplace.[95] Second, through their policy of providing free airtime to any member of Congress who desired it, CBS and NBC did much to undercut any budding insurgency. Moreover, it was the network lobbyists who were responsible for scheduling members of Congress for their broadcasts. For example, between January 1931 and October 1933, U.S. senators made 298 free appearances over NBC.[96] As Morgan put it, "The politicians are too eager to use radio to come out for reform."[97]

One first-term member of the House of Representatives, Thomas R. Amlie, Republican of Wisconsin, laid out the situation in stark terms in a confidential letter to the NCER in 1932. "I wanted to do something that would call attention to the inherent evils of our present commercialized form of broadcasting," he wrote. Amlie then described how after he sponsored legislation that would have prohibited radio advertising on Sundays, the broadcasters of Wisconsin formally condemned him, the NAB attacked his bill and it was dropped by the pertinent House committee "without as much as a voice of protest on the Floor of the House." Amlie attributed this to the fact that "members of Congress are dependent upon these stations for many favors." He concluded that "this is a factor you must overcome if you are to get anywhere with your program."[98] Amlie's letter seemingly confirmed the prediction of the CBS executive who confided to Perry late in 1930 that the newly formed NCER "would fail because the political cards were stacked against them."[99] Despite this self-confidence, however, the radio lobby would leave nothing to chance in the early 1930s. Its fear was always that the reformers' critique would develop a significant base of support among the citizenry before the system was fully in place and no more susceptible to political challenge than any other major U.S. industry.

The Battle on Capitol Hill

On 8 January 1931 Senator Simeon Fess, Republican of Ohio, introduced a bill, soon dubbed the Fess bill, calling for the FRC to reserve 15 percent of the channels for educational institutions. Fess, the former president of Antioch College, did so after meeting with Joy Elmer Morgan. The radio lobby opposed the bill; indeed, before 1933 it was opposed to passage by Congress of any radio legislation since it was quite happy with the manner in which the FRC was stabilizing the airwaves for commercial exploitation.[100] The broadcasters' agenda was assisted by two factors. First, the economic depression dominated the thinking of Congress. "Were it not for the disturbing economic situation," *Broadcasting* observed, "Congress might blunder into the political radio morass camouflaged by these lobbying factions."[101] Second, while there was support for reform among rank-and-file members of Congress, perhaps reflecting the degree of public antipathy to the status quo despite the strength of the radio lobby, the ranking members of the congressional committees that handled radio legislation, especially James Couzens, Republican of Michigan, and C. C. Dill, Democrat of Washington, were staunch defenders of the industry. This became most apparent when a bill to set up a national nonprofit radio channel to be operated by organized labor passed the House and Senate in 1931, only to be squelched by the committee chairs in conference. "If it were not for a little group of reactionary leaders in both branches of Congress," the chief labor radio lobbyist observed, "this legislation would have been passed."[102]

The Fess bill never made it out of committee that winter, but the NCER was convinced that its prospects were outstanding in the session of Congress that would convene in December 1931. Bolton was less certain. Using her numerous contacts on Capitol Hill, she determined that there was considerable support in Congress for the idea of broadcast reform, but most members found the Fess bill an unacceptable alternative.[103] In the fall of 1931 Evans moved to Washington, D.C., to begin active lobbying as the representative of the *Ventura Free Press*. "Things look awfully good here," he noted after gauging the degree of hostility to commercial broadcasting on Capitol Hill, but, like Bolton, he soon realized that the Fess bill was unpassable.[104] Moreover, he recognized that there was a pressing need to come up with a workable piece of legislation. "Mr. Average Congressman is undoubtedly dissatisfied with the present condition of radio," Evans informed Woehlke. "But I doubt if he will be likely to give up the present system for one the merits of which cannot be definitely ascertained."[105] While the NCER continued to lobby for the Fess bill, Evans threw his support behind a measure that called for a complete congressional investigation of broadcasting, with the purpose of gathering facts for establishing a new broadcast setup.

The winter of 1931–1932 was the high-water mark of discontent with commercial broadcasting. It was clear to congressional defenders of the status quo that some radio legislation would almost certainly pass Congress and that the legislation would probably be harmful to industry interests. Accordingly, Couzens and Dill proposed and got passed Senate Resolution 129 in January 1932, which called for the FRC to make a thorough study of the various criticisms of broadcasting and report back to Congress by the summer. This was a devastating blow to the reformers, since the congressional leaders could now claim that no radio legislation should be considered until the FRC completed its study. Moreover, that the FRC would endorse the status quo was a foregone conclusion. In December 1931, to quell the rising tide of criticism, the FRC had released a statement commending the "American system of broadcasting" as the "best . . . in the world" and asserting that no reforms were necessary.[106] Davis insisted that the *Free Press* continue to "make every possible effort to get action at this session of Congress." He told Crandall that "it would be very difficult to keep the radio matter alive through another year."[107]

Since the FRC was now conducting a study, the bill Evans had favored mandating a congressional study of radio was withdrawn. From February to April Evans pushed relentlessly on behalf of new legislation that would put sharp limits on the amount of advertising permitted over the air. Davis repeatedly implored Crandall to get the NCER to support Evans's activities. Although Perry agreed with Davis, since Fess had withdrawn his measure in January after SR 129 had passed, Morgan refused to cooperate, informing Davis that he supported only the NCPT's resolution calling for the complete nationalization and decommercialization of broadcasting. "Mr. Joy Elmer Morgan," Davis wrote to Crandall incredulously, "does not even approve the campaign he is conducting."[108] By now the NCER's lobbying had assumed an almost surreal quality. While Tyler spent the spring urging educators to support the Fess bill, which was no longer viable, Morgan supported a measure that no one was seriously considering, all the while informing NCER members that reform legislation would almost certainly pass "during the next winter."[109] When the *Free Press* advertising limits proposal failed in April, the two branches of the Payne Fund's radio activities were heading in opposite directions. In a sober memorandum shortly thereafter, Crandall was unsparing toward the NCER as a lobbying agency, stating that it made "no effort . . . to understand the entire political situation in Congress and out of it regarding radio legislation."[110]

In June the FRC issued its response to SR 129. The report, *Commercial Radio Advertising*, was lavish in its praise of the status quo and dismissed all criticism unconditionally. The commercial broadcasters were elated, arguing that this settled the matter for all time. The reformers were distraught; Davis called the report "a joke."[111] The summer of

1932 was a somber period for the broadcast reform movement. "We expected to get several bills," Davis despondently noted to Woehlke, "and we failed to get any."[112] The only heartening development for the reformers took place in Canada, where, after years of study and public hearings, the Parliament had formally resolved to establish a nonprofit broadcasting system in April 1932. Indeed, the only American to testify in Ottawa that spring had been Joy Elmer Morgan, who urged the Canadians to avoid commercial broadcasting in no uncertain terms. "Until your visit," the Canadian leader of the movement for nonprofit, noncommercial broadcasting later wrote Morgan, "the committee had regarded the American situation as largely satisfactory."[113] The U.S. reformers believed that if they could get a similar study authorized by Congress to be conducted by independent citizens not affiliated with the industry, as the FRC clearly was, it could only resolve for a noncommercial system like that in Britain or Canada.

Thus, when Congress reconvened, the *Free Press* put all its effort behind legislation to establish an "investigation of the whole field of radio broadcasting." "If the federal investigation of radio fails," Evans wrote to Davis, "we are practically sunk anyway."[114] The NCER also formally announced its support for a study, after being encouraged to do so by Crandall.[115] The campaign for a radio investigation never got anywhere, however. On one hand, *Commercial Radio Advertising* had been the result of such a study, albeit by the FRC, and that was enough to satisfy most members of Congress that another study was unnecessary. On the other hand, virtually all of the members of Congress who had worked for broadcast reform had been defeated in the 1932 elections. Whether the radio lobby was responsible for these defeats is not clear; in any case the message was probably clear to those who came to Congress in the winter of 1932–1933. "In both Houses of Congress there is no one," Evans informed Woehlke after a month of lobbying, "with whom we can play ball to get ahead in radio."[116] Finally, in January 1933, Evans acknowledged defeat. "I must say that the situation has developed to a point," he wrote to the NCER, "where I am convinced that further radio agitation in Washington is futile at the present time."[117]

In this context, the Payne Fund asked Evans to prepare a memorandum concerning whether the Fund should drop its campaign for broadcast reform and, like the NACRE, simply accept the status quo and cooperate with the commercial broadcasters. Evans acknowledged that the reform movement probably would never "successfully undermine commercial broadcasting in this country." He insisted, however, that the "fundamental structure of broadcasting" was still "absolutely unsound" and that the public remained dissatisfied with "excessive commercialism." Evans concluded that the Payne Fund should stay the course, as "the whole structure needs to be reorganized."[118]

The Payne Fund accepted Evans's counsel and then made two fundamental decisions. First, it terminated the *Ventura Free Press* radio campaign. In California, Woehlke and Carew were released, while Evans returned to work at the Payne Fund offices in New York, where he would act as a consultant on radio and other matters. With the termination of the *Free Press* radio campaign, the mood at the Payne Fund regarding its radio projects was rapidly transformed from one of enthusiasm, even euphoria, to one of despair. H. O. Davis would later inform Crandall how much he "regretted" that it had been "impossible for us to carry the campaign to a successful end."[119] Second, Crandall advised the NCER to suspend its lobbying as well and to "concentrate all their forces on creating local opinion which would later be reflected in Congress."[120]

To this end, the NCER hired a field organizer to travel across the nation, meet with educators and the public at large, make speeches and generally drum up support for broadcast reform. The field organizer, Eugene Coltrane, did so at a breakneck pace throughout 1933, until failing health and the prospect of a job as a college president led him to resign the post early in 1934. The NCER also managed to have broadcast reform made the official college and high school debate topic for the 1933–1934 academic year. The commercial broadcasters were terrified by the debate topic, since it would expose broadcast reform issues to fifteen hundred college and six thousand high school debate teams in thirty-three states. The networks and the NAB went to great expense to promote a positive view of the status quo, and they were able to defuse the situation. "We were able to comply with the objective without damage," NBC president Merlin Aylesworth informed RCA's David Sarnoff.[121] In short, without any appreciable increase in press coverage, these NCER attempts to rouse public opinion had little visible impact.

The one hope remaining for the NCER was to gain the support of Franklin D. Roosevelt, who was inaugurated as president in March 1933. "Unless the big business [*sic*] has somehow entrenched itself with President Roosevelt," an NCER board member noted, "the program of protecting radio for its best public purpose would fit admirably into his entire program."[122] The reformers were encouraged by the presence of several broadcast reform sympathizers in the Roosevelt administration, including Adolph A. Berle and chairman of the Tennessee Valley Authority (TVA), Dr. Arthur Morgan, who argued that not only radio but the entire mass media should be operated on a nonprofit basis, "just as are the public schools."[123] The most outspoken advocate of reform was the ambassador to Mexico, Josephus Daniels, perhaps Roosevelt's most trusted friend in politics, who repeatedly implored the president to nationalize radio broadcasting in his correspondence from Mexico City.[124] Nonetheless, the president elected not to ally with the reformers and take on an uphill fight with the powerful commercial broadcasters. To some extent, he did not want to jeopardize his ability to take to the airwaves whenever he desired, which the broadcasters granted him, thereby bypassing the largely Republican newspaper industry.[125] Moreover, the communications industry tended to be Democratic and to support the overarching agenda of the New Deal.[126]

By this time the broadcasters were in favor of passing legislation that would establish the permanent regulation of broadcasting, thus providing a "thoroughly stabilized" industry and thereby eliminating the basis for the annual "attacks by unfriendly groups" in Washington.[127] In February 1934 Dill introduced a bill to establish the permanent regulation of broadcasting and create a Federal Communications Commission (FCC) to replace the FRC. Otherwise the bill rephrased the Radio Act of 1927 mostly verbatim. A similar bill was introduced in the House. The Roosevelt administration and the NAB announced their support of the bills. Given these conditions, and the lack of any active reform lobbying on Capitol Hill, "all signs pointed to a quick passage," as broadcast historian Philip T. Rosen has noted.[128]

Then, most unexpectedly, Father John B. Harney, Paulist Fathers' superior general, whose station had recently lost an ongoing struggle with the FRC to gain more time on the frequency it shared with a CBS station, entered the fray. In March, Harney went to Washington and arranged to have Senators Henry Hatfield, Republican of West Virginia, and Robert Wagner, Democrat of New York, introduce an amendment that would require the new FCC to set aside 25 percent of the channels for the use of nonprofit groups. With little media coverage, Harney and the Paulists launched a whirlwind campaign among national Catholic organizations, generating more than sixty thousand signatures on petitions in three weeks in April.[129] The radio lobby seemingly had been caught flat-footed; whereas with labor, education and the press it had carefully cultivated allies over the years, it was unprepared for this onslaught from the previously dormant Catholics. By the end of April, the trade publication *Variety* warned that the Wagner–Hatfield amendment stood "better than a 50–50 chance of being adopted." The NAB proclaimed that it "brings to a head the campaign against the present broadcasting set-up which has been smoldering in Congress for several years."[130] To defuse the momentum for reform, Dill added a clause to his communications bill, Section 307(c), that required the new FCC to study the Wagner–Hatfield proposition and then report back to Congress with recommendations early in 1935.

While Harney received the support of organized labor in his lobbying effort, he was unable to get any help from the NCER despite repeated, at times frantic, overtures in March and April. Indeed, Tyler informed Harney that he thought Dill's Section 307(c) would be a victory for the reform movement.[131] Harney was astounded that Tyler could regard Dill as "at all in sympathy" with broadcast reform.[132] He implored Perry to bypass Tyler and take the matter up with others in the NCER. "We must not let this opportunity knock at our door in vain. A better day will hardly come in our lifetime."[133] Although Perry found some support from college broadcasters across the nation, the NCER's other Washington-based operatives, Tyler and Morgan, could not be aroused, believing that the reform cause could do even better in the coming sessions of Congress. An exasperated Perry began to express his deep reservations about the NCER leadership to Crandall, confessing his "feeling of personal responsibility" for the "exasperatingly slow progress made."[134]

In early May the radio lobby attacked the Wagner–Hatfield amendment as if "its passage obviously would have destroyed the whole structure of broadcasting in America," as the NAB's chief lobbyist put it.[135] Behind Senator Dill, the measure was defeated on the floor of the Senate 42–23 on 15 May; Dill's communications bill passed on a voice vote later the same day. Dill's inclusion of Section 307(c) was the decisive factor that convinced many wavering senators that it was better to let the "experts" on the new FCC evaluate the 25 percent idea before putting it into law. The House soon passed its version of the same bill and Roosevelt signed the Communications Act of 1934 into law on 18 June. "When we read it," the NAB's lobbyist later commented, "we found that every point we had asked for was there."[136] Now only one opportunity remained for the reformers to advance their cause: the FCC hearings on whether to reserve 25 percent of the channels for nonprofit institutions as mandated by Section 307(c). Harney and organized labor, the groups mostly responsible for the hearings, refused to participate, regarding them as "a pro forma affair, designed to entrench the commercial interests in their privileged position."[137] Indeed, two of the three FCC members who would conduct the October hearings informed the NAB convention in September that they would refuse to recommend any change in the status quo.[138]

Ironically, the NCER agreed to direct the side arguing on behalf of the 25 percent measure, although it informed the FCC that it "had not suggested the enactment of the specific legislation under discussion." Perry agreed with the position of the Paulists and labor on the fraudulent nature of the hearings, while Tyler and Morgan believed that the FCC hearings "would be better than no study at all."[139] The subsequent hearings were a colossal mismatch; the NCER did not even attempt to coordinate the statements of its witnesses and the educators' combined testimony consisted mostly of contradictory statements. After both sides had made their presentations, NBC's chief lobbyist informed New York headquarters that the industry case "was done to perfection" and "was simply overwhelming so far as the opposition's case was concerned."[140] Morgan thought he had a breakthrough when he and Tyler used their contacts with the TVA to have a TVA representative appear at the hearings on one of the final days and make a statement calling for the establishment of a chain of noncommercial government stations. The stunned broadcasters immediately demanded an explanation from the White House, which then forced the TVA to withdraw its statement.[141] A frustrated Morgan continued to insist that the original TVA statement was actually the New Deal position on radio, but his efforts to do so only drew him condemnation from all sides in view of the second TVA statement.

When the FCC hearings drew to a close in early November, the stark reality facing the NCER began to sink in. "It seems to me that the commercial broadcasters have got such a firm grip on the situation," one college president and longtime NCER loyalist wrote Tyler, "that it is going to be difficult for it ever to be broken up." In a confidential memorandum on the NCER to Bolton, Crandall noted that "the organization and administration of the committee from the beginning has been unsatisfactory," and she recommended that the Payne Fund let the group dissolve when its grant expired in 1935, unless the NCER had entirely new leadership.[142] The 20 November meeting of the NCER was marked by severe criticism of Morgan and his handling of the FCC hearings, with Morgan responding by shouting "insults," as Perry put it, to the assembled educators.[143] In January 1935 the FCC released its report to Congress in response to Section 307(c); to no one's surprise it recommended against the fixed-percentage proposal. When Congress reconvened that month, it showed no interest in broadcast reform legislation, regarding the matter as settled with the passage of the Communications Act and the formation of the FCC, which itself now regarded commercial broadcasting as the officially authorized system unless informed otherwise by Congress. The political battle for the control of U.S. broadcasting, including television as well as radio, as much as it ever existed, was now formally concluded.

That point was not immediately clear to the NCER. In March, under the direction of the president of the University of Wyoming, Arthur Crane, who would soon replace Morgan as NCER chairman, the NCER announced an ambitious plan to have the federal government establish a series of nonprofit, noncommercial stations to be supported by tax dollars.[144] The NCER hoped to capitalize on the lessening hostility toward government ownership as the New Deal entered its most liberal phase. Instead, the proposal did not receive a trace of recognition and was quietly dropped by the early summer. The NCER then abandoned its lobbying efforts forever.

If the economic and political consolidation of commercial broadcasting was accomplished by 1935, the ideological consolidation was completed in the remainder of the decade. With the collapse and disappearance of organized opposition, this process was quick, almost inexorable. As RCA president David Sarnoff informed a nationwide NBC audience in 1938, "Our American system of broadcasting is what it is because it operates in American democracy. It is a free system because this is a free country."[145] CBS president William S. Paley informed a group of educators in 1937 that "he who attacks the American system" of broadcasting "attacks democracy itself."[146] Only a few years earlier the same comment would have been met by derision; in 1937 it barely received notice. The system was now off-limits to fundamental attack. Not only was the capitalistic basis of U.S. broadcasting unchallenged in legitimate discourse, it was elevated to the point where such criticism was unthinkable. Commercial broadcasting would continue to receive substantial criticism in subsequent years; however, with the dominant role of the profit motive sacrosanct, critics were left arguing for making the marketplace more competitive, not eliminating it. Besides being ineffectual, this criticism left the core relations unquestioned.

The Payne Fund responded to the shifting currents, with the encouragement of the broadcasting industry. As Perry noted in 1934, "The industry fully understands that if it can get the Fund to withdraw its support commercial radio will have an almost clear field." In September 1935 two NBC executives made a presentation to Bolton to impress upon her the network's commitment to educational programming. One week later, a friend of Bolton's in the House of Representatives confidentially informed her that if she persisted in funding a group that advocated that "the present broadcasting structure be scrapped," it might put the Payne Fund in "danger."[147] Bolton then decided to renew the NCER but under the condition that it "refrain from controversy or an attack" on the industry and that it be "restricted to educational" work. In short, the new NCER would work through the existing system. Tyler, Morgan and Perry all resigned and the NCER offices in Washington, D.C. were closed. Evans took charge of the NCER in January 1936 with a two-year $15,000 grant, working out of the Payne Fund's New York headquarters. Evans never abandoned his personal hatred for commercial broadcasting and his belief in the need for radical structural reform, describing himself in 1936 as "advocating Christianity in a world that is decidedly pagan," but he reconciled himself to the impossibility of reform and the Payne Fund's explicit mandate to the reformed NCER to work within the status quo.[148]

As Perry commented in December 1935, the capitulation of the NCER and the entrenchment of the commercial broadcasters seemingly made the NACRE the apparent winner in the battle to determine the course of educational broadcasting.[149] Ironically, however, precisely as the NCER found itself embracing the status quo, the NACRE released a major study of its relations with NBC from 1932 to 1935 that denounced cooperation between educators and commercial broadcasters as unworkable and failed.[150] Outraged, NBC, perhaps because it no longer needed the NACRE for public relations purposes, made it clear that it had no desire to reconcile the differences between the organizations. The Carnegie Corporation disbanded the NACRE the following year.

The years that followed were difficult times for educators concerned with broadcasting. They had to come to grips with their marginal situation and hope to exact concessions from the FCC and the networks with minimal leverage. In this context, the Payne Fund quietly terminated the NCER in 1941 after the resignation of Evans, who was increasingly frustrated by the group's lack of influence over policy. With the possibility of suggesting fundamental structural changes in the broadcasting setup verboten, those who wished to encourage educational or nonprofit public service radio and television found themselves in an absurd position. Their efforts could be successful or secure only to the extent that they did not interfere with the profitability, existing or potential, of the commercial broadcasters – that is, to the extent that they were ineffectual.

Conclusion

This appendix has chronicled the role the Payne Fund played in attempting to establish a public debate over how the United States might best structure its broadcasting system and, furthermore, in leading the drive to establish a significant, even dominant, nonprofit and noncommercial sector. It is remarkable in two respects. First, the Payne Fund broadcast reform campaign indicates the extent to which the Fund was willing to challenge powerful institutions in pursuit of its principles, even against great odds. In this regard it displayed a degree of courage, a willingness to take on the powers that be that has been all too absent in the liberal major foundations of the 1930s and thereafter. To some extent this may be attributed to the period and to the fact that the commercial broadcasters were not yet sacrosanct in U.S. political culture. The fact remains, however, that the Payne Fund alone recognized the fundamental importance of the ownership and control of broadcasting in a democratic society and was then willing to devote resources to bringing about radical change.

Second, whereas many other democratic nations had extensive public hearings and debates before determining the types of broadcasting systems they eventually established, in the United States these decisions were made quietly, behind closed doors, by self-interested elites, with minimal public participation. Regardless of the obvious limitations of the *Ventura Free Press* radio campaign and, in particular, the NCER, and the uphill fight they would have faced in even the best of circumstances, the fact remains that the Payne Fund is largely responsible for whatever fundamental debate there has been about the merits of a network-dominated, profit-motivated and advertising-supported broadcasting system in the United States. Considerable scholarship suggests that many of these concerns regarding the concentration and commercialization of the media are perhaps more pressing today than ever before.[151] In addition, the advent of revolutionary communication and information technologies, along with dramatic changes in the world political economy, is forcing a global reappraisal of how societies can best organize their communication systems. The Payne Fund experience may provide a tradition to draw from as we face important questions of the relationship of communication to democracy, and the complex problems associated with generating answers to these questions, in the years to come.

The Motion Picture Experience as Modified by Social Background and Personality

PAUL G. CRESSEY

Systematic research upon the theatrical motion picture has established many significant facts concerning its effects upon the information, the attitudes, and behavior of children and youth. That children and young people see many films, that these are exceedingly varied as to content,[1] and that they remember much from the plots of these photoplays, has been definitely demonstrated. It is equally well established that social attitudes and racial prejudices, at least upon "debatable" issues and type characters, can be affected by photoplays. Peterson and Thurstone, by measuring attitudes *before* and *after* their subjects had seen certain films, have shown convincingly that appropriate photoplays affect the social attitudes of youth toward such stereotyped groups as "Negroes," "Chinese" and "Germans," and upon controversial issues such as warfare, patriotism and the punishment of criminals.[2]

When properly interpreted, other findings from recent research may be accepted. That children and young people when seeing films can be disturbed emotionally, *i.e. physiologically,* in a manner and degree recordable upon laboratory instruments, and that the film content which stimulates in this way varies greatly with age and maturity, is well established.[3] That photoplays can provide young people with patterns for make-believe play, for phantasy and daydreaming, and for conscious or "unwitting" imitation of dress and beautification, of lovemaking techniques, of mannerisms and gestures, and that theatrical films can furnish schemes of life which are utilized experimentally by young people in their own social activities, has been shown clearly by Blumer and others.[4] Even though some critics may seek a broader perspective for

Reprinted from *American Sociological Review*, 3 (August 1938), pp. 516–525.

interpreting such findings, they cannot disregard the simple facts that boys and young men, when suitably predisposed, sometimes have utilized techniques of crime seen in the movies, have used gangster films to stimulate susceptible ones toward crime, and on occasion in their own criminal actions, have idealized themselves imaginatively as possessing the attractive personality or as engaging in the romantic activities of a gangster screen hero.

Such attempts at summarization of our present knowledge are inadequate, but at least they show the problems involved are very complex and that the widespread loose thinking, the public controversy and the prejudice which have prevailed, make scientific study in this field even more difficult. In practice, one must constantly buttress all these generalizations with supplementary explanations and with reiterated statements of the limitations of his evidence. Thus, in the above statement of the relation in certain cases of motion pictures to crime, one must follow it with the explanation, however gratuitous, that he does not mean that movies have been shown to be a "cause" of crime, that he does not mean that thoroughly "good" boys are enticed into crime by gangster films; in short, that he merely means what he has said, namely, that boys and young men responsive to crime portrayals have been found on occasion to use ideas and techniques seen at the movies. Similarly, in summarizing motion picture influence on imitation, daydreaming and thinking, we always must add that we merely mean that the motion picture, together with other socializing agencies, has been found at times to be a source for the individual's patterns of thought and behavior.

We are confronting here at least two distinct "levels" in the interpretation of cinema influence. Some have been content to cite evidence that motion pictures are sometimes sources of various patterns utilized in subsequent behavior and in the formation of attitudes. Others have contended that such findings cannot be true. They have attacked both those studies showing the cinema as an occasional source for crime patterns and ideation and those indicating it as a source in the formation of attitudes and behavior by asserting that the data do not "prove" the photoplays "caused" these crimes and personality changes – something, obviously, that the monographs had not attempted to demonstrate.

This confusion is due primarily to inadequate conceptualization of the problem. We must make clear the methodological distinctions between a study of the cinema as *a source* for patterns of thought, feeling and behavior and a study of its *net contribution* in terms of the total social situation, or "configuration," in which it is experienced. Fundamentally, the motion picture is an instrument of communication and informal education and it can be best studied sociologically when so conceived. Recognition of the education potentialities of the theatrical film, ably demonstrated in experimental settings and specific social situations, must not be allowed to obscure an equally significant consideration, viz., that the cinema's "effect" upon an individual, a community or a society never can be gauged accurately if the motion picture experience is studied only segmentally and never in its essential unity. "Going to the movies" is a unified experience involving always a specific film, a specific personality, a specific social situation and a specific time and mood; therefore, any program of research which does not recognize all essential phases of the motion picture experience can offer little more than conjecture as to the cinema's net "effect" in actual social settings and communities. Moreover, because the cinema *in itself* is merely and instrument of communication, the responses to it must always be a product of the interplay of all the above mentioned variables. It is, therefore, a serious misconception of social process to assume that accurate knowledge of the cinema's "contribution" can be deduced from particularistic studies of the motion picture experience.

This failure to include all the phases essential to the motion picture experience has misled not only the above critics of published studies, but also many "popular" writers and speakers. Disregarding the social background and personal interests of their subjects, they have made sweeping statements about the motion picture's "effect," even though their information pertained to but one phase of the cinema experience. Thus, some have argued, solely from a sampling of film content, that young people who see "undesirable," "immoral," or even criminal conduct upon the screen will go out and do likewise, or at least will tend inevitably to acquire corresponding attitudes and values. Others, merely from knowledge of instances of conduct and attitudes patterned after specific screen action or values, have jumped to the conclusion that the cinema "caused" these changes in behavior or attitudes. While it is possible to deduce from these latter instances the simple, though not unimportant, fact that the photoplay had been *a source* for the acquisition of these specific patterns or values, it is not possible to infer from such information alone that the film has "caused" these changes. Social causation is entirely too complex a problem to be explained by any such simplistic interpretation of incomplete data.

What is most needed today is an adequate frame of reference for studying the motion picture which is acceptable to all the special disciplines involved in such research. Its absence is the cause of much misunderstanding and fruitless controversy; our inability to use many specialized research findings is largely due to this lack of a common frame of reference. Such a conceptual scheme must recognize the cinema's function as an instrument of communication and informal education and must provide a formulation by which later quantitative and experimental research may be enabled to supply more precise knowledge concerning this function. It should provide a conceptualization of the whole motion picture experience by which we may be able to study the cinema's "contribution" under various circumstances and social situations and to perceive more fundamentally its role in the growth of attitudes and personality. Such a frame of reference must be sufficiently comprehensive to provide as a basis for study a "unit of interrelationships," *i.e.* a *closed system*,[5] which includes all of the essential phases of the motion picture experience.

One necessary step in that direction is a better understanding of the motion picture situation itself. It is not essentially a social situation, since it does not involve social interaction. The spectator obviously is not a part of the screen milieu and, whatever his wishes, he can never participate in the screen action. There is none of that mutual responsiveness and adaptation of actor and audience which characterizes the legitimate theater. Except for emotional "contagion," the incidental and quite extrinsic interaction among spectators, social participation is wholly absent. Yet the motion picture situation involves important social features. The spectator's reactions to the screen, his interests and affects are socially conditioned, and what he "carries away" with him is altered by later social contacts. Strictly conceived, the motion picture situation is neither wholly "social" nor wholly "nonsocial"; it is *extrasocial*. It denotes a distinctive type of semisocial behavior which, because of such inventions as movies and radio, is becoming more common. It merits much more attention from sociologists and educators than it has yet received.[6]

Instead of facilitating social interaction, the cinema serves chiefly to set up imaginative states. In these, imaginative participation and *identification* become the means by which a semblance of vitality and substance can be discovered in the movies. It is significant that this imaginative participation constitutes really the essence of social participation, as Mead, Cooley, Stern,[7] and others have shown in studies of "role-taking" or "personation"; and that the spectator at the cinema is but continuing, in this more symbolic form, the type of behavior which is basic to all face-to-face social interaction. *Identification* also connotes, as White has suggested, a certain "vagueness in the province of the self."[8] It is perhaps because of this "vagueness" in the imaginative delimitation of self and social world that one discovers in a screen milieu values, sentiments, and activities of consequence to oneself.

This is suggested by the three distinct modes or "imaginative adjustments" in identification which have been noted in our New York study. Using the formulation of social psychiatry, these may be described as *projection, introjection,* and *displacement. Projection,* described by Kimball Young as the "thrusting upon others imaginatively" of "qualities which we ourselves possess,"[9] appears to be the most frequent imaginative adjustment to the screen and is found in some degree whenever any sense of "participation" is reported. *Introjection,* on the other hand, is an intermittent imaginative adjustment involving momentary loss of both social orientation and self orientation and is found among those who experience identification in a "more complete" form. Whereas *projection* implies an unwarranted delimitation of the province of the self, *introjection* is an "incorporation of a part of the environment into the concept of the self."[10] *Displacement,* however, denotes a partial substitution of certain personalities and values of one's own social world for the characters and objects in the screen milieu while continuing, *as oneself,* to experience imaginative participation in the screen action. It is a derived imaginative adjustment, used quasiconsciously as a means of enhancing the film's affective significance, and, in contrast to introjection, involves only social disorientation, not self disorientation. Through such imaginative adjustments, the spectator bridges the gap between himself and the screen milieu and gives the latter affective significance to himself.

It is of interest also to note that imaginative screen participation never can be "complete" in any sense that this imaginative and ideational interrelationship must always remain quite "relative." The illusion of reality is achieved through the spectator's ability to find in the screen action and plot some satisfaction of personal interests and feelings, to perceive there attributes which appear to him in some way "human," or to find in the film social values, sentiments, and behavior which, upon the basis of his experience and insights, seem "true to life." However, while it is necessary for the film to present enough familiar attributes to make it interesting and pleasurable, it is equally desirable that it should not possess so great an identity of elements as to make it "too realistic" or "painful." Especially because the theatrical motion picture is primarily a medium of entertainment, the maintenance of an appropriate, or *optimum,* "psychiatric distance" between film content and the constantly shifting public interests and tastes is most important, and is possibly the most vexing problem confronting producers and directors.

A second phase of any frame of reference which is adequate for the problem must be inclusion of a point of view and procedures for systematic consideration of differentials in personality and social backgrounds of spectators as these impinge upon and modify their responses to the motion picture. This conceptualization must take cognizance of the interrelationships between film content and the spectator's personality and social background, his special interests and values, and the events which are subsequent to the motion picture experience but which may serve to redefine it. This is necessary because the cleavage between the motion picture situation and the patron's social background and other personal experiences is more apparent than real. At the cinema, he is physically but not psychologically detached from his own background and at least some of his responses are necessarily affected by his earlier association, his present interests, and his other contacts. What he perceives or fails to perceive upon the screen, what he feels or does not feel, what he remembers or fails to remember, and what he does or does not imitate, are inevitably affected by his social background and personality as much, or more than, by the immediate motion picture situation. Likewise, the ultimate meaning of the cinema experience cannot be determined without consideration of subsequent events which have reference to it.

In practice, such an approach calls for procedures and considerations which may not be required in other research. It involves not only detailed study of personal and social background data but also the attempt to gain greater understanding of the cinema's "net contribution" through analysis of all other essential phases of the motion picture experience which are imaginatively or socially interrelated. This requires not only a comprehension of specific personalities and social backgrounds, but also a knowledge of collateral experiences, of the imaginative response to movie patterns and ideas, *before, during* and *after* cinema attendance, and of later successes and failures in utilizing movie patterns, ideas, and values. It also involves tracing the imaginative and social interrelationships between screen and subject and between the subject and his social world in an effort to perceive the cinema's "contribution" in the light of this broader perspective.

In this approach, the cinema is evaluated from a wholly different configuration, or *gestalt,* and from different premises. Its "influence," instead of being revealed by observing and recording disjunctive items of screen content and postcinema behavior, as commonly is thought to be the case, is recognized as being intertwined complexly with the entire web of social and imaginative processes which arise with reference to the motion picture.[11] The cinema, moreover, is seen to acquire its meanings, its definitions for its patrons, in the interaction between imagination and social behavior; its valuations and utilizations, its effects, in turn, result from the efforts to relate film content to personal interests, values, or to overt activities. Thus, the cinema is interpreted neither as a prime "cause" nor a prime "effect" of the social and personal manifestations subsequent to the motion picture experience. Rather, its "contribution" is regarded as the product of the interplay of forces in which it may be both "cause" and "effect" and by which its own social role is established.

Such a conceptualization conceives the cinema, not as a unilateral social "force," but as a reciprocal interrelationship of screen and spectator, of screen patterns and values, and of social patterns and social values. When the motion picture is viewed only "externally," it certainly appears to be only unilateral, *i.e.,* the patrons are wholly passive agents who are merely "played upon" through the arts and skills of cinematography. We have, however, abundant evidence that this is an erroneous conception. Through imaginative participation, identification, random reflection, phantasy before and after cinema attendance, and through the impact of prior interests and values, the cinema experience is redefined in many ways and may affect the patron in forms only incidentally associated with film content. It is for this reason that it is impossible accurately to describe cinema influence as a "contribution" or an "effect" unless these familiar words are used in such a way as to imply something more than a unilateral relationship.

To ascertain the cinema's "net contribution" to personality or community and to develop an adequate frame of reference for conceptualizing it will require further study of concrete community situations in which sufficiently complete data are available. These should include other types of community settings than the interstitial areas studied at New York University.[12] Assemblage and collation of enough such studies give promise of providing a basis for valid generalizations regarding the motion picture experience in typical community settings and social situations and with reference to personalities differing in age, sex, intellectual and emotional "maturity," and in cultural and ecological antecedents. It would also provide a basis for obtaining inductively a valid set of principles which might be of great practical assistance in determining public policies relative to the motion picture. These formulations would not deny the cinema's incidental function as an instrument of communication and informal education, but they might make possible, ultimately, an objective and critical evaluation of those other aspects of cinema "influence" now the subject of so much futile controversy.

Immediately, moreover, this approach to the problem gives promise of averting much of the popular misinterpretation and the public misrepresentation which have attended earlier studies. The fact that the findings as reported must always include consideration of the entire motion picture experience, of social background and personality differentials, may prevent the uncritical from making unwarranted inferences from partial findings and may forestall premature judgment as to whether the cinema's "contribution" in specific cases is "socially desirable" or "socially undesirable." Thus, to take but one illustration, the knowledge that the motion picture had been in certain instances a source of crime techniques later used by delinquents is not allowed to stand alone but always is related to the subject's social background, personal values, character, and interests, insofar as these can be seen to have been related to his screen responses. While this procedure confirms findings from earlier studies that gangster and crime films *occasionally* have supplied patterns later used in crime, *at times* have evoked criminal responses and attitudes, or have been a means *occasionally* by which a delinquent romantically might idealize himself, it reveals also that *in most instances,* if not in all, there were individual values and preconceptions, personal problems, and immediate interests which clearly served in some degree to condition these screen responses.[13] Reporting these socially undesirable "effects" only when careful consideration is also given to significant contributing factors may serve to deter hasty judgment by many readers. On so controversial an issue, it is probably impossible to prevent misconstruction and misinterpretation, especially by the zealots at each extreme, but such a procedure at least will direct the reader's attention to the essential problem.

The chief importance of this comprehensive approach, however, is the different order of findings obtained. The cinema's role in general conduct is found for the most part to be *reflexive,* to take its specific character from the social configuration, the social-psychological "frame" in which the motion picture is experienced and in which responses to it arise. While this approach does not disprove the finding that in certain cases the cinema's incidental "contribution" as reported has seemed to be "socially desirable" and in other cases definitely "undesirable," it adds the significant conclusion that the types of conduct in which cinema influence is discernible appear to be determined largely, if not entirely, by the subject's previous experiences and associations, his problems and interests at the time, and by the pleasure or displeasure later experienced with this conduct. Some of these associations and experiences can be, of course, cinematic in origin but, except for cases involving intense personal conflict and crises in which the subject is a problem to himself, or in cases of psychopathic personalities, all cases thus far intensively studied reveal that the *immediate* behavior has been so conditioned and modified. Behavior which is affected by the cinema is found to constitute either *suggestion, i.e.,* "a release of attitudes and tendencies" already a part of the subject's personality, the "unwitting" acquisition of mannerisms and gestures, or the "conscious" or deliberate imitation of screen patterns.[14] All three forms involve a response to prior conditioning, interests or values. Moreover, the subject's continuance of this behavior when he already has experienced it, and his returning to film showings of a type known to be stimulating, implies some tolerance of this conduct by the subject or his friends and a further selection of screen reactions through social control.

Social attitudes as well as general and special information are also refashioned through the interplay of social and personal background, but in these fields there is indubitable evidence of a significant "net contribution" by the cinema. In contrast to overt behavior, in which only a limited divergence in conduct is usually tolerated by the group, a wide range of individual differentiation in the acquisition of attitudes and information is permitted and even encouraged. This at least partially explains the fact that the cinema's "net contributions" are found in those areas of knowledge for which children and young people do not have other more adequate sources of information; screen representations are accepted only so long as other more "authoritative" knowledge is unavailable and only when they do not *seem* to contradict the mores, codes, and the axiomatic "truths" accepted by the subject and his group. Thus, though many cinema stereotypes are found to be reflected significantly in the attitudes of children and young people, they are effective only in connection with inadequate social background and individual limitations in intellect and alertness. In acquiring general information, what one perceives or fails to perceive in a film, or what he remembers or fails to remember, appears to be similarly affected. In the acquisition of special information, however, there is involved not only an inadequacy of other sources but the presence of positive interests which impel toward learning. It is perhaps for this reason that much cinema learning involves "techniques" for meeting special situations and personal problems.

Though these findings indicate that the cinema is *reflexive* in its influence, it is unwarranted to describe [it] as "negative." In a society in which there are many factors making both for disorganization and social amelioration, the cinema is an important social and educational force contributing directly and incidentally to both. Under certain circumstances, it has been found to influence greatly the shaping of attitudes and the acquisition of information, and even to affect overt behavior in certain situations. The *nature* of these "effects" is determined by many forces external to the motion picture but the fact of its educational and social role cannot be denied for that reason. Moreover, even though the motion picture's influence is reflexive, it is still possible to discover certain characteristic circumstances in which the cinema's contribution to ideation and conduct is great. In fields of vital interests not adequately met through other community institutions and agencies, in fields where prestige is attached to the acquisition of the "latest thing," as in fashion, popular songs, and slang, and in fields where the movie facilitates trends in standards of public opinion which are already under way, the motion picture makes some of its most distinct "contributions." Careful study of these special circumstances and comparison of them with other settings in which the cinema's contribution does not appear to be appreciable gives promise of more precise knowledge of the circumstances under which the motion picture's specific "effect" becomes exceptionally significant.

Notes

Primary documents are cited according to the following system:

PFP: Records of the Payne Fund, Inc., held at the Western Reserve Historical Society, Cleveland, Ohio. The records are identified by the carton and file number. For example, C28 f555 indicates file number 555 in carton 28. An excellent finding aid in the form of a Register to the Collection is available, written by Leslie Solotko, Edward C. Cade and John J. Grabowski.

MPRC: Papers of the Motion Picture Research Council held in the Archives of the Hoover Institution on War, Revolution and Peace, Stanford University, Stanford, California. A five-page finding aid is available. The records are identified by box number and by file name, for example, Box 16, Thrasher file.

CP: Papers of W. W. Charters, research director of the Payne Fund Studies, which are deposited in special collections in the library of Ohio State University, Columbus. These are in unnumbered boxes, unnumbered files. A rudimentary finding aid is available.

Introduction

1. Shils (1980), pp. 215–220; this view is shared by Matthews (1977). In addition to these sources, the following were consulted: Faris (1967); Bulmer (1984); Smith (1988).
2. Matthews (1977), p. 75.
3. Bulmer (1984), p. 69; cf. p. 79.
4. Mitchell (1929).
5. Ross (1991), pp. 226–227.
6. Park (1915).
7. See MPRC, Box 12, Blumer file. Park's proposal to study the influence of movies on juvenile delinquency pretty much describes what Blumer, and

Blumer and Hauser, carried out. His other suggestions, a study of young women who go to Hollywood and become movie actresses, and a study of the consequences of overstimulating young people, were not followed up. On the former, however, see Peters (1971).

8. The records of the Boys' Club study are held at the Rockefeller Foundation Archive.

9. Janowitz (1968); Larsen and Mock (1939).

10. The research director, W. W. Charters, summarizing thirty years earlier, had a different estimate: "From all these data collected about the content of motion pictures the conclusion is inevitable that from the point of view of children's welfare the commercial movies are an unsavory mess. For adults the selection of movies is their own business, to be controlled by whatever means they want to use. But children have crashed the gate in millions – eager minded, ripe for learning; and three weeks out of four on their once-a-week trips to the movies they see a crime picture, a sex picture. The producers ought to have a heart" (Charters 1933, p. 55).

11. In the later 1930s, when commercial sponsorship entered the field, yet another agenda extraneous to purely scientific concerns was introduced. Paul F. Lazersfeld, a product of Karl and Charlotte Bühler's Psychological Institute at the University of Vienna, was instrumental in much of this (see Chapter Three). Thus he had difficulty in making full use of the refugees from the Frankfurt Institute of Social Research, and, indeed, his empirical and administrative approach was later attacked by them as "positivism."

12. An indication of the changes going on is Young's editorial Introductory Note (1931). Introducing work by students and colleagues of W. I. Thomas, he writes: "It is true that important beginnings are underway among psychologists and sociologists, especially by such men as Allport, May, Rice, and Thurstone, to devise methods of treating certain aspects of social attitudes by statistical techniques. But the material here is of the case study or historical-genetic series and in dealing with these data we have not yet discovered adequate quantitative instruments for collecting the essential facts nor mathematical terms in which to couch the concepts necessary for their adequate interpretation" (p. vii).

13. See Clausen's (1966) indicative if descriptively dated paper, esp. pp. 234–235. These examples illustrate how theoretical perspectives bedevil rational debate. The participants operate with conflicting ideas about social causation and hence draw different conclusions about possible remedies.

14. K. Davis (1937). Davis was published in the new academic quarterly set up as a rival to the *American Journal of Sociology*, which had been founded by Albion W. Small at Chicago in 1895.

15. It is unclear whether functionalism ever admitted causes – stresses in the system, sometimes called its dysfunctional aspects.

16. Lasswell (1939); Cantril (1940); Merton and Lazarsfeld (1944). See further discussion in Chapter Three.
17. Forman (1932 a, b, c).
18. See Samuel Renshaw's letter of 4 November 1932 to Short (MPRC, Box 16, Renshaw file) reiterating his objection to the *McCall's* articles: "It is my judgment that the publication of the 'popular' articles in advance of the publication of the documents on which they are based is bound to lead to ... misconstruction."
19. Moley (1938).
20. From philosophical premises he had reached a conclusion that dovetailed neatly with the emerging functionalist approach. Both lines of thought counseled a very critical and self-conscious approach to the isolation of any social feature as a problem.
21. It is very clear from the mass of internal paperwork that the social scientists involved in the PFS felt their position as scientists would be damaged if they were directly involved in any kind of partisan campaign, regardless of the fact that some of them were strong critics of the movies.
22. The issue of the role of social control and censorship in American films is currently undergoing a major revision. See Black (1994).
23. Cressey (1938a).
24. The careers of all the significant dramatis personae can be found at the front of this book.
25. Herbert Blumer became the leader of symbolic interactionism at the University of California, Berkeley; L. L. Thurstone and Mark A. May had distinguished careers in psychology.
26. For historical material see Jowett, Reath and Schouten (1977) and K. Davis (1976). *Report of the Royal Commission* (1977), pp. 382–497, has a useful country-by-country chronology of research, studies and policies on the media.
27. Katz and Lazarsfeld (1955), p. 17n, claim that Herbert Blumer was still articulating this view as late as 1946.
28. Cressey (1938a).
29. Delia (1987), p. 40.
30. Jarvie (1966).
31. Randall (1989) writes as follows: "The movies ... were the first medium without roots in either elite or folk culture. Their appeal to an undifferentiated mass public was untempered by any tradition of providing news and opinion. From the outset their tremendous representational power was used almost exclusively to entertain and divert. Where the mass circulation newspaper reached news *readers,* the movies reached new audiences of the literate and nonliterate alike. They were exclusively a public medium, not to be wrapped up, taken home, and savored in private. They came from

outside the community and were not indebted to it. With few exceptions, no advertisers influenced their content; financially they depended almost entirely on those who paid to see them" (p. 188).

32. Lewis (1933).

33. It is no excuse to note that Handel (1950), p. 229, must have done the same thing.

1. Social Science as a Weapon

1. Seabury (1926), p. 187.

2. It is interesting that the Payne Fund, a private philanthropic organization, was mentioned only in the original book frontispiece reproduced here, and not in the published title of the studies themselves. However, over the years the collective body of work has acquired the name of the sponsor.

3. Sklar (1975); Jowett (1976).

4. In recent years, a few film scholars have used the PFS in their research. Jacobs (1990) examined the studies in some detail, especially that by Edgar Dale on motion picture appreciation. Of more significance, Balio (1993), in the fifth volume of the prestigious History of American Cinema series, devotes only a few paragraphs to the PFS, and does so in conjunction with an examination of censorship and self-regulation in the motion picture industry. See Maltby (1993), p. 56.

5. Rowland (1983).

6. Wartella and Reeves (1985); Delia (1987), p. 40.

7. Lowery and De Fleur (1988), p. 53.

8. Munsterberg (1970/1916), p. 95.

9. The history of this period is covered in great depth in Musser (1990) and Bowser (1990), vols. 1 and 2 of the History of American Cinema series.

10. The reaction to the motion picture as a social and cultural force in this early period is discussed in Jowett (1976) and Sklar (1975).

11. For a discussion of the rise of movie stars see DeCordova (1990); Schickel (1985); Fowles (1992).

12. L. May (1980).

13. H. F. May (1959); Carmen (1966); Randall (1968).

14. Jowett (1976), pp. 74–76.

15. Siegfried (1927), p. 33.

16. Gusfield (1963).

17. In the *Mutual* decision, the unanimous Supreme Court, speaking through Justice McKenna, ruled: "It cannot be put out of view that the exhibition of moving pictures is a business pure and simple, originated and conducted for profit, like other spectacles, not to be regarded, nor intended to be regarded as part of the press of the country or as organs of public opinion. They are

mere representations of events, of ideas and sentiments published or known; vivid, useful and entertaining, no doubt, but ... capable of evil, having power for it, the greater because of their attractiveness and the manner of exhibition." *Mutual Film Corporation v. Ohio Industrial Commission* 236 US, 230 Supreme Court, 1915, p. 242.

18. Jowett (1989).

19. It is interesting that, while neither restriction lasted, Prohibition was repealed as early as 1932; the Supreme Court did not review the issue of movie censorship for another thirty-seven years after the *Mutual* case, in 1952.

20. At one time in the early 1920s, thirteen states had film censorship boards; however, in 1922, censorship bills were introduced into thirty-two state legislatures (Jowett 1976, p. 167).

21. Hays used all of his political talents in marshaling forces to defeat this referendum. His tactics were later the subject of a congressional hearing. See Jowett (1976), pp. 166–171; U.S. Congress, House (1926), pp. 398–404.

22. The studios' reluctance to assert their "free speech" rights has long intrigued film scholars. There is no easy explanation, but much can be traced to the deep concern of the largely Jewish heads of the studios about fomenting large-scale anti-Semitic outbursts from Protestant reformers. Certainly, there were occasional veiled references to "foreigners" pushing their values through the medium of the movies. For more information see Gabler (1988).

23. Good evaluations of the role of movies in workers' lives by social workers are Butler (1909) and Byington (1910).

24. Addams (1909), pp. 75–76.

25. Addams specifically cites two stories – one involving a robbery and murder, with a ten-year-old boy avenging his father's death; the other involving a robbery and murder of a Chinese laundryman by two young boys in order to feed their starving mother and younger sister. The latter murder, Addams claimed, ended with "a Prayer of thankfulness for this timely and heaven-sent assistance" (1909, pp. 78–80).

26. Ibid., p. 86.

27. Ibid., p. 103.

28. Healy (1915), p. 307.

29. Ibid., p. 308.

30. For details of the intense public relations effort of the Hays Office see Shenton (1971).

31. U.S. Congress, House (1914, 1916, 1926).

32. U.S. Congress, House (1926), pp. 24–25.

33. Robert Davis (1976) provides an excellent examination of the rhetorical devices used by both sides in the arguments surrounding the introduction of the various mass media in the twentieth century.

34. The other reformer groups continued to meet, but achieved very little. As an example, the Federal Motion Picture Council was formed as a direct result of three conferences called by the Presbyterian church in 1922, 1924 and 1925. The title of the organization was imposing, but in reality it had very few members, and no local chapters, relying upon the local support of groups like the Women's Christian Temperance Union. See Shenton (1971), p. 92.

35. Short to National Committee for the Study of Juvenile Reading, 3 June 1925, PFP, C28 f542. This letter was written on a letterhead from *Christian Work – A Religious Weekly Review*, edited by Fred Eastman, who would later become significant in promoting the published PFS.

36. Clymer to Short, 7 June 1926, PFP, C28 f542. Obviously, Short had brought up his relationship with Lucking sometime in the preceding year. Short was well connected because of his previous work with a variety of peace organizations and was constantly dropping names. (He included former president William Howard Taft on his resume.)

37. Short to Clymer, 9 June 1926, PFP, C28 f542. This letter was written on a Rollins College Project letterhead.

38. Short to Lucking, 15 July 1926, PFP, C28 f554.

39. Short to Crandall, 6 August 1926, PFP, C28 f542.

40. Crandall to Short, 27 August 1926, PFP, C28 f542.

41. Undated report, "A Proposal for: Out-of-School Education Through Recreational Reading," PFP, C28 f542.

42. There are many examples of this attitude toward Short in the voluminous correspondence in the Payne Fund files. Crandall and Clymer were very suspicious of Short's fervent moral agenda, often counseling Mrs. Bolton to be cautious of him and to maintain a public distance.

43. Short to Taft, 13 July 1927, PFP, C28 f542.

44. MPRC, Box 1, MPRC history file, p. 1.

45. Terry Ramsaye wrote that "Dr. Short hit so high a mark in bristling discipline and efficiency as business manager of Rollins College in Florida that the students tossed him into the park lake and thereafter kept his motor tires in a constant state of puncture until he sought other fields." *Motion Picture Herald*, 30 June 1934, p. 9

46. Seabury to Short, 14 March 1927, MPRC, Box 15, Seabury file.

47. MPRC, Box 1, MPRC history file.

48. Short, "Historical Sketch of the Payne Fund Studies," August 1928, MPRC, Box 1, MPRC history file, p. 2.

49. Ibid., p. 3.

50. Crandall to Blossom, 22 September 1927, MPRC, Box 5, Payne Fund file.

51. MPRC, Box 1, MPRC history file, p. 4.

52. Short to Clymer and Crandall, 27 September 1927, PFP, C28 f542.

53. MPRC, Box 1, MPRC history file, p. 4.

54. Memorandum from Seabury, 3 September 1927, MPRC, Box 15, Seabury file.

55. Seabury's memorandum outlining what types of action this new organization should be engaged in was extracted from the more fully developed ideas offered in *The Public and the Motion Picture Industry* (1926). In that book he declared that "it is each nation's duty to declare the [motion picture] industry to be a public utility and to treat it as such" (p. 169). Certainly Seabury's clearly articulated conception of the motion picture as a major international social and cultural force, equivalent in its impact to the telegraph, telephone and radio, and therefore subject to some form of government monitoring, was way ahead of most other perspectives at this time. However, Seabury, like many others of his background, was also deeply suspicious of the Jewish control of the motion picture industry, which he disguised as a concern for the "foreign" influence on movies. In an undated statement found in the MPRC files, he noted: "Mr. [Terry] Ramsaye . . . admits that the so-called upper strata of control of the motion picture industry in the United States is now about 90% Jewish. Objectionable, not because they are Jewish but because it is as unthinkable that America shall continue to entrust the amusements of her children to alien and uneducated men as it would be to turn over her schools, her pulpits or press to such men." Seabury, "The Kind of Men Who Control the Motion Picture Industry," n.d., MPRC, Box 15, Seabury file.

56. Short to Clymer, 15 November 1927, quoted in Short, "Historical Sketch," p. 5.

57. Sklar (1975), p. 134.

58. Short (1927), pp. 69–70.

59. Lyons (1969).

60. MPRC, Box 1, MPRC history file, p. 7.

61. Seabury to Short, 10 October 1927, MPRC, Box 15, Seabury file.

62. Short, handwritten note, n.d., but probably preparatory to Short letter to Seabury of 18 October 1927, ibid.

63. Short to Seabury, 18 October 1927, ibid.

64. Seabury to Short, 13 December 1927, ibid.

65. Ibid.

66. Short to Seabury, 14 December 1927, ibid.

67. Short to Seabury, 27 December 1927, ibid.

68. Minutes of 15 December 1928, ibid.

69. A letter from Clymer to Short reveals that Short had offered to contact Chief Justice William Howard Taft on behalf of the efforts of the Payne Fund to obtain backing for this endeavor. This letter also contains a fascinating paragraph in which Clymer asks Short, "Will you be thinking in any odd moments about a letter you might write to Colonel Lindbergh?"

Apparently "a number of people . . . are endeavoring to show Lindbergh why he should not accept offers being made which would require a year and a half of his time in Hollywood on a motion picture. . . . The general idea is to show Lindbergh that he can serve the nation better by not affiliating with the motion pictures, which are not endorsed by 50% of our intelligent people, but rather keeping clear for a real service through youth." Clearly, at this stage the Payne Fund officers were as enthusiastic about challenging the morality of movies as was Short. Clymer to Short, 3 November 1927, MPRC, Box 5, Payne Fund file.

70. "Discussion with Mrs. Bolton," 15 November 1927, PFP, C28 f542.

71. Clymer to Bolton, 12 January 1928, MPRC, Box 5, Clymer file.

72. Clymer to Short, 23 January 1928, ibid.

73. For more information on this aspect of the Hays Office's operations see Shenton (1971).

74. In a letter to Mrs. Bolton in December 1928, Short quoted Skinner as saying that "Mr. Bolton is very much afraid that your name will be brought in, in some way, as part of an attack on the motion picture industry with consequences to Mr. Bolton politically which would be ruinous." Short to Mrs. Bolton, 15 December 1928, PFP, C1 f24.

75. Of course, from the historian's point of view, this deliberate attempt to maintain secrecy about the organization of the research program is precisely why we knew so little about the history of the PFS until the archival documents were made available.

76. Report from Short to file, 6–9 July 1928, PFP, C28 f542.

77. "Program of Business," 22 August 1928, PFP, C28 f555.

78. Clymer to Short, 25 September 1928, MPRC, Box 5, Clymer file.

79. Short to Clymer, 27 September 1928, ibid. It was also in this letter that Short indicated a potential for the production of films, presumably under the auspices of the junior extension university that Mrs. Bolton was trying to create. He noted: "If, however, this situation [the vertical integration of the motion picture industry] should be changed either by divorcing the producing and distributing agencies from theater ownership, or by the growth in the homes in the country of a demand for pictures of a kind and grade that are not now in existence, production might be feasible." This discussion would periodically surface during the next four years. George A. Skinner, former president of Educational Film Corporation of America, tried to enlist the Payne Fund in producing educational films, and there was some discussion of this issue. See the memorandum from Crandall to Short, 1 October 1928, PFP, C28 f555.

80. Clymer and Crandall to Short, 19 October 1928, MPRC, Box 5, Clymer file.

81. PFP, C28 f555, p. 2.

82. Short to Bolton, 5 November 1928, PFP, C28 f555.

83. Clymer to Bolton, 21 November 1928, PFP, C28 f555.
84. Ibid.
85. Seabury to Short, 13 December 1928, MPRC, Box 15, Seabury file.
86. Short to Seabury, 14 December 1928, ibid.
87. Clymer to Bolton, 27 November 1928, PFP, C28 f555.
88. Clymer to Bolton, 18 December 1928, PFP, C2 f24; emphasis added.
89. Ibid.
90. Ibid.
91. In a letter to Mrs. Bolton dated 20 December 1928, Ella Crandall also discussed the committee meeting earlier that month. Her impressions were a little more forthcoming about how the "friends of the movies" really felt. She noted: "What he [Short] does not know is that Mrs. Gilman has positively contradicted herself regarding her belief in Mr. Short's program. Obviously she and Miss Stecker were deeply influenced by Mr. Seabury's [resignation] letter. Mr. Skinner never granted any practical value for the psychological studies. Yet all of these people voted emphatically for them at the meeting." Crandall also suggested that Short would "be compelled to reconstruct his Committee" as a result of this conference. PFP, C2 f24.
92. Letter of contract from Maxwell to Short, 28 December 1933, PFP, C29 f566.
93. Crandall to Short, 2 March 1934, ibid.
94. Crandall to Short, 15 March 1934, ibid.
95. Maxfield to Blaine, 14 November 1934, ibid.
96. Finley to Crandall, 18 February 1935, ibid.
97. Crandall to Finley, 25 February 1935, ibid.
98. Camille Cavalier to Mrs. Walter McNab Miller, 5 April 1935, MPRC, Box 1, MPRC history file.
99. The MPRC files contain material dated as late as 1946, but some of it may have come from Wilbur's own files. There is no clear date of the dissolution of the MPRC; it just seems to have faded away.
100. In 1929 the estimated total spent on admission to movies was $720 million; this declined to a low point of $482 million in 1932, but was back up to $735 million by 1940. Jowett (1976), p. 473.
101. For details on this issue see Jowett (1976), pp. 233–259; Maltby (1993) pp. 37–72; and Black (1994).
102. In his letter to Crandall on 4 December 1934, Charters reviewed his work with the Payne Fund since 1928. At the end of this lengthy recounting, he wrote: "I will have had seven years of sport during which a germ of investigation grew into a sturdy tree with fruits of substance, during which the findings of research were translated into action, while hundreds of thousands of children were developing discriminatory tastes toward the movies and while the cultural forces of the nation were being welded to

produce an instrument of integration, coordination and improvement." PFP, C28 f551.

2. Movie-Made Social Science

1. See Furner (1975); Ross (1991). On numerous occasions Charters praised Short's grasp of the studies. See, e.g., "Report of 29–31 May 1931 Conference," "General Remarks after Afternoon Session, 31 May," p. 15, MPRC, Box 15, file 1931.
2. Short, "Historical Sketch of the Payne Fund Studies," August 1928, MPRC, Box 1, MPRC history file, pp. 4–5.
3. Charters, "A Ten Year Adventure, 1928–1938," PFP, C7 f130, p. 2; Short to Clymer, 13 March 1928, PFP, C30 f595; Short, "Historical Sketch," pp. 4–5.
4. See Bulmer (1984).
5. Short, "Director's Report," July 1928, PFP, C30 f595; Waples (1953), p. 33; see also Charters (1927).
6. Short, "Director's Report."
7. Short, "Historical Sketch," p. 9. Securing adequate funding for the massive research program would be Short's ongoing concern.
8. Charters, "A Ten Year Adventure," p. 2; Short, "Director's Report"; see also Thurstone (1928). Personal connections shaped the research staff in many ways. W. W. Charters, Freeman, Thurstone, Park, Blumer, Hauser, Peterson, Jessie Charters, Dale, Thrasher and Cressey were all University of Chicago faculty or alumni/alumnae. Charters recommended numerous friends, such as Stoddard, Peters, Renshaw and Ben Wood for involvement in the PFS.
9. Charters, "A Ten Year Adventure," p. 2.
10. See Munsterberg (1916); Lynd and Lynd (1929); Fox (1983); see also extensive bibliographies in Jowett (1976) and Austin (1989). Thrasher (1927) included a chapter titled "Movies and Dime Novels."
11. Waples (1953), p. 33; Short, "Historical Sketch," p. 9; Short to Charters, 8 November 1928, MPRC, Box 5, Charters file; Dale (1953).
12. "Organization of the Study Program of the National Committee for the Study of Social Values in Motion Pictures; a Digest from the Minutes of December 15, 1928," PFP, C30 f596, p. 7.
13. See Bulmer (1984) and Hammersley (1989) for historical treatments of this issue.
14. Short, "Director's Quarterly Report," January–March 1929, PFP, C30 f596.
15. Charters to Clymer, 23 February 1929, PFP, C28 f542.
16. Charters recalled, "Professor Snedden and Mr. Short tried their hands at it

but nothing that was prepared seemed to the Director of the study [Charters] to quite do justice to the demands for breadth of conception and adequacy of style." Charters, "A Ten Year Adventure," p. 3; Short, "The Motion Picture as a Molder of the National Character," 13 June 1930, MPRC, Box 5, Short file; Short to Charters, 14 June 1929, CP, Short file; "Moving Picture Study," 1928 (mimeograph copy marked up c. 1934), CP, Short file.

17. See Holaday and Stoddard (1933); Forman (1932b), p. 54.

18. Short, "Payne Fund Motion Picture Research Project," 1 July 1929, PFP, C30 f595, p. 9; Charters to May, 3 May 1932, CP, May file; Short to Charters, 5 December 1929, CP, Short file.

19. Chisman (1976), p. 39; May to Charters, 21 December 1928, CP, May file; see also Fleming (1967).

20. Short to Charters, 11 September 1929, PFP, C28 f543.

21. May to Charters, 25 April 1932, CP, May file; Charters to May, 3 May 1932, CP, May file; see also May and Shuttleworth (1933).

22. See Peterson and Thurstone (1933).

23. See Dysinger and Ruckmick (1933) and Forman (1932b), p. 16.

24. Short to Charters, 3 September 1929, CP, Short file; see also Renshaw, Miller and Marquis (1933).

25. Park, "Suggestions for a Study of the Influence of Moving Pictures on Juvenile Delinquency," [1928], MPRC, Box 12, Blumer file.

26. Ibid., p. 3. Park thought the possibility that movies led young women to dream of going to Hollywood would be interesting and useful to study. "My impression is that the movies have had much greater influence upon young women than upon young men" (p. 4). See transcript of November 1928 conference in Columbus, CP, file DB400, pp. 289, 300; Park to Short, 23 January 1929, MPRC, Box 12, Blumer file; Short to Park, 21 April 1930, PFP, C28 f558.

27. Park to Short, 22 December 1928, MPRC, Box 12, Blumer file; Blumer to Charters, 19 April 1929, MPRC, Box 5, Charters file.

28. Thrasher to Charters, 11 February 1929, CP, Thrasher file.

29. As Charters recalled," Studies were laid out in conference. The investigators went home and worked. At least once a year they came back in conference, reported progress and accepted mutual criticism." Charters, "A Ten Year Adventure," p. 17; Charters to May, 3 May 1932, CP, May file; Short to Charters, 5 December 1929, CP, Short file.

30. Thurstone to Charters, 17 September 1929, MPRC, Box 5, Charters file.

31. Short, "Payne Fund Motion Picture Research Project," 22–23 June 1929, PFP, C30 f595, p. 10; Short, "Director's Report, August 1–October 15, 1929," PFP, C30 f597; L. C. Marshall, an economist in the law program at Johns Hopkins University (and another old acquaintance of Charters), proposed an investigation of the influence of Hollywood films and the movie

business around the globe. Despite Short's championing of Marshall's plan, the Payne Fund declared that studies of any facet of the movie industry itself fell outside the PFS, and turned the project down. Short, "Director's Report, May–July 1929," PFP, C30 f597.

32. Charters to Crandall, 7 November 1929, PFP, C28 f542; Short to Charters, 11 September 1929, PFP, C28 f557; Short to Charters, 26 September 1929, CP, Short file.

33. Charters to Short, 1 October 1929, CP, Short file; Short, "The Motion Picture as a Molder of the National Character."

34. Figures cited in "Report of May 29–31, 1931 Meeting," p. 23.

35. Charters to Clymer, 23 February 1929, PFP, C28 f542; Charters to Short, 4 October 1929, MPRC, Box 5, Charters file; Charters to Short, 13 December 1929, MPRC, Box 5, Charters file.

36. See Dale (1953). Content analysis is thought to have been fully developed only with Bernard Berelson's *Content Analysis in Communications Research* (1952); see Chisman (1976), p. 42. See also Short, "Proceedings of Annual Research Conference, June 1929," 1 July 1929, CP, Short file, pp. 7, 16.

37. Thurstone, "Summary of Work of the Payne Fund," 9 June 1930, CP, Thurstone file, pp. 1–10; see also Peterson and Thurstone (1933), pp. 13–15.

38. Short to Charters, 19 December 1929, CP, Short file.

39. Short to Charters, 13 February 1920, MPRC, Box 5, Charters file; Short to May, 2 July 1930, PFP, C28 f558.

40. "Report of May 29–31, 1931 Meeting," p. 24.

41. See Peters (1933). Short's frustration with Peters stemmed from Peters's statements that he attended the movies frequently with his wife and did not think they did any harm. Short to Peters, 16 June 1931, CP, Peters file.

42. "Report of May 29–31, 1931 Meeting," "Publications Session, 31 May," p. 7.

43. Orville Crays, "Report to Dr. W. W. Charters – Boys' Club Study of Motion Pictures," 9 May 1929, MPRC, Box 5, Charters file; Thrasher, Nelson, Crays and Whitley, "The First Year of the Motion Picture Study at New York University," June 1930, MPRC, Box 5, Charters file. Thrasher reported that Nelson and Whitley would take over; Short to Charters, 5 May 1920, MPRC, Box 5, Charters file.

44. "Report of May 29–31, 1931 Conference," Blumer summary, p. 12; Short to Blumer, 11 January 1932, MPRC, Box 4, Blumer file.

45. See Blumer (1933); Blumer and Hauser (1933).

46. Blumer, "Private Monograph on Movies and Sex," MPRC, Box 5, Blumer file; Hauser, "Motion Pictures in Penal and Correctional Institutions: A Study of the Reactions of Prisoners to Movies," Master's thesis, University

of Chicago, 1933, pp. 36, 48, 66. Blumer was willing to continue plugging away on links between film viewing, delinquency and crime, but Charters was skeptical: "I am inclined to think that Dr. Blumer would not be able after an extended period of study to establish the causal relationship between the movies and crime," he wrote Short. "I am lead [sic] to this conclusion in part because Shuttleworth and May could not establish it. The best they could do was to say that delinquency and frequent attendance at the movies went hand in hand. You will note further that in the same area Thurstone's assistants felt that they were unable to establish a causal relationship." Charters to Short, 13 October 1931, MPRC, Box 4, Charters file.

47. "Report of May 29–31, 1931 Conference," "May 31, General Remarks" section, pp. 1–2, 5.
48. Ibid., pp. 2–3.
49. Ibid., p. 1.
50. Ibid., pp. 6–7.
51. Ibid., p. 8.
52. Ibid., pp. 3, 5, 14.
53. Ibid., pp. 9–10.
54. Ibid., pp. 11, 13.
55. See Ross (1928), pp. 76, 179; Short to Charters, 3 May 1929, MPRC, Box 5, Charters file.
56. Short to Charters, 15 May 1929, PFP, C30 f597.
57. Charters to Short, 20 May 1929, PFP, C30 f597.
58. Charters to Crandall, 31 January 1920, PFP, C28 f542. Charters wrote, "We ought to get this material if we can get it without notoriety. I do not feel that it is so important that we should make ourselves into martyrs, but there is no necessity of making martyrs of ourselves, if we are careful not to cut across the taboos in the minds of unscientific people." The Payne Fund board would go along with a sex behavior study if it was sponsored and partially funded by some other responsible agency, such as the YMCA or YWCA. In the spring of 1930, Short unsuccessfully applied to the Ys and to the American Social Hygiene Association for research support. Crandall to Charters, 28 January 1930, PFP, C28 f542; Short to Charters, 14 March 1930; Short to Charters, 5 May 1930; Charters to Short, 20 May 1930, all MPRC, Box 5, Charters file; Charters to Thrasher, 10 June 1932, MPRC, Box 5, Charters file.
59. Short to Charters, 14 March 1930, MPRC, Box 5, Charters file.
60. Cressey to Short, 27 November 1931, MPRC, Box 5, Cressey file.
61. Short to Charters, 1 December 1931, MPRC, Box 5, Charters file.
62. Thrasher to Charters, 14 June 1932, CP, Thrasher file; Charters to Thrasher, 20 June 1932, MPRC, Box 5, Charters file.

63. Cressey to Charters, 2 March 1934, CP, Thrasher file.
64. In May 1931, Whitley had reported that what went on in the movie theater was just as important as what was on the screen, and that movies were often just "accentuating a pattern already in existence." "Report of the May 29–31, 1931 Conference," Thrasher group presentation, pp. 6–7. See Thrasher (1938), p. 469; Cressey (1932a), pp. 238–240; Cressey, "The Community – A Social Setting for the Motion Picture," unpublished typescript (c. 1932), MPRC, Box 5, reprinted in Chapter Four of this volume.
65. Short to Charters, 15 January 1932, MPRC, Box 5, Charters file; Research staff of NYU Motion Picture Study to Charters, 1 August 1934, CP, Thrasher file; Cressey to Charters, 5 August 1934, Cressey to Charters, 15 February 1935, both CP, Cressey file; Thrasher to Charters, 10 February 1936, CP, Thrasher file.
66. "Nearly all the investigators wanted more space to tell their story to the public than was available," Dale (1953) later recalled. Stoddard wrote apologetically to Charters: "It is much worse than I thought from casual inspection. Holaday has displayed a positive genius for saying things the wrong way, and with the greatest amount of tedium." Stoddard scrawled on the cover of Holaday's report, "This mss simply doesn't come to life in its present form. Even though I am familiar with the problem, the style (general and detailed) acts as a detriment, a frustration, an obfuscation! In short it is the rottenest mss that ever disguised a study of this scope." Stoddard to Charters, 18 November 1931, CP, Stoddard file; May to Charters, 25 April 1932, CP, May file; Charters to May, 3 May 1932, CP, May file; Stoddard to Charters, 26 January 1933, MPRC, Box 5, Charters file; May to Charters, 25 April 1932, CP, May file; Short to Charters, 8 January 1932, MPRC, Box 5, Charters file; Blumer to Short, 8 July 1933, MPRC, Box 4, Blumer file; Short to Blumer, 11 July 1933, MPRC, Box 4, Blumer file.

3. Aftermath

1. Schumach (1964); Randall (1968).
2. See Inglis (1947). Under the Production Code, the Hollywood West became populated by cowboys and outlaws, but there were no prostitutes – only jolly "dancing girls." Giving birth in Hollywood films became a behind-closed-doors process that required a lot of hot water.
3. Including B pictures, serials and, eventually, in 1937, feature-length animated cartoons.
4. Modeled on the teetotaler pledge, these were pledges not to patronize "indecent" films; see Facey (1945), Table I. The emergence of the Legion of Decency's publications is detailed in Facey (1945), pp. 65–68.

5. The reference is probably to Chapin Hall, "Attack on Movies Stuns Hollywood," *New York Times*, 8 July 1934.

6. Report on the work of the Payne Fund, 1935, PFP, C6 f127.

7. Adler (1937).

8. Forman (1932 a, b, c).

9. The widespread coverage is attested to in the extensive files of press clippings, PFP, Cc33–34 ff629–646. One or two syndicated articles by Short appeared after his death in January 1935. Ibid.

10. Kellogg (1933); Rorty (1933a, b).

11. Forman himself reviewed them in the *New York Times Book Review*, 24 December 1933, which to contemporary eyes was scandalous.

12. On 6 November 1935, Charters reported to the authors that there had been strong sales of his own volume and of Dale's *How to Appreciate Motion Pictures,* and that as for the rest of the volumes about half the stock had been sold. PFP, C63 f1229. A letter to the Payne Fund from Macmillan, 11 June 1947, proposed selling the remaining stock to a jobber, which was agreed to. PFP, C63 f1229.

13. *Hollywood Reporter*, 25 May 1934.

14. Adler (1937), pp. 274–275.

15. Ibid., p. 269.

16. Short (1928).

17. In a speech to the Society of Motion Picture Engineers on 24 April 1933 (PFP, C66 f1284), Short imagined printing having just been invented. "Suppose ... that the first use it was put to was of the risqué sort, so that it began its career in disrepute, in back alleys, among the educationally and socially unelite. Suppose half a dozen quick and enterprising men, highly able but uneducated and of alien viewpoint, seized hold of it and developed a rip-roaring tabloid press, directed at the intellectual fourteen year-olds. ... The high hat portion of the people still love, cherish and devote themselves to their beautiful handmade books and manuscripts. Instead of helping even to develop the printing art for the lower classes, suppose the main concern of culture had so far been to check and safeguard the printing art by half-hostile criticism and censorship.... Would not a situation exist which would be ripe for the intervention and leadership of a group of socially-minded leaders, social workers, social scientists, laymen and women? – would it not be fitting ... to seek to find out who the potentially revolutionary powers [are] ... [who] should be harnessed and put to work in the service of civilization?"

18. Short, "Unoccupied Motion Picture Fields," PFP, C66 f1284.

19. Coolidge to Crandall, 8 March 1934, PFP, C30 f594.

20. Before her marriage, Mrs. Belmont was the British actress Eleanor Robson, for whom Shaw wrote *Major Barbara.*

21. See *Educational Screen*, 1 April 1934.

22. Short (1934).

23. "Trade gossip to the effect that Mrs. Belmont, like Dr. Lawrence A. Lowell, who preceded her, retired from the number one post after a disagreement with Rev. William A. Short, moving spirit of the organization, was derided by the executive committee." *Variety*, 3 July 1934.

24. "This week Dr. Short and his cabinet spent mostly in New York wondering who might be cast in the role so recently abandoned by Mrs. August Belmont, who went a-summering up in Maine and resigned the presidency just as the Motion Picture Research Council's publicity went into the deep eclipse shadows cast by the rise of the Legion of Decency." *Motion Picture Herald*, 14 July 1934.

25. Conant (1960).

26. Farber (1971).

27. On Protestant–Catholic differences see Schumach (1964), pp. 94–95; see also the detailed work of Black (1994).

28. Edgar Dale authored the final volume of the Payne Fund series in 1935, combining two studies, "Children's Attendance at Motion Pictures" and "The Content of Motion Pictures."

29. But see Jacobs (1990) for a beginning and Field (1952) for a British history.

30. These names are gleaned from letters in various files in the MPRC papers.

31. See R. S. Woodsworth, "Preliminary Report on Psychological Research on Motion Pictures Conducted in Columbia University in 1926," PFP, C66 f1283. May had earlier, however, written to Short that he was "very much impressed" with the overwhelming evidence amassed in *A Generation of Motion Pictures*: "I congratulate you heartily on the excellent beginning you have made." He knew, perhaps, on which side his bread was buttered. See May to Short, 14 August 1928, PFP, C28 f555. Short at one time considered May Charters's "strongest ally in the undertaking"; Short to Crandall, 3 February 1929, PFP, C28 f542.

32. These are preserved in MPRC, Box 12, Shuttleworth (1931–1932) file.

33. Mark A. May, "How Are the Movies Molding our Children?", address before members of the Massachusetts Civic League, n.d., probably early 1933, ibid; Shuttleworth (1932). Short's suspicions that May was less than a committed critic of the present state of the movies was correct. May was later recruited by Hays to his Advisory Committee on the Uses of Motion Pictures in Education, and in the group portrait reproduced by Moley (1945, p. 161) May is standing directly behind and leaning on Hays's chair. Incidentally, to Hays's right in that photograph is Edward E. Day, president of Cornell University, who was approached in 1945 to succeed Hays. He declined, and the offer was made to Eric Johnston. In 1946 Frederic Thrasher lent his name to a celebration of Hollywood's achievements

(Thrasher 1946). As "editor" he contributed a short, laudatory preface. No author is given, but the text celebrates gangster movies, saucy musicals and other material that was of concern to Short.

34. May to Short, 11 May 1933, MPRC, Box 12, Shuttleworth (1931–1932) file. May also reported that he had not seen the whole of the Forman manuscript, or any of the other final reports of the studies; see May to Short, 13 April 1933, ibid.

35. Memo, 19 November 1928, from the National Committee for the Study of Social Values in Motion Pictures [NCSSVMP] to the Payne Fund, PFP, C25 f555; also quoted in Short to Bolton, 5 November 1928, PFP, C25 f555.

36. Short to Clymer, 28 September 1928, PFP, C25 f555.

37. See NCSSVMP to the Payne Fund, ibid.

38. Short to Charters, 18 March 1931, MPRC, Box 5, Charters file.

39. Charters to Fisher, 24 June 1931, CP, general 1931 file.

40. Before his Payne Fund commission, Forman had published *In the Footprints of Heine* (Boston: Houghton Mifflin, 1910); *The Ideal Italian Tour* (Boston: Houghton Mifflin, 1911); *London: An Intimate Picture* (New York: McBride Nast, 1913); *The Captain of His Soul* (New York: McBride Nast, 1914); *Fire of Youth* (Boston: Little Brown, 1920); *The Man Who Lived in a Shoe* (Boston: Little Brown, 1922); *The Enchanted Garden* (Boston: Little Brown, 1923); *Guilt* (New York: Liveright, 1924); *The Pony Express, a Romance* (with scenes from the photoplay; New York: Grosset and Dunlap, 1925); *Sudden Wealth* (New York: Boni and Liveright, 1925); *Grecian Italy* (London: Jonathan Cape, 1927); and *The Rembrandt Murder* (New York: R. R. Smith, Inc., 1931). In his own curriculum vitae sent to Short (attachment to Forman to Short, 29 February 1932, MPRC, Box 13, Publication of Findings file) Forman listed another novel printed by the last-named publisher, *The Shadowed Garden*. Oddly, this is not listed in the *National Union Catalogue*.

41. Forman (1932a, b, c).

42. Charters to Thurstone et al., 2 January 1932, MPRC, Box 5, Charters file.

43. Charters to Forman, 21 January 1933, CP, Forman file.

44. See Charters to Short, 25 March 1933, MPRC, Box 5, Charters file.

45. See Short's twelve pages of detailed notes on the manuscript in MPRC, Box 8, Forman file, in which he, too, explicitly warns against seeming to have a bias against the movies. Yet his own views were also extreme: "The movie theater is an educational system, a school of conduct. . . . What the young child sees on the screen he accepts with much the same trustfulness as the fledgling in the nest accepts food from the mother bird." Short, "Unoccupied Motion Picture Fields." The place of women in his metaphors is often ambivalent. In his notes of a discussion with Dr. Ben D. Wood of Columbia we read: "An evil girl in a community will infect a whole group of boys in

spite of the fact that there are good girls in the same community." Short, notes on meetings, 15 and 16 August 1928, PFP, C28 f555. We might term this the "venereal theory of film influence." Compare Thrasher's proposal for "Special Case Studies of Motion Picture Theaters which are known or suspected to be Foci of Moral Infection," Thrasher notes to Charters, 9 May 1929, MPRC, Box 16, Thrasher file.

46. Forman to Charters (holograph), 27 January 1933, CP, Forman file.

47. Charters to Forman, 14 February 1933, MPRC, Box 5, Charters file.

48. Charters to Short, 25 March 1933, ibid.

49. Stoddard to Charters, 26 January 1933, ibid.

50. In a section called "Mirror of the World's Opinion," 17 November 1932, the *Christian Science Monitor* printed a short text headed "Movies and Morals" with the source line *New York Times*. The piece consists of two paragraphs reporting some unfavorable findings of the May–Shuttleworth study at Yale. There is no trace of it in the *New York Times* itself.

51. May letter, 3 January 1933, clipping in MPRC, Box 5, Charters file.

52. Short to Charters, 19 January 1933, ibid.

53. Charters to Short, 26 January 1933, ibid.

54. Short to Charters, 31 January 1933, ibid.

55. Short to Charters, 16 February 1933, ibid.

56. Thurstone to Charters, 29 September 1933, MPRC, Box 16, Thurstone file.

57. Cressey to Thrasher, 9 January 1933, MPRC, Box 5, Charters file.

58. Cressey memo to Thrasher, 17 March 1933, CP, Thrasher file.

59. Cressey (1938a); Inglis (1947), p. 22.

60. Thrasher to Charters, 20 March 1933, CP, Thrasher file.

61. The identification of the Mr. Rorty referred to in the MPRC papers as James Rorty is tentative. The report quoted in the text certainly differs in style from Rorty (1933a, b, c).

62. Rorty to Crandall, 16 January 1933, enclosed with Crandall to Charters, same date, PFP, C67 f1316.

63. Ella Phillips Crandall, secretary of the Payne Fund, wrote to Mrs. Bolton that Rorty's negative opinion of Forman's book led Charters to consider not publishing it and so "spare the Board of Directors an otherwise very difficult and unhappy task." Among other things, the Payne Fund had been persuaded to prefinance the book and would be reimbursed only from anticipated royalties. Crandall to Bolton, 17 January 1933, PFP, C28 f542.

64. Short, "Unoccupied Motion Picture Fields," p. 2.

65. *Motion Picture Herald*, 10 June 1933.

66. For details see Facey (1945). Regarding Jowett's claim (1976, pp. 226–227) that Hays, anticipating the outcry, convened the MPPDA Board of Directors on 7 March to reaffirm their responsibility and renew their commitment to the highest moral standards: either Hays was extraordinarily prescient

(since Forman's book did not appear until two months later) or he was responding to the general alarm among pressure groups, including the ever-noisier threats from the Roman Catholic hierarchy.

67. This provoked Terry Ramsaye to the rather brutal thought that the MPRC had ceased to serve any function: "A considerable part of the reason for the existence of the MPRC would appear to be to supply a career and activity for its staff, headed by Dr. William Harrison Short"; see *Motion Picture Herald*, 30 June 1934.

68. The formula for compromise was that there be "compensating moral value" for any venality that was portrayed. See Sargent (1963); Jowett (1990); Vaughn (1990); Black (1994).

69. Conant (1960).

70. Thrasher (1938); Cressey (1934, 1938a).

71. Charters, "A Ten Year Adventure," PFP, C7 f130, p. 18. In this document Charters also maintains that the PFS "crystallized public action . . . at the psychological moment." He also mentions that Edgar Dale sat in on some Legion organizing meetings and that the Payne Fund paid for the printing and distribution of two important speeches. "This indicates conclusively in my judgment that the Legion of Decency was a direct outcome of the Payne Fund Studies. For obvious reasons we should not want to make this claim in public but it is nevertheless a valid claim." Short also knew on which side his bread was buttered.

72. Young (1935). Short's notes of 14 August 1928 to the Payne Fund, PFP, C66 f1283, say that Young suggested Thrasher to Short during the latter's 1928 trip to the University of Michigan. Young did graduate work at Chicago from 1917 to 1919 and edited *Social Attitudes,* a group of papers by former students and colleagues of W. I. Thomas, including a distinguished roster of contributors such as Ellsworth Faris, Florian Znaniecki, Emory S. Bogardus, Robert Park, L. L. Barnard and Ernest W. Burgess. Thrasher was included and his paper dealt briefly with movies in the lives of boys.

73. Cantril, Gaudet and Herzog (1940). The research was conducted under the aegis of Paul Lazarsfeld.

74. Cantril (1935), p. 239.

75. Willey (1935), pp. 288, 289.

76. Louttit (1934), pp. 307, 315.

77. Krasker (1934), p. 383.

78. Meltzer (1935), p. 240; Shuttleworth and May (1933), p. 83.

79. See Thurstone (1931). A complete issue of the *Journal of Educational Sociology* (vol. 6, 1932) was devoted to papers explaining how the PFS research was being carried out. The guest editor was Frederic Thrasher.

80. Lasswell (1948).
81. Short, in "Unoccupied Motion Picture Fields," wrote of "half a dozen quick and enterprising men, highly able but uneducated and of alien viewpoint." Short was echoing phrases he may first have come across in Seabury's brief statement," "The Kind of Men Who Control the Motion Picture Industry," MPRC, Box 15, Seabury file. Zeroing in on Adolph Zukor, Marcus Loew, William Fox and Carl Laemmle, Seabury declared three of them to be of foreign birth. He cited Ramsaye as his source for the information that Laemmle was a former haberdasher; Fox a former cloth sponger; and Zukor a furrier as late as 1912. H. L. Mencken is quoted as describing "those in the industry who determine what subject matter the public of the world shall see as 'blacksmiths and pantspressers.' Mr. Ramsaye in the same article frankly admits that the so-called upper strata of control of the motion picture industry in the United States is now about 90% Jewish. Objectionable, not because they are Jewish but because it is unthinkable that America shall continue to entrust the amusements of her children to alien and uneducated men as it would be to turn over her schools, her pulpits or press to such men." This strain of nativism apparently wanted a glass ceiling over first-generation immigrants.
82. See Berelson (1952); Lazarsfeld and Rosenberg (1955); Danielson (1963). An instructive example is Linton and Jowett (1977), including their methodological Appendix B.
83. Fearing (1947); Handel (1950); Sklar (1975); Jowett (1976); Delia (1987).
84. Lowery and De Fleur (1988).
85. Klapper (1959).
86. See Mark A. May (1937, 1946, 1947); May and Lumsdaine (1958).
87. Thrasher (1946). Thrasher joined the Board of Directors of the National Board of Review. He also wrote a classic critique of the panic over horror comics and drew a parallel with the reformers' distress over movies, citing Cressey's work as squelching the latter (Thrasher 1949). In that article he lists himself as a member of the Attorney-General's Conference on Juvenile Delinquency and as a former secretary of the Society for the Prevention of Crime.
88. Baugh (1990).
89. See Thrasher, "The First Year of the Motion Picture Study" (1929), at New York University (Boys' Club Study, Frederic M. Thrasher, Director), MPRC, Box 16, Thrasher file. Jennifer Platt (1983) treats Cressey as a pioneer of the method of participant observation. An indication of how hard and deeply Cressey was thinking about these problems is a 104-page legal-sized typescript in MPRC, Box 6, Cressey file, entitled "A Chronological Review of Scholarly Interest and Research in the Psychological and

Social Influence of the Motion Picture." This is a critical *bibliographie raisonée* covering works up to 1933. It is a fitting precursor of Klapper (1959) and supplements the bibliography found in Jarvie (1970).

90. Katz and Lazarsfeld (1955), p. 16.

91. Thrasher (1938).

92. Adler is an interesting figure. Though born a Jew, he converted to Roman Catholicism. (Intriguingly, he never mentions the efforts of his fellow Catholics in the Legion of Decency in his 1937 book.) He had degrees in both philosophy and jurisprudence. His previous book had been on the social scientific study of crime (Adler 1933). He was an influential figure in Robert Hutchins's University of Chicago, where he was the brains behind the Great Books program (Adler 1977, chap. 8).

93. Both the statements of Moley (1938, p. 7) and Hays (1955, p. 459), in suspiciously similar wording, are ambiguous about the role they played in the making of Adler's book. The book's preface tells us that the industry asked Adler to write a report on the PFS. Adler gives a later version (1977, pp. 191–194).

94. Adler was notably severe with his Chicago colleague Herbert Blumer, although it must be admitted that Blumer seemed the most convinced of the researchers that Short's dire view of the movies was correct. Blumer had coveted the research director's job and tried to get the Payne Fund to finance his further research ideas.

95. Adler (1937), pp. 424–425; see Hays (1955), p. 459.

96. There was a piquant confrontation between Moley, Forman and C. C. Pettijohn (the MPPDA's Washington lobbyist) recorded in State of New York, *Proceedings of the Governor's Conference on Crime, the Criminal and Society, September 30 to October 3, 1935,* Albany, pp. 31–37, 306–322. Even heckling was a tactic the industry employed: Short was heckled by the MPPDA official Carl E. Milliken when he appeared before the Senate Inquiry into Rackets; see *New York Herald Tribune,* 25 November 1933. The same newspaper reported on 18 April 1934 that Pettijohn had "confronted" Forman at a luncheon speech at the Town Hall Club in New York City.

97. In a balanced and forceful review of Adler, Cressey (1938b) demolished his pretensions and did his very best to restore the scientific integrity of the Payne Fund Studies.

98. Hays (1955), pp. 458–459.

99. On the nature of public opinion in the United States see Jarvie (1992), pp. 13–14.

100. Lazarsfeld (1941).

101. See Lazarsfeld (1947); Austin (1983).

102. Lazarsfeld had been trained in Vienna under Buhler and was clearly, in this article, influenced by his encounter with Adorno.
103. Lazarsfeld (1941), p. 16.
104. Lazarsfeld in Kendall (1982), p. 61.
105. Adorno (1941); Herzog (1941, 1944); Arnheim (1944); Lowenthal (1944).
106. Wiese and Cole (1946); Kracauer (1947); Warner anthology (1948); Wolfenstein and Leites (1950).
107. Merton and Lazarsfeld (1943).
108. Psychologism is the doctrine that human society is not more than an aggregate of individual humans and their psychologies. The laws of society are envisaged as psychological laws. Sociologism, by contrast, emphasizes that social institutions cannot be explained by psychological laws; if anything, the reverse is the case. On the confusion of sociology with the psychology of social consciousness see Jarvie (1970).
109. Lasswell (1939); Cantril, Gaudet and Herzog (1940); Herzog (1941, 1944); Merton and Lazarsfeld (1944); Adorno (1941); Adorno et al. (1950); Warner and Henry (1948); Hovland, Lumsdaine and Sheffield (1949); Fearing (1950).
110. Jarvie (1985, 1987); Randall (1988).

4. The Lost Manuscript

1. MPRC, Box 5, Blumer file.
2. Because of the manner in which Blumer collected material through the autobiography method, these two studies are often considered to be the most controversial and also the most interesting.
3. These theories of "uniform" or "direct influences" originated in the concept of mass society developed by European social theorists at the turn of the century. Shearon Lowery and Melvin De Fleur (1983) note that "the mass society concept yielded a theory of mass communication effects in which the media were seen as powerful, and their effects both uniform and direct among the members of the mass society" (p. 21).
4. Cressey (1938a), p. 518.
5. Cressey to Short, 15 January 1934, MPRC, Box 5, Cressey file.
6. Cressey to Charters, 5 August 1934, CP, Cressey file.
7. Cressey to Charters, 15 February 1935, ibid.
8. Thrasher to Charters, 10 February 1936, CP, Thrasher file.
9. Cressey to Charters, 11 November 1936, CP, Cressey file.
10. Charters to Cressey, 19 November 1936, ibid.
11. Thrasher writes of it being on deposit there (1949, p. 199, n. 13).
12. See Thrasher (1932); Thrasher, Introduction to "The Final Report of the

Jefferson Park Branch of the Boys' Club of New York," Bureau of Social Hygiene Papers, Series 3.3, Boxes 11, 12, 13, Rockefeller Archive Center, North Tarrytown, New York.

THE COMMUNITY – A SOCIAL SETTING FOR THE MOTION PICTURE

1. [*Ed. note:* For more information on the community of Intervale, see the introduction above.]
2. Public Health Reports, New York City.
3. May Case Marsh, "Life and Work of Churches in Boys' Club Area" (Ph.D. dissertation, New York University, 1932), p. 57. [*Ed. note:* Marsh's study is referenced Thrasher (1932), p. 173; an excerpt from Marsh's dissertation is also listed as Appendix 11 of Thrasher, "Final Report of the Jefferson Park Branch of the Boys' Club of New York."]
4. Janet Fowler Nelson, "A Comparison of Boys' Club Members and Eligible Non-Members in Terms of Intelligence, Emotional Stability, and Educational Achievement; also a Comparison of Delinquents (in institutions) with Non-Delinquents, Living in a Delinquency (Boys' Club) Area in Terms of Intelligence and Emotional Instability," p. 19. [*Ed. note:* Nelson's report is listed as Appendix 13 of Thrasher, "Final Report of Boys' Club Study."]
5. Public Health Reports, New York City.
6. Quoted by Marsh, "Life and Work of Churches," pp. 55–56.
7. From U.S. Census data of 1920, 1930, and from the ecological studies of the area by Professor Thrasher. Another reflection of this congestion is seen in frequency of deaths of children in traffic. In but one year, 1927, in this community fifteen children were killed in traffic accidents. Marsh, "Life and Work of Churches," p. 24.
8. See Harvey W. Zorbaugh's discussion of "natural areas" in Ernest W. Burgess, *The Urban Community* (Chicago: University of Chicago Press, 1926), pp. 219–229.
9. John E. Jacobi, "Juvenile Delinquency in Boys' Club and Related Areas" (unpublished mss). [*Ed. note:* Jacobi's report is referenced in Thrasher, "Related and Subsidiary Studies of the Boys' Club Study."]
10. Quoted in Marsh, "Life and Work of Churches."
11. Quoted in Salvatore Cimilluca, "History of Boys' Club Community from 1880s to Date" (unpublished mss). [*Ed. note:* Cimilluca's report is referenced in Thrasher, "Related and Subsidiary Studies of the Boys' Club Study."]
12. Quoted in Marsh, "Life and Work of Churches."
13. Frederic M. Thrasher, "The Social Attitudes of Superior Boys in an Interstitial Community," in *Social Attitudes*, ed. Kimball Young (New York: Henry

Holt, 1932), pp. 256–258. [*Ed. note:* The "superior boys" attended DeWitt Clinton High School.]

14. Time after time in conducting this study it was discovered that a change in residence of but one or two short city blocks has resulted in the boy's giving up his old chums for ones residing in the same block. The boy's own explanation is typically as follows: "I don't chum with him now, he moved over to the next block; we just talk to each other now."

15. Robert L. Whitley, "Bad Boys" (unpublished mss), pp. 3–4. [*Ed. note:* This book manuscript probably no longer exists; the author most likely incorporated in it material from his published articles. See Whitley (1930, 1931, 1932a, b); see also Whitley, "Analysis of Case Studies of Problem Boys, Members and Non-Members of the Boys' Club, with Reference to the Influence of the Club upon Problem Behavior," Appendix 20 of Thrasher, "Final Report of the Boys' Club Study."]

16. Whitley, "Bad Boys."

17. Whitley, "Bad Boys."

18. Sydney R. Ussher, "Community Organization in a Boys' Club Area" (unpublished mss). [*Ed. note:* Ussher's report is referenced in Thrasher, "Related and Subsidiary Studies of the Boys' Club Study."]

19. See Annual Report for 1930 for the Committee of Fourteen of New York City, pp. 28–29, 40–41; see also Paul G. Cressey, *The Taxi-Dance Hall: A Sociological Study in Commercialized Recreation and City Life* (Chicago: University of Chicago Press, 1932).

20. Whitley, "Bad Boys," p. 55.

21. Adapted from Whitley, "Bad Boys," pp. 42–43.

22. Ussher, "Community Organization in a Boys' Club Area."

23. [*Ed. note:* See Shaw and Burgess (1930).]

24. It should be noted that it is not necessary that the account of this boy's activities be authentic in every detail for the document to be valid for use here. In any event this interview reveals much of the ideation and values of this young man and suggest the social world in which his life is being molded.

25. [*Ed. note:* Dates added in brackets are years of film's first release, taken from *Film Daily Yearbook*. Films may not have played in "Intervale" neighborhood theaters until six to twelve months later.]

26. Several instances are on record in which acquaintanceships made by boys, incidental to a recreational program, have paved the way for delinquency careers. In one instance, boys who were introduced to each other and became close friends through such a program later deserted these interests, became a predatory gang, and after quite a career were finally apprehended by Federal officers for extensive robbery from local mail boxes.

27. For the results of scientific research demonstrating the concentration of

delinquency see Clifford R. Shaw, *Delinquency Areas: A Study of the Geographic Distribution of School Truants, Juvenile Delinquents and Adult Offenders in Chicago* (Chicago: University of Chicago Press, 1929) and Shaw and Henry D. McKay, *Social Factors in Juvenile Delinquency* (National Commission on Law Observance and Enforcement Cause of Crime, Volume II, Government Printing Office, 1931). See also Frederic M. Thrasher, *The Gang, A Study of 1,313 Gangs in Chicago* (Chicago: University of Chicago Press, 1927). For conception of the interstitial area and delinquency, see Thrasher, *The Gang,* pp. 22–25.

28. Frederic M. Thrasher, "Juvenile Delinquency and Mercenary Crime," in *Crime for Profit: A Symposium on Mercenary Crime,* ed. Ernest D. MacDougall (Boston: Stratford, 1933).

29. Frederic M. Thrasher, "Social Attitudes of Superior Boys in an Interstitial Community."

30. See Nels Anderson and E. C. Lindeman, *Urban Sociology* (New York: Crafts, 1928), pp. 208–210; Niles Carpenter, *The Sociology of City Life* (New York: Longman, 1932); Cressey, *Taxi-Dance Hall,* pp. 240–243, 287.

31. Nelson, "Comparison of Intelligence and Emotional Stability."

32. Whitley, "Bad Boys," p. 39.

33. Ernest W. Burgess, *The Urban Community.*

34. Robert E. Park and Ernest W. Burgess, *The City* (Chicago: University of Chicago Press, 1925).

35. See articles by Roderick D. McKenzie in Burgess, *The Urban Community,* and Park and Burgess, *The City.*

36. Shaw, *Delinquency Areas.*

37. Adapted from Thrasher, *The Gang,* pp. 22–25.

38. Adapted from Thrasher, "Juvenile Delinquency and Mercenary Crime."

39. Thrasher, *The Gang,* pp. 22–23.

40. See Thrasher, "Juvenile Delinquency and Mercenary Crime" and Paul G. Cressey, "The Social Role of Motion Pictures in an Interstitial Area," *Journal of Educational Sociology* 6:4 (December, 1932), pp. 238–243.

41. From the reports of Orville Crays, 1930.

42. As an incidental part of this study the feature films offered each week in every theater in the area for 1929, 1930, and 1931 have been recorded. From a study of these reports it has been possible to make the above generalizations.

43. [*Ed. note:* Cressey may be using the term "mine run" in the same sense as the old colloquial phrase "run of the mine," meaning an average sample of what the industry turns out.]

44. From unpublished manuscript of Leo Rubin, student, New York University.

45. Rubin, unpublished mss.

46. Rubin, unpublished mss.

47. The questionnaires included one which was a sampling of the Boys' Club membership, another a group of boys affiliated with another recreational agency in the community, another a high school group, another a continuation school group, another approximately seven hundred boys of the seventh and eighth grades in public schools, and also a group of boys who had dropped out of the Boys' Club.

48. It should be noted that these replies are merely the boys' own estimates of their frequency in attendance at movies. The boys were asked in every case to be as careful as possible in estimating attendance and their replies in most cases represent their sincere efforts to judge attendance. Yet their replies are subject to all the variables which operate in such estimates. For instance, the greater movie attendance by Boys' Club members, as reported in Table I, may not indicate really that they attend more frequently. Instead, it may reflect merely that because Boys' Club members have been found to be more unstable emotionally, they may be merely more inaccurate in estimating their attendance. . . .

49. Obviously such replies as "seldom," "often," etc., cannot be reduced to numerical frequency. Deducting also those who report that they "never attend the movies" and those whose movie frequency is not known the net figure is 1,784.

50. Estimating the net time in school as 25 hours per week and 36 weeks per year as the conventional school calendar it may be said that the average child is in public school approximately 900 hours a year.

51. [Ed. note: At this point, Cressey presents Janet Fowler Nelson's comparative research on the intelligence test scores, emotional instability, educational achievements, truancy and delinquency rates, and frequency of movie attendance of various groups of boys in the interstitial area. This text and tabular material have been deleted here, but can be located in the original manuscript. This research is also discussed in Nelson (1932), and in text and appendixes of Thrasher, "Final Report of the Jefferson Park Branch of the Boys' Club."]

52. Average [intelligence score] for school boys in this community is, of course, low − 89 +.

53. Out of the 571 Boys' Club members who answered a question upon favorite "hobbies" only 6, but 1.05 percent of the group, mentioned attendance at motion pictures. Yet, of this Boys' Club group, the report is that they attend at an average rate of 1.98 times per week and but 9 report that they "never" attend the movies.

54. Whitley, "Bad Boys," Chapter 8.

55. Whitley, "Bad Boys."

56. Whitley, "Bad Boys," pp. 25–26.

57. A specialist in the community who deals much with cases involving venereal disease told me in an interview of six cases in the previous three months in which married women had met men in local movie theaters and subsequently had contracted a social disease from them.

58. Whitley, "Bad Boys."

59. Whitley, "Bad Boys."

60. From reports of a special investigator.

61. Report of an interview with a motion picture proprietor in the community.

62. Report of a special investigator.

63. Report of a special investigator.

64. See Part One of this report.

65. The practice in some community theaters, for instance, of asking notorious local gangsters to help on occasion in quelling by intimidation the boisterous conduct of some in the children's section of the theater has sometimes served to enhance the gangster's prestige in the eyes of the boy and on occasion has served to bring a youngster to the attention of the local "big shots."

66. From life histories materials of New York University Motion Picture Study.

67. Reports of a careful census conducted informally of attitudes towards movie actors and actresses by special investigator.

68. Report of a special investigator.

69. For a discussion of the significance of public stereotypes in conditioning/ attitudes toward an individual or groups of individuals or toward certain aspects of life, see Walter Lippmann, *Public Opinion* (New York: Harcourt Brace, 1922).

70. Dictation of a superior boy.

71. See Hugo Munsterberg, *The Photoplay: A Psychological Study* (1916) for a thorough discussion of this technological advantage of the cinema.

72. See discussion of this research method in Paul G. Cressey, "The Social Role of Motion Pictures in an Interstitial Area," *Journal of Educational Sociology* 6:4 (December, 1932), pp. 238–243.

73. [*Ed. note:* Cressey would develop this idea further in Cressey (1934).]

74. Report of a special investigator.

75. "Doorway to Hell" [1930], featuring Lew Ayres.

76. Report of a special investigator.

77. There is no evidence that this was actually used later in crime.

78. Report of a special investigator.

79. Report of a special investigator.

80. Report of a special investigator.

81. It should be clearly understood that there is no attempt here to claim that

motion pictures, as such, are the "cause of crime." Rather, it should be understood that the cinema is here regarded as contributory only in that it provides patterns for conduct later duplicated in the behavior of those who saw and apparently remember with considerable clarity the criminal acts shown in these photoplays. It should also be noted that in a large proportion of the cases investigated, the criminal patterns of delinquents were in no way traced to the motion picture. By way of illustration, see Part One of this report.

82. Giving names of notorious racketeers in the community. Names here are substituted.

83. Report of a special investigator.

84. In point of numbers, this film was second only to "Over the Hill" [1931] in the frequency with which boys indicate that it stirred them greatly and caused them to want to "do better."

85. Report of a special investigator.

86. Cagney and Robinson, without doubt, during 1930–1931 were the unquestioned "favorite actors" for the boys and young men in this community.

87. Whitley, "Bad Boys."

88. Report of a special investigator.

89. The attempt to compare the replies of 25 delinquent and 25 non-delinquent boys in this community to a standardized interview questionnaire.

90. The education indication of this "carry over" of patterns can be found in the frequent way of special words and phrases and certain familiar acts of movie heroes as well as mimicry. In one case . . . the mother reported that certain phrases were contained in the children's chatter for weeks and even months after witnessing the photoplay in which these particular words and phrases were used.

91. Report of a special investigator.

92. See by way of illustration the documents on file in this study indicating in part the use of a gangster photoplay as a means for "nerving oneself up" to do a "job."

93. Whitley, "Bad Boys."

94. It should be noted that the motion picture is not the only or in fact the chief source for sexual stimulation in this community. The talk on the street corners reeks with sex and there is in this community a clandestine description of pornographic pictures but also the recent development of pornographic films for use in the portable 16 millimeter projection machine. Also in this community there flourish burlesque shows which also pander to the sexual interest of the adolescent. The following is one account by an adolescent boy that has visited a burlesque show: "Burlesque, they show you good

stuff. Girls dance. They come out with little over their breasts. When something good dances out you get hot. Girls come out on boards in a middle of the orchestra. A couple of weeks ago they had some guys dancing with the girls on the stage. One old guy got hot and wanted to go for the girl on the stage. They threw him out. The bouncers are tough as hell. One guy offered a girl money once, in a box. These girls are street women. The guys pay their board. Some guy on my block had one. I wouldn't like that: hell, no."

5. The Intervale Study

1. Cressey to Charters, 5 August 1934, CP, Cressey file.
2. As Kathryn Fuller discovered from the alumni records of his alma mater, Oberlin College.
3. Cressey (1934, 1938a, b).
4. Once functionalist approaches became widespread in sociology (see Chapter Three), "social breakdown" became the preferred term.
5. The allusion is to Sumner (1907).
6. This issue of the intrusion of outside influences into local cultures was a key finding of the Lynds in 1929 and 1937. Cressey appears to be stressing how whole "patterns of life as unities" strike such communities as foreign and therefore unapproved.

NEW YORK UNIVERSITY MOTION PICTURE STUDY – OUTLINE OF CHAPTERS

1. [*Ed. note:* We believe the "Preliminary report" to be "The Community – A Social Setting for the Motion Picture"; see Chapter Four.]
2. [*Ed. note:* The Cinema Shops were a chain of women's ready-to-wear boutiques opened in department stores in U.S. cities in the 1930s that sold inexpensive copies of costumes worn by female stars in their current films. See Eckert (1978).]
3. [*Ed. note:* Cressey listed the research materials he had obtained by 1934: 43 movie life histories written by local boys; 60 movie life histories written by adults from outside the area; 10 case studies; 80 of the 850 movie essays written by DeWitt Clinton High School boys; 296 interviews on 19 films; 110 controlled interviews; 57 interviews with area delinquent boys; and 13 interviews with outside delinquents "who had been reported to have committed offenses 'because of the movies.' "]
4. Howard Becker, "Some Forms of Sympathy: A Phenomenological Analysis," *Journal of Abnormal Psychology and Social Psychology* 26 (1931–32), pp. 58–68.

5. Malcolm M. Willey and S. A. Rice, "Communication," in President's Research Commission on Social Trends, *Recent Social Trends in the United States* (New York: McGraw-Hill, 1933).

6. Student Movie Autobiographies and "Movies and Sex"

1. Blumer to Charters, 1 February 1929, CP, Blumer file. See Fuller (1992).
2. Blumer reported to Charters on this early, "fragmentary" evidence in April 1929: "I have started some preliminary analysis of these documents and am realizing the recurrence of certain definite experiences. There is no longer any question in my mind concerning the extent to which children's play becomes modeled after the picture shown on the screen. It is also clearly evident in the copying of mannerisms, gestures, poses, ways of dressing and beautification, and, last but not least, in the improvement of one's sex charms, in flirting, making love, kissing, and so forth. . . . What I am particularly interested in now is the extent to which motion pictures create interest, desires, ambitions and temptations rather than what is imitated after these are formed." Blumer to Charters, 6 April 1929, PFP, C29 f572. "Blumer Plan – Study of Motion Pictures," n.d. [c. 1929], PFP, C29 f572. The third and fourth autobiographies in the appendix of *Movies and Conduct* were also found in the MPRC collection. Short to Blumer, 2 April 1929, MPRC, Box 4, Blumer file.
3. See "Autobiography of My Motion Picture Experiences" and "Autobiography of Number 30," this chapter.
4. Three recent Blumer intellectual biographies hardly mention the two Payne Fund studies, which account for half of Blumer's published monographs.
5. Blumer (1933), p. xi.
6. Blumer to Charters, 2 March 1929, MPRC, Box 4, Blumer file.
7. Ibid. Blumer played college football at the University of Missouri and professional football for the Chicago Cardinals for six seasons, from 1925 to 1930 and in 1933. He was named an all-American college player (guard) in 1928, the year of his doctoral defense.
8. Blumer to Short, 22 December 1931, MPRC, Box 4, Blumer file; Short to Charters, 8 January 1932, MPRC, Box 5, Charters file. Short soon learned that "Movies and Sex" would be difficult to publish. He showed the manuscript to one adviser, sociologist Ben Wood of Columbia University, who warned that it was "fit only for medical and professional readers." "I think the monograph should be very limited in its circulation," Wood noted, "because of the unavoidable pornographic elements in the materials presented." Short to Wood, 15 January 1932; Wood to Short, 20 January 1932, both MPRC, Box 4, Blumer file.
9. Blumer to Short, 14 March 1933, MPRC, Box 4, Blumer file; Blumer to

Charters, 16 January 1933, MPRC, Box 4, Blumer file; Blumer to Forman, 16 January 1933, MPRC, Box 4, Blumer file.

THE MOTION PICTURE AUTOBIOGRAPHIES

1. For the films we could identify, date given is year of film's release to first-run theaters. Viewers at small-town and neighborhood movie theaters, however, may not have seen these films until six to twelve months later.
2. Paragraph used in Blumer (1933), p. 171; writer identified as "female, 20, white sophomore."
3. "A quiet, refined, able college girl" is handwritten across the top of the manuscript page.
4. Passage found in Blumer (1933), pp. 18–19; writer identified as "female, 19, white college junior."
5. Passage found in Blumer (1933), p. 181; writer identified as "female, 20, Jewish college sophomore."
6. Passage found in Blumer (1933), p. 163; writer identified as "female, 20, white college sophomore."
7. Passage found in Blumer (1933), p. 185; writer identified as "female, 20, white college sophomore."
8. Passage found in Blumer (1933), p. 177; writer identified as "male, 20, white, Jewish, college junior."
9. Passage found in Blumer (1933), p. 130; writer identified as "female, 21, white college junior."
10. Passage found in Blumer, "Movies and Sex"; writer identified as "male, 21, white university senior."
11. Passage found in Blumer (1933), p. 81; writer identified as "female, 20, white college sophomore."
12. Three paragraphs found in Blumer (1933), pp. 105–106; writer identified as "college girl of nineteen."
13. Passage found in Blumer, "Movies and Sex;" writer identified as "male, 20, white university junior."
14. Passage found in Blumer, "Movies and Sex;" writer identified as "female, 21, white college junior."
15. Passage found in Blumer (1933), p. 63; writer identified as "female, 19, white college sophomore."
16. Passage found in Blumer (1933), p. 43; writer identified as "female, 17, white high school junior." In the book, Blumer omitted the phrase "I know better now."
17. Two paragraphs found in Blumer (1933), pp. 154–155; writer identified as "female, 16, white high school junior."

18. Passage found in Blumer (1933), p. 47; writer identified as "female, 16, white high school junior."
19. Passage found in Blumer, "Movies and Sex;" writer identified as "male, 21, university senior."

PRIVATE MONOGRAPH ON MOVIES AND SEX

1. Passage found in Blumer autobiographies, "Case 7: [Untitled]," in this volume.
2. Passage found in Blumer autobiographies, "Case 6: The Effects the Movies Have Had on Me," in this volume; manuscript page 35 in Blumer.
3. Passage found in Blumer autobiographies, "Autobiography Concerning the Effect of Moving Pictures on My Life" (not included in this volume), manuscript page 26.
4. Passage found in Blumer autobiographies, "Case 10: My Movie Experiences," in this volume; manuscript page 63 in Blumer.
5. Passage found in Blumer autobiographies, "Movies and Their Effect upon Me" (not included in this volume), manuscript page 21.

Appendix A

1. Summary of the Payne Fund's Activities in Radio, undated memorandum, approximately June 1933, PFP, C40 f768.
2. Ibid.; Charters to Morgan, 31 January 1931, PFP, C68 f1343; Agenda, Meeting of the Board of Directors of the Payne Fund, 18–20 April 1930, PFP, C56 f1066.
3. Perry to Clymer, 7 January 1931, PFP, C68 f1343.
4. See, for classic statements, Bagdikian (1992); Herman and Chomsky (1988). For a more extended treatment of this theme see McChesney (1991a).
5. I review this aspect of U.S. broadcasting history in greater detail in McChesney (1993a), ch. 2. Most of the issues discussed in this appendix concerning radio broadcasting are covered at length in this book. For those wishing only a summary of the book's argument, see McChesney (1993b).
6. "The Menace of Radio Monopoly," *Education by Radio*, 26 March 1931, p. 27; "The Power Trust and the Public Schools," *Education by Radio*, 10 December 1931, p. 150; "Radio Censorship and the Federal Communications Commission," *Columbia Law Review*, 39 (March 1939): 447; 97 percent figure cited in Boddy (1990), p. 36.
7. Martin Codel, "Networks Reveal Impressive Gains," undated, sometime in January 1931, entry in scrapbook for North American Newspaper Alliance, news service that covered radio, among other topics, for approximately

sixty U.S. daily newspapers in the early 1930s. In Martin Codel papers, State Historical Society of Wisconsin, Madison, vol. 61 (hereafter cited as NANA); Hilmes (1990), p. 52.

8. Volkening (1930), pp. 396–400; Rosen (1980), p. 12; Barnouw (1966), p. 270.

9. Armstrong Perry, "The Ohio School of the Air and Other Experiments in the Use of Radio in Education," 29 May 1929, PFP, C69 f1353.

10. Perry to Clymer, 6 April 1929, PFP, C56 f1067.

11. Ibid; Clymer to Executive Committee, Department of Superintendence, National Education Association, 6 April 1929, PFP, C56 f1067.

12. Perry to Clifton, 21 August 1929, PFP, C56 f1068.

13. *Official Report of Proceedings Before the Federal Communications Commission on Section (307)s of the Communications Act of 1934,* Smith & Hulse, Official Reporters (Washington, D.C.: Federal Communications Commission, 1935), pp. 180–249.

14. Advisory Committee on Education by Radio (1930), pp. 35–37.

15. Ibid., p. 76.

16. Cooper to Shipherd, 31 March 1930, Office of Education papers, RG 12, National Archives, Washington, D.C., Box 31 (hereafter cited as OEP); Perry to Crandall, 17 March 1930, PFP, C56 f1069.

17. Cooper to Presidents of Land Grant Institutions Having Broadcasting Stations, undated, Summer 1930, OEP Box 32; Perry (1930), pp. 80–81.

18. Crandall to Perry, 9 July 1930, PFP, C56 f1070.

19. Crandall to Perry, 17 July 1930, PFP, C56 f1070; Crandall, "Memorandum of Conference with Mr. Perry," 23 July 1930, PFP, C69 f1352.

20. Much of this correspondence is in the Herbert Hoover papers, Herbert Hoover Presidential Library, West Branch, Iowa, Commerce series, Box 148. See, in particular, Cooper to Wilbur, 8 December 1930; for RCA's attempt to influence Bolton see memorandum of meeting between Mrs. Bolton and Mr. Dunham, 29 October 1930, PFP, C69 f1352.

21. Perry to Crandall, 14 October 1930, PFP, C56 f1070; "Proposed Plan of Action," 2 October 1930, PFP, C69 f1352.

22. Minutes of the Conference on Educational Radio Problems Stevens Hotel, Chicago, 13 October 1930, at the Invitation of the U.S. Commissioner of Education, OEP Box 31.

23. The nine groups included the NEA, the National Association of State Universities, the National University Extension Association, the Association of College and University Broadcasting Stations, the Association of Land Grant Colleges and Universities, the National Council of State Superintendents, the Jesuit Education Association, the National Catholic Education Association and the American Council on Education.

24. Minutes, 13 October 1930, OEP Box 31; Morgan to Davis, 8 March 1932, PFP, C47 f901.

25. Crandall to Perry, 2 December 1930, PFP, C56 f1071.

26. Bolton to Morgan, 17 June 1932, PFP, C42 f812.

27. Darrow to Clymer, 3 February 1931, PFP, C68 f1343.

28. Perry to Klauber, 9 March 1931, PFP, C55 f1052.

29. J. E. Morgan (1931b), p. 10.

30. Wright to Reid, 26 May 1930, PFP, C41 f796.

31. Perry (1935), p. 26; Perry, "Report of the Service Bureau," March 1931, PFP, C38 f743; Lohnes to Tyler, 10 January 1933, PFP, C44 f854.

32. See Morgan and Bullock (1911); for an example of Morgan's anticorporate beliefs see J. E. Morgan (1934a), pp. 227–229.

33. J. E. Morgan (1931a), p. 128.

34. Ibid., pp. 123, 128.

35. Ibid., pp. 120–121.

36. J. E. Morgan (1932), p. 79; Morgan to McAndrew, 20 September 1932, Joy Elmer Morgan papers, National Education Association, Washington, D.C., 1932 correspondence, FCB 2, Drawer 3.

37. Tyler to Cunningham, 2 November 1933, PFP, C47 f916.

38. "The Fittest Survive," *Broadcasting*, 15 January 1933, p. 16; " 'Listeners Society,' " *Broadcasting*, 1 April 1933, p. 14; "When Educators Differ," *Broadcasting*, 1 June 1933, p. 20; "Exit Mr. Morgan," *Broadcasting*, 15 September 1935, p. 30.

39. Coltrane, "A Brief Statement in Support of Representative Fulmer's Resolution for a Study of Radio Broadcasting," 2 March 1933, PFP, C54 f1034.

40. Brackett to Beaird, 15 December 1931, National Association of Educational Broadcasters papers, State Historical Society of Wisconsin, Madison, Box 1a, General Correspondence 1932 (hereafter cited as NAEBP).

41. Perry, "Institutes for Education by Radio," December 1935, PFP, C52 f986.

42. Brackett to Charters, 27 August 1931, NAEBP, Box 1a, General Correspondence, 1929–1931.

43. Summary of Miss Crandall's Discussions with Dr. Charters, 14 March 1931, PFP, C69 f1352.

44. Radio Research Work at Ohio State University, 6 December 1933, PFP, C69 f1352.

45. Morgan to Coltrane, 22 November 1932, PFP, C41 f783.

46. Evans to Woehlke, 18 October 1932, PFP, C60 f1167; Memorandum re Conference, Dr. Joy Elmer Morgan and Miss Crandall, 1 October 1932, PFP, C42 f812; Perry, "National Education Association," December 1935, PFP, C52 f986.

47. Tyson (1934), p. 15.
48. Perry, "National Broadcasting Company," December 1935, PFP, C52 f986; Aylesworth (1932), p. 3.
49. Tyson to Keppel, 2 January 1934, Carnegie Corporation of New York papers, Columbia University, New York, NACRE Box 1, NACRE 1934 (hereafter cited as CCP).
50. Tyson to Keppel, 4 December 1929, CCP, NACRE Box 1, NACRE 1929.
51. Tyson to Patterson, 29 November 1932, National Broadcasting Company papers, State Historical Society of Wisconsin, Madison, B12 f15 (hereafter cited as NBCP).
52. Evans to Harris, 8 October 1934, PFP, C69 f1350.
53. Crandall, "Memorandum to Mr. Perry re General Situation of Radio in Education," 29 December 1930, PFP, C69 f1352.
54. Tyson to Keppel, 28 October 1930, CCP, NACRE Box 1, NACRE 1930; Tyson to Keppel, 2 January 1934, CCP, NACRE Box 1, NACRE 1934.
55. Crandall to Bolton, 23 June 1932, PFP, C52 f983.
56. *Proceedings of the Nineteenth Annual Convention of the National University Extension Association, Volume 17, 1934* (Bloomington: Indiana University Press, 1934), p. 86.
57. Barnouw (1966), p. 261; Avery and Pepper (1980), p. 127.
58. Crandall to Davis, 15 April 1931, PFP, C59 f1142.
59. Ibid.
60. Davis to Maxfield, 12 June 1931, PFP, C59 f1142; Evans to Bernays, 3 March 1932, PFP, C69 f1350; Crandall to Davis, 13 October 1931, PFP, C59 f1143.
61. Evans to Williams, 9 December 1932, PFP, C60 f1174; Davis to Evans, 30 July 1931, PFP, C59 f1142.
62. Walter Woehlke Memorandum, undated, Summer 1931, PFP, C49 f945.
63. H. O. Davis to H. L. Williamson, 25 September 1931, NBCP, B5 f65.
64. Woehlke to Evans, 1 September 1931, PFP, C60 f1163; Evans to Davis, 5 September 1931, PFP, C59 f1143.
65. Davis to Bolton, 9 September 1931, PFP, C40 f764; Evans, "Memorandum re Payne Fund Relationship with Davis Radio Campaign," 18 September 1931, PFP, C49 f945.
66. For Davis's final proposal as such, see Davis (1932), p. 99.
67. McChesney (1991b). I deal with the topic in more detail in McChesney (1993a), esp. ch. 7.
68. Summary of Expenditures of Ventura Free Press Radio Project, June 1932, PFP, C59 f1145; "Free Press Most Widely Quoted Newspaper West of the Rockies," *Ventura Free Press*, 28 July 1932, pp. 1, 3.
69. "A Vicious Fight Against Broadcasting," *Broadcasting*, 1 December 1932, p. 10.

70. Randall to Mason, 3 July 1934, NBCP, B25 f58.

71. "Editors Favor American Plan," *Broadcasters' News Bulletin,* 13 June 1931.

72. Davis to Bolton, 9 September 1931, PFP, C40 f764.

73. Crandall to Perry, 3 June 1931, PFP, C56 f1072.

74. Woehlke to Evans, 25 November 1931, PFP, C60 f1164.

75. Bolton to Davis, 1 September 1931, PFP, C59 f1143.

76. Crandall to Davis, 1 October 1931, PFP, C59 f1143; Memorandum re Discussion at Board Meeting Held October 30, 1931 Regarding the Ventura Free Press Campaign Against Radio Monopoly, 30 October 1931, PFP, C61 f1178.

77. All of these groups are profiled in McChesney (1993a), ch. 4. For a discussion specifically of the role played by organized labor, see McChesney (1992a).

78. J. E. Morgan (1933), p. 82.

79. Woehlke to Evans, 22 December 1932, PFP, C60 f1147.

80. "Neither Sponsors nor Stations Heed Listeners' Grumbling," *Business Week,* 10 February 1932, pp. 18-19; cited in "From the Newspapers," *Education by Radio,* 5 March 1931, p. 14.

81. J. E. Morgan (1934b), pp. 26, 28.

82. Davis to Lighter, 1 December 1931, PFP, C59 f1143.

83. "Report of the Committee on Radio Broadcasting," in A. H. Upham, ed., *Transactions and Proceedings of the National Association of State Universities in the United States of America 1931, Volume 29* (National Association of State Universities, 1931), p. 150; J. E. Morgan (1931a), p. 130; J. E. Morgan (1933), p. 93.

84. Perry (1932), p. 223.

85. Coltrane (1933), p. 36.

86. See, e.g., J. E. Morgan (1932), p. 83.

87. Perry to British Broadcasting Corporation, 17 December 1935, PFP, C58 f1110.

88. Perry to Charters, undated, early summer 1930, PFP C56 f1069.

89. Woehlke to Evans, 22 December 1932, PFP, C60 f1167.

90. Perry to Crandall, 8 March 1932, PFP, C59 f1144.

91. Evans to Woehlke, 15 February 1932, PFP, C60 f1165.

92. Bliven (1934), p. 201; "I'm Signing Off," *Forum,* February 1932, p. 114. For a particularly acute example of blaming the audience for the alleged asininity of commercial programming, see "The Dominant Moron," *Catholic World,* May 1934, pp. 135–137.

93. This topic is addressed in McChesney (1991b).

94. Tyler to Baldwin, 26 October 1933, American Civil Liberties Union papers, Princeton University, Princeton, N.J., 1933, vol. 599.

95. For two classic statements along these lines, see National Association of Broadcasters (1933); National Broadcasting Company (1935).

96. Paul F. Peter, NBC Chief Statistician, "Appearances by U.S. Federal Officials over National Broadcasting Company Networks, 1931–1933," November 1933, NBCP, B16 f26.

97. Morgan to McCracken, 2 August 1932, PFP, C42 f801.

98. Amlie to Tyler, 24 May 1932, PFP, C43 f825.

99. Perry, "Columbia Broadcasting System," December 1935, PFP, C52 f986.

100. "Better Business," *Broadcasting*, 15 December 1931, p. 18.

101. Sol Taishoff, "Session of Radio-Minded Congress Nears," *Broadcasting*, 1 December 1931, p. 5.

102. Nockels (1931), p. 2.

103. Bolton to MacCracken, 9 October 1931, PFP, C40 f768.

104. Evans to Woehlke, 22 December 1931, PFP, C60 f1164.

105. Evans to Woehlke, 29 February 1932, PFP, C69 f1358.

106. FRC, "In re: The use of radio broadcasting stations for advertising purposes," 21 December 1931, PFP, C60 f1159.

107. Davis to Crandall, 23 February 1932, PFP, C59 f1144.

108. Davis to Crandall, 8 March 1932, PFP, C59 f1144.

109. Tyler to Marsh, 7 April 1932, PFP, C39 f744; Morgan to Bolton, PFP, C42 f812.

110. Crandall, "Review of the Program of the National Committee on Education by Radio," 11 August 1932, PFP, C56 f1075.

111. Davis to Brooks, 5 October 1932, PFP, C59 f1145. For a copy of the FRC report, see Federal Radio Commission (1932).

112. Davis to Woehlke, undated, Summer 1932, PFP, C60 f1167.

113. Spry to Morgan, 2 May 1932, PFP, C42 f822.

114. Evans to Davis, 18 November 1932, PFP, C59 f1145.

115. Evans to Woehlke, 7 October 1932, PFP, C60 f1167.

116. Evans to Woehlke, 19 December 1932, PFP, C69 f1358.

117. Evans to Coltrane, 25 January 1933, PFP, C41 f783.

118. Memorandum Concerning Payne Fund Cooperation with Commercial Radio Stations, 15 November 1932, PFP, C69 f1352.

119. Davis to Crandall, 20 September 1934, PFP, C59 f1148.

120. Crandall to Cooper, 19 February 1933, PFP, C68 f1337.

121. Aylesworth to Sarnoff, 20 August 1934, NBCP, B32 f7.

122. Crane to Tyler, 19 March 1934, PFP, C41 f785.

123. A. E. Morgan (1934), p. 81.

124. See McChesney (1993a), ch. 7.

125. Martin Codel, "President Aided by Radio Chains," undated, March 1933, NANA, v. 61; "F.D.R.'s Radio Record," *Broadcasting*, 15 March 1934, p. 8.

126. See Ferguson (1991); Ferguson (1989); Allen (1991); Domhoff (1990).
127. Sol Taishoff, "'War Plans' Laid to Protect Broadcasting," *Broadcasting*, 1 March 1933, p. 5.
128. Rosen (1980), p. 177.
129. Petitions and letters found in Robert F. Wagner papers, Georgetown University, Washington, D.C., Legislative Files, Box 223; United States Interstate Commerce Committee papers, National Archives, Washington, D.C., Sen. 73A-J28, Tray 155.
130. "Air Enemies United Forces," *Variety*, 8 May 1934, pp. 37, 45; "Wagner Amendment Up Next Week," *NAB Reports*, 5 May 1934, p. 375.
131. Tyler to Harney, 30 March 1934, PFP, C44 f850.
132. Harney to Tyler, 3 April 1934, PFP, ibid.
133. Harney to Perry, 4 April 1934, PFP, C59 f1132.
134. Perry to Crandall, 15 June 1934, PFP, C56 f1079.
135. Henry A. Bellows, "Report of the Legislative Committee," *NAB Reports*, 15 November 1934, p. 618.
136. Ibid., p. 618.
137. "Commercial Control of the Air," *Christian Century*, 26 September 1934, pp. 1196–1197.
138. "Government Interference Fears Groundless, Say Commissioners," *Broadcasting*, 1 October 1934, p. 18.
139. Tyler to Dill, 5 June 1934, PFP, C43 f824.
140. Russell to Hard, 23 October 1934, NBCP, B26 f28.
141. Early memo, McIntyre memo, 20 October 1934, 22 October 1934, Franklin D. Roosevelt papers, Franklin D. Roosevelt Presidential Library, Hyde Park, N.Y., OF 136, 1934; "More About TVA Proposal," *Education by Radio*, 22 November 1934, p. 53.
142. Futrall to Tyler, 15 December 1934, PFP, C49 f941; Crandall memorandum to Bolton, Maxfield, 5 November 1934, PFP, C69 f1352.
143. Perry to Evans, 28 November 1934, PFP, C56 f1080.
144. See Crane (1935).
145. Cited in "In Their Own Behalf," *Education by Radio*, June–July 1938, p. 21.
146. Paley (1937), p. 6.
147. Perry to Evans, 18 March 1934, PFP, C56 f1079; Patterson, Jr., to Norton, 5 September 1935, NBCP, B36 f38; Memorandum to Bolton from Evans, 16 September 1935, PFP, C69 f1351.
148. Excerpt from Minutes of Executive Committee Meeting on National Committee on Education by Radio, 18–19 January 1936, PFP, C69 f1147; Evans to Crane, 19 June 1936, PFP, C69 f1147.
149. Perry, "National Advisory Council on Radio in Education," December 1935, PFP, C52 f986.

150. Committee on Civic Education by Radio of the National Advisory Council on Radio in Education and the American Political Science Association (1937).

151. See note 4 above; see also McChesney (1992b).

Appendix B

1. Edgar Dale, *Children's Attendance at Motion Pictures*, Motion Pictures and Youth Series (Payne Fund Studies), New York, 1933; Alice M. Mitchell, *Children and Movies*, chap. 3, Chicago, 1929; Edgar Dale, *Content of Motion Pictures* (Payne Fund Studies), New York, 1933; C. C. Peters, *Motion Pictures and Standards of Morality* (Same Series), New York, 1933; P. W. Holaday and G. D. Stoddard, *Getting Ideas from the Movies* (Payne Fund Studies), New York, 1933.

2. Ruth C. Peterson and L. T. [*sic*] Thurstone, *Motion Pictures and the Social Attitudes of Children* (Payne Fund Studies), New York, 1933. See also S. P. Rosenthal, *Change of Socio-Economic Attitudes Under Radical Motion Picture Propaganda*, Columbia University Archives of Psychology, No. 166, 1934.

3. W. S. Dysinger and C. A. Ruckmick, *Emotional Responses of Children to the Motion Picture Situation* (Payne Fund Studies), New York, 1933; S. Renshaw, V. L. Miller, and D. Marquis, *Children's Sleep* (Payne Fund Studies), New York, 1933.

4. H. Blumer, *Movies and Conduct* (Payne Fund Studies), New York, 1933; H. Blumer and P. Hauser, *Movies, Delinquency and Crime* (Same Series), New York, 1933.

5. F. Znaniecki, *Methods of Sociology*, 10–20, New York, 1934.

6. Though courses in literature, art appreciation, and photoplay appreciation are among those which attest to the fact that such *extrasocial* situations are believed to be culturally significant, sociological study of such situations is hardly begun. See, however, Katherine Niles, "Sociology of Reading," M.A. thesis, University of Chicago, 1935.

7. G. H. Mead, *Mind, Self and Society*, Chicago, 1935; C. H. Cooley, *Human Nature and the Social Order*, New York, 1902; William Stern, *Psychology of Early Childhood*, 316–323, New York, 1930.

8. W. A. White, *An Introduction to the Study of the Mind*, 76, Washington, D.C. [no date].

9. These are usually described as "dynamisms," "mental mechanisms" or as "imaginative processes," but the above conception of them as "modes in cinema identification" or as "imaginative adjustments" does not differ from their more precise usage. K. Young, *Social Psychology*, 135–136, New York, 1930; T. D. Eliot, "The Use of Psycho-analytic Classifications in

Analysis of Social Behavior," *Proceedings of the American Sociological Society,* 1927, 21: 185–190.

10. J. K. Folsom, *The Family,* 85, New York, 1934; S. Ferenczi, "Introjection and Transference," *Contributions to Psycho-Analysis,* Boston, 1916; Folsom, *op. cit.,* 84 defines *displacement* as the "substitution of another object, goal or idea for the original object of the emotion, while the emotion itself remains the same."

11. Studies of direct bearing on this specific problem are few; cf., however, M. Halbwachs, *Les Cadres Sociaux de la Memoire,* Alcan, Paris, 1925; Karl Mannheim, *Ideology and Utopia,* New York, 1936; F. C. Bartlett, *Remembering: A Study in Experimental and Social Psychology,* New York, 1932; Muzafer Sherif, *Psychology of Social Norms,* New York, 1936.

12. *Journal of Educational Sociology,* Dec. 1932, 238–244, and April 1934, 504–518; also, *Proceedings of the American Sociological Society,* 1934, 28: 90–94.

13. From findings of special study of this question, later to be reported. Conversely, evidence that behavior affected by the cinema is sometimes exclusively of a socially desirable sort cannot be accepted as *ipso facto* proof that other less desirable elements were not presented in the films which were seen, as some have claimed. Rather, absence of such screen responses may signify only the stable character and socialized training of these patrons.

14. See esp. E. Faris, "The Concept of Imitation," *The Nature of Human Nature,* 61–83, esp. 75–78, New York, 1936; G. Humphrey, "The Conditioned Reflex and the Elementary Social Reaction," *Journal of Abnormal and Social Psychology,* 1922–1923, 7: 113–119; E. Faris on "unwitting" imitation, *op. cit.,* 75–76; F. Znaniecki, *Social Actions,* New York, 1936, on "impersonative imitation," 304–309; E. Faris, *op. cit.,* 76 and 79–80, and F. Znaniecki, *op. cit.,* 309–311, on "conscious" or "independent imitation."

Bibliography

The major portion of the bibliography for this book consists of the primary sources cited in the notes.

Addams, Jane, 1909, *The Spirit of Youth and City Streets* (New York: Macmillan).

Adler, Mortimer J., 1933, *Crime, Law and Social Science* (New York: Harcourt Brace).

Adler, Mortimer J., 1937, *Art and Prudence* (New York: Longmans Green).

Adler, Mortimer J., 1977, *Philosopher at Large* (New York: Macmillan).

Adorno, T. W., 1941, "On Popular Music," *Studies in Philosophy and Social Science (Zeitschrift für Sozialforschung)*, 9, pp. 17–48.

Adorno, T. W., Else Frenkel-Brunswick, D. J. Levinson and R. N. Sandford, 1950, *The Authoritarian Personality* (New York: Harper).

Advisory Committee on Education by Radio, 1930, *Report of the Advisory Committee on Education by Radio Appointed by the Secretary of the Interior* (Columbus: F. J. Heer).

Allen, Michael Patrick, 1991, "Capitalist Response to State Intervention: Theories of the State and Political Finance in the New Deal," *American Sociological Review*, 56, pp. 679–689.

Arnheim, Rudolf, 1944, "The World of the Daytime Serial," in Paul F. Lazarsfeld and Frank Stanton, eds., *Radio Research, 1942–43* (New York: Duell, Sloan and Pearce), pp. 34–85.

Austin, Bruce A., 1983, *The Film Audience: An International Bibliography of Research* (Metuchen, NJ: Scarecrow Press).

Austin, Bruce, 1989, *Immediate Seating: A Look at Movie Audiences* (Belmont, CA: Wadsworth).

Avery, Robert K., and Pepper, Robert, 1980, "An Institutional History of Public Broadcasting," *Journal of Communication*, 30:3, pp. 126–38.

Aylesworth, Merlin H., 1932, "Broadcasting Today," *Dun's Review*, 5, p. 3.

Bagdikian, Ben H., 1992, *The Media Monopoly*, 4th ed. (Boston: Beacon Press).

Balio, Tino, ed., 1993, *Grand Design: Hollywood as a Modern Business Enterprise, 1930–1939* (New York: Scribners).

Barnouw, Erik, 1966, *A Tower in Babel* (New York: Oxford University Press).

Baugh, Kenneth Jr., 1990, *The Methodology of Herbert Blumer* (New York: Cambridge University Press).

Berelson, Bernard, 1952, *Content Analysis and Communication Research* (New York: Free Press).

Black, Gregory D., 1994, *Hollywood Censored: Morality Codes, Catholics, and the Movies* (New York: Cambridge University Press).

Bliven, Bruce, 1934. "For Better Broadcasting," *New Republic*, 3, p. 8.

Blumer, Herbert, 1933, *Movies and Conduct* (New York: Macmillan).

Blumer, Herbert, and Philip Hauser, 1933, *Movies, Delinquency and Crime* (New York: Macmillan).

Boddy, William, 1990, *Fifties Television: The Industry and Its Critics* (Urbana: University of Illinois Press).

Bowser, Eileen, 1990, *The Transformation of Cinema, 1907–1915* (New York: Scribners).

Bulmer, Martin, 1984, *The Chicago School of Sociology: Institutionalization, Diversity and the Rise of Sociological Research* (Chicago: University of Chicago Press).

Butler, Elizabeth Beardsley, 1909, *Women and the Trades: Pittsburgh, 1907–08* (New York: Charities Publication Committee).

Byington, Margaret F., 1910, *Homestead: The Households of a Mill Town* (New York: Charities Publication Committee).

Cantril, Hadley, 1935, "Review of First Volume of the Payne Fund Studies," *Journal of Abnormal and Social Psychology*, 29, pp. 238–239.

Cantril, Hadley, Hazel Gaudet, and Herta Herzog, 1940, *The Invasion from Mars* (Princeton, NJ: Princeton University Press).

Carmen, Ira H., 1966, *Movies, Censorship and the Law* (Ann Arbor: University of Michigan Press).

Charters, W. W., 1927, *The Teaching of Ideals* (New York: Macmillan).

Charters, W. W., 1932, "A Technique for Studying a Social Problem," *Journal of Educational Sociology*, 6:4, pp. 196–203.

Charters, W. W., 1933, *Motion Pictures and Youth* (New York: Macmillan).

Chisman, Forest, 1976, *Attitude Psychology and the Study of Public Opinion* (University Park: Penn State University Press).

Clausen, John A., 1966, "Drug Addiction," in Robert K. Merton and Robert A. Nisbet, eds., *Contemporary Social Problems*, 2nd ed. (New York: Harcourt Brace and World), pp. 193–235.

Coltrane, Eugene J., 1933, "A System of Radio Broadcasting Suited to American Purposes," in E. R. Rankin, ed., *Radio Control and Operation* (Chapel Hill: University of North Carolina Extension Bulletin).

Committee on Civic Education by Radio of the National Advisory Council on Radio in Education and the American Political Science Association, 1937. *Four Years of Network Broadcasting* (Chicago: University of Chicago Press).

Conant, Michael, 1960, *Anti-Trust in the Motion Picture Industry* (Berkeley and Los Angeles: University of California Press).

Crane, Arthur, G., 1935. "Safeguarding Educational Radio," in Levering Tyson and Josephine H. MacLatchy, eds., *Education on the Air . . . and Radio and Education 1935* (Chicago: University of Chicago Press), pp. 117–125.

Cressey, Paul G., 1932a, "The Social Role of Motion Pictures in an Interstitial Area," *Journal of Educational Sociology*, 6:4, pp. 238–243.

Cressey, Paul G., 1932b, *The Taxi-Dance Hall: A Sociological Study in Commercialized Recreation and City Life* (Chicago: University of Chicago Press).

Cressey, Paul G., 1934, "The Motion Picture as Informal Education," *Journal of Educational Sociology*, 7:8, pp. 504–515.

Cressey, Paul G., 1938a, "The Motion Picture Experience as Modified by Social Background and Personality," *American Sociological Review*, 3, pp. 516–525.

Cressey, Paul G., 1938b, "A Study in Practical Philosophy" (review of Adler [1937]), *Journal of Higher Education*, 9, pp. 319–328.

Dale, Edgar, 1932, "Method for Analyzing the Content of Motion Pictures," *Journal of Educational Sociology*, 6:4, pp. 244–250.

Dale, Edgar, 1933, *How to Appreciate Motion Pictures* (New York: Macmillan).

Dale, Edgar, 1935, *Children's Attendance at Motion Pictures and The Content of Motion Pictures* (New York: Macmillan).

Dale, Edgar, 1953, "The Student of Curriculum Problems," *Educational Research Bulletin* (Ohio State University, Bureau of Educational Research), 11 (February), pp. 37–41.

Danielson, Wayne A., 1963, "Content Analysis," in R. O. Nafziger and D. M. White, eds., *Introduction to Communication Research* (Baton Rouge: Louisiana State University Press), pp. 180–206.

Davis, H. O., 1932. *Empire of the Air* (Ventura, CA: Ventura Free Press).

Davis, Kingsley, 1937, "The Sociology of Prostitution," *American Sociological Review*, 2, pp. 744–755.

Davis, Robert E., 1976, *Response to Innovation: A Study of Popular Argument About New Mass Media* (New York: Arno Press).

DeCordova, Richard, 1990, *Picture Personalities: The Emergence of the Star System in America* (Urbana: University of Illinois Press).

Delia, Jesse G., 1987, "Communication Research: A History," in Charles Berger and Steven H. Chaffee, eds., *Handbook of Communication Sciences* (Newbury Park, NJ: Sage), pp. 20–98.

Domhoff, G. William, 1990, *The Power Elite and the State: How Policy Is Made in America* (New York: Aldine-De Gruyter).

Dysinger, W. S. and Christian A. Ruckmick, 1933, *The Emotional Responses of Children to the Motion Picture Situation* (New York: Macmillan).

Eckert, Charles, 1978, "The Carole Lombard in Macy's Window," *Quarterly Review of Film Studies* 3:1, pp. 1–22.

Facey, Paul W., 1945, "The Legion of Decency: A Sociological Analysis of the Emergence and Development of a Pressure Group," Ph.D. dissertation, Fordham University; reprint, New York: Arno Press, 1974.

Farber, Manny, 1971, *Negative Space* (New York: Praeger).

Faris, Robert E. L., 1967, *Chicago Sociology, 1920–1932* (San Francisco: Chandler).

Fearing, Franklin, 1947, "Influence of Movies on Attitudes and Behavior," *Annals of the American Academy of Political and Social Science,* 254, pp. 70–79.

Fearing, Franklin, 1950, *Motion Pictures as Medium of Instruction and Communication* (Berkeley and Los Angeles: University of California Press).

Federal Radio Commission, 1932, *Commercial Radio Advertising* (Washington, DC: U. S. Government Printing Office).

Ferguson, Thomas, 1989, "Industrial Conflict and the Coming of the New Deal: The Triumph of Multinational Liberalism in America," in Steve Fraser and Gary Gerstle, eds., *The Rise and Fall of the New Deal Order* (Princeton, NJ: Princeton University Press), pp. 3–31.

Ferguson, Thomas, 1991, "Industrial Structure and Party Competition in the New Deal: A Reply to Webber," *Sociological Perspectives,* 34, pp. 493–526.

Field, Mary, 1952, *Good Company: The Story of the Children's Entertainment Film Movement in Great Britain, 1943–1950* (London: Longmans Green).

Fleming, Donald, 1967, "Attitude: The History of a Concept," *Perspectives in American History,* 1, pp. 287–368.

Forman, Henry James, 1932a, "To the Movies – But Not to Sleep!" *McCall's,* September, pp. 12–13 +.

Forman, Henry James, 1932b, "Movie Madness," *McCall's,* October, pp. 14–15 +.

Forman, Henry James, 1932c, "Molded By Movies," *McCall's*, November, pp. 17+.

Forman, Henry James, 1933, *Our Movie Made Children* (New York: Macmillan).

Fowles, Jib, 1992, *Starstruck: Celebrity Performers and the American Public* (Washington, DC: Smithsonian Press).

Fox, Richard Wrightman, 1983, "Epitaph for Middletown: Robert S. Lynd and the Analysis of Consumer Culture," in Richard W. Fox and T. J. Jackson Lears, eds., *The Culture of Consumption: Critical Essays in American History, 1880–1980* (New York: Pantheon), pp. 101–141.

Freeman, Frank, 1933, "The Technique Used in the Study of the Effect of Motion Pictures on the Care of the Teeth," *Journal of Educational Sociology*, 6:5, pp. 309–311.

Freeman, Frank, and Benjamin Wood, 1929, *Motion Pictures in the Classroom* (Boston: Houghton Mifflin).

Fuller, Kathryn H., 1992, "Shadowland: American Audiences and the Movie-Going Experience in the Silent Film Era," Ph.D. dissertation, Johns Hopkins University.

Furner, Mary O., 1975, *Advocacy and Objectivity: A Crisis in the Professionalization of American Social Science, 1865–1905* (Lexington: University of Kentucky Press).

Gabler, Neal, 1988, *An Empire of Their Own: How the Jews Invented Hollywood* (New York: Crown).

Gusfield, Joseph R., 1963, *Symbolic Crusade: Status Politics and the American Temperance Movement* (Urbana: University of Illinois Press).

Hammersley, Martyn, 1989, *The Dilemma of Qualitative Method: Herbert Blumer and the Chicago Tradition* (New York: Routledge).

Handel, Leo A., 1950, *Hollywood Looks at Its Audience: A Report of Film Audience Research* (Urbana: University of Illinois Press).

Hauser, Philip M., 1932, "How Do Motion Pictures Affect the Conduct of Children?" *Journal of Educational Sociology*, 6:4, pp. 231–237.

Hauser, Philip M., 1933, "Motion Pictures in Penal and Correctional Institutions: A Study of the Reactions of Prisoners to Movies," Unpublished M.A. thesis, University of Chicago.

Hays, Will H., 1955, *The Memoirs of Will Hays* (Garden City, NY: Doubleday).

Healy, William, 1915, *The Individual Delinquent* (Boston: Little, Brown).

Herman, Edward S., and Noam Chomsky, 1988, *Manufacturing Consent: The Political Economy of the Mass Media* (New York: Pantheon).

Herzog, Herta, 1941, "On Borrowed Experience," *Studies in Philosophy and Social Science (Zeitschrift für Sozialforschung)*, 9: 65–90.

Herzog, Herta, 1944, "What Do We Really Know About Daytime Serial

Listeners?" in Paul F. Lazarsfeld and Frank Stanton, eds., *Radio Research, 1942–43* (New York: Duell, Sloan and Pearce), pp. 3–33.

Hilmes, Michele, 1990, *Hollywood and Broadcasting: From Radio to Cable* (Urbana: University of Illinois Press).

Holaday, P. W., and George D. Stoddard, 1933, *Getting Ideas from the Movies* (New York: Macmillan).

Hovland, Carl I., A. A. Lumsdaine, and F. D. Sheffield, 1949, *Experiments in Mass Communication* (Princeton, NJ: Princeton University Press).

Inglis, Ruth A., 1947, *Freedom of the Movies: A Report on Self-Regulation from the Commission on Freedom of the Press* (Chicago: University of Chicago Press).

Jacobs, Lea, 1990, "Reformers and Spectators: The Film Education Movement in the Thirties," *Camera Obscura*, 22, pp. 29–49.

Janowitz, Morris, 1968, "Mass Communication Research," in *Encyclopedia of the Social Sciences* (New York: Macmillan), vol. 3.

Jarvie, I. C., 1964, *The Revolution in Anthropology* (London: Routledge).

Jarvie, I. C., 1966, "Academic Fashions and Grandfather-Killing: In Defense of Frazer," *Encounter*, 26, pp. 53–55.

Jarvie, I. C., 1970, *Movies and Society* (New York: Basic Books).

Jarvie, I. C., 1985, *Thinking About Society: Theory and Practice* (Dordrecht: Reidel), ch. 25, "Methodological and Conceptual Problems in the Study of Pornography and Violence."

Jarvie, I. C., 1987, "The Sociology of the Pornography Debate," *Philosophy of the Social Sciences*, 17, pp. 257–275.

Jarvie, I. C., 1992, *Hollywood's Overseas Campaign: The Film Trade in the North Atlantic Triangle, 1920–1950* (New York: Cambridge University Press).

Jowett, Garth S., 1976, *Film: The Democratic Art* (Boston: Little, Brown).

Jowett, Garth S., 1989, " 'A Capacity for Evil': The 1915 Supreme Court *Mutual* Decision," *Historical Journal of Film, Radio and Television*, 9:1, pp. 59–78.

Jowett, Garth S., 1990, "Moral Responsibility and Commercial Entertainment: Social Control in the United States' Film Industry," *Historical Journal of Film, Radio and Television*, 10, pp. 3–31.

Jowett, Garth S., Penny Reath, and Monica Schouten, 1977, "The Control of Mass Entertainment Media in Canada, the United States and Great Britain: Historical Surveys," in *Report of the Royal Commission on Violence in the Communications Industry* (Toronto: Queen's Printer), vol. 4, pp. 1–104.

Katz, Elihu, and Paul F. Lazarsfeld, 1955, *Personal Influence* (Glencoe, IL: Free Press).

Kendall, Patricia L., 1982, *The Varied Sociology of Paul F. Lazarsfeld* (New York: Columbia University Press).

Klapper, Joseph, 1959, *The Effects of Mass Communication* (Glencoe, IL: Free Press).

Kracauer, Siegfried, 1947, *From Caligari to Hitler* (Princeton, NJ: Princeton University Press).

Krasker, Abraham, 1934, "Review of Motion Pictures and Youth," *Education*, 54, pp. 382–384.

Larsen, Cedric, and James R. Mock, 1939, "The Lost Files of the Creel Committee of 1917–19," *Public Opinion Quarterly*, 3, pp. 5–29.

Lasswell, Harold D., 1939, *World Revolutionary Propaganda: A Chicago Study* (New York: Knopf).

Lasswell, Harold D., 1948, "The Structure and Function of Communication," in Lyman Bryson, ed., *The Communication of Ideas* (New York: Harper and Bros.), pp. 32–51; reprinted in Bernard Berelson and Morris Janowitz, eds., *Reader in Public Opinion and Communication* (New York: Free Press, 1966), pp. 178–189.

Lazarsfeld, Paul F., 1941, "Remarks on Administrative and Critical Communications Research," *Studies in Philosophy and Social Science (Zeitschrift für Sozialforschung)*, 9, pp. 2–16.

Lazarsfeld, Paul F., 1947, "Audience Research in the Movie Field," in Gordon Watkins, ed., *The Motion Picture Industry*, vol. 254 of Annals of the American Academy of Political and Social Science, pp. 160–168.

Lazarsfeld, Paul F., and Morris Rosenberg, eds., 1955, *The Languages of Social Research* (Glencoe, IL: Free Press).

Lewis, Howard T., 1933, *The Motion Picture Industry* (New York: Van Nostrand).

Linton, James, and Garth S. Jowett, 1977, "A Content Analysis of Feature Films," in *Report of the Royal Commission on Violence in the Communications Industry* (Toronto: Queen's Printer), vol. 3, pp. 465–580.

Louttit, C. M., 1934, "Review of Motion Pictures and Youth," *Journal of Applied Psychology*, 18, pp. 307–316.

Lowenthal, Leo, 1944, "Biographies in Popular Magazines," in Paul F. Lazarsfeld and Frank Stanton, eds., *Radio Research, 1942–43* (New York: Duell, Sloan and Pearce), pp. 507–548.

Lowery, Shearon A., and Melvin L. De Fleur, 1988, *Milestones in Mass Communications Research*, 2nd ed. (New York: Longmans).

Lynd, Robert, and Helen Lynd, 1929, *Middletown: A Study in Modern American Culture* (New York: Harcourt, Brace).

Lynd, Robert, and Helen Lynd, 1937, *Middletown in Transition: A Study in Cultural Conflicts* (New York: Harcourt, Brace).

Lyons, Gene M., 1969, *The Uneasy Partnership* (New York: Russell Sage).

Maltby, Richard, 1993, "The Production Code and the Hays Office," in

Tino Balio, ed., *Grand Design: Hollywood as a Modern Business Enterprise, 1930–1939* (New York: Scribners), pp. 37–72.

Matthews, Fred, 1977, *Quest for an American Sociology: Robert E. Park and the Chicago School* (Montreal: McGill-Queen's University Press).

May, Henry F., 1959, *The End of American Innocence* (New York: Knopf).

May, Lary, 1980, *Screening Out the Past: The Birth of Mass Culture and the Motion Picture Industry* (New York: Oxford University Press).

May, Mark A., 1937, "Educational Possibilities of Motion Pictures," *Journal of Educational Sociology*, 11, pp. 149–160.

May, Mark A., 1946, "The Psychology of Learning from Demonstration Films," *Journal of Educational Psychology*, 37, pp. 1–12.

May, Mark A., 1947, "Educational Projects," *Educational Screen*, 26, pp. 200–201+.

May, Mark A., and A. A. Lumsdaine, 1958, *Learning from Films* (New Haven: Yale University Press).

May, Mark A., and Frank Shuttleworth, 1933, *The Social Conduct and Attitudes of Movie Fans* (New York: Macmillan).

McChesney, Robert W., 1991a, "An Almost Incredible Absurdity for a Democracy," *Journal of Communication Inquiry*, 15:1, pp. 89–114.

McChesney, Robert W., 1991b, "Press–Radio Relations and the Emergence of Network, Commercial Broadcasting in the United States, 1930-1935," *Historical Journal of Film, Radio and Television*, 11:1, pp. 41–57.

McChesney, Robert W., 1992a, "Labor and the Marketplace of Ideas: WCFL and the Battle for Labor Radio Broadcasting, 1927–1934," *Journalism Monographs*, 134.

McChesney, Robert W., 1992b, "Off-Limits: An Inquiry into the Lack of Debate over the Ownership, Structure and Control of the Mass Media in U.S. Political Life," *Communication* 13, pp. 1–19.

McChesney, Robert W., 1993a, *Telecommunications, Mass Media, and Democracy: The Battle for the Control of U.S. Broadcasting, 1928–1935* (New York: Oxford University Press).

McChesney, Robert W., 1993b, "Conflict, Not Consensus: The Debate over Broadcast Communication Policy, 1930-1935," in William S. Solomon and Robert W. McChesney, eds., *Ruthless Criticism: New Perspectives in U.S. Communication History* (Minneapolis: University of Minnesota Press), pp. 222–258.

Meltzer, H., 1935, "Review of Motion Pictures and Youth," *Journal of Educational Psychology*, 26, pp. 238–240.

Merton, Robert K., and Paul F. Lazarsfeld, 1943, "Studies in Radio and Film Propaganda," *Transactions of the New York Academy of Sciences*, series II, 6.

Merton, Robert K., and Paul F. Lazarsfeld, 1944, "The Psychological Analysis of Propaganda," *Writers' Congress* (Berkeley and Los Angeles: University of California Press), pp. 362–380.

Mitchell, Alice Miller, 1929, *Children and Movies* (Chicago: University of Chicago Press).

Moley, Raymond A., 1938, *Are We Movie Made?* (New York: Macy-Masius).

Moley, Raymond A., 1945, *The Hays Office* (Indianapolis: Bobbs-Merrill).

Morgan, Arthur E., 1934. "Radio as a Cultural Agency in Sparsely Settled Regions and Remote Areas," in Tracy F. Tyler, ed., *Radio as a Cultural Agency: Proceedings of a National Conference on the Use of Radio as a Cultural Agency in a Democracy* (Washington, DC: National Committee on Education by Radio).

Morgan, Joy Elmer, 1931a, "The National Committee on Education by Radio," in Josephine H. MacLatchy, ed., *Education on the Air: Second Yearbook of the Institute for Education by Radio* (Columbus: Ohio State University), pp. 3–14.

Morgan, Joy Elmer, 1931b, "Education's Rights on the Air," in Levering Tyson, ed., *Radio and Education: Proceedings of the First Assembly of the National Advisory Council on Radio in Education, 1931* (Chicago: University of Chicago Press), pp. 120–136, 144–147.

Morgan, Joy Elmer, 1932, "The Radio in Education," in *Proceedings of the Seventeenth Annual Convention of the National University Extension Association 1932* (Bloomington: Indiana University Press), vol. 15, pp. 74–87.

Morgan, Joy Elmer, 1933, "The New American Plan for Radio," in Bower Aly and Gerald D. Shively, eds., *A Debate Handbook on Radio Control and Operation* (Columbia, MO: Staples), pp. 81–111.

Morgan, Joy Elmer, 1934a, "The Corporation in America," *Journal of the National Education Association, 23*, pp. 227–229.

Morgan, Joy Elmer, 1934b, "A National Culture – A By-Product or Objective of National Planning," in Tracy F. Tyler, ed., *Radio as a Cultural Agency: Proceedings of a National Conference on the Use of Radio as a Cultural Agency in a Democracy* (Washington, DC: National Committee on Education by Radio), pp. 23–32.

Morgan, Joy Elmer, and E. D. Bullock, 1911, *Selected Articles on Municipal Ownership* (Minneapolis: Wilson).

Munsterberg, Hugo, 1916, *The Photoplay: A Psychological Study* (New York: Appleton); reprint, New York: Dover, 1970.

Musser, Charles., 1990, *The Emergence of Cinema: The American Screen to 1907* (New York: Scribners).

National Association of Broadcasters, 1933, *Broadcasting in the United States* (Washington, DC: National Association of Broadcasters).

National Broadcasting Company, 1935, *Broadcasting* (New York: National Broadcasting Company), vols 1–4.

Nelson, Janet, 1932, "Statistical Aspects of the Boys' Club Study," *Journal of Educational Sociology*, 6:2, pp. 31–42.

Nockels, Edward N., 1931, "Labor's Rights on the Air," *Federation News*, 7.

Paley, William S., 1937, "The Viewpoint of the Radio Industry," in C. S. Marsh, ed., *Educational Broadcasting, 1937* (Chicago: University of Chicago Press), pp. 74–87.

Park, Robert E., 1915, "The City: Suggestions for the Investigation of Human Behavior in the City Environment," *American Journal of Sociology*, 20, pp. 577–579.

Park, Robert E., 1938, "Reflections on Communication and Culture," *American Journal of Sociology*, 44:2, pp. 187–205.

Perry, Armstrong, 1930, "The Status of Education by Radio in the United States," in Josephine MacLatchy, ed., *Education on the Air: First Yearbook of the Institute for Education by Radio* (Columbus: Ohio State University), pp. 79–89.

Perry, Armstrong, 1932, Comments following talk by C. M. Jansky, Jr., in Levering Tyson, ed., *Radio and Education: Proceedings of the Third Annual Assembly of National Advisory Council on Radio in Education, Inc., 1932* (Chicago: University of Chicago Press), pp. 221–225.

Perry, Armstrong, 1935, "Weak Spots in the American System of Broadcasting," in Herman S. Hettinger, ed., *Radio – The Fifth Estate*, vol. 117 of the Annals of the American Academy of Political and Social Science, pp. 22–28.

Peters, Anne Kling, 1971, "Acting and Aspiring Actresses in Hollywood: A Sociological Analysis," Ph.D. dissertation, University of California, Los Angeles.

Peters, Charles C., 1932, "The Relation of Motion Pictures to Standards of Morality," *Journal of Educational Sociology*, 6:4, pp. 251–255.

Peters, Charles C., 1933, *Motion Pictures and Standards of Morality* (New York: Macmillan).

Peterson, Ruth, and L. L. Thurstone, 1933, *Motion Pictures and the Social Attitudes of Children* (New York: Macmillan).

Platt, Jennifer, 1983, "The Development of the 'Participant Observation' Method in Sociology: Origin Myth and History," *Journal of the History of the Behavioral Sciences*, 19, pp. 379–393.

Randall, Richard S., 1968, *Censorship and the Movies* (Madison: University of Wisconsin Press).

Randall, Richard S., 1989, *Freedom and Taboo: Pornography and the Politics of a Self Divided* (Berkeley and Los Angeles: University of California Press).

Renshaw, Samuel, 1932, "Sleep Motility as an Index of Motion Picture Influence," *Journal of Educational Sociology,* 6:4, pp. 226–230.

Renshaw, Samuel, Vernon L. Miller and Dorothy P. Marquis, 1933, *Children's Sleep* (New York: Macmillan).

Report of the Royal Commission on Violence in the Communications Industry, 1977 (Toronto: Queen's Printer), vol. 3.

Rorty, James, 1933a, "New Facts About Movies and Children," *Parents,* 8 (July), pp. 18–19 +.

Rorty, James, 1933b, "How the Movies Harm Children," *Parents,* 8 (August), pp. 18–19.

Rorty, James, 1933c, Review of *Our Movie-Made Children, New Republic,* 11 (October), p. 255.

Rosen, Philip T., 1980, *The Modern Stentors: Radio Broadcasting and the Federal Government, 1920–1934* (Westport, CT: Greenwood Press).

Ross, Dorothy, 1991, *The Origins of American Social Science* (New York: Cambridge University Press).

Ross, Edward Alsworth, 1928, *World Drift* (New York).

Rowland, Willard D., 1983, *The Politics of TV Violence* (Beverly Hills, CA: Sage).

Ruckmick, Christian, 1932, "How Do Motion Pictures Affect the Attitudes and Emotions of Children?" *Journal of Educational Sociology,* 6:4, pp. 210–216.

Sargent, J. A., 1963, "Self-Regulation: The Motion Picture Production Code, 1930–1961," Ph.D. dissertation, University of Michigan.

Schickel, Richard, 1985, *Intimate Strangers: The Culture of Celebrity* (Garden City, NY: Doubleday).

Schumach, Murray, 1964, *The Face on the Cutting Room Floor* (New York: Morrow).

Seabury, William M., 1926, *The Public and the Motion Picture Industry* (New York: Macmillan).

Seabury, William M., 1929, *Motion Picture Problems: The Cinema and the League of Nations* (New York: Avondale Press); reprint, New York: Arno Press, 1978

Shaw, Clifford, and Ernest W. Burgess, 1930, *The Jack-Roller: A Delinquent Boy's Own Story* (Chicago: University of Chicago Press).

Shenton, Herbert, 1931, *The Public Relations of the Motion Picture Industry* (New York: Federal Council of Churches of Christ in America, Department of Research and Education); reprint, Englewood Cliffs, NJ: Jerome S. Ozer, 1971.

Shils, Edward, 1980, *The Calling of Sociology* (Chicago: University of Chicago Press).

Short, William H., 1928, *A Generation of Motion Pictures: A Review of*

Social Values in Recreational Films (New York: The National Committee for the Study of Social Values in Motion Pictures).

Short, William H., 1932, "The Effect of Motion Pictures on the Social Attitudes of High School Students," *Journal of Educational Sociology,* 6:4, pp. 220–226.

Short, William H., 1934, "An Intelligent Movie Program," *Education,* October, pp. 104–108.

Shuttleworth, Frank K., 1932, "Measuring the Influence of Motion Picture Attendance on Conduct and Attitudes," *Journal of Educational Sociology,* 6:4, pp. 216–219.

Shuttleworth, Frank K., and Mark A. May, 1933, *The Social Conduct and Attitudes of Movie Fans* (New York: Macmillan).

Siegfried, Andre, 1927, *America Comes of Age* (New York: Harcourt, Brace and World).

Sklar, Robert, 1975, *Movie-Made America* (New York: Random House).

Smith, Dennis, 1988, *The Chicago School: A Liberal Critique of Capitalism* (London: Routledge).

"Society," in Lyman Bryson, ed., *The Communication of Ideas* (New York: Harper and Bros., 1948), pp. 37–51; reprinted in Bernard Berelson and Morris Janowitz, eds., *Reader in Public Opinion and Communication* (New York: Free Press, 1966), pp. 178–190.

State of New York, 1935, *Proceedings of the Governor's Conference on Crime, the Criminal and Society,* Albany.

Stoddard, George, 1932, "Measuring the Effect of Motion Pictures on the Intellectual Content of Children," *Journal of Educational Sociology,* 6:4, pp. 204–209.

Sumner, William Graham, 1907, *Folkways: A Study of the Sociological Importance of Usages, Manners, Customs, Mores and Morals* (New York: Ginn).

Thrasher, Frederic M., 1927, *The Gang: A Study of 1,313 Gangs in Chicago* (Chicago: University of Chicago Press).

Thrasher, Frederic M., 1931, "Social Attitudes of Superior Boys in an Interstitial Community," in Kimball Young, ed., *Social Attitudes* (New York: Henry Holt), pp. 236–264.

Thrasher, Frederic M., 1932, "The Boys' Club Study," *Journal of Educational Sociology,* 6:1 (September), pp. 4–16.

Thrasher, Frederic M., 1938, "The Sociological Approach to Motion Pictures in Relation to Education," *Education,* 58, pp. 467–473.

Thrasher, Frederic M., 1940, "Education versus Censorship," *Journal of Educational Sociology,* 13, pp. 285–306.

Thrasher, Frederic M., 1946, *Okay for Sound* (New York: Duell, Sloan and Pearce).

Thrasher, Frederic M., 1949, "The Comics and Delinquency: Cause or Scapegoat?" *Journal of Educational Sociology,* 23, pp. 195–205.

Thurstone, L. L., 1928, "Attitudes Can Be Measured," *American Journal of Sociology,* 33:4, pp. 529–554.

Thurstone, L. L., 1931, "Influence of Motion Pictures on Children's Attitudes," *Journal of Social Psychology,* 2, pp. 291–305.

Thurstone, L. L., and E. J. Chave, 1929, *The Measurement of Attitude* (Chicago: University of Chicago Press).

Tyson, Levering, 1934, "Where Is American Radio Heading?" in Josephine H. MacLatchy, ed., *Education on the Air: Fifth Yearbook of the Institute for Education by Radio* (Columbus: Ohio State University Press), pp. 5–19.

U.S. Congress, House, 1914, Committee on Education, *Hearings: Motion Picture Commission,* 63rd Congress, 2nd Session.

U.S. Congress, House, 1916, Committee on Education, *Hearings On H.R. 456: Bill to Create a Federal Motion Picture Commission,* 64th Congress, 1st Session.

U.S. Congress, House, 1926, Committee on Education, *Hearings on H.R. 4094: Proposed Federal Motion Picture Commission.* 69th Congress, 1st Session.

Vaughn, Stephen, 1990, "Morality and Entertainment: The Origins of the Motion Picture Production Code," *Journal of American History,* 77, pp. 39–65.

Volkening, Henry, 1930, "Abuses of Radio Broadcasting," *Current History,* 33, pp. 396–400.

Waples, Douglas, 1953, "The Man and the Educator," *Educational Research Bulletin* (Ohio State University, Bureau of Educational Research), 11 February, pp. 29–36.

Warner, W. Lloyd, and William E. Henry, 1948, "The Radio Daytime Serial: A Symbolic Analysis," *Genetic Psychology Monographs,* 37, pp. 3–71.

Wartella, Ellen, and Byron Reeves, 1985, "Historical Trends in Research on Children and the Media: 1900–1960," *Journal of Communication,* 35:2, pp. 118–133.

Whitley, Robert L., 1930, "The Observation of the Problem Boy," *Journal of Educational Sociology,* 3:6, pp. 326–340.

Whitley, Robert L., 1931, "Interviewing the Problem Boy, Parts I and II," *Journal of Educational Sociology,* 5:2–3, pp. 89–100, 140–151.

Whitley, Robert L., 1932a, "The Case Study as a Method of Research," *Social Forces,* 10:4, pp. 567–573.

Whitley, Robert L., 1932b, "Case Studies in the Boys' Club Study," *Journal of Educational Sociology,* 6:1, pp. 17–30.

Wiese, M., and S. Cole, 1946, "A Study of Children's Attitudes and the Influence of a Commercial Motion Picture," *Journal of Psychology*, 21, pp. 151–171.

Willey, Malcolm, 1935, Review of Forman and four of the Payne Fund Studies, *Annals of the American Academy of Political and Social Science*, 177, pp. 288–289.

Wolfenstein, Martha, and Nathan Leites, 1950, *Movies: A Psychological Study* (Glencoe, IL: Free Press).

Young, Kimball, ed., 1931, *Social Attitudes* (New York: Henry Holt).

Young, Kimball, 1935, Review of the Payne Fund Studies, *American Journal of Sociology*, 41, pp. 249–255.

Index of Names

The letter *q* indicates that a person is quoted.

Index of Subjects

The letter *q* indicates that a source is quoted; *t* denotes a term that is defined or discussed. Italic titles not followed by an author's name in parentheses are film titles, except, obviously, for journal and periodical titles.